A Southern Music

A Southern Music

The Karnatik Story

T.M. KRISHNA

HarperCollins *Publishers* India

First published in India in 2013 by
HarperCollins *Publishers* India

Copyright © T.M. Krishna 2013

ISBN: 978-93-5029-821-3

2 4 6 8 10 9 7 5 3 1

T.M. Krishna asserts the moral right
to be identified as the author of this work.

The views and opinions expressed in this book are the author's own and
the facts are as reported by him, and the publishers are not in
any way liable for the same.

HarperCollins *Publishers*
A-53, Sector 57, Noida, Uttar Pradesh 201301, India
77-85 Fulham Palace Road, London W6 8JB, United Kingdom
Hazelton Lanes, 55 Avenue Road, Suite 2900, Toronto, Ontario M5R 3L2
and 1995 Markham Road, Scarborough, Ontario M1B 5M8, Canada
25 Ryde Road, Pymble, Sydney, NSW 2073, Australia
31 View Road, Glenfield, Auckland 10, New Zealand
10 East 53rd Street, New York NY 10022, USA

Typeset in 10.5/14 Galliard BT
by Jojy Philip, New Delhi 110 015

Printed and bound at
Thomson Press (India) Ltd

To
Sangeetha Sivakumar
musician
my conscience
my wife

Contents

Foreword

It is all too rare that a great artist reflects deeply, systematically and in a communicative manner on the particular artistic tradition of which he or she is a part. The very idea of such reflection is rather exotic, indeed improbable: a musician sings, a painter paints, a poet writes verses. The attempt to explain what goes on in the hidden reaches of the artist's mind may even be inimical to the actual business of making art happen. A Telugu verse, still circulating orally, tells us that it is fruitless, even ridiculous, to ask a poet about his own productions:

> *The beauties of a poem are best known*
> *by the critic.*
> *What does the author know?*
> *The beauties of a woman are known*
> *only to her husband.*
> *What does a father know?*

But in the case of music, for example, who exactly is the father (or, for that matter, the husband)? The doubt voiced by the poem applies, *mutatis mutandis*, to great performers, who are, as everyone knows, creative artists in their own right. In short, 'doing' and 'reflecting' may well be mutually contradictory. Some egregious examples come to mind, such as Glenn Gould's incomprehensible recorded talks on Bach's Goldberg Variations (a composition for which he gave us two very different, equally unforgettable renditions, the first recorded in 1955 and the second, shortly before his death, in 1981). When I first listened to the pedantic near-gibberish of these talks, I thought to myself: 'Please stop the torrent of words, just play the pieces!' A great musician always tells us – very eloquently – what he or she thinks just by making music, as a dancer does by dancing.

But occasionally there is an exception to this rule, and the book before us surely fits this description. T.M. Krishna is my favourite male vocalist of Carnatic music in this generation. He is a consummate master of the intricacies of this most subtle of musical traditions, with its vast expressive range enlivened by disciplined precision, sensitivity and nuance. I think he preserves, in some natural and unprepossessing manner, something of the intimate, gentle, profoundly emotional character that was clearly central to modern Carnatic singing in its earlier, formative phase – at the Maratha Tanjavur court, for example, and later in the new middle-class salons that sprung up in places like Manali (near early-colonial Madras) and Ettayapuram. This artist is also very well aware of his place within the continually evolving tradition, and he has much to say about the practices of performance in its theoretical frame and historical contexts. He has, in effect, given us a detailed meditation on all major aspects of Carnatic music – a glimpse, one might say, from behind the visible surface of the kacceri, from some point deep within the artist's heart and mind, remote from the microphones and even from the magic of what we can hear with our ears. Interestingly, he also has much to say on ultra-modern musical forms, including film songs and popular music, which to his great credit he sees as, in some senses, continuous with the classical tradition.

There are fascinating discussions of specific, sometimes quite technical topics and domains (the long chapter on rhythm, for example; and the fine presentation of what raga means to a performer). We also see an unusual historical sensibility informing the entire book and coming to sustained expression in the chapter on the evolution of Carnatic music over the last four centuries. A connoisseur of Carnatic singing will find here surprising articulations of what goes on in the mind of a supremely skilled performer in the course of a full-scale concert. How much is conscious at the moment when sound emerges from the throat (or perhaps from some more unfathomable place in the body)? How does the long process of training, replete with criss-crossing technical knowledge on many levels, translate into the gift of active interpretation of the musical and verbal texts? There are things that we, the listeners, will never know (and probably should not think too much about) – and yet a window, at moments amazingly transparent, has been opened for us by a performer of unimpeachable authority.

If I had to pick one topic of special importance, I would go for those passages where T.M. Krishna speaks of the performer's creative role vis-à-vis the composer and his texts. One could argue that, in this respect, both the Carnatic and the Hindustani streams allow, even require, the performer to go well beyond what is considered normative in Western classical music. Indeed, it is impossible even to begin to understand a Carnatic kriti in live performance without an awareness of this critical, active re-creation by the skilled performer. It is not only a matter of improvisation, at various possible points; rather, the creative Carnatic singer in some sense mingles with the composer throughout, a not unconstrained, yet surprisingly autonomous, partner to the expressive process. We have reason to be grateful to an artist who not only embodies this truth in practice, but who has also found accessible words to make sense of it.

This is a passionate book written by a person capable

of strong feeling – capable, that is, of love. You can hear this personal quality, along with the tremendous force of practice and experience, in the way he writes: 'The raga exists in a trained listener's mind even before it is heard.' 'Time is not only a measure; it is a living entity that defines and redefines our sense of ourselves as individuals and as a people... The most beautiful part of time in music is the idea of created time.' 'Creativity that is born out of purely structural rules that are imposed on a raga lacks the organic quality of creativity.' The author is therefore interested, as he tells us, in the way 'rules cease to be conditions'. He is sometimes ironic: 'We think of both a person standing on his head for twenty-four hours and a rendition of raga bhairavi by a vidvan as "awesome".' He can be refreshingly irreverent: 'The biggest problem with musicologists is that they study Carnatic music as a science.' Though he embodies a tradition given to various competing orthodoxies, he is open to experimentation. Thus, needless to say, passages of his book sound deliberately provocative and will certainly generate controversy, as befits a vital artistic tradition that has proven capable of repeatedly renewing, even re-imagining, itself over the course of six or seven generations. This book is testimony to that vitality. My hope is that it will reach readers who love Carnatic music without knowing much about it – without knowing why they love it – and that it will move people who have never heard a Carnatic kriti to discover what they have missed. As for the connoisseurs, T.M. Krishna has given them a candid view of how a true master of the art conceives of what he does, what he hears, what he has learnt, and what he thinks is still to come.

David Shulman
Hebrew University, Jerusalem

A Note on Reading

Dear Reader,

How would you read a book – or this book? 'Just pick it up and start reading.' True, and much as that would be entirely your call, I'm tempted to leave you with one more thought. With a book of poems, you hop, skip and jump, but with a novel you would follow the author's stream. In a book of essays, the continuity exists in the overarching idea the author holds and which permeates the whole book. But that idea reveals itself to greater effect if the essays are read in a certain order. This is a personal note on how I would read this book, if at all I were the one picking it up!

A Southern Music has been arranged into three broad sections: the Experience, the Context and the History. Each section is self-contained, but the chapters in the second section of the book, the Context, can be read in any order at any time. However, I would advise the reader not to move to the History before going through the Experience. After all it is experience that gives us insight into history. Within sections, you could do crossovers if you wish, except in the Experience section, which is ideally read as is. I have avoided diacritical signs to make the reading easier.

However, this requires the reader to be conscious of the nuances in Indian languages.

I hope this letter will help you to not just read but enjoy the book.

Warm regards,

TMK

Book 1

The Experience

'When I paint my object is to show what I have
found and not what I am looking for.'
– Pablo Ruiz y Picasso

Music

A Narrative

No one journeys through life alone. From nowhere almost, a companion joins in and keeps step right through – music.

Whether flowing out of the hollow of the bamboo or taking complex forms in the musical imagination, music has been and remains an integral part of human existence. It mirrors every moment of a person's life, not just one specific time. It is life itself. Music is something intimate, a friend, guide, teacher, protector, challenger, aphrodisiac, stimulator and much more. Even in those who believe that they are tone-deaf or not musically inclined, certain songs and tunes rouse emotions.

We know this, but what *is* music? A difficult question, because how do we view something so intimate with detachment? Can it be defined? Even more importantly, does it need to be defined? But whether it needs to be defined or not, it certainly needs to be understood; so important it is to our beings. It needs to be understood in order to give us a concept of what it is we hold so close. It also needs to be understood because, by understanding something so vital to us, we understand something of ourselves.

The specific combination of sounds that becomes music can be explained in technical terms, but to the receiver, it is a stimulus – an intricate stimulus. It is not the sounds themselves, but what they do to us that makes those sounds 'music'. The senses define something to us as music.

So the sounds need to have a certain quality to be called music. This 'quality' is not a technical property of the sounds, but acoustic and emotive. It is in and through this that we discover the musicality of sounds, discover music. One may argue that, in order to make this interaction happen, there has to be a technical relationship between the sounds that are generated and our aesthetic receptors. While this may be true, when we respond to music, we are not responding to or sensing the technical quality, we are sensing the acoustic and emotive quality. It is in this experience of being made and being experienced that music may be said to 'happen', or be created. I use the word 'created' advisedly: music lies not in the sounds, but in the way they arise, unfold and travel to the receiver like great creations. The receiver includes the person generating the sounds. We are all receivers, the maker of the music as much as the listener.

Is music the creation of human activity? All of us say that birds sing, but do they? What is it about the chirping of some birds that makes it a song? It is the human relationship with what we believe is 'song'. The idea that the bird sings is ours, not the bird's. Its sounds are related to its own existence and life cycle, perhaps hormonal changes or physical reactions. The bird does not intend to make music. A mating call, for instance, is a signal to prospective partners. Does this sound need to be beautiful? For their purposes, probably. But what is beautiful to us is not necessarily beautiful to the bird; we are defining the beauty of the sound as we perceive it. Whatever acoustic, emotive or biological stimulus the bird responds to, it is not to the music in the sound – at least not as we understand music to be. When humans respond to the music in a bird's song, we are being conditioned by our experience of music in life. Music in nature is not nature's music. It is by human yardsticks that we determine beauty, symmetry, essence and the like.

Even among humans, what is considered music today is completely different from what was considered music a thousand years ago. There is a claim that animals, birds and plants respond to music. If they do, what music are we referring to? Would we say that they too evolve in their response to music? The claim that non-human life too responds to music has been debated by scientists with no clear conclusion.

But the veracity of that claim is not the issue here. The fact remains that the response, or lack thereof, of any other being does not impact the creation of music. Music is a human activity and so is its experience. It is not an accident, but a conscious expression of life defined within the human sphere. Many would say that music, indeed art itself, deals with a person's personal feelings conditioned by experience. The reader may feel that I find this assertion acceptable.

Let us break this assertion down. With both the artist and the conscious connoisseur, the experience of art can leave the sphere of personal feeling. Art removes one from the site of personal sense to that of an impersonal sense of experience. This is not a sterile or self-fulfilling movement, but an immensely wholesome and fulfilling one. Let me explain. The individual is drawn completely into the world of the art, and there develops a personal relationship with it. The personal nature of the experience lies within this created space, yet it remains impersonal because the felt experience is not just about the individual's own conditioned feelings as much as it is about the quality of the art being experienced in itself. This experiencing of the art is definitely far more than a manifestation of personal human feelings or needs.

In the construction of this essay, I have placed two types of experiences that art can give us: one that is about ourselves, and another that is purely about the created. Both exist, of course, and all of us experience them. There are two elements that play a role in defining the experience: the art form itself and the receiver. Not all forms of art intend to transport the receiver beyond the realm of his or her personal self. Some forms cater squarely to the personal nature of one's being. But there are art forms that intend to move every individual beyond the space of personal feeling towards one of created emotion: the space of the created art. In order to experience music beyond personal confines, the receiver also needs to be a serious seeker of art and aware of the art itself. Without that insight, the receiver may not be able to inhabit that created space, for the music will be received as personal feeling alone, and to that extent be incomplete. At the same time, a truly evolved connoisseur may be able to draw out a sense of emotional abstraction from an art form that is primarily aimed at personal emotion, purely by her attitude towards it. The seriousness and appropriate attitude towards understanding art have to be cultivated by every art seeker.

Aesthetics

Coming back to the idea of defining and understanding music, there is a specific word that comes to mind: aesthetics, from the Greek 'aisthetikos'. Unless we spend some time with this word, it will be impossible to formulate ideas regarding music. We use aesthetics to describe personal tastes and sensibilities, or in the context of pretty, beautiful or pleasant things. A culturally conditioned sensibility. What is aesthetic to an Indian may not be so to a Russian. If we hold to this understanding, it will make a discussion on music a non-starter. We need to rethink – or rather think more deeply about – our understanding of aesthetics.

Aesthetics is primarily about the senses, as in aesthesia. But it is not about what you sense, but how to sense. This may seem illogical; how is it possible to tutor one on how to sense? But this is exactly what aesthetics is about. In aesthetics, one is not overly worried about an individual's preferences, but more about the object that has generated a certain feeling in him. The point of reference is not the person but the object. Greek words ending with 'tikos' relate to a body of empirically arrived ideas, that is, through serious observation and experience.

Therefore, aesthetics is a body of philosophy that tries to understand the aspects of an art form that give it its identity and content. Aesthetics in arts is about the understanding of art. It would include an understanding of intent, structure, form, changes, developments and history, thereby also examining why an art form is what it is. Aesthetics does not judge art on the basis of taste. Through this understanding, one tries to discuss and critique art.

It is also possible for an individual to hold a personal liking for an aspect of something – music, for instance – and yet understand that what is liked is aesthetically destroying the essence of a specific aspect of the music. Here I have presented aesthetics as an objective rather than a subjective idea.

Now if we look at music in terms of aesthetics and see it as a combination of sounds that gives us an aesthetic experience, we have a completely different understanding of music. At a personal level, it gives us pleasure through our senses, but from an objective point of view, it is a combination of sounds that have been given a certain form, content and organization, which has an impact on the senses. Aesthetics is the understanding of this form, content and organization. Let us look at beauty within this context. It has a personal manifestation and a sense beyond the personal. We need to go beyond the personal in order to grasp the *idea* of beauty. Similarly, we must develop the capacity to critique music on the basis of the aesthetics that define it, rather than our personal sensibilities. In the course of these essays, I will strive to write from this impersonal, objective stand, not my personal predispositions, instincts or sensibilities.

Instinct in Musical Experience

The human response to music is initially instinctive. As soon as we hear any form of music, there is an involuntary reaction, a flicker of recognition, an acknowledgement of an earlier association reflected in a deep breath. The standard understanding of instinct is that it is an involuntary response, independent of reason or experience. How much of 'instinct' is genetically coded – can it even be? The amorphous nature of ideas such as art and knowledge makes such associations futile, in fact irrelevant. For the sake of social parity, it is better left alone. We already have communities claiming greater intelligence based on prejudiced and discriminatory science. But this I can say: even if instinct is an unpremeditated and unrehearsed prompting, it is finessed by the sounds that we heard in our homes and the environments in which we grew up. These stimuli connect the subconscious mind with our past experiences. Every lived experience places a layer of impressions on our mind, and we build on it right through life – layers of resultant opinions, likes and dislikes. Our initial response to the stimuli of music emerges from all these.

Conversely, when we hear music that does not relate to any of our experiences, most often, the immediate response is of unease. This is rare, as more often than not, the mind makes immediate connections with our previous experiences of music. But when it does happen, there is discomfort and even dislike for the strange music. If we hear it over and over, new connections are created, which may allow us to build a relationship with the musical form that had seemed unfamiliar, even unwelcome.

Purely at the level of feelings and memory, music triggers images and emotions that also establish our relationship with it. We must realize that these responses are more about us than the music. When music reiterates feelings that touch us at a deep level, it seems closer. It reminds us of places, people, thoughts and dreams and can sift even the most distant event from our memory. Music transcends melody and rhythm; it is a deeply personal emotive experience that connects to our life through our senses. This is what makes music meaningful in our normal life. Beyond comprehension, grammar and form, what makes music intimate is its ability to reveal ourselves to us. Therefore, when a person likes or dislikes a form of music, there are possibly many layers of cause and effect encompassing the musical, social and, of course, the personal. From this personal space of an instinctive response, with its subtle ambient texturing, the aesthetic moves on to the larger created space of shared art. But I want to take a step back now, to the 'original' moment of response to music.

The Fleeting Moment

I wonder whether there exists something else as well – something that lies just before the 'instinctive' response. Is there a slice of a moment, a space so thin as to be invisible almost, where stimuli and sense intersect? In this minuscule time frame exists an experience that does not admit of even the narrowest baggage of conditioning. But this space passes quickly, so quickly that we may not even realize that it was ever there. There are times when a stimulus appears all of a sudden – like a beautiful ray of sunlight from behind a mountain when we least expect it – and for a moment, there is just 'pure sense'. That slice of a moment precedes the recognition of the ray of light as beautiful or even as sunlight.

Response to stimuli is not linear – pure sense, instinct and cognitive response – though it may often appear in that order. Music can give us a pure sense experience that lasts for a merest moment as also, equally, for a long time, coming much after instinctive and cognitive reactions. I would like to connect this experience with what I referred to earlier as an 'impersonal' sense of experience. Impersonal and pure senses are not counter-indicative. In this state, the experience is at the cusp of the sensual, and the music is devoid of the individual's own identity. This is not only rare, but also requires that the experiencer be an aesthetically evolved person. It is interesting that an individual has to reflect the instinctive and be simultaneously immersed in the cognitive to finally live in the art itself. The final state is that of the true aesthete.

Serious engagement with music cannot be dependent on instinct. It has to be cultivated through aesthetic study. The receiver grows from unconscious predisposition to conscious disposition. The highest form of conscious disposition, though, is completely unselfconscious.

The reason that instinctive experience lasts for only a fraction of a second is that we react to the stimulus of music by creating identities and categorizing it. This is an essential function of our mind that gives us a sense of security. This identification process gives us the strength to say 'I recognize' or 'I know'. Quite often, a classical musician will say, 'This film song sounds like such-and-such raga.' The opposite too can happen. A lay listener could say, 'This raga sounds like that film song.' These are examples of creating associations based on known qualities. These associations are relevant to both the listener and the musician. Both do exactly the same thing, the only difference being that the understanding of music comes from their differing roles and the intensity of engagement. When a musician sings, he is creating identities based on his conditioned comprehension. It is therefore very important to understand how these connections with identity define the essential character of each musical form. After all, it is musicians who define the music. It is their mind that fashions the form, shapes its essence.

The Musician and the Self

I would like to look at these interconnections in two ways: first, when they are created by organic and evolutionary processes though enhanced by individual expression, and second, when they are the result of the musician's own battle for self-identity. In evolutionary change there is no doubt a role for the individual self, but the role is governed by the threads that have been handed down to him. In the self-oriented change, that thread is lost.

When we look at history, we find that the process of identity recognition led to the development of various schools of thought. We can philosophize about the need for this process, but the fact remains that it exists. The reiteration of an identity by successive contributing musicians establishes a form. This does not mean that the identity is a closed box of inflexibility, for the possibility of change, improvisation and evolution continues to exist. Inside every impression, there lies a possibility of redefinition.

A living thought is never idle; it is being constantly redefined and rejuvenated, and over a period of time, is perceived as an original idea. The beauty lies in the fact that there exists a continuum within every level of thought when it is a part of the organic evolutionary process. This continuum is created because thinkers recognize the essential elements that build the form and create their own story from them. After a while, there appear different versions of the same story, each keeping the core characters and principles intact. Each story also changes when handled by different storytellers, thereby increasing the depth, with the core remaining intact. This is what I call tradition, and many of the organic changes in Karnatik music seem to have evolved through this fascinating metamorphosis.

The word 'tradition', of course, can be interpreted in so many different ways that we seem to understand it as something that a large number of people have done repeatedly over a period of time. Understanding what tradition is becomes especially relevant in the context of classical art forms. In the world of Karnatik music, we use the word tradition, or sampradaya, to justify almost every act for which we have no explanation. This is essentially an escape route. Tradition is not a repetitive act; it is change that retains within it the essential threads that define the whole. Every banyan tree is different; in many ways, each tree is so unique that it can be defined individually. Banyan trees have also changed through millions of years of evolution, and yet, all of them share certain qualities. These are the elements which, when put together, define a banyan tree. This is tradition.

When we do not view it in this manner, we battle with problems of identity and form. Is identity then just the will of a person? Can the will of every individual create divergent forms? In this case, the identity we are battling is not music, but ourselves. In the search for self-identity, we are willing to ignore or not seek the threads that have been handed down. This is a problem we face not just in contemporary music, but right through musical history.

There have been musicians and musicologists of various periods who, in the battle within their own selves, have changed tradition. It is not an issue of what is right and what is wrong, but something we need to comprehend, so that we may gauge what we have lost, gained or changed. Where a certain change that is not in sync with the musical evolutionary thought is implemented and even accepted, the music is adapted in order to include it. And very soon, the new adaptation becomes tradition. Sometimes, as individuals, we do not spend enough time to understand the evolutionary process, and make decisions on the basis of influences that are outside it. I would prefer not to use the terms 'internal' or 'external', as every influence is a result of the interaction between the two. But it is important to understand the form, change and development of thought in an art form in order to absorb external influences, and yet retain the essential elements that make the music. When there is a lot of external influence on a musician lacking internal introspection, the end result is a musical direction that is disconnected. The acceptance or the lack of that is not the issue, but the aesthetic repercussions of such directional changes is a matter of concern.

Convention, Tradition and Sampradaya

These terms are interchangeably used in the context of music. Conventions are accepted norms that are followed by the community, and tradition is viewed as ideas that are repeated and passed down. We have already discussed the nuanced view of tradition. In Karnatik music, the word sampradaya means both conventions and traditions. The differentiation between the two is probably thought of as irrelevant – the result of which is a situation where all changes are considered to be within the spectrum of sampradaya. This gives all musicians the right to claim something as their sampradaya, while simultaneously abdicating the responsibility of comprehending these traditions, if at all they exist. This is a licence that we wield to establish our connection with the past.

Many of the practices that we follow come under the category of convention, which are often the result of a single musician's actions. Once this is followed by her students and emulated by other musicians, it comes to be established as a sampradaya. These conventions (sampradaya) are often at loggerheads with tradition (sampradaya), but reconciliation is not what we seek. We accept convention as being a part of the whole traditional system. It is interesting that we do not see conflict. This is due to two main reasons: first, the stature of the musician who created this convention supersedes logical analysis. Second, its wide, inherited acceptability creates a sense of collective history, which secures our belief systems in the antiquity of the music itself.

Conventions are also generated due to social, religious and political influences, necessitated by the need for acceptability within a context. These changes can either be true to the musical tradition or divergent, but the context makes them acceptable. Religious beliefs too play an important role in influencing art forms. These lead to complete changes in the essence of the music as the very survival or the popularity of the art is challenged.

For example, Tamil ritual theatre forms today present stories from contemporary themes to sustain viewer interest. One could view these as superficial changes, as the form, style and presentation are retained. But techniques used to portray contemporary stories may lead to changes in storytelling methods. In my view, even when the context demands a change, it is important for artists to be sensitive to the form and intent of the art form. In a challenging environment, though, it is very difficult to strike a balance. This is similar to the challenges faced by people working in traditional textiles and trying to modify their designs and products for today's customers. This directly influences design tradition, but the need for survival is a serious and essential concern.

One wonders whether there is another way of dealing with this problem. Can we bring society around to rediscovering the beauty of the traditional form rather than compromising the form to meet social needs? It is far from easy, of course, to negotiate the complexity of evolving social tastes and preferences. As an integral part of social thought, religion directly influences artistic expression. The birth of most art forms came from the search for the mystical and unknown, a fascination with nature's mysteries, creation and connection to the gods. It is true of every civilization that many conventions are borrowed from religious beliefs and accepted into artistic tradition. Usually, these changes result in a major realignment in the art form.

Tradition in musical evolution is the result of the movements of the past leading to change in the present, while retaining the essential core elements. It may be influenced by individuals and the social context, but all these are secondary to the integrity of the musical form. Individual changes and conventions are driven by the need of the individual or by factors of survival, which take precedence over the art form. History reveals that all these various changes – whether traditional, individual or social – interact with each other. In the unravelling of this complex basket of interactions lie the form, structure and intent of an art form.

In my opinion, for the better understanding of music as it is today, it is imperative that every musician explores the idea of sampradaya. This involves sieving through collective organic thought, and individual and socio-political conventions. This process of introspection will also come to define every musician's own musical thought. Being part of the organic history of music is the way to retain qualities that give each musical form its unique identity. This becomes even more relevant in an age when we have stimuli from so many different sources. These stimuli, without doubt, influence our orientation towards Karnatik music. In this environment, unless we comprehend our music as a continuous river that travels in time, adapting and changing to different environments, we will not be one of the travellers on that river. We may create a dam and divert the water, but this will change the natural flow. It is up to each one of us to decide how we want to experience music and, by experiencing it, contribute to its journeys.

2

The Intent of Music

What does music mean to me?

This is a question that every music lover engages with. The connections between the music and the listener are both intellectual and emotional. These create preferences for different forms of music, different hierarchies and gradations in our mind. These hierarchies are not fixed; they can meander and change in the course of our lives, with certain constants holding their ground.

In spite of these gradations, it is still perfectly possible for two totally different forms of music to generate equally strong emotional responses. The excitement generated, for instance, from listening to a song by the Beatles can be the same as that from a composition in the raga kadananakutuhalam. The cultural background, instruments, system and intonation in those two are completely different, yet they evoke a similar experience. Technically, of course, it is possible to establish commonalities. Be that as it may, the almost similar emotional response generated by two distinct musical forms remains intriguing. This sometimes results in the naïve belief that the intent of all music is the same.

We do need to investigate the following questions: If we can relate emotionally to different forms of music in the same way, what is it that sets apart one form from the other? Is all music then the same? Are all the differences that we perceive based purely on our conditioning? These thoughts lead us to a deeper investigation of the nature of music, the role of music in society and what it means to an individual.

Let us attempt such an investigation. Our emotional response to music is driven by the senses. As discussed in the previous essay, various factors contribute to that response. Many people believe that, irrespective of the form of music and its nature, or what may be called the 'kind' of music, its most important function is to touch our hearts. For some, the important thing about music is the 'excitement' it generates, or some other such response. It is important to remember that the kind of music we listen to also connects with and reflects our own character and psychological state at a given point of time. Depending on one's emotional state, some kinds of music may prove to be deeply affecting, even disturbing.

Quite apart from that emotional charge, every form of music has its own historical and contemporary role based on the social and cultural scaffolding that society has raised around it. Here, the role of music is the result of the nature of its origin, its journey and its function within the social construct. This social and externally positioned intent drives its form, governs its nature and performance, and controls the environment in which it operates. We must note that sometimes the scaffolding is constructed even as the music is evolving. When this occurs, the intent that existed before the social framework could begin to evolve in a different direction.

The word 'intent' is, therefore, essential to an understanding of why music takes on a certain form. Unravelling this is rendered difficult by various factors including tradition, convention and the personal choices of individuals. Nevertheless, this investigation and the resultant discovery open our mind to why it is that we can get so deeply involved with a specific art form over others. Consider for a moment the structure of a house and that of an office. Both buildings will host human beings, but the very nature of why they were built governs the use of the space and material, as well as factors like structure and accessibility.

What is the purpose of an art form? It can vary from being religious, playing a supportive role to other art presentations, community building, societal and personal events, or it could be a form that in its intent is purely art itself. All these have a direct impact on the form and development of the art. As socio-political formations evolve, so does the art form; it constantly adapts in its own subtle manner to these changes. Critically and analytically understanding the various societal roles of an art form is necessary if we are to identify the ways in which the form has changed over the years. It is imperative that this examination be separated from studies of emotional responses, since it is clear that diametrically opposite art forms can evoke similar emotions.

Sometimes, as an art form is influenced by social, political or religious factors, it can modify and even change character in order to adapt to the circumstances. Of course, when I say the art form 'changes', I am referring to the role of the form's practitioners. This can, at times, lead to a blurring between two art forms – the result of an overlapping of intent between the two. These modifications can lead to an overlap in the emotions that they evoke. The cognitive relationship between an individual and two art forms can then come together. This leads to dichotomous responses and perceptions and can go on to a realignment within the form and structure of the art. It is, therefore, neither feasible nor quite correct to analyse the journey and evolution of a form of music at an emotional level, as that will lead to emotive correlations between completely divergent stimuli without reference to the larger and more complex causes of this similarity and its significance.

Another aspect of the social nature of music is that each form has its audience groupings, the nature of which is defined by cultural backgrounds, exposure and social divisions – the field ripe for the creation of hierarchies. The role of the form in society and the generic perceptions of it define its access to people as well as the size of audience groupings. It is also true that musical forms that have very clear community roles tend to have larger audiences. The social composition of the group too is usually defined by the origin and nature of the music. Classifications exist within and between these communities, so there is no avoiding these complex social formations.

Certain art forms are considered by their practitioners and patrons as 'elevated', by others as elitist. Other forms are held in disdain by the so-called elite, even regarded as crass or uncultured. These differences are often determined by social hierarchy, depending on the communities that nurtured and supported the art. This differentiation too needs to be excised from the discussion in order to pursue the question of intent. Sophistication, a sense of culture and refinement, is a subjective perception. For the British in the seventeenth century, Indians as a category were uncultured. What was the basis of this notion? It was nothing more than the wholly false notion that culture as practised in British society was superior. Today most Indians, especially those living in urban India, nurse similar perceptions of what is crude and what is sophisticated. For instance, in Tamil Nadu, most people tend to be overtly expressive and have heightened emotional reactions. Unsurprisingly, many so-called English-educated sections of society are uneasy with such responses. What does this show? Just this, that these sections are influenced by Western notions of what is cultured and nurse the classist illusion that holds unrestrained emotional expressiveness as being somehow inferior.

The idea of sophistication also seems to imply it is something that requires a higher order of sensitivity, a certain cultural plinth reflective of the higher social echelons. This leads to the conviction that the art and culture practised, preserved and propagated by this class is of a higher standard than that of those in the 'lower' levels of society. It is significant that this idea is not the hallmark of the relevant 'class' alone; it is prevalent in the social environment as a whole. People who have improved their financial position tend to imitate the behaviour of those already at that level of society, and enthusiastically support the preferred art forms in order to be regarded as part of that category of taste and discrimination. The support and appreciation of these art forms are considered hallmarks of an evolved human being. In reality, this is a social phenomenon. The appreciation of all art forms is a product of cultivated association. Art forms are not to be compared with one another.

Obviously, the intent governing the formulation of the art form will drive its evolution, just as the social factors do too. A notable and noticeable feature in the evolution of an art form is internal stylization. Stylization is only relevant within each art. The process of evolution – the differentiation from previous interpretations – results in the separation of various styles based on internal comparison. The word 'internal' here refers to the fact that these changes occur within the spectrum of the art itself. This does not take away from the fact that all such changes are also being guided by 'external' dynamics that come from society.

Let us now look at the various forms of music in south Indian society and try to understand their role within the larger canvas of the arts.

Folk Music

I am reminded of a conversation I had with Dr Harold Powers, the well-known ethnomusicologist from Princeton University, many years ago. He said, 'The classifications of folk and classical are purely social. As musical forms are appreciated by more people in the higher sections of society, the music transforms into classical and the aesthetic is reconstructed.'

This was the first time I heard of this interpretation. Like any classical musician, until then, I had assumed that folk forms are less systematized or developed and are intended to so remain. This leads me to the big question: what is folk?

We refer to forms like kootthu (a theatre form from Tamil Nadu) or even Yakshagana as 'folk', implying that they belong to a less evolved genre. This is misleading. Almost all performance art forms that we describe as folk are highly evolved – in the sense of what in actual fact constitutes the art form, and not perceptions about it. It might then be asked: why then the categorization, why refer to these form as folk music? I think Dr Powers's remark was extremely insightful.

Our perception of folk art is purely social and is class-based. The audience groups for these art forms are drawn from rural environments, or the underprivileged and lower-income groups. These folk performances, usually held in temples or at local congregations, are integral to the social or religious calendars of the communities. These art forms are used to represent traditional narratives that connect with living social beliefs and practices. They are sustained by a community of artists whose training in these forms is traditionally carried on by families or communities that have grown into these art forms for centuries.

A superficial observation of these arts would lead us to untrue and simplistic conclusions. To arrive at an understanding, we must address grammar and theory. Grammar and systems can be written or oral. Even written grammar was not handed down to us as the final word. It is the result of gradual changes in practice. Therefore, the perceived prerequisite that a classical form must have a written grammar is not, strictly speaking, appropriate. While folk art forms do have a well-developed grammar and organized system, these are not necessarily written down as formal theory. The learning process, which is practice passed down the generations, may be more by observation than a codified training methodology. Therefore, students imbibe the inherent grammar, theory and systems at a subconscious level. The theoretical base has evolved over a period of time, in which practitioner, listener, student and society have been interacting. It would therefore be erroneous to believe that these forms do not have a developed theory. What we could say is that, in some performing arts, the line of theorization and the schools of musicology are active partners to practice; while in others these are not developed as separate areas of study.

Some forms are part of ritual performances. This is an interesting and important dimension where these forms have an aesthetic structure, presentation and system, but their intent is an integral part of a community's religious practice. Therefore, when we take them out of the context of a ritual rite or requirement, and present them as an individual art presentation within our modern perception of performance, they lose an integral part of their identity. At the same time, we cannot exclude the distinct possibility of the transformed nature of their out-of-context, but nonetheless authentic, presentation creating an altogether new aesthetic identity and intent. The creation of Bharatanatyam from Sadir (its form in the days when it was practised only by the devadasis), which was a ritual-related yet distinct art form, is a case of transformed existence. It is also very likely, as in the case of Sadir, that even while functioning within its ritualistic 'home' environment, the art form had evolved into something more than a ritualistic offering. The seeds for this evolution are anterior to its ritualistic identity. Sometimes changes are forced upon them, and that is when these forms, no longer a part of their roots in ritual practice, can find their very survival under threat.

So then, what is folk music?

Folk music refers to music or songs that are part of a community's lore – lullabies, songs sung during festivals or during important events in life, like birth, weddings and funerals.

There is no audience, as that term is commonly understood, to receive this expression of music. The receiver and the giver together express aesthetic intent through their emotional state. Anybody who is part of the community that has inherited a specific song can render it. This natural expression through music of elemental emotions at landmark occasions can be said to fall within the description of folk music. This music does not have a subconscious system that governs its identity, but is defined by the community's own context and cultural history. Therefore, let us be careful, respectful and mindful when we classify music as 'folk'.

Film Music

In the Indian context, this is the musical expression that dominates our sense receptors. Radio and TV channels present cine-music through the day. Its popularity is as unquestioned as it is unprecedented. Films are made in almost every Indian language, and their songs hover on people's lips. It is impossible to be part of contemporary society in India today and escape the sounds of film music. The reach of cinema is, of course, the central reason.

Cinema is the most dominant form of artistic expression globally, and especially so in India. As a direct result, film music too is unmistakably the driving force of popular musical aesthetics. But film music did not materialize in a vacuum. Interestingly, and even incredibly, in its earlier and formative phase, film music depended heavily on classical music. Its melody and rhythms were derived from classical music and many actors, who sang their own songs those days, were either classical musicians or had received training in classical music.

Over time, this changed and music for films evolved into a separate genre. Just as stories, storytelling methods and techniques changed in Indian cinema, so did its music. Film music is a versatile and amorphous form that constantly reinvents and reinterprets itself in response to the major influences of the day. In that sense, film music does not have to retain any specific musical quality – a fact that makes its identity difficult to define. The only constant in film music is its highly resilient and adaptive relevance within the context of the cinema.

It is important to note here that dance is a very important part of music in Indian cinema. The role of music in the context of cinema makes for an interesting study. It is part of our cultural history and not a recent interpolation – a natural extension of the symbiotic connection between drama, music and dance in the Indian cultural context. Theatre in ancient Indian art presentations included all these forms of expressions. Ancient Indian theatre art was inseparable from music and dance. This is reflected both in ancient Sanskrit and Tamil literature. Today Koodiyattam, Yakshagana and Bhagavata Mela are living examples of this tradition. Even Indian theatre in the early part of the twentieth century followed this practice, with actors using songs and dialogues to express themselves. Therefore, music and dance in our cinema are a continuation of our cultural history, very much a part of our theatrical tradition.

What is the role of music in cinema?

It is very clear that its role is to support, enhance and express emotional situations. Every song is positioned to provide the viewer with a deeper experience of a particular moment in the story or the character's state at specific moments. Therefore, songs appear to express love, sorrow, longing, separation and so on. Beyond this, music also plays a subtle role as a background score within scenes, between dialogues and during silent moments. In fact, the more 'frightening' scenes would impact the viewer far less if there were no sound, no music to enhance the visual. The music that we hear enhances, even constitutes, the visual experience. The dance sequences in the movies also help express the same changes.

Does this mean that film songs do not have an intrinsic value?

Do not people hear the songs even before they see the movie and continue to play them, later, independent of the film? Of course they do, and this is significant. The intrinsic musical value of the songs cannot be denied. But the fact remains that if the movie did not exist, these songs would never have been composed. Sometimes we even relate songs to actors and identify voices of certain playback singers with certain actors. This too is a result of the relationship between music and cinema. Enjoying film music for its beauty is definitely possible, but the intent of its creation still remains rooted in cinema.

Namasankirtana and Bhajan

These religious musical performances, specific to Hinduism, are prevalent all over India and form a very important part of the religious fabric of society. Parallels in other religious streams include choral singing in Christianity, qawwalis in the Sufi tradition and shabadkirtan in Sikhism.

Three great saints – Shridhara Ayyaval, Bodhendra Sarasvati and Sadguru Svami of Marudanallur – who lived between the late seventeenth and early nineteenth centuries in south India, propagated the practice of Namasiddhanta, or chanting the lord's name. Another saint-singer, Sadashiva Brahmendra, contributed to its spread. The basis of this movement was the belief that chanting the lord's name was the easiest way to moksha. This developed into a tradition where songs were sung in praise of the various gods and goddesses. Therefore, Namasankirtana was encouraged, developed and spread to involve people in the collective singing of the lord's name. This was an important tool to keep Hindus together and spread Hinduism.

Over many centuries, Namasankirtana has gained a very important place in the lives of south Indian Hindus, especially the brahmin community. It is believed that this musical tradition was originally structured by Bodhendra Sarasvati, though the present format is credited to Sadguru Svami, who evolved a performance practice that is still current, using compositions written by saints from various parts of the country. The performance practice was standardized and the range of composers greatly enlarged. This made Namasankirtana acceptable to people of different languages as it included the abhangs of Tukaram, kirtanas of Purandaradasa and Annamacharya, the bhajans of Mirabai, ashtapadis of Jayadeva, tarangas of Narayana Tirtha and the outpourings of Tamil composers like Arunachala Kavi.

Namasankirtana presentations in the south have one main singer, with one or two additional singers who support and provide chorus, accompanied on the violin and mrdanga. Sometimes the tabla and dholak are also included in the percussion ensemble.

It must also be mentioned that Namasankirtana seems to have evolved in Tamil-speaking regions during the Maratha rule (seventeenth to nineteenth century) since the kirtan tradition had long been popular in west India.

Collective bhajan singing is but an extension of the Namasankirtana tradition. In collective bhajan renditions, there is usually a group that leads the community in singing compositions on various gods and goddesses. The result is a highly charged atmosphere. Sometimes people go into a trance. There is no audience here; every individual is a participant who contributes to this religious fervour and the increased devotional and emotional heightening that many experience.

What is the role of music here? It is obviously to contribute to the religious experience. The music is such that everyone can sing; the tunes are simple and repetitive. One does not need musical training to sing along in this tradition, only religious fellow feeling. The focus is on the lyrics, which are largely eulogies to gods and their names. The multiple repetition of lines heightens the experience.

Namasankirtana involves a trained group of musicians who render religious songs to a group of believers. Therefore, there is a performance-like aspect to it. Yet the audience will join in at specific points as directed by the lead singer. Even if these are presentations by trained musicians, their role is similar, since the lyrics focus on religious fervour, the names of gods, mythological stories or spiritual messages dressed in beautiful music. The focus is on giving oneself up to a religious experience triggered by singing the lord's name and being entranced by the stories and the philosophical import of the songs. The singer provides this with the fervour with which he sings.

Harikatha

Harikatha or kathakalakshepam arose in the nineteenth century with the migration of kirtankars such as Ramachandra Bava and Morkar Bava from Gwalior to Tanjavur. This is a beautiful form of storytelling that remains vibrant in many parts of south India. It is a musical presentation where mythological, religious and spiritual stories come to be narrated. The main presenter uses history, music, poetry, mythology, philosophy and contemporary experiences to communicate the story. The aim is to convey through stories what is regarded as the moral, religious and spiritual values expressed in Indian philosophy to a listener. The storyteller is usually accompanied by musicians. The story is woven within a prescribed traditional format, but the choice of songs and narration are left to the exponent. During the course of the narration, the performer constantly cross-refers to various other mythological stories, quotes and treatises to emphasize the religious idea. The intent of traditional Harikatha – as the name suggests – is to relate the 'story of the lord'. These stories convey various aspects of the lord's character, deeds and benevolence. The compositions, by various poets and composers, are not necessarily presented as a whole. Specific sections are selected to convey emotions, messages of moral values that are woven into the movement of the story. This makes the Harikatha exponent a multifaceted personality with innumerable talents – a linguist, musician, scholar, historian, didactician and, of course, storyteller par excellence – with the ability to switch from one role to another during the performance.

As far as the role of music in Harikatha goes, the focus is on the lyrical content of the compositions. While we cannot deny the musical ability of many great Harikatha exponents, the fact remains that their focus is on the meaning of the lyrics and not on the musical value of their presentation. Harikatha exponents give special emphasis to the lyrics; the music is subservient to the story.

Western Popular Music

Many forms of popular Western music over the last century can be traced to the African American community in the United States. From its Spirituals came Gospel and Blues. From these rose rhythm and blues (R&B) and the earliest forms of jazz, American folk music, country music, rock 'n' roll and bluegrass. Hip Hop arose from later forms of jazz, and all forms of rock progressed from rock 'n' roll. Many musical forms developed among the African American community were an expression of social inequalities and an assertion of identity; it was musical entertainment that also empowered.

The fact that a lot of modern popular music arose from social and religious protests, especially among the African American community, has influenced its lyrical content. Right through history, these forms have been used to express protest, rage against oppression, proclaim freedom and strength. Whether it is slavery, war, sexuality or gender inequalities, popular music has brought these issues boldly into public purview. This was especially evident during the 1960s and 1970s when musicians such as Pete Seeger, Woody and Arlo Guthrie, Bob Dylan, John Lennon and CSNY used their music to raise awareness of social issues. David Crosby,

Graham Nash, Pete Seeger and Arlo Guthrie were even seen recently during the Occupy Wall Street protest of 2012. Out-and-out popular singers have composed songs that speak about various issues – Michael Jackson on race, for instance.

At the same time, the role of stage performances, music videos and discos give us an insight into another important facet. For performers like Elvis Presley or Michael Jackson, the dance and the physicality of the presentation were as important as the music itself. Similarly, the audience's involvement in that visual experience is an equal part of the music. In fact, they are inseparable.

Popular music is part of the popular dance culture. Discos and dance floors constantly play many popular numbers, and the music, along with the lighting, is part of the experience. Dancing is an integral part of many of these musical forms, and the intent of the music is very closely knit with participatory dance. The exhilaration from this experience is a very important intent of the music. Therefore, these forms of music generate a sense of excitement in an individual, which the lights and the atmosphere of the performance enhance.

Music videos too interpret the music to give the viewer a visual experience of intrigue, thrill and excitement. The whole package together is the experience. This interrelationship between the visual interpretations, innovative lighting and music is what makes popular Western music interesting. Here the function is not just music itself but the larger experience built on dance, lights and music. This also makes the music participatory, leading to a communal experience. Once again, the origins of these musical forms seem to have a role in this subtext. One must note that dance and physicality refer here not only to a forceful dance expression, but includes even the slowest and subtlest moves that popular music evokes.

As we can see, there are two very strong elements that unite Western popular music. Depending on the genre and the performer, the weightage of the two aspects vary, but they do, nevertheless, exist. Some believe that popular music has not been used as a powerful social tool over the last couple of decades and has completely focused on movement, with electronic and dance music dominating.

There are some forms of non-classical Western music that do not fall into this category and need to be understood and treated differently. Jazz, for example, has evolved to become art music, which we shall discuss next, while blues and Hip Hop remain a social musical expression.

Over the last century, Western popular music has become an important part of the listening culture of urban south India. In its popularity, it is now only second to cinema music. There are many Western music bands in the south playing different genres, some even trying to create the 'same music' using south Indian languages.

Karnatik Music as Art Music

Karnatik music is a most interesting form in its function within the social fabric and its own evolution. What makes it so is that its function is based on the musical aspects that constitute its existence. These are: raga, tala, composition and improvisation.

The function of the musician is to express the various melodic and rhythmic aspects of the music with a complete understanding of its aesthetics and grammar. The musician is neither conveying a social message nor helping interpret a certain theatrical act or delivering a religious experience. The experience begins and ends with the musicality of the form. Like many musical forms, Karnatik music has a complex religious history. But I do believe that even while it was practised in courts and temples in different presentations, it had collectively far more than the immediately perceived religious, social or political intent. The history of the music and its aesthetic formations naturally moved the music beyond its social and religious context. Some ritual practices of which Karnatik music was a part were such that they encouraged an art music temperament. The music, as a collective musical identity, has always had a strong art music orientation despite its various socio-political contexts and practitioners. Within the modern context, Karnatik music has a presence separate from the temples and courts. But this is only an extension of the collective art music identity that the form had developed in those spaces. Over the centuries, Karnatik music evolved to explore the abstract areas of melody, rhythm and prosody, creating an aesthetic unit that is experienced as a whole. Karnatik music, like other art music forms, has also developed a line of study in theory that constructs and deconstructs the music.

There is no denying the fact that most lyrics in the Karnatik music repertoire are religious in nature. This creates a serious overlap of experience for the listener. The challenge of perception is when compositions with religious import are rendered in art music presentations. This is due to two factors. One, many compositions that were created for the art music repertoire found their way into other forms, like Harikatha, due to the religious nature of their lyrics. Two, many poems that were religious outpourings also found their way into Karnatik music.

The role of lyrics, meaning and syllabic form will be discussed separately. But I must mention here that, within the context of an art music form such as Karnatik music, lyrics go far beyond linguistic meaning. The nature of the composition changes, depending on the intent of the performance. A Karnatik music composition, when presented as part of Namasankirtana, has a different role when compared to its presentation in a Karnatik concert. In Namasankirtana, the composition is a religious passage conveyed through the vehicle of music. This is why sometimes you find performers explaining the meaning, relating an incident or story about the deity referred to in the lyrics.

When presented in a Karnatik music concert, the focus is on the beauty of the language, its sounds, syllables and their interactions with the raga and tala. The musician has to bring out the various shades, yet contain them within the aesthetic spectrum. This complete musical experience is what we refer to as art music. Art music is about creating art objects that are abstract creations, which give birth to an aesthetic form. The interaction between various components that constitute the music creates these artistic images. The result is an aesthetic experience without external intent.

A Karnatik musician has a responsibility towards this intent. During a concert, the musician delves deep into the aesthetic identity of the music. In this journey, she takes the audience along. This does not mean that the music becomes dry or devoid of feeling. This is a misconception. Raga, tala, composition and improvisation are not mere technical tools; they exist only if they have emotional quality. An object of art is a creation of emotion, not of theory. The music is a manifestation of the musician and will contain the essence of his lived experience.

A person's understanding of emotion is born from life experiences. In life, the stimuli for a certain emotional state may be definable, its nature identifiable, but the feeling itself is only the experience and cannot be defined. This nature of emotion naturally leads to the abstraction of this experience in pure art, including art music.

This does not mean that the musician is transferring a life experience into the musical creation. The transference is in the emotional idea that is being abstracted. Whether or not the musician is actually feeling that emotion at the moment of creation is immaterial. What matters is her ability to bring the abstraction of the emotional world into the music. The constructions of an art music form allows for the expression of this abstraction. The musician's personality is directed towards the art objects, and this involvement is complete. In order to achieve this, the musician uses melody and rhythm. This emotion is not about the lyrical meaning or the musician's feelings.

Art music is about giving the idea of emotion a representation in music. This representation is impersonal as it is about capturing and giving to the world the essence of different shades of human emotion. Music is a piece of art, which creates an aural world of emotions. The lyrical content may be religious or social, but that is not the musician's focus.

However, as the musician is also an individual, his religious or social beliefs will influence his thought. Should he set them aside? While in the world of art music, the musical intent should supersede the personal, I would be the first to admit that this happens only in an ideal situation. A true understanding of art music will be when the musician realizes that, within the context of art music, there is no reason for the creation of music other than the music itself.

Forms referred to as classical music have traditionally been categorized as art music and possess the characteristics discussed above. Originally, along with developed grammar, rules, forms and history, art music was also expected to have a written tradition – possibly because the theories of art music began in the West. But, as awareness of music systems around the world increased, it was noticed that highly developed art music systems did not always have a written tradition. These musical systems were transferred orally, but had the characteristics of art music forms. The intent to express music as itself within set parameters and to create objects of art, celebrated as aesthetic creations, is a distinct quality of art music. There exist forms of music beyond the traditionally accepted realm of 'classical' that are also art music forms, such as jazz. Hence, it is important when making these distinctions in art forms, to lift from descriptions of art music, the heavy mantle of the term 'classical'.

Does this mean that other forms of music do not create art objects? They definitely do, but these objects are not self-contained, as the intent of the music is not to create purely melodic or rhythmic art objects. These art objects are but a result of a larger role that the music plays within the context of its intent.

The various musical systems discussed here have audiences in different parts of south India. This is not a comprehensive discussion on the various performing art traditions that use music, but just a sample of the different roles music plays within each form. This distinction gives us an understanding of music for music's sake, not as a philosophical stance, but as the basis of art music. Any discussion on the aesthetics of Karnatik music must be driven by this clear intent that the form has when presented as art music. Only such a discussion can lead us to a comprehensive understanding and give us the strength to question prevailing notions about Karnatik music.

3

Imagination, Creativity, Improvisation

To imagine is to live in the reality of today and also in the essence of tomorrow. Imagination is the ability of the mind to think of that which does not exist today – combining what exists now in ways that have not been done before, or even bringing together older experiences in newer ways.

Every individual imagines numerous possibilities around living one's life in the normal course. But life is not just about living; it is also about the possibility of creating worlds that do not exist, sounds that have never been heard before or sights that seem improbable. These are real in the mind. In this imagination lies the courage to fight for today, to work and find the happiness of the day. Every possibility drives humans to push the boundaries of living. If not for this, there would be no tomorrow to look forward to and no reason for action in our daily existence.

Yet imagination arises from the present through human interaction with the world around. The possibilities generated by imagination are not pulled out of thin air, but born out of what exists, which in turn is the result of the past. When we link the past and present, we see a continuum, and within this change exists. In the spark of the imagination is born this constant environment of change.

Imagination may be born out of the complexities, even the frustrations of reality, the sheer beauty around us or the compelling needs of the present. If we take this line of thought a little further, we can ask: Is the imagined indeed new when it has its roots in today? If today did not exist, what would we imagine? Imagination is viewed as the source of creating something new. The basis for this is the continuum of the past and present. Therefore, the newness is not in the source, but in how that source is transformed as a result of the human ability to imagine. We are creating a world in our mind, where the known is relearnt, twisted, shifted, expanded, exploded and transformed. This view is as applicable to life itself as it is to an endeavour. Within each field, the known changes, the environments are different, the history is specific but the process of imagination is the same.

Can Everyone Imagine?

Yes, of course. Then how is it that certain people seem more imaginative than others? This differs from person to person, but there is scarcely a person who does not imagine, each in a different, even unique way. But does one recognize imagination? Not by looking for it in the act itself, but in the openness to receiving life around us as a stimulus and recognizing its capacity to transform thought. Often all the stimuli from life pass us by, and we do not even realize that they were actually gifts. Once we recognize all life's experiences as ways of opening our thought, we become aware of imagination. This awareness is the birthplace of imagination. In a state of ignorance, without that awareness, we may even miss the moment of imagination when it passes us. This does not mean a lack of imagination, but it does reflect a lack of openness to life. Once we sense this, every stimulus is an opportunity – and from it is born the capacity to create images that are beyond our interaction with the world through our senses.

In the arts, the words imagination and creativity are often used as synonyms and all artists are deemed to possess this quality. However, I see the two words as being different, even if they refer to the conjuring up of things that are fresh or not experienced before. While imagination is an activity that remains in the world of the mind, creativity is the result of it leading to a tangible creation in the temporal world. Therefore, great imagination need not result in creativity, but it is the source of creativity. The spark for imagination is experience, and the spirit of creativity is imagination. The act of creation is closely linked to the instinct of imagination. When humans 'imagine', they are experiencing their creations in the mind. These do not translate into creativity unless moved from the mind into the real world. Creativity involves the actual act of creation. This in a way is the translation of 'that which is imagined' into the reality of the present. Great artists are those who are able to make this move.

While all of us imagine, why is it that the imagination of everyone does not lead to creativity? Because if imagination has to be creative, it has to be accompanied by something else as well: deep understanding. This is essential for the spark of imagination to be more than fantasy. Essentially, the creative individual needs depth of perception. This depth is multilayered, with the past and present serving as a continuum as well as a stimulus to further evolution. Even the most radical and path-breaking ideas come from the same deep understanding within which acceptance and rejection play a part. I do not refer here to studied learning, but to a process of seriously comprehending the elements, their existence and various perceptions of them. The understanding I speak of is a result of observation and introspection.

Another 'essential' for creativity is skill. An artist may translate the images in her mind onto the canvas to create paintings, but a person without the skill to paint cannot do so. Here, skill plays the role of an enabler. It enables better understanding and creativity. Without this, it would be impossible for ideas to transform into tangible creations.

This then leads us to look at imagination and creativity in a slightly different way. Every individual has imagination; it is awareness that differentiates the imaginative from the others. Similarly, if one recognizes imagination, develops understanding and skill, every individual could be creative. I am not a scientist, but I do not believe that creativity is purely the result of genetic predisposition. In fact, we do not know exactly how genes play a role in influencing amorphous ideas such as imagination and creativity. The circumstances of one's environment and life provide different stimuli, which in turn can transform one into a creative individual. All things remaining the same, all of us have the capacity to be creative in our own ways and in our chosen areas. One should not compare two individuals on the basis of who is more creative, but instead appreciate the process of creativity that is alive in both. This is what I mean by saying that every individual has the potential to be creative.

It is important to also understand that it is the constant interaction between a field of activity and society at large that stimulates imagination and leads to creativity. This is why imagination can be born only from the understanding that the environment in which one is placed, indeed life as a whole, is a stimulus for creativity. When this combines with a deep insight into the specific field, it leads to wonderful creativity that could redefine it.

There is therefore a continuum between the reality of one's physical environment and the imagination that leads to creativity. Unless this chain is interlinked, the creative process is not complete.

Is Everything 'New' Creative?

Today, the word 'creativity' is used rather loosely, merely to signify something that is new. A sound that has not been heard before, a gymnastic act that has not been seen, a new product are all viewed as results of creativity. In such an environment, it becomes very difficult to separate true creativity from the rest. There is a difference. Just because we have not seen something before, it need not be creative.

Creativity is more than an action of difference. It is also much more than a display of ability or skill, which are merely enabling factors for creativity, not the cause of it. An individual's ability can result in actions that have not been attempted before or in the creation of new articles. This is a result of skill development. A truly creative exploration occurs when this creation is facilitated by ability but has added to the aesthetic, functional or experiential body of the field. How does a certain expression contribute to the specific field?

In music, for example, true creativity contributes to the aesthetic dimensions of the art, that is, both its technical and experiential qualities. It is when a musician is able to blend the two not adhesively but organically that he makes his precise contribution. This is born out of introspection on the various elements that go into the making of music. There is a larger picture to be viewed when we talk about creativity that is beyond the individual. Every truly creative action transforms and changes the nature of the field in question, yet remains rooted in the past and present. The rootedness is in the understanding, interpretation, negation or acceptance of the past and present.

That leads us to the next logical question: does creativity exist in an act repeated through time by many? If vases in the same design are made over centuries, does that constitute creative art? This question has haunted theorists for a long time. Is this art or craft? In music, does the same phrase in a raga rendered numerous times by many musicians reflect creativity? My position is that both are creative if they still induce in the receiver the illusion from abstraction that is the essence of art. Who could deny that a phrase in a given raga does not have the same freshness, or move one to the same extent when rendered by all musicians? Only some can take a listener beyond the actuality of the phrase and induce an emotional abstraction. We may know the phrase – even understand its exact form – yet the experience is real. One may argue that this is due to familiarity. If that were the case, the phrase would evoke the same response, no matter which musician rendered it. But it does not, not even if all the musicians render it technically in the same fashion.

Artists who take the phrase beyond its technicality, infuse it with creative emotion. In their rendition of the phrase, there exists a transformation from the actual to the abstract. The vase too is art and a creative act if it is possessed of this quality of creating an idea of emotion from artistic abstraction.

Creativity in music, along with its actual existence in the real world, also plays a very important part in what may be called the world of pure abstraction, which is akin to the world of pure thought or philosophic experience. Creative music creates an illusion beyond the technical qualities of raga, tala and the like. It transports the mind into the realm of an abstract experience, which has a deep emotional quality that is beyond oneself and is yet personally completely absorbing. The spark of imagination leads to introspection and from the understanding that follows comes the creation. The process need neither be sudden nor gradual. It is not the speed, but the quality of that which is created that matters.

Such creativity comes from the natural introspection of a truly committed musician. Over a period of time, it bursts out into creative expressions. This is a continuous subconscious activity, where the various inputs, stimuli and ideas combine with ability, introspection and understanding. When these factors come together in perfect unison, creativity can appear to be 'sudden'. The individual is not necessarily conscious of the creative flow. To a superficial mind, such creative expressions may seem sudden, but to a deeper consciousness their evolution will be clear.

On the stage of creativity, there is yet another player – improvisation. Integral to Indian art music, improvisation is what sets every individual apart from every other. Improvisation is defined as the ability to perform, recite or compose with no premeditation, extempore, whether in music, poetry or any other field. While performing, there are numerous ways in which the Karnatik musician explores melodic and rhythmic possibilities without any conscious thought. But this is not completely devoid of preparation. Musicians prepare almost constantly, leading to a level of internalization where the rules of the music and its aesthetics are embedded in the psyche. In this state, true creativity emerges through improvisation. It is unrehearsed and extempore, but behind it lies a vast hinterland of preparation that cannot be discounted. Without creativity, the very objective of improvisation is lost and we will be stuck in the conscious known.

Creative Freedom

When the ideas of creativity and improvisation are discussed, there comes in another vital concept: freedom. To be creative is understood to mean going beyond the received parameters, prescribed and 'understood' possibilities; to break conditions with no restrictions whatsoever. Here it is assumed that, in conditions of such complete freedom, a musician has the opportunity to do whatever he wants. But that is a rushed understanding of freedom in the world of creativity. With creativity, ability, freedom of thought and action comes a great deal of responsibilities of keeping the aesthetics of the artistic form in place. Again, true creativity cannot exist if the artist is not continuously mindful about the past and the present.

In this understanding of the rights and responsibilities of the creative imagination also lives, very importantly, the right of negation. The negation I refer to is not a frivolous act. It is a serious movement taking art in a certain direction. When we negate something, it is not a question of saying 'I disagree', but an act of understanding. Negation is neither negative nor rebellious. True negation is sensitive. It has to be sensitive, as the strength of negation is the result of an understanding of that which we want to negate. Therefore, sensitivity towards that which exists or existed is imperative. This sensitivity is impersonal, dispassionate and brutally honest. It is an honesty born out of the very same introspection that leads us to acceptance. 'I negate because I understand, I negate because I truly feel and I negate because it is not about me' – even in negation, a creative expression is connected. The world of freedom exists within the spectrum of the aesthetics that constitute the basic nature of the art form. The form, structure and intent of the art are the bases on which an individual has to build her creativity. Thus, freedom is also generated from within the aesthetic construction. When a creative interpretation negates an artistic thought, it is doing so on the basis of the insight from the aesthetics. Freedom, therefore, must respect these fundamentals.

The Musician's Inner Being

The creative changes that a musician can contribute are determined by her inner being and her attitude to artistic freedom and responsibility. Freedom is unlimited in creativity, but needs to be tempered by the individual's sincerity towards the world she seeks to influence and change. This is what separates creativity from anarchy.

The artist's personal imagination – transforming into creativity through introspection, understanding and improvisation – is what imbues her with an identifiable and distinct creative personality and a true artistic quality. Not that acquiring such a personality should be the artist's goal, of course.

To imagine, create and to touch the old world anew is what makes the magical journey of the artist. Artists neither belong to any special community, nor are they a unique set of people. To be an artist is in the essence of a human being. It is in every one of us to breathe life with the expanse of imagination, embrace it in our thoughts and give with our body. We are all artists.

4

The Fundamentals

In the very instant that we hear a melody or an instrument we are used to, we can identify the music or at least its nature. In fact, the sound evokes in our conscious mind a cognate melody or a beat. We feel and imagine the music of which we have heard only a snatch. In this imagination lies the distinctive identity of the music: its melodic movement, the rhythmic interplays, the poetic flow and its overarching impact.

The core nature of the sound, its essential movement and rhythm remain constant across the different styles of musicians or instruments within a form. This constant is the unique and distinctive thread that binds all musicians to a common idiom. It is not a restrictive bond, but an empowering one, allowing every musician to build her own interpretation around a stable core. It is from within this mutuality that the musicians live, identify and create magical identities of their own from which they create the composite sound that lies at the heart of their music. This is the sound that emanates from the form of music itself, its essence – the indefinable filament between the listener and the music. To understand the nature of this 'sound' and its facets is to understand the nature of the music itself.

The distinctive character of a musical form has many components, which gives it a unique nature beyond the technical details. The form's emotive layers are built using this quality. Within this we have structures that have evolved over centuries. Of course, the sound that we hear today is not the same as the one heard 200 years ago. But the relationship between now and then is beautifully etched within the landscape of music. We can analyse these aspects in terms of technicalities, but they will make no sense unless we try and capture the experience of the sound both for the trained and the untrained ear. This is as much about the listener as about the musician. The process of the listeners' evolution is important, as sensitivity to various nuances and subtleties play a very important role in their appreciation of the music.

Karnatik Music

To many, Karnatik music is an acquired taste. It is not something most people will seek out or want to spend an evening with unless they have acquired a taste for its unusual nature. Unusual because – though it has similarities with its north Indian cousin, Hindustani music – its essential melodic and rhythmic sounds do not relate easily to what is superficially considered beautiful. Those who seek to bring this experience within the accepted, generic parameters of appealing musical sounds may find the music difficult to accept.

Words like 'melodious', used in the traditional sense, may not readily apply to Karnatik music. This is because what people may believe to be out of tune or 'besur' in Hindustani are illusions derived from the habituated experience of what is considered tuneful in another form. I do not intend to even remotely suggest that Karnatik music is intrinsically out of tune – not at all. It is to stress that the understanding of its tune and pitch requires nuancing.

In order to truly grasp this concept, we need to understand svara in the very specific context of Karnatik music.

Svaras

All musical sounds are expressed in terms of notes, which we refer to as svara. We usually perceive svaras as fixed pitch positions (an idea I will come back to). The exact positions of these svaras have been identified by the human ear, and not by mathematical analysis, a separate area of study available today. All melodic forms have their basis in svaras, which are articulated as sa, ri, ga, ma, pa, dha, ni in ascending and sa, ni, dha, pa, ma, ga, ri in descending pitch positions. These are truncations of words that refer to each pitch position: shadja, rishabha, gandhara, madhyama, panchama, dhaivata, nishada.

In Karnatik music, if we were to sing the svaras, beginning with sa sequentially in the ascending order, we will move higher in pitch position. Once we reach ni, we will repeat the svara sa. This sa is in the higher octave. Similarly, when we move from sa down to ri, we reach sa in the lower octave. Basically, when svaras are repeated on higher octaves, they are double the frequency of the previous manifestation and, at lower octaves, half the frequency of the previous manifestation.

Five svaras (ri, ga, ma, dha, ni) have multiple pitch positions within an octave. Each svara – other than sa and its fifth pa – have two to three pitch positions. For example ri has three positions; they are all ri, but each sounds different and are assigned different names. Similarly, a few svaras share the same pitch position, but the interpretation depends on the melody they represent. The history of these pitch positions is over 1,500 years old, and there is a reason for the present set of twelve svaras and sixteen names (see Chart 1).

Chart 1: The twelve svaras and their sixteen names

Pitch Position	Svara	Name
1	Sa	Shadja (S)
2	Ri1	Shuddha Rishabha (R1)
3	Ri2/Ga1	Chatushruti Rishabha (R2) / Shuddha Gandhara (G1)
4	Ri3/Ga2	Shatshruti Rishabha (R3) / Sadharana Gandhara (G2)
5	Ga3	Antara Gandhara (G3)
6	Ma1	Shuddha Madhyama (M1)
7	Ma2	Prati Madhyama (M2)
8	Pa	Panchama (P)
9	Da1	Shuddha Dhaivata (D1)
10	Da2/Ni1	Chatushruti Dhaivata (D2) / Shuddha Nishada (N1)
11	Da3/Ni2	Shatshruti Dhaivata (D3) / Kaishiki Nishada (N2)
12	Ni3	Kakali Nishada (N3)

Every pitch position increases in pitch as we ascend the octave. Therefore, each pitch position of ri is higher than the previous ri as we ascend the octave. Now I will try and describe why there are two names given to the same pitch position (see Chart 2). Depending on the melodic context, the third pitch position given to ri (shatshruti rishabha) can be the first pitch position of ga (shuddha gandhara). Though their pitch position and frequency are exactly the same, in one melody they will be uttered as ri and the other melody as ga. The melody will define whether it is ri or ga. The specific role of each svara in the melody and the relationship between svaras will determine whether the svara is ri or ga. In other words, you could have two melodies wherein the same pitch position is ri in one and ga in another. Readers must understand that all these pitch positions are uttered as sa, ri, ga, ma, pa, dha, ni in music, and not by the descriptive words given to them. In all that history, these positions were determined by the test of the ear. Music can be viewed as the specific use of these svaras within definite melodic contexts, but that is not how Karnatik music, or for that matter Hindustani music, derives melodies.

Chart 2: Pitch positions with variable identities

Pitch Position	Svara	Name
3	Ri2/Ga1	Chatushruti Rishabha (R2) / Shuddha Gandhara (G1)
4	Ri3/Ga2	Shatshruti Rishabha (R3) / Sadharana Gandhara (G2)
10	Da2/Ni1	Chatushruti Dhaivata (D2) / Shuddha Nishada (N1)
11	Da3/Ni2	Shatshruti Dhaivata (D3) / Kaishiki Nishada (N2)

The Tambura

We must turn here to the one instrument that can be said to hold within itself the very essence of classical music. So unobtrusive is this instrument, so self-effacing in its positioning on the stage and so tender of nature, that it is almost taken for granted. And yet it is absolutely indispensable. I refer, of course, to the tambura or tanpura, as it is known in Hindustani music. This instrument usually has four strings that are tuned to specific pitch positions and provide a melodic foundation for the music. This is a constant.

What is this constant? Sa takes the role of the 'tonic': this requirement comes from the fact that all melodies are based on the identity of the svaras, which can be stabilized only if there is a reference pitch position in the beginning. If we do not have this fixed reference, every pitch will sound like a different svara each time, which would mean that melodies cannot be defined. This is referred to as the tonic. Once the tonic is fixed, all the other notes move and express themselves with reference to it. Therefore, every svara is positioned on the basis of the sa. Moving up in pitch position from the tonic sa to ni is referred to as madhya sthayi (middle octave). If we move to the next higher pitch position, which would be sa once again, we will be rendering the same sequence in tara sthayi (higher octave). If we were to move lower in pitch position from the madhya sthayi sa, we will be rendering the svaras in mandara sthayi (lower octave) (see Chart 3). Now to be even more precise, the madhya sthayi sa is the tonic.

Chart 3: The three octaves

Sthayi (Octave)	Mandara Sthayi							Madhya Sthayi							Tara Sthayi						
Svara	S	Ṛ	G̣	Ṃ	P̣	Ḍ	Ṇ	**S**	R	G	M	P	D	N	Ṡ	Ṙ	Ġ	Ṁ	Ṗ	Ḋ	Ṅ

Tonic

Note: A dot above the svara represents Tara Sthayi. A dot below represents Mandara Sthayi.

This tonic is fixed not on a musical basis, but on the basis of the singer's voice or the instrument's timbre. Every human being talks at a different pitch; similarly, each person's natural singing pitch is different. In the case of a solo instrumental performance, the tonic is fixed based on the timbre quality sought by the musician. Once this tonic is established, it cannot be changed during a concert. The role of the tambura then becomes to establish and sustain this tonic – the base or foundation on which every melodic expression is woven. Every piece is presented with the same tonic reference, thereby creating, through the tambura, a constant aesthetic reference for music.

The tambura is tuned so as to highlight the tonic sa in madhya sthayi and tara sthayi along with pa, the fifth svara from sa in the madhya sthayi. Here occur two concurrences around 'shruti'. First is the sound that emanates from a perfectly tuned tambura, and the second an equally important connotation meaning the tonic itself.

The human voice or any melodic instrument has a limited range of about three octaves once tuned to a given tonic (see Chart 4). Therefore, all Indian classical music in general can be expressed within a range of two octaves, one complete octave plus half in a higher and half in the lower octave. In this, the tambura gives the musician unique and irreplaceable support.

Chart 4: The usual range of the human voice

Sthayi (Octave)	Mandara Sthayi							Madhya Sthayi							Tara Sthayi						
Svara	S	R	G	M	P	D	N	S	R	G	M	P	D	N	S	R	G	M	P	D	N

Typical Musical Range

Beyond that, the tambura means much more to Indian music and the musician. It is the life-giver, the soul of our music. In the sublime resonance of its four strings lies the matrix of Indian classical music. This might seem eulogistic, but it is exactly what a musician feels. The experience of the tambura exists in the collective sound of the four strings. The tuning of the four strings is a difficult task. The subtlety that lies in tuning each string and the correlation between them, which leads to the final moment when all four are in unison, is indescribable. A whole world of melodies comes together, yet lies hidden in the tambura's unified sound. Only a musician who has experienced this sanctity can be a true musical vehicle. In the internal absorption of the tambura's resonance, music happens.

When a person enters an auditorium and hears the sound of the tambura, he internalizes its resonance. Many see it as meditative. To me, it is even more – the very sound of musical reality, a musical awakening that is beyond feeling. I have even met people who have found the sound of the tambura overpowering. It is as if the sound would not leave them; it haunts their senses to such an extent that nothing else registers. In a way this is true, but as we grow into the sound, the musical experience is quieter.

The Gamaka

Any discussion on Karnatik music has to visit the life of the svara in that world. An important inhabitant there, with a mobility, fluidity and character of its own, is the three-syllabled word, the gamaka. It is known widely in the Karnatik world, has been developed into an intricate system with subtle variations and nuances each of which bears a character, it is recognized instantly, valued immensely, applied with diligence by musicians and observed closely by experts. Yet, there is something elusive about it. The gamaka can be described in approximations to its meaning, it can be illustrated, it can be explained, but it cannot really be defined. It is described in terms of the svara's oscillation.

Gamakas have been explained as melodic ornamentations applied to svaras, giving them mobility around their specific pitch positions. The moment we accept this explanation, our understanding of a svara turns visual. It appears as a fixed entity with a given identity around which the gamaka is devised. This would imply that each svara is a distinct musical unit that pre-exists independently of the gamaka. This is not true. As svara enters the realm of music, it acquires the shape of a micro-musical versatility. When that happens, a svara moves from being a mere sound to becoming music. This metamorphosis is complete when the svara draws the concept of gamaka into its own meaning. The gamaka becomes part of the svara's own voltaic energy. The two concepts, two words – svara and gamaka – are not independent of each other. The svara is a musical form only because of the gamaka. Therefore, within Karnatik music, gamaka is an expression of the svara and the svara's musical identity binds it to the gamaka. In other words, the svara does not exist without gamaka. The term that can be used to describe a pitch position would be 'svarasthana'.

The svara's main function in Karnatik music is to give us a microcosm of the larger melody. But it cannot do this entirely on its own. It does so through a process of interaction. The svara, acts with other svaras to create smaller melodic units, which in turn define the larger melody. How does a svara, the 'micro', express the macro? It does so by representing an aspect of the larger melody, not by its fixity or rootedness, its immobility on a scale, but through its movable nature. Therefore, every svara can move, bounce, slide, glide, shiver or skip. How and to what extent a svara can be expressive depends on the nature of the larger musical identity it is part of and the nature of the other svaras within that macro identity. Svaras in some ways are like cells in a body. The cells (svaras) are determined by the content and function of the tissues (smaller melodic units), yet the larger human being (melody as a whole) is embedded in every cell, within the DNA.

Each svara has a clear role within the smaller melodic unit and the larger melody, but here lies what may be called the svara's beauty. While doing what it does to the larger melody, it also goes through a certain activity within itself. There, inside its 'self' lies, like a genome, the macro identity of the entire melody. Thus, the svara is a complex melodic unit that has different interpretations, depending on where and when it occurs in the melody; it is unique yet contains the macro identity. Without these interpretations then, the svara does not exist as a melodic atom.

In the modern context, it is accepted that about eight different types of gamakas constitute the svara identity. Within the svara's complex melodic identity also lies the possibility that it could be expressed as a stationary pitch position. One should also remember that even these eight ways of rendering svaras can be further divided, depending on the musician and her musical interpretations. Yet, the primary intention, which is to reinforce the identity of the macro melody, cannot be lost.

What does this mean to the listener? Someone listening to Karnatik music for the first time may notice a shake, jump, roughness and toughness in the music. This leaves one with the feeling of a lack of pitch or tonality – a perception that arises from the fact that svaras are like a set of moving sounds that subtly merge with each other to create a flow of melody. The beauty of these svaras is that the same svara has numerous ways of presenting itself within the same melody. Each time the svara is rendered, it presents yet another feature of the larger canvas with minute changes having occurred in its form. Each such shade provides another window to the melody, another approach to the musical passages. The svara seems to be exploring nooks and corners between pitch positions. Each expression is within the music, and none is arbitrary. If anything, it is very precise. This makes the effect very different from musical genres that express themselves mainly through pure and clear pitch positions.

Sometimes, this leads to a perception that Karnatik music lacks feeling when compared to other forms. This is because of our conditioning in emotive reactions to music. Every musical movement in Karnatik music has emotive appeal, if only we can open our minds to possibilities beyond conditioned grooves.

The Raga

While I have used the word 'melodies' as being the defining aspects of svaras, the appropriate term is raga. There is a reason why I have refrained from using this term until now, and it is because the prevailing descriptions do not adequately express the idea of the raga. It is not an easy concept to understand, but once understood, it unlocks musical understanding. The raga is a musical, technical, acoustic, emotional and psychological identity. Many musicologists have tried to define a raga, but have been unable to do so conclusively. A classical description of the raga is 'that which delights the mind' or 'sound that is embellished by musical tones'. Some scholars have recognized two aspects of a raga – the experience of its melody and its aesthetics structures.

Intrinsically, raga is both a technical and an experiential identity. The factors that go into a raga are svaras, in the holistic sense as described earlier, and the phrases (smaller melodic units) that have been formed through the ages, as established by compositions in their core. Every raga usually has a minimum of five svaras;

the maximum is, of course, all seven. Phrases are melodic motifs that collectively give a raga its aesthetic form. They contain combinations of svaras that are based on the aesthetic value of the phrase and are not derived from a manipulation of the svaras. Every svara, phrase, movement or pause has evolved organically over centuries in the hands of musicians and composers. This is encapsulated in the compositions that have been orally handed down. We cannot sing a raga by just knowing the svaras that go into it; it is not a play of permutations and combinations. Each svara has a different role in a raga; the context within a phrase determines the svara and the svara determines connections between phrases. All these have to constantly establish the image of the raga. The svara has numerous identities within each raga. Its relationship with other svaras constantly changes its form, making their interplay contextual.

The phrases themselves are interesting ideas. They are not clearly defined with a demarcated beginning and an end. Each phrase is an open-ended idea. While a core identity is recognized, each time a musician renders these phrases, the form will vary. The way each phrase connects to another will also change. Like a creeper, the raga, even as it turns and twists in the musician's hands, remains the same.

Does the singing of these phrases make a raga? No. Every movement is a manifestation of the raga's unspoken qualities, which constitute its emotional charge. The svaras and phrases themselves evolve over time into emotional triggers. These are formed as much by their sound and texture, as they are by what we are used to and the emotional images that musicians create.

Musicians use various methods to express the raga. Voice texture, intonation, volume and other vocal methods are used to transmit the raga emotion. But this is not a conscious or taught action. The emotional charge may differ each time the raga is sung, but the raga itself will be the same. The emotional charge of the day will determine even the technical movements, but rests in the raga without disturbing the essential technical components of its identity. We must also factor in the composition's textual contribution to the raga's emotional landscape. The lyrics create a subconscious canvas of emotions, which charge the mood of the raga and reinforce its identity. This does not foreclose any expansion of the canvas, but the established emotional connections remain strong. While I believe that, in art music, the actual linguistic meaning is not the primary function of the lyrics, I cannot deny that it influences the musician's emotional state.

Psychologically, the raga exists in a trained listener's mind even before it is heard, because of constant listening, practice and conditioning. The phrases and emotional experience lie deep inside. When even a single svara is heard, the connected listener starts singing the raga in her mind. The nuances are generated as much in the mind as they are by the musician. This imaging is essential for the raga's identity. The cognition that is brought about by constant listening and performing is an important part of the raga continuum. When a musician starts rendering a raga, his first intent is to tap into the listener's ingrained cognition. Once the raga identity has pervaded the listeners, the musician will venture into a deeper exploration. When a new phrase is rendered, it could reiterate older phrase associations, or it could initially register as an unusual occurrence, and may even seem out of place. Once again, constant rendition and listening establishes the phrase and brings it within the raga.

Does this mean that any phrase can be added? What then remains constant?

The svaras, their associations and established phraseology are the raga's primary constant determinants. The raga's aesthetic and experiential identity lies within its musical atom: the svara (the holistic svara + gamaka). This is why, in Karnatik music, compositions play a crucial role in raga definition. We are handed down the raga's musical shape through compositions. All changes that occur have to be within this established 'given'. It seems like some mega principle of vague value, but is actually the working methodology in which lie the strength and character of raga identity. Every raga also has a certain acoustic identity, which gives its svara, phrase and the raga itself a traditional range of persona. Within this range lies the raga. If this is breached, the musician is not rendering the said raga, but melodic lines sans the raga form. I like to refer to this acoustic identity as the 'sound' of the raga. That sound extends from the micro to the macro, and is closely associated with cognition.

There are, of course, certain points of acoustic crossovers between ragas, which are part of their aesthetic evolution. Musicians must be aware of this while rendering the raga.

In its totality, a raga is a combination of musical heritage, technical elements, emotional charge, cognitive understanding and aural identity.

The Idea of Time

As much as melody gives Karnatik music a distinct identity, the rhythmic side of the form gives it a structure that is unique in the world of music. This is possibly the best-known fact about Karnatik music: its complex rhythmic system and the techniques of playing various percussion instruments.

Before we address rhythm, we need to understand the role of time in music. Among its meanings, the word 'time' also refers to a limited stretch of continued existence and a moment at which, or duration in which, things happen. These suggest that time refers to some kind of movement. It also means that there is a connection between that which is stretched and that which is not. In these two aspects of movement and connection exists time. Time has existed both as a horological and philosophical question in most civilizations, with varying interpretations given to its significance and impact. When the thought of time occurs to us, we tend to recollect events that have happened in the past, or are happening at the present moment, even what lies ahead. This clearly establishes that time exists because there are events or actions.

Time, however, is not perceived by these 'action' moments alone. It is perceived no less by the interim of seeming inaction, inactivity or inertness between the active occurrences. This interim is not an empty dormancy or lassitude, but an active mediation between two highlighted events. No timepiece strikes the resounding hour, which has not stood in sixty minutes of utter silence. And so, for a complete awareness of time, we need to perceive both: the differentiated events and, equally, the interval between them.

This interval is not to be perceived as a blank between two forms, but as a form in itself. If we were to perceive life as a seamless continuity, in complete awareness of every action or event, without placing any intellectual or emotional accent on any event, integrating seemingly inactive intervals with the seemingly active, would time still retain any meaning? In short bursts, all of us experience this. Sportsmen speak about a 'zone', musicians immersed in music forget themselves, and connoisseurs of art remain 'still' in front of a masterpiece. If this experience were to be extended right through life, what would happen to time?

Since we yet hold that time exists, how and where are we to capture its beginning, middle or end? How do we measure it?

To measure time, we need equally distributed or orderly actions as reference. Then we could use these references to place all irregular events within. The rotations of the earth and the moon are regular events that can be measured and mathematically related to the next event. One of the greatest horological challenges of the ancient world was to reconcile the duration of the moon's movement around the earth and the earth's around the sun. This finally led to the time systems we follow today. So the concept of time is dependent on events and intervals, and its measurement on the regularity of certain events. Human behaviour is in general irregular, but time measure gives this irregularity a structure.

One could argue that every living being relates to changes in nature, like changing seasons or the ageing process of the body. Does this mean that time is built into nature? Many natural changes occur due to factors that are usually chemical. If we let tea leaves soak for a very long time, the nature of the brew changes. Here, time indicates the difference between tea brewed for a short while and that brewed for a long time. But, as a process, the continued brewing changes the chemical state of the tea and the water, thereby changing the end product.

Where does time come into this? It comes into the picture as the relationship between the two states and the interval between them. Time is not the factor that changes the state, but time is what brings its elements together. The duration of the whole reaction is crucial to the change. The moment we use the words 'duration' and 'change', we are discussing the relationships between all the factors; and time exists in this relationship. Therefore, though change is the natural mode of life, to relate it to time is a human function. If there was no time, would the change occur?

Often when we see a person after many years, we say that he looks exactly the same. What we mean is that the person does not look older though the clock has moved and the person has changed biologically. We perceive time in terms of the calendar, clock and memory, not that person. If we did not have memory or a measure of time, would we perceive change in relation to that person? So, then, now and all that is in between are all important. If any of these pieces are missing, our idea of time changes.

Recently, my little daughter asked if we could go to a certain place, and reminded me that we had gone there 'a very long time ago'. I told her that it was not a very long time ago, but only about ten days. She insisted that it was a long time ago. So I asked her, 'Then what is recent?' Her answer: 'a week'. To her, ten days ago was a very long time ago and a week was recent. To me, a very long time ago may be a year and recent about ten days. Both my daughter and I are using the same measure of time but our 'sense' of time is very different. This is a very important aspect. Depending on the person, her age, place and lifestyle, the sense of time changes. All of us feel that some days are longer and others shorter. An hour is slower on one day, but too fast on another. The clock would say that the hour was the same, but we feel different. This is sensed time. This is, in a way, created time. It is created because it is a product of the mind and not a measurable quantity. But this created time has the quality of changing our mental state, actions and life experience.

Another aspect of sensed time is also seen in different fields. Biological time, geological time and archaeological time are all different. The meaning of ten years, thousand years or a million years within each sphere is unique. In fact, to a geologist, ten years are of no consequence. The change that each field is looking for and its relevance varies. The measure of time is the same, but the experience is vastly different in each.

Time influences not just actions, but also its nature. Certain actions are done only at certain times of the day, which makes time a place holder for actions. Our sense of organization, nature of work and mental state are affected by the sense of time. Similarly, social behaviour is influenced greatly by time. The sense of occasion, the nature of social events and our own interaction with society are wedded to this idea.

Time is very closely knit with events that shape our personal, social and political life. It helps us relate to history, wars and political events and contributes to the emotional relationship between the event and ourselves. For example, our relationship with India's independence is as important as the date: 15 August. The date and the event are so inseparable that we invest the date with a great deal of significance.

But there is another way in which time can relate to history. This is in the signification that certain events acquire for society. The exact time of the event's occurrence ceases to be relevant. The meaning is derived from the incident itself and what it comes to mean to society. With every successive generation, its relevance grows. Events that occur subsequently are then imbued with the significance of that earlier one. Thus two different events, which may be far apart in time, are connected through the values they stand for. It may even be said that they are felt only because of the recurring perception of connectedness – a cyclical perception of time that indirectly shapes social values. Consider, for instance, the events described in the lives of many of India's revered saints and the recurring themes that link them: the rejection of the financial benefits offered by a king, or an encounter with a 'low-caste' person who is in fact God in disguise. These personages lived centuries apart, yet these stories string their sagas together. They are parcels of values that society hopes to carry forward and, therefore, are linked through memory and time. These recurring themes are not only intra-cultural, but even seen across cultures, for example, the parting of the sea to provide a path.

Time is not only a measure; it is a living entity that defines and redefines our sense of ourselves as individuals and as a people. It is thereby both the author of change and its witness.

Within Karnatik music, we bring all these aspects together. It is a linear movement bound by regular events and is relevant only when cyclical. It is a measure, a structure and a character definer; it conditions the abstract, creates space for movements and, importantly, reiterates its existence by repeating itself. Therefore time, as viewed in life, is brought into the musical idiom and abstracts the nature of life within music.

The most beautiful part of time in music is the idea of created time. Within every Karnatik music piece, the various layers of melody, svara, syllables and rhythmic structuring create multiple senses of time. Each raga has movements that create different experiences of time embedded in its identity. In fact, these created illusions are built into the melodic phrases that form the raga. If we were to alter the created time experiences, the beauty of the phrases would be lost. The svaras rendered also create senses of time depending on the musician's emphasis. An intense accent on a svara can make it seem slower than the others. A lighter intonation on a collection of svaras can make them seem faster. Every part of the lyrics also contributes to created time, both because of its intrinsic syllabic structure and relationship with the melody. When all this is placed within a rhythmic structure, the relationship of all these different aspects collectively gives the listener a unique sense of time, which is purely a creation of the music. Of course, we need an engaged listener to truly experience this.

Laya and Tala

These various features of time are marked primarily by two elements – laya and tala – and the various aspects built around them.

Laya is a beautiful term. In a generic sense, it refers to speed. Within a musical presentation, speed is sensed by the interval between artificially created rhythmic divisions – that is, based on the frequency with which these divisions are placed. For example, if every division appears within one second of each other, it would be faster than a division appearing after three seconds. But, in Karnatik music, speed is not equal to an exact mathematical value. It is generally measured as slow, medium or fast (chauka, madhyama, durita). If one is to ask what exactly is fast, there is no value to be attached to it. A range of accepted speeds are sensed and placed in these three categories. Therefore, speed itself is a sense, a feeling and a conditioning. What we refer to as slow now could have been very different a hundred years ago. It is the collective musical psyche of a specific period that defines our sense of speed. This sense is critical to the aesthetics of Karnatik music. The raga form is shaped on the basis of this sense and changes according to this sensed speed. It is in this feeling that emotional layers are placed on music and human connections established with the listener.

Laya is that which gives space within a rhythmic structure by creating intervals. These intervals that create space become the playground for melodic exploration.

However, this space is not independent of the divisions. Only when there are divisions to a rhythmical form does the interval exist. Laya also means 'to adhere' or 'to cling'. Every interval clings to the beat that is the division. Though we discuss the interval and the division independently, they exist together. This interval is further divided into smaller units, and the melodic flow adheres to these subdivisions. This adherence is not necessarily perceivable. It is often not stressed upon, but is naturally maintained by the divisions within the structure. In this, the structural beauty provided by laya gives melody a definite pulse to operate within. Laya gives to tala what emotion gives to reason.

This idea of laya is not unique to music; it exists in the raindrops, in the falling of the leaves, in the heartbeat, in the birth of a child – wherever there exists a feeling of time encased within an event. As in Karnatik music, these are not experienced by a measurable number, but by a general sense of time. Any change in the laya of these events changes our emotional responses to them.

Other than a general sense of speed, laya also refers to the measure of the interval between every division. To give you an analogy, if two people were asked to walk a distance of ten feet and one person took nine steps and the other seven steps to travel this distance, taking the same amount of time, it would seem that the former was faster. This is because the time between each step shrinks. Similarly, within a fixed interval between two rhythmic divisions, we could melodically fill the interval with five or four svaras. When we do this, the former would be faster than the latter though the length of the interval is the same. Therefore laya can change in two ways, with an actual increase or decrease in the interval between two divisions or by melodically placing less or more svaras within the same interval. There is a subtle difference in these two methods. In the first, there is a change to the duration of the interval, but the second is a change to the melody placed within the interval.

When laya comes together with a fixed number of divisions, a composite rhythmic unit, or a tala, is created. A tala is a concrete method of dividing time: a creation for the purposes of music and not a natural phenomenon. Pulsation is found in many places, but it is not considered a tala unless it is created by melody. It is only when melody is placed that tala is created, to exhibit its sense of structure, division and space. Tala also creates a sense of time for melody, defining and highlighting it. Sans the melody, tala is non-existent. A tala is consciously created in music to divide time, so that melody can be placed and measured within it. Laya provides the space and the division within the tala that gives it its body.

A tala is linear, in the sense that it allows the melody to move forward, but cyclical in order to hold together the whole linear melodic movement within one repeated rhythmic matrix. Every tala is cyclical in that it repeats its form in exactly the same way right through a composition. Melody itself may not be completely linear, but with the completion of every cyclical reiteration moves forward. The ideas of cyclical or linear are not literal, but abstract, referring to the sense of movement that the music generates. A tala is not complete unless this composite unit also has an actual physical manifestation in presentation. This would mean that a tala is not only a rhythmic concept but also has an actual physical form.

Laya and the divisions that define it are the cornerstones of the tala and give it a form in two ways. First, they define the tala's mathematical form and subdivide the total number of beats into identifiable groups. Second, they give these divisions physical manifestations in an action by which both the musician and the listener can identify the tala structure. These divisions within a tala are known are kriyas. Every kriya is a beat, and the total number of beats equals the total number of kriyas in a tala. As I said earlier, laya and kriya exist together and are not to be understood independently. Between every kriya is an interval and this duration determines the laya of the tala.

Kriyas are not just divisions, but also clear physical actions that visually define the tala structure. Kriyas can be of two types: those that make a sound (sashabda kriya), the slap on the thigh, and those that make no sound (nishabda kriya), a finger count or flip of the palm. The first kriya in every tala is referred to as the sama – the beginning, always the slap on the thigh.

The sum total of the beats in a tala is divided into smaller structures by combining various kriyas. This gives every tala a distinctive form and provides stability. Most talas in the Karnatik system are made up of various combinations of these kriyas. Kriyas combine to form three structural groups: Laghu (a slap on the thigh followed by finger counts of variable number), druta (a slap on the thigh followed by a flip of the palm) and anudruta (only a slap on the thigh). While druta always has two beats and anudruta one, the laghu is a variable form that can have 3, 4, 5, 7 or 9 beats. The laghu, along with the druta and anudruta, defines the total number of beats in a tala. These three structural groups are known as tala angas.

The values 4, 3, 7, 5, 9 (chaturashra, tisra, mishra, khanda, sankirna) are essential to all the different tala structures and the laya. The variability of the laghu mentioned above is defined by these values. Every laghu begins with a kriya, which is a slap on the thigh. Following this are finger counts, which could be 2, 3, 4, 6, 8. Adding the finger counts to the slap on the thigh you get the laghu values of 3, 4, 5, 7 or 9.This is referred to as 'laghu jati' (with an elongated 'aa'), meaning that the laghu has five jatis (categories): chaturashra (4), tisra (3), mishra (7), khanda (5), sankirna (9).Other than the laghu, depending on the tala, drutas and anudrutas will be used. One complete tala form, with its tala angas, is called an avartana – and this avartana is cyclical within a specific musical presentation.

In Karnatik music, there are seven talas that form the basis for the tala structures. These are combinations of laghu, druta and anudruta, and are known as the suladi sapta tala. Most talas in use today are some variations of these seven primary talas.

Chart 5: The seven talas

Tala	Structure	Total
Dhruva	Laghu (4) + Laghu (4) + Druta (2) + Laghu (4)	14
Matya	Laghu (4) + Druta (2) + Laghu (4)	10
Rupaka	Druta (2) + Laghu (4)	6
Jhampa	Laghu (7) + Anudruta (1) + Druta (2)	10
Triputa	Laghu (3) + Druta (2) + Druta (2)	7
Ata	Laghu (5) + Laghu (5) + Druta (2) + Druta (2)	14
Eka	Laghu (4)	4

To these seven, if we bring in the variability of the laghu measure, we get thirty-five talas (seven talas x five jatis).

Chart 6: The seven talas and five jatis

Tala	Structure	Total
Dhruva	Laghu (4) + Laghu (4) + Druta (2) + Laghu (4)	14
	Laghu (3) + Laghu (3) + Druta (2) + Laghu (3)	11
	Laghu (7) + Laghu (7) + Druta (2) + Laghu (7)	23
	Laghu (5) + Laghu (5) + Druta (2) + Laghu (5)	17
	Laghu (9) + Laghu (9) + Druta (2) + Laghu (9)	29
Matya	Laghu (4) + Druta (2) + Laghu (4)	10
	Laghu (3) + Druta (2) + Laghu (3)	8
	Laghu (7) + Druta (2) + Laghu (7)	16
	Laghu (5) + Druta (2) + Laghu (5)	12
	Laghu (9) + Druta (2) + Laghu (9)	20

Tala	Structure	Total
Rupaka	**Druta (2) + Laghu (4)**	**6**
	Druta (2) + Laghu (3)	5
	Druta (2) + Laghu (7)	9
	Druta (2) + Laghu (5)	7
	Druta (2) + Laghu (9)	11
Jhampa	Laghu (4) + Anudruta (1) + Druta (2)	7
	Laghu (3) + Anudruta (1) + Druta (2)	6
	Laghu (7) + Anudruta (1) + Druta (2)	**10**
	Laghu (5) + Anudruta (1) + Druta (2)	8
	Laghu (9) + Anudruta (1) + Druta (2)	12
Triputa	Laghu (4) + Druta (2) + Druta (2)	8
	Laghu (3) + Druta (2) + Druta (2)	**7**
	Laghu (7) + Druta (2) + Druta (2)	11
	Laghu (5) + Druta (2) + Druta (2)	9
	Laghu (9) + Druta (2) + Druta (2)	13
Ata	Laghu (4) + Laghu (4) + Druta (2) + Druta (2)	12
	Laghu (3) + Laghu (3) + Druta (2) + Druta (2)	10
	Laghu (7) + Laghu (7) + Druta (2) + Druta (2)	18
	Laghu (5) + Laghu (5) + Druta (2) + Druta (2)	**14**
	Laghu (9) + Laghu (9) + Druta (2) + Druta (2)	22
Eka	**Laghu (4)**	**4**
	Laghu (3)	3
	Laghu (7)	7
	Laghu (5)	5
	Laghu (9)	9

Using the same values of 4, 3, 7, 5, 9, the interval between every kriya (essentially the laya) can also be altered by the number of svaras sung between them (or the number of rhythmic sounds produced between them). The value for the interval between two kriyas is referred to as nadai, or gati. If we were to render a composition where there were three svaras sung between every kriya, we would refer to the nadai as tisra nadai. Based on the number of svaras present between each kriya in the tala, the laya of the tala would change. If we were to also include the variability of the nadai to the thirty-five talas, we would get 175 different talas (thirty-give talas x five nadai).

One may wonder why I have stated these values as 4, 3, 7, 5, 9 and not as 3, 4, 5, 7, 9. This is because it is traditionally accepted that four and three are fundamental rhythmic values from which every other value emerges. But this logic is not infallible.

We should remember that while changes in laya can be in the form of nadai, they can also manifest by doubling or halving the five basic numbers of svaras sung between each kriya. For example, you could have a laya of 4, 8, or 16. Though all these are from the base form of 4, they still vary the laya, as the number of svaras being sung between each kriya changes. But all multiples will still be viewed as manifestations of the basic chaturashra, tisra, mishra, khanda, sankirna.

In Karnatik music, we also employ a method of increasing the length of the tala without actually changing the laya. When I say that we do not change the laya, I mean that the number of svaras being sung between every kriya is the same, and there is no slowing down or increasing the frequency of the kriyas, yet the length of time covered by the tala will be more. In order to do this, the musician employs a very simple technique of doubling every kriya. In a tala with six kriyas, rupaka tala, if every kriya was presented after a gap of one second, then, in order to increase the length of the tala, the composer or musician would double each kriya so the total becomes twelve, but retain the same one-second gap between every kriya. Similarly, when each kriya is presented four times, retaining the same one-second gap, the length of the tala increases to twenty-four kriyas. But the number of svaras being rendered between each kriya would be the same. When a tala is presented in its doubled form, it is called 'rendu kalai' (in Tamil, rendu is two) and in its quadruple form 'naalu kalai' (naalu is four) and so on.

Chart 7: The three kalais and the beats they encompass in Rupaka tala

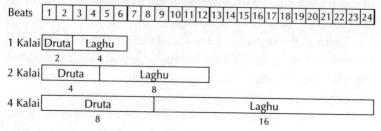

I should mention here that there are a few talas, like mishra chapu and khanda chapu, that do not find a place in this structure. And yet they have been absorbed with natural ease into Karnatik music. These two talas do not have the tala angas – laghu, druta and anudruta. Mishra chapu is a tala with seven beats, the slap on the thigh (sashabda kriya) being the only form of kriya. This tala starts with a slap on the thigh for the first beat followed by a slap on the thigh for the second, fourth and sixth beats. The seven beats in mishra chapu are taken as a combination of 3+4 and not 1+1+1+1+1+1+1. This gives the tala an internal structure. Some musicians use a flip of the palm rather than a slap on the thigh for the first two beats of the tala. This change may have been introduced later in order to identify the beginning of the avartana. Mishra is understood to mean mixed, but it also means blended, combined and connected. Mishra chapu is a blend or combination of three (tisra) and four (chaturashra). These are, after all, two of the basic rhythmic values used in music. I am not

sure whether this was the reason for the name, but the word's
original meaning certainly invites attention.

Khanda chapu has five beats with a slap on the thigh on the
first, third and fourth beats. The five beats are a combination of
2+3. Khanda means 'break' or 'fragment'. But does Khanda chapu
have a fragment of something? It actually does – of chaturashra. It
has half of four: two. The most important difference between these
two talas and the other talas is the non-uniform interval between
the kriyas. In all the other talas, whether made up of laghu, druta or
anudruta, the interval between every kriya is the same. This means
that if there is a one-second gap between the first and second kriya,
the same would be maintained between all the kriyas. But in these
two talas it is uneven. In mishra chapu, the interval between the
first (first beat) and second kriya (second beat) is shorter than the
interval between the second (second beat) and third kriya (fourth
beat) and the third (fourth beat) and fourth kriya (sixth beat). In
khanda chapu, the interval between the first (first beat) and second
kriya (third beat) is larger than the interval between the second
(third beat) and third kriya (fourth beat). Unlike all other talas, in
mishra chapu and khanda chapu, the number of beats is not equal
to the number of kriyas. This unusual distribution of kriyas lends
these two talas a distinct aesthetic form.

'Chapa' is an intriguing word. Sanskrit etymology gives us
'chaapam' meaning bow. Chapa in Hindi, interestingly enough,
means pressure. In both mishra chapu and khanda chapu, the
only kriya is a slap on the thigh – pressure, maybe?

Chart 8:

Mishra Chapu – 7 beats, 4 kriyas

Kriya 1	Kriya 2	Kriya 3	Kriya 4
Beat 1	Beats 2 & 3	Beats 4 & 5	Beats 6 & 7

Khanda Chapu – 5 beats, 3 kriyas

Kriya 1	Kriya 2	Kriya 3
Beats 1 & 2	Beat 3	Beat 4 & 5

Of the different talas in Karnatik music, adi tala, rupaka tala, mishra chapu and khanda chapu are the most widely employed. Adi tala has an independent history of its own which I shall elaborate later in the book. But it is nonetheless regarded as a variety of triputa tala – chaturashra jati triputa tala. Rupaka tala is a form that consists of one druta followed by a laghu of the chaturashra variety, making the total number of beats six. But in practice, musicians render this tala as three beats consisting of two slaps on the thigh and a flip of palm and call it rupaka tala. This version of rupaka tala has been in vogue for quite sometime. Though we refer to this tala also as rupaka, since it is only half the number of beats of the 'original' rupaka tala, it would be more appropriate to call it tisra chapu.

These features of Karnatik music comprise its aesthetic foundations. They are not absolute in form, but clarity emerges when we look into the abstraction that exists within their nature. In this discovery lies the true aesthetics of Karnatik music.

5

The Tune in the Word

The word 'composer' is derived from the Latin 'cum' (meaning 'with') and from the late Latin 'pausare' (meaning 'to pause'), blended with 'ponere' (meaning 'to lay down, set, place in') and 'positum' (meaning 'place in its proper position'). So, etymologically speaking, it means 'to reflectively create an entity that has all its ingredients set in their proper assigned positions'. It also means 'to combine elements'. One who accomplishes these is then a composer.

As there is composing in music, so also in art, literature and photography. In fact, in printing, the word quite literally refers to assembling material on a page. The etymology of 'compose' does not, therefore, point to an original creation, but to the act of placing material together. And to the fact that this amounts to an original exercise in itself. But the prevalent use of the noun in music denotes one who produces original work, as opposed to one combining already existing music. In Western classical music, for instance, the composer creates new and original work. Depending on the compositional intent, the composer gives his music an aural form by combining various instruments using different musicians.

In fact, one of the definitions of composer is 'a person who writes music'. I would like to discuss this, as it will help us understand the concept of a Karnatik music composer. The two operative words here are 'write' and 'music'. Let us, first, look at 'write'.

Obviously, the image of the composer as one who writes music has evolved from the tradition of Western classical music where composers *wrote* music. Though Indian music has been an oral tradition, we need to recognize that our music also had a written form in the past and, in fact, continues to be written even now. Ancient classical music traditions from the sixth century evolved a method to write music. The svaras have been written as sa, ri, ga, ma (as sung) from that period. Some ancient compositions have been published in treatises. The quality of these notations, in terms of how much they help us recreate the music, is a different question. Still, the fact that Indian music was written down is of importance to the subject of this essay: the theory and practice of compositions.

Modern (twentieth century) Indian classical music has developed a unique culture-centric notation system. More specifically, Karnatik music has, over the last century, developed an interesting way of writing music. I call it 'interesting' because, due to its complex nature, notating was always an issue with Karnatik musicians. Over the years, many of them have very innovatively used symbols to try and represent Karnatik music in written form.

Does this mean that the Karnatik music composer wrote – and writes – music? At least until the mid-nineteenth century, the process of composing seems to have been intellectual work passed on orally. It was recorded by students who learnt directly from the composer. They may have written it during the learning process, or the writing may have occurred years later. But the act of writing music was not an inherent part of the process of composing, and definitely not part of teaching. The writing was primarily a record. And so to encapsulate the position, one could say that writing of music has been known, but unlike in the Western tradition, it has been essentially an ancillary exercise.

Compositions, Their Nature and Evolution

In such a situation, we need to understand the nature of a composition that arises in the composer's musical imagination, which is then taught orally and is not written down by the composer himself. This impacts on what is perceived to be an 'authentic' version of the composition. When a composition is taught and transmitted orally, changes in it occur quite naturally over a period of time. These are the result of the way successive generations recall it from memory.

Various other aspects that were absorbed by the individual also influence the process of recall: such as the influences of other musicians, as well as the musician's own insight acquired from experience, exposure and study. And so the composition evolves, retaining the essential aspects that the original composer transferred to the student, intact. As the changes increase with every new generation, they become more obvious, and older versions begin to sound more authentic. The more they deviate from what might have been the composer's idea, the more conspicuous the changes become. This is where the authenticity issue comes in. But the fact is that authenticity itself is not a static entity. It is the living value of the composition, its essential core. The whole process of a composition's organic evolution is part of its authenticity. We are looking at a nuanced idea here: that the 'quality' of evolution is built into the tradition of oral transmission. Whether in the rendition of the Vedas, a musical composition or a dance, we tend to believe and say that they are now as they were hundreds of years ago. But they have changed, and the fact that they were not written down in some original and immutable text is an important enabling reason. The beauty of the oral tradition lies in the fact that it has enabled creativity. Here I must stress that no composer has actually given any musician the right to change his composition. But every composer must have known, without doubt, that the musical imagination of successive generations singing or playing their composition will invest something of their own genius on it, while retaining the essential integrity of its structure and spirit. This process, in its true sense, can be called organic.

It is, however, crucial that we distinguish between organic change and change made consciously without an understanding of the composition and the versions that have come down through the guru–shishya parampara. In Karnatik music, most composers have handed down their music through the guru–shishya parampara.

This is the lineage of teachers and students beginning from one specific musician. It grows out of a certain style of music, along with the compositions and thought, handed down the generations through an ideationally linked line of teachers and students. Any changes made by musicians who ignore this link to tradition cannot be included in this organic change.

Many modern composers write their own compositions, but even in these there is a possibility of reinterpretation. The method of notating essentially consists of providing the compositional framework. This means that every musician who learns the composition from the notation reinterprets the music with her own sensibilities. This makes a composition sound very different when handled by different artists. To the extent that artists adhere to the composer's notated framework, their renditions are considered 'authentic'. When artists' interpretations move away from the notation, arbitrary changes become a distinct possibility.

Unfortunately, this happens with many compositions in vogue today. Irresponsible reinterpretations have led to the compositions completely losing the composer's intent. This has happened even to compositions of the twentieth century. Within a decade or so, the renditions have become very distant from the original. Therefore, it is a reality that, along with organic changes, there have been changes made by musicians based on their perceptions of music, ignoring renditions handed down by the guru–shishya parampara.

Essentially, the oral guru–shishya tradition has given us many authentic versions of compositions by important composers in Karnatik music. We need a more sensitive approach to understand the relationship between the composition and the composer and also re-calibrate the role of notation in Karnatik music.

The 'Music' that Is Written

Let us turn to 'writing music' now. In some cases, a poet may have written the lyrics, while the musician-composer sets the music. In many popular traditions, the lyricist or songwriter is mentioned separately from the composer. The same person may do both, but 'composer' refers specifically to one who composes music.

In Karnatik music, we have a beautiful word – vaggeyakara – to refer to the composer. It encompasses the two primary roles, and is derived from 'vak' (meaning 'word' or 'language') and 'geya' (from the root 'gi', which means, among other things, 'to sing'). Clearly, the role of a composer is related both to text and music. The term 'to sing' here refers to the melodic content. Unless an individual is proficient in both, he cannot be a vaggeyakara. A reference to a composer in Karnatik music means one who creates both the text, often called the 'poetry' and the music. These are not considered separate from each other. The perfecting and embellishing may happen later, but the composition is usually a spontaneous creation of both melody and poetry. The most exquisite compositions in the Karnatik oeuvre seem to have sprung from a creative flow of melody and text together, creating the aesthetic identity of the composition. This simultaneous evolution makes the relationship between the text and melody intimate, making it impossible to identify one without subconsciously hearing the other. This relationship gives the compositions a distinct quality, as the same person is responsible for the emotional core of both the poetry and the music, giving the listener an intimate experience of the composer's expression of music embedded in the poetry. The vaggeyakara also establishes the authorship of the composition with a signature – either his name or a pseudonym – usually at the end. This is their signet, nom de plume, known as a mudra or ankita.

An issue arises when we define a vaggeyakara's role in terms of word and music. There are compositional forms where the texts are linguistically void, instead using syllabic sounds that represent percussion strokes or svaras. These 'sound texts' do not have word meaning. Can composers of such compositions also be referred to as vaggeyakaras? This is an interesting conundrum. It requires us to look at and understand 'vak' not as a word, but as any text with its remarkable original meaning: 'that which is said'. In such compositions, the role of the text is different from that of compositions, which have text with linguistic meaning. We then have compositions where the text is either verbal or syllabic. Where the svaras are both the text and the melody, they acquire a dual role.

We must now turn to an important concept and word in Karnatik music – 'sahitya'. Normally, sahitya is used to refer to the written word, while 'sangita' refers to music. As sahitya specifically refers to text with linguistic meaning, the syllabic text does not constitute sahitya. This does not privilege one kind of text over the other. Both remain equal and interrelated. The general term used to refer to the textual part of a composition is 'matu', while the melody is 'dhatu'. To students of music, these words are introduced as part of classroom conversation on the beauty of composition. Students are told that 'matu', text, is the mother and dhatu, melody, is the father. The coming together of the two leads to the creation of a composition. These associations are used to impress upon the student that word and word meaning are the essence of a composition, and the melody has to enhance the word.

A closer investigation of the words 'dhatu' and 'matu' leads us in a different direction, though. Dhatu among its many meanings in Sanskrit denotes the soul, essence and supreme spirit. Matu may not even be a Sanskrit word. In Kannada, matu means word, 'that which is said' and conversation, or the expressed word. This must have been why in music it is used for text. The word matrka in Sanskrit refers to the mother and alphabets. This could have led to matu being interpreted as mother. The father association in dhatu may come from the fact that, among its many connotations, dhatu also means seminal fluid.

Many musicians set verse written by other poets to music. These can result in beautiful creations of art, but such musicians are not accepted as composers. The converse can happen as well. There are many compositions by vaggeyakaras for which the words remain, but the music has been lost. Since the lyrics are available, musicians set them to music. This is a sensitive task indeed, as the musicians need to understand not just the word meaning of the lyrics, but also their inner energy, the syllabic form of the poetry and its inherent metre. A true musician tries to capture all these when investing a piece of verse with music.

In this endeavour, there is yet another challenge. In the case of some great vaggeyakaras, there are documents or inscriptions that mention the name of the raga in which the composition was tuned by the vaggeyakara. But if that raga is not extant or active – like samanta, saurashtragujjari and padi – we face a real difficulty.

If a musician is to revive the composition, what is he to do? If the musician re-tunes the sahitya, should he do so only in that raga?

There are two opinions on this issue. Some believe that since the actual raga is no longer current, or can even be regarded as extinct, it makes no difference if the musician tunes the lyrics in another raga. The other view, to which I subscribe, is that it does make a difference. If we want to refer to these composers as vaggeyakaras, we need to respect the raga in which they composed. If not, we are removing the only link we have with the vaggeyakara. This in turn means that we have to, wherever possible, retrieve the original raga from its retreat.

The other option is not to refer to them as the vaggeyakaras for those texts, since the matu is incomplete without the dhatu.

It is a reality that some of the ragas mentioned in inscriptions are irretrievably lost. In such cases, some believe that we have no option but to tune the poetry in a raga of one's own choice. However, we could take the position – and I do – that trying to reconstruct the raga from collateral sources and internal evidence in relevant textual history would still be a worthwhile effort, though the raga we recreate will not be the original one.

The role of compositions in Karnatik music is diverse, giving it raga understanding, tala comprehension and matu. An understanding of the elements, form and expression in compositions is vital for an insight into the aesthetics of the music.

Understanding Raga

The struggle for a student of music is to try and understand a raga. What is its identity? What are the crucial svaras, phrases, expressions? In the answers to these questions lie the seeds of musical imagination. Every composition is a storehouse of the facets that give a raga its image. A composition interprets the raga through the melody in a unique way, giving musicians a different perspective, opening a new window to it. Each composition builds a whole range of ideas and approaches to a raga in a musician's mind. The raga identity is not something that comes the moment a musician learns a composition or its technical aspects. The raga is being learnt and relearnt continuously right through life, every time a new composition is learnt. This keeps the raga fresh and the musician evolving. Compositions contain various speeds in raga phrases and multiple speeds within the same composition. This again is a very important contribution to raga comprehension. Every melodic phrase in a raga transforms itself depending on the speed of rendition. This, in turn, is built into raga identity, which is learnt from composition.

The question then is: how was raga identity first established? In Karnatik music, a raga is accepted as one only when there is at least one composition in it. This is significant. It is accepted that the first true expression of a raga within the system lies with the vaggeyakara, not the performing musician. The musician may have explored a new melodic idea, but this is not established unless encapsulated in a composition. A new raga comes into its own only when it is embedded in a composition. The composition's framework lets the composer establish the various facets of the raga, capturing the raga's core essentials. These become the points of reference for every musician. The raga is then built upon constantly by the contributions of other composers and the creativity of musicians. Significantly, though some performing musicians have been vaggeyakaras, not all vaggeyakaras have been performing musicians.

Unravelling Tala

Tala is the life rhythm of compositions. As I have explained previously, tala is a tactile method of dividing time, specifically created for music. It consists of a fixed number of divisions between which exists a measurable pause. This composite unit is repeated cyclically. All musical compositions in Karnatik music are set to tala. Though there is a tradition of singing poetry in a free-flowing style sans tala, known as viruttam or shloka, this is not considered a musical composition. It is an improvised musical interpretation of poetry.

The tala form can be understood only when it finds a place in compositions. Apart from giving tala a melodic identity, compositions exploit the various parts of the tala, its divisions and its laya in order to present it in its complete form.

While we can theoretically describe a tala, we can never truly understand its relevance until we see it bound to the composition. We can physically demonstrate a tala without a composition or a melody, but a true understanding of the tala and an appreciation of its role comes when the layers of melody are placed within the rubric of the tala. The tala gives dhatu and matu a defined space within which to build musical and textual structures. Every composition, therefore, uses tala, laya and its various angas to give itself sections, textual structures and defined melodic phrases.

For a composer, the possibilities of exploring the structured space to create melodic imagery within a single tala are immense. A study of compositions by great vaggeyakaras shows that the same tala has been used differently each time. When this happens, a tala comes alive, gives a composition strength of support through its internal division, sets the raga flowing through its laya and creates complete musical identities through its form and cyclical nature. The choice of tala for a composition is dependent on the text and the raga's melodic movement

Within the tala structure, the composer defines the exact places where every line of a composition begins and ends. This means that, first, the melodic laya and the textual laya have to be in sync and, second, they must have a direct relationship with the tala structure. In every composition, there is usually a certain fixed structure with regard to how the dhatu, matu and tala relate to each other. Therefore, the beginning of the melody, the textual and melodic stresses and the ending of the melody within every avartana are related, if not constant, within each composition.

So it is the vaggeyakara who fixes the raga, tala and melodic structure of the composition.

Unfolding Laya

As explained earlier, laya refers generically to speed, but within the context of Karnatik music, it has different connotations, each with a specific meaning. Laya can refer to a feeling of speed while rendering or listening to a piece of music, which is determined by conditioning or the specific length of the pause between two divisions within a tala or the number of svaras or emphasis between two divisions within a tala. What is left of laya when matu is simply not there? When tala is counted without the rendition of any composition, laya remains tangible and sensed only in the indefinable speed within the pause between each beat. Beyond this we do not have any other layering. Once we render a composition, laya unfolds into myriad colours. The composition's syllabic stress in conjunction with melodic flow establishes the laya. The language and syllabic form of the text and the aesthetics of the raga embrace the bare framework of the tala and infuse it with melody. Laya is born to immense musical effect in this triangular relationship. Its journey proceeds based on the aesthetic intent of each compositional form.

Sahitya

Sahitya in the world of musical compositions refers to linguistically meaningful texts.

In compositions, sahitya plays a very important role, both in the nature of its sound and the meaning it conveys. The sound of every syllable and its relationship with the melody contributes to the aesthetic experience of a composition. When I use the word 'melody', I am referring to the svaras that are part of every raga's identity and lie behind every melodic line rendered with text. Every syllabic sound is closely related to its specific musical context. In any quality composition, it will be found that the length of the syllable is related to that of its specific melody. Therefore, a longer syllable will have a longer melody or phrase and vice versa, thereby influencing the melodic flow. In some compositions, we find that a stress on a specific syllable also translates to a stress on a svara relevant to the raga. So every line is a unique part of the musical form, with the melody constantly interacting with the syllables and the tala to give the raga an integrated form (svarupa). We should include here the aesthetics of the sound created by the pronounced word.

Sahitya also frames musical lines, defines the beginning and the end of a musical statement within a composition. This is, of course, bound by the tala structure, but a collection of raga phrases, which is a line of melody, can extend to multiple cycles of a tala, because it is defined by sahitya's poetic form.

We cannot ignore the fact that every language brings a different aesthetic dimension to a composition. The structural form combines with the sound's aesthetic form to influence the composition's raga and tala.

In Karnatik music, compositions are mainly in Sanskrit, Telugu, Tamil, Kannada and Malayalam. Musicians will find that the aesthetics of the melody seems different when the same musical phrase is sung in two different languages. This is primarily because of the sound of the syllables, which are the pillars on which the melodic phrase is structured. This could be partly psychological – the result of the mind interpreting the melodic flow differently when other syllables are placed in the same position. The syllables and the compound sounds unique to each language register differently in our mind, making the structure of the phrase seem different.

Sahitya in a composition gives emotional colour to the raga. Among other things, the composer is trying to express the sensitivity of the lyrics through the raga, which in turn influences raga development. The texture of the raga is also being defined. Every time a different subject is handled lyrically in a raga, its emotional range expands. This is part of the musician's learning and an accepted experience. That said, it is important to remember that the primary objective of art music is not to communicate the meaning of sahitya.

As much as sahitya influences the raga movements in a composition, the raga's emotive qualities also influence the way we pronounce sahitya. The pronunciation is influenced both at the syllabic and the word level. Through the manner of rendering, melodic movements in a raga have developed a certain emotive texture through the ages. The volume and quality of sound given to the various parts of the movement contribute to this. Certain parts of the phrases are stressed more and have a brighter expression, where others are made subtle. These stresses are reflected in the phrase when it appears in a composition that contains lyrics. The lyrics themselves are sung with similar expression. Brilliant composers have been aware of this and their choice of words match the raga's flow.

Linguistically Void Text

Can there be a text that is linguistically void?

In music, yes. Some musical forms use the verbal syllabic representations of percussion sounds as text. These include sounds like ta, taka, kita, tarikita, tam, dhim, dhirana, tarikitatom. In some Karnatik compositions, the svaras themselves can form the text, without the use of a single word in the linguistic sense. Therefore, the musician will render the composition by singing the svara.

For example:

    Raga: Kalyani

    Tala: Adi

Melody: S -- NDPDMGRNRS -- NRGMGMPDN

Text: S NDPDMGRNRS   NRGMGMPDN

The hyphens present in the notation are time measures of the pauses of the svara preceding the marking. This compositional form is known as jati svara and used extensively in Bharatanatyam.

Text that is linguistically void carries as much musical import as sahitya, because its syllabic structures combine with melodic movements to create composite melodic units in the compositions. These texts are syllabically valuable.

Can a linguistically void text give emotion to a composition? Emotion is registered by texture, stress on word and syllable. The harder or tougher sounds relate to stronger emotions, while softer, delicate sounds seem to communicate a feeling of love, sympathy, empathy, etc. Our minds make these connections on the basis of human thought, action and behaviour. The matu reflects these whether the texts are meaningful or not. Therefore, texts influence these melodic movements. If the texts consist of svaras, they directly manifest their character within the raga in the specific context.

This intimate relationship between sahitya or linguistically void text and sangita makes it imperative for a vaggeyakara to be proficient in both. Musicians who want to set poetry written by others to music find that not all great poetry is suitable for music. From the sound of the syllables to the pronunciation of the words, everything about the sahitya – external and internal – affects the raga. Therefore, the choice of the linguistic text or poetry must be made with great sensitivity to raga and tala. A composition can be described as an amalgam of raga, tala, syllabic sound and meaning. It is one side of the musical coin, the other being manodharma sangita which is inadequately translated as 'improvisational music' for a lack of a better phrase.

Among the various types of compositions in Karnatik music today, each is unique in the way it combines raga, tala and text.

Every composition is divided into sections that are a development of dhatu and matu. The importance given to these elements and the way they interact with each other gives each compositional type a specific identity. The linguistically void text of a composition plays the same role in its interaction with dhatu and tala as sahitya. Every syllable of the text is therefore inextricable from the melody it contains. No syllable is independent of the melody, irrespective of whether it has linguistic meaning or not. In spite of all the differences between compositional forms, there is an underlying structural similarity. Let us look at this before we go into the different types of compositions and their aesthetics.

Pallavi

Almost all compositional forms in Karnatik music open with the section called 'pallavi', literally, the shoot of a plant. This also indicates its position in the composition – the starting point. The pallavi opens a composition and in so doing directs the raga's melodic flow. It establishes the musical focus and laya of the raga, melody and the tala, which in turn influence the various nuances that occur within every svara. From the rendition of the pallavi, it is possible to feel the texture of the raga that is to develop in the composition.

Lyrically too the pallavi makes the opening poetic statement of the sahitya and establishes the vaggeyakara's ideational intent and introduces or sets the tone for the core issue of the composition. The pallavi is usually made up of one or two lines, covering one to four avartanas.

Anupallavi

Next comes the anupallavi, the melodic movements of which tend to explore the raga in the higher octave. This is common to most compositions. This section continues to lyrically expand the subject of the pallavi. Unless it is specifically indicated, it is sometimes difficult to recognize where the anupallavi begins by looking only at the melody. However, there is a poetic method to do so. Poetry uses a technical form, prasa or alliteration, where the same syllable is repeated in different lines, but at the same place in the poetic metre, either as the first, second or last syllable (prathamakshara prasa, dvitiyakshara prasa, antimakshara prasa). This technique seems to have been perfected in the south, specifically in Tamil poetry, and is widely used in Telugu, Kannada and Malayalam as well. In Sanskrit poetry, the technique can be seen in works from the south, though not from other parts of the country. There are three examples below:

Prathamakshara Prasa

> _manasu svadhinamainayaghanuniki_
> _mari mantra tantramulela_

> Vaggeyakara: Tyagaraja
> Language: Telugu

Dvitiyakshara Prasa

> _himachala tanaya brocutaki_
> _di manci samayamu rave amba_
> _kumara janani samanamevarila_
> _nu manavati shri brhannayaki_

> Vaggeyakara: Shyama Shastri
> Language: Telugu

Antimakshara Prasa

> _dakshinamurte_
> _vidalita dasarte_
> _cidananda sphurte_
> _sada mauna kirte_

> Vaggeyakara: Muttusvami Dikshitar
> Language: Sanskrit

The anupallavi is identified by the occurrence of the dvitiyakshara prasa in the pallavi's opening line and in the first line of the anupallavi. Below is an example.

Pallavi

*da**nda**yudhapanim dandita daitya shrenim*
dayanidhim bhajare hrdaya satatam sura vinutam

Anupallavi

*cha**nda**mshushata koti sankasham jagadisham a*
khanda rupam andaja muni mandala maya kundaladi
manditanga sukumaram khandita taraka shuram
panditatara navaviram chandikeshavataram

Vaggeyakara: Muttusvami Dikshitar
Language: Sanskrit

There is also a beautiful pattern to the way prasa appears in a composition. Within the tala flow the position of the dvitiyakshara syllable is usually at the same position in both the lines. This further binds the sahitya and sangita within the tala. Along with the dvitiyakshara prasa we have to look at whether the meaning of the anupallavi sahitya directly connects with the pallavi, which is the refrain, and also take into account the number of avartanas of the pallavi and anupallavi. Clearly, it is not possible to identify the anupallavi on the basis of melody, although, in the case of some composers, the melodic flow can be indicative even if it is not definitive. In spite of sahitya being our primary indicator here, it is still not foolproof. Scholars and musicians have different opinions regarding many kirtanas (a compositional form) where the anupallavi is not explicitly mentioned. The problems in identifying the anupallavi are usually found in kirtanas, and not other compositional forms. We should also remember that though the dvitiyakshara prasa is used to identify the anupallavi, the composition may also have other prasas. When the anupallavi is present in a composition it is always rendered immediately after the pallavi and before any other section.

Charana

Another section found in most compositional types is a charana. Its length varies, depending on the type of composition. The prasa used in the charana is usually independent of the prasa in pallavi or anupallavi, and is consistent within itself. Below is an example of a composition where the prasa of the pallavi and anupallavi are the same, and that of the charana is different.

Pallavi

ra__ma__ ninne namminanu nijamuga sita

Anupallavi

ka__ma__janaka kamaniya vadana nannu
kavave karunya jaladhe

Charana

ra__ja__ raja vandita
bhu__ja__ nayaka sura sa
ma__ja__ shrikara tyaga
ra__ja__ manasa sa
ro__ja__ kusuma dina
ra__ja__ pankti ratha
ra__ja__ tanaya shri

Vaggeyakara: Tyagaraja
Language: Sanskrit

The reader might legitimately ask what the purpose of prasa is. It is essentially a mnemonic device, which also happens to be aesthetically appealing. Obviously, compositional forms that use texts that are linguistically void do not need to follow the technique of poetic alliteration.

Compositional Forms

In the threefold structure of compositions, the pallavi is invariably a constant, but there is some variability about the anupallavi and charana. Almost all compositional forms are made up of one or the other of these combinations:

Pallavi–Anupallavi–Charana
Pallavi–Anupallavi–Multiple Charanas
Pallavi–Anupallavi
Pallavi–Multiple Charanas

While these are the primary combinations, many compositional forms add some other sections between these, giving each form a different aesthetic structure. Though most compositions are contained in a single raga and set to one tala, others can occur in multiple ragas and talas.

The singer can take a deliberate pause between the pallavi, anupallavi and charana. These pauses help in emphasizing, stabilizing and developing the melodic and lyrical aspects of the composition. The pauses are not arbitrary, but positioned to allow the avartana to end after the conclusion of a section; the next section is taken exactly at the point fixed in the tala. When the compositional form requires continuity between certain sections, they are rendered without these pauses.

Let us now try and understand the aesthetics of some important compositional forms.

Gita

Gita is the first type of composition that a student learns. This form seems to be an exception to the earlier statement made by me that all compositions in Karnatik music is derived from a pallavi–anupallavi–charana base. Though the word 'gita'can refer to any melodic structure, composition or song, here it refers to a specific compositional form. Gitas are simple constructions of raga, tala and sahitya. Musicologists who have published notations of gitas have refrained from presenting them in the pallavi–anupallavi–charana structure. Gitas contain multiple two-line verses that dovetail to the refrain. We can try placing them into the standard format, but this is inadvisable due to the lack of structural commonality between them and differences in the format of rendition.

Musically, these compositions are simple and easy to comprehend. The melodic structure does not have too many complex movements. The tala structuring is also straightforward, and the sahitya specifically emphasizes the tala's structural divisions. Sahitya is usually composed in Kannada, Sanskrit or Telugu. Sometimes it has extended melodic movements containing vowel sounds that have no linguistic meaning. Important composers of gitas are Purandaradasa (1484–1564), who is considered the father of Karnatik music, and Paidala Gurumurti Shastri (eighteenth century).

A form of gita that is not usually learnt is the lakshya gita. These are clearly older compositional forms, which retain sections that connect closely to an older musical tradition called the chaturdandi and specifically to the composition type called the prabandha. These are not divided into the pallavi and charana structure, but into dhruva, antari and javada. The structure and flow are very different from what we are used to, and cannot be related directly to compositions that are the mainstay of Karnatik music today. However, some scholars believe that the modern kirtanas may have originated from the prabandha. In general, gitas are not part of concert music repertoire.

Varna

The varna is an exquisite musical form, the complexity of which lies in the melody and use of tala structure, because the sahitya is not significant. Varna expands the pallavi–anupallavi–charana structure and includes other sections in between. Its aesthetics is very significant in any discussion on Karnatik music.

The sections of a varna are: pallavi, anupallavi, muktayi svara, charana and ettugada svaras (chitta svara).

Each section has a texture of its own. The pallavi is usually of two avartanas and is connected directly to the anupallavi, which is of the same length. The second avartana of the anupallavi explores the higher octave. Both the pallavi and anupallavi contain sahitya. The sahitya is invariably dedicated to a deity, although it usually contains romantic or erotic imagery.

After the anupallavi, the composition moves into a section called muktayi svara, which is rendered as svaras. This section can vary from two to four avartanas, depending on the varna's length. These svara structures traverse across two octaves, presenting the raga in the svara form. The muktayi svara connects back with the pallavi. In some varnas, even the muktayi svara has sahitya, in which case the svaras are rendered first, followed by the sahitya. Once the pallavi is rendered again, the first segment (purvanga) of the varna is considered to have ended.

The next segment (uttaranga) begins with a single avartana that contains sahitya. This is the charana. It forms the nucleus around which multiple svara structures are composed. Each svara pattern returns to the charana, which is the musical refrain. These svaras are called ettugada or chitta svaras. Their length increases as we move from the first to, say, the fourth ettugada svara. There could be anywhere from four to six ettugada svaras in a varna. An analysis of the ettugada svaras reveals some uniformity in the musical structures of each. The first svara structure is normally of one avartana and contains many long svara pauses; the second is of the same length, but is a combination of long and short svaras; the third is usually longer (two avartanas) and contains only short svaras with no pauses, or very few that emphasize the same points in the tala cycles. If the fourth svara is the last, it is longer, traversing the whole range of the raga, beginning with a long pause either on a svara important to the raga or on sa/pa.

There are, of course, exceptions. Some varnas contain sahitya for every ettugada svara. In these cases, the svara is rendered first, leading to the charana refrain, followed by sahitya. The format is the same for all ettugada svaras.

At the end of the last ettugada svara, the varna ends by repeating the charana. But many varnas are structured in such a way that the meaning of the charana is complete only when it is linked back to the pallavi. There was a tradition of connecting the charana to the anupallavi and concluding with the pallavi. In older varnas, there are a few more avartanas to the charana, which are rendered after the ettugada svaras. This was then connected to the pallavi, usually through the anupallavi.

Let us now look at the two types of contrastive varnas: tana varna and pada varna.

The tana varna is easily identifiable by its compositional form and rendering. As the name indicates, the aural texture of the tana varna is similar to the manodharma form, tana. Every line has a regimented structure, with every svara being emphasized by the repetition of the vowel ending of the previous syllable. This aesthetic is evident in the pallavi and anupallavi. Chart 9 is a small sample of how this could be written.

As the example shows, there are multiple vowel extensions, Es and As that are sounded on every svara though there is no sahitya for those sections. This gives the tana varna a very rigid and stiff structure. The pallavi and anupallavi are usually rendered in two speeds. Sahitya is minimal and requires extension of the syllables in the melody. This means that, for every avartana, the sahitya contains only a word or two. Artists have to render the varna with continuity between the syllables to present each line as a cohesive melodic unit. This requires a great deal of breath control and a conscious understanding of where the melodic movement can be paused and a breath drawn. Textual meaning has little importance in tana varnas, where the primary objective is to highlight the melody.

Chart 9: Tana Varna

S	–	–	R	N	–	Ḍ	–	Ṇ	–	S	–	R	–	–	G	S	–	R	–
a				a	a		a	vi		ri		bo			o	o		o	

G	R	G	G	R	–	–	–	G	G	R	G	M	P	D	M	P	G	R	S
ni	i	i	i	i				ni	i	i	i	i	i	i	i	i	i	i	i

Ṇ	S	M	G	R	S	N	S	R	G	S	R	N	N	Ḍ	N
ne	e	e	e	e	e	ko	o	o	o	o	o	o	o	o	o

S	G	R	N	S	N	Ḍ	P	Ṗ	Ḍ	Ṗ	Ḍ	Ṇ	N	Ḍ	P	Ḍ	Ṇ	S	R
ri	i	i	i	i	i	i	i	ma	a	a	a	ru	u	u	u	lu	u	u	u

Ṗ	Ḍ	Ṇ	S	R	G	M	P	M	G	R	G	M	N	D	P	M	G	R	Ṇ
ko	o	o	o	o	o	o	o	nna	a	a	a	di	i	i	i	i	i	i	i

S	R	G	M	G	R	G	G	R	–	–	–	Ṡ	N	D	P
i	i	i	i	i	i	i	i	ra				a	a	a	a

Vaggeyakara:	Pacchimiriyam Adiyappaiyya
Language:	Telugu
Raga:	Bhairavi
Tala:	Khanda Jati Ata
Lyrics:	viriboni nine kori marulu konnadira

The pada varna, on the other hand, is a continuous melodic movement that sounds more like the musical form pada. There are no obvious stresses on svaras; every syllable is enunciated and the rest of the svaras are not emphasized with a vowel sound. Each svara is in a seamless flow, and not acting as defined support posts. The pada varna has more sahitya in every avartana and is usually rendered in a slower laya. Hence, it is also referred to as a chauka varna. The internal sections of both these compositional types are the same, but the aesthetics are different. Chart 10 is a sample of a pada varna.

Chart 10: Pada varna

N	–	–	–	S̊	–	–	–	–	–	Ṙ	–	Ṡ	–	–	Ṡ	–	–	Ṡ	N	N	D	P	–
Mo				*ha*						*ma*		*na*			*en*			*mi*				*dhil*	

N	–	S̊	–	N	–	–	–	N	D	P	–	M	P	G	R	G	–	M	–	P	–	D	P
ni								*in*				*da*			*ve*			*la*		*yil*			

Vaggeyakara:	Ponniah Pillai, Tanjavur Quartet
Language:	Tamil
Raga:	Bhairavi
Tala:	Rupaka
Lyrics:	mohamana en midhil ni indha velayil

Though the tana varna is usually distinguished from the pada varna on the basis of the sahitya for the muktayi and the ettugada svaras, this is not always the case. There are some tana varnas that have sahitya for these svara sections. The difference lies in the aesthetics of the composition, not the structure.

Importantly, in a tana varna, the pallavi, anupallavi and charana sections, which have sahitya, are not taught only as raga melodies. The svaras are taught first, followed by the sahitya. This is not followed when pada varnas are taught.

Svarajati

The svarajati has two distinct forms. The older svarajati, which may have predated the varna, is very similar to it in structure. The only major difference is the existence of 'jatis' after the anupallavi in the muktayi svara section. Jatis, or sollukattus, are the verbal syllabic sounds given to all rhythmic strokes played on the percussion instruments. These jatis are sometimes interspersed in the muktayi svara section. The ettugada svaras of a svarajati always have sahitya. In terms of the structural aesthetics, there is not much that differentiates the svarajati from the varna.

The more common form of svarajati is inextricably linked

with the legendary composer Shyama Shastri. Three of his compositions are in this form (though one of them does not conform to what we understand the structure of the svarajati to be). This type of svarajati contains a pallavi with two sahitya lines, followed by multiple charanas.

There are some beautiful aspects to the way these charanas are structured. They are composed to begin successively in the ascending order of the svaras of the raga. Which means that the svarajati in bhairavi has each charana beginning with sa, ri, ga, ma, pa, dha, ni, sa in the same order. Second, the match between the length of each syllable and the svara is perfect, creating a unique musical aesthetic. Whether rendered as svara or sahitya, the definitions of the melodic structures remain the same. While rendering the svarajati, the svara and sahitya of every charana has to be connected to the pallavi. The length of every charana increases between the first and last, though many could be of the same length. Among the three svarajatis composed by Shyama Shastri, the compositions in ragas bhairavi and yadukula kambhoji fall within these structural definitions, but the one in raga todi does not.

There is also a composition called svarajati that is learnt soon after the gitas. These consist of a pallavi and multiple charana, but do not have the specific characteristics of Shyama Shastri's svarajatis.

Kirtana/Kriti

The kirtana is the most important compositional form in Karnatik music. It carries with it the absolute identity of Karnatik music as we experience it today. The popularity of this form makes it the most recognizable, and the format of the twentieth-century Karnatik music concert, still current, is based upon the aesthetics of this form. The eighteenth-century composers Tyagaraja (1767–1847), Muttusvami Dikshitar (1775–1835) and Shyama Shastri (1762–1827), known as the 'trinity', were masters of this form.

Aesthetically, the kirtana is a beautiful balance between the three integral elements of a composition: dhatu, matu and tala. While most other compositional forms emphasize one or the other, the kirtana balances these elements, giving the listener a fused form.

The exploration of melody within this compositional type covers the entire gamut of raga possibilities. Many older ragas have over a dozen compositions in this format. The pallavi is the opening of the kirtana. It is between one and four avartanas, depending on the tala. The raga is introduced in this section, and forms the melodic basis for its development through the entire composition. The opening line establishes the melodic emphasis of the raga. Every melodic line with its phraseological movement has a laya, which is closely related to the tala and its own laya. The overlaying of one on the other is what defines the texture of every kirtana. This is again defined in the pallavi. The sahitya, unlike in the tana varna, is very significant. In a kirtana it does not contain any unnatural syllabic extensions. The density of sahitya in a kirtana is much more than that of the pallavi or anupallavi in a tana varna. It varies, depending on raga, tala and laya. A kirtana's lyrical content is usually bhakti. How important this is to art music can be debated, but we cannot ignore the kirtana's sahitya.

The structure of a kirtana explores all four possibilities in the pallavi–anupallavi–charana structure mentioned before.

Pallavi–Anupallavi–Charana
Pallavi–Anupallavi
Pallavi–Anupallavi–Multiple Charanas
Pallavi–Multiple Charanas

The pallavi is always the melodic and lyrical refrain of the composition. Therefore it is constantly reiterated. So when the pallavi ends, there is a pause, followed by the anupallavi, after which the pallavi is rendered again. The anupallavi's lyrical and melodic flow is connected to the pallavi. Again, after a pause in the pallavi, the charana is rendered, followed by the pallavi. In compositions where there is no charana, the anupallavi ends with a few lines of sahitya in a laya faster than the established laya of the composition. This is known as madhyama-kala sahitya, which means, for example, in adi tala there will be two or four syllables or stresses per beat, depending on the laya of rest of the composition. At the end of this, the pallavi is once again rendered. Sometimes, madhyama-kala sahitya can occur even in the charana. This technique of using madhyama-kala sahitya in the anupallavi and charana was Muttusvami Dikshitar's contribution to kirtana aesthetics. The use of madhyama-kala sahitya at the end of the anupallavi or charana creates a contrast in laya. The change in laya between the anupallavi's earlier section and the madhyama-kala sahitya, leading to a reversal in laya when linked to the pallavi, brings seamless shifts in feeling. If I were to explain that visually, I would say, think of a bird gliding in the sky before diving to the surface of the lake only to return to the airflow to once again glide.

In the case of a kirtana with pallavi, anupallavi and multiple charanas, the pallavi is repeated after the rendition of every charana. The same is followed in the case of kirtanas with a pallavi and multiple charanas. The lengths of the pallavi–anupallavi–charana are usually connected. In general, the pallavi is of one, two or four avartanas depending on the tala. The length of the anupallavi is related to the pallavi and so is the charana. Therefore, when the pallavi is one avartana long, the anupallavi is two and the charana four. Though this is true in most compositions, it is not a rule. There are kirtanas with an odd number of avartanas in the pallavi and sometimes the length of the anupallavi is not arithmetically related to the pallavi.

The kirtana introduced an important melodic idea to Karnatik music, which brought improvisation into the gamut of compositional music, as a part of the composed structure. This added a further nuance to the idea of a fixed composition. A

set of melodic variations was brought to certain lines within a
kirtana. These variations are not arbitrary. They are determined
by the raga, melody, laya, tala and texture of the raga within the
line, and the positions of the syllables of the sahitya within the
tala matrix. Melodic variations, known as sangatis, are composed
keeping all this in mind. These can be present in any line in the
kirtana and vary from composer to composer.

Here an important question is always asked: does the composer
compose all the sangatis? The answer is definitely no. The sangatis
have been added by the various musicians who handle the
kirtana. This leads us back to the problem of the authenticity of
compositions. The added sangatis should not change the kirtana's
melodic flow and must use the fundamental melodic line as the
base. This means that every sangati in its departure from the basic
melodic line is actually reiterating it. Each sangati becomes relevant
to the fundamental melodic line and to the composer.

But there is a problem here as well: the aesthetic sensibility of
each musician. Each musician perceives the melodic changes to
a line from a different perspective, making it possible to connect
between his sangati conceptually with the fundamental melodic
line. This allows for great differences in the sangatis between
different guru–shishya paramparas. The only way to reconcile
this problem is to objectively analyse the different versions of
the compositions and scrutinize the sangatis that have been
handed down through the direct guru–shishya parampara of
the vaggeyakara. This should give us a clearer idea of whether
there is an aesthetic connect between the sangatis incorporated in
the kirtana and the structure as handed down by tradition. This
dispassionate analysis is certainly required in order to reassess the
kirtanas that we render today.

Apart from a kirtana's structure, its musical identity has two
distinct versions. One established by Tyagaraja and the other by
Muttusvami Dikshitar. While later composers have followed the
Tyagaraja style, the kirtana's handling by Dikshitar is unique.

In most Tyagaraja kirtanas, each line of the composition – though linked with each other – stand out as clear melodic statements. These are linked with all the others in a logical melodic set-up. The anupallavi almost always explores the higher regions of the middle and the higher octave, finally connecting back to the pallavi. This is true even in kirtanas where the pallavi itself may begin in the higher regions of the middle octave. The charana clearly begins at the lower end of the middle octave, sometimes exploring a little of the lower octave before the last two lines repeat the melody of the anupallavi. This musical structure is found in almost all Tyagaraja compositions, with some exceptions, of course. The Tyagaraja kirtanas give us clearly defined nuggets of the raga's phrases in almost every line.

Muttusvami Dikshitar has not followed this melodic structuring. He has looked at the whole kirtana as one body of melodic movement. This makes comprehension of the composition more difficult, because even within one section, many melodic movements end only after a few avartanas or lines of sahitya. The raga flows in a very unstructured manner. This is not to imply a lack of clarity, but to an absence of obvious divisions within melodic patterns. The raga reveals itself as one composite form. The feeling that one gets from a Muttusvami Dikshitar kirtana is of a melody with numerous nuances slowly moving across octaves, unveiling the raga.

Though the kirtanas of Shyama Shastri may not be distinctly different from Tyagaraja's kirtana structuring, the quality that sets his compositions apart is the use of laya and rhythmic structures within the melody in contrast to the tala of the kirtana. This gives his kirtanas a special texture that has to be experienced.

In some kirtanas, vaggeyakaras add a few avartanas of svaras after the anupallavi or charana and connect with the pallavi; these are known as chitta svaras. At times, performing musicians too compose these chitta svaras, and add them to kirtanas of other vaggeyakaras. The inclusion of chitta svaras by musicians in kirtanas can be beautiful and seem to enhance the overall appeal of the composition. But whether this addition infringes upon the aesthetic vision of the vaggeyakaras need to be considered.

Pada

The pada is not structurally very different from the kirtana. It has a pallavi, anupallavi and charana or multiple charanas. The difference lies in its laya, sahitya and presentation. The sahitya is always romantic or erotic. The laya is always slow, creating large spaces for the raga to be beautifully expressed within the sahitya. The pada is a slow unfolding of the raga, containing many intricately ornamented movements that fit tightly within the tala. The listener may imagine that slow movements mean a loose structure, but this is not true. The movements are clearly established and have to fit within the divisions in the tala. The beauty of the pada lies in this clarity within the slow laya. Padas too have sangatis. Though the sahitya is almost as dense as the kirtana, it feels like there are fewer lyrics due to the laya. The oral tradition of rendering padas is such that the rendition begins with the anupallavi. Though this is accepted, some scholars question the practice, as the meaning of the pada requires that the compositions begin with the pallavi. Once again, we find ourselves facing the question about the role of sahitya in art music.

Javali

The javali is a smaller fast-paced composition of romance and eroticism. Structurally, there is nothing unique about it. These compositions follow the pallavi–anupallavi–charanas or pallavi–charanas format of the kirtana, with the melody being repeated in every charana. Some scholars suggest that the musician is allowed to take more liberties with the raga in a javali. The many non-traditional usages of ragas in javalis seem to substantiate this argument. Javalis have also been composed in Hindustani ragas that have been absorbed into Karnatik music.

Tillana

The tillana is a distinct compositional form, and one that has hardly any sahitya. In fact, here the major purpose of the sahitya is to serve as the vehicle for the composer's mudra. The entire composition is presented using jatis (pronounced without an elongated 'a'), or sollukattus (which are the oral syllabic sounds given to rhythmic strokes played on the percussion), making for a very different aesthetic experience. There is a distinct difference between vocalizing linguistically meaningful text and text that is linguistically void. This is true even if the lyrics are in a language that the musician does not understand. The aesthetics of the language structure is different from the aesthetics of the jati structure, but there could be an influence of language in compound jati forms. Though born from percussion sounds, some of the jati patterns are unique to Bharatanatyam. There are certain rules born out of traditional rhythmic structures that are used while composing jatis both in percussion and Bharatanatyam. In a tillana, these are rendered in musical form. Within these jatis, some sounds are softer, while others are stronger, giving the tillana an emotional quality.

The tillana, in general, is structured with very crisp melodic lines, which do not leave room for curves and niceties. Each line is clear and defined, and the presence of the jatis gives a feeling of rigidity. The tillana is structured in a pallavi–anupallavi–charana format. Melodically, the anupallavi expands on the opening pallavi to explore the higher regions of the middle and higher octave to end again with the pallavi. The charana, which is the only section that has sahitya, is connected to another set of jatis, which are sung to link with the pallavi. The musical movements of the charana are independent of the anupallavi or pallavi. The only connection is in the re-establishment of the pallavi at the end. Sometimes the charana is linked to the jatis of the anupallavi, leading to the pallavi. The laya of the tillana is always madhyama or durita kala.

Ragamalika and Talamalika

Ragamalika and talamalika cannot be referred to as compositional forms. As the names indicate, they mean a garland of ragas or talas. They contain multiple ragas or talas, or a combination of both, that can be used in any compositional form. In creating a ragamalika or talamalika, a lot of thought goes into the relationship between every chosen raga or tala. The point of transfer is not whimsical, but a result of careful selection with reference to mutual compatibility and aesthetic pleasure.

In this discussion I have focused only on the compositions of vaggeyakaras. There are other forms, like tiruppugazhs, which are rendered in Karnatik music performances, but are not musical compositions. These are poems that have been set to music and have now acquired a musical identity of their own. I have also not included musical forms that have entered Karnatik music over the last century, including bhajans and abhangs, as the development of their aesthetic identity was not linked specifically to Karnatik music.

Every compositional type has a clear aesthetic personality. It adds new dimensions to the idea of a composition and thereby to the colour of the musical form. This expands the understanding of ragas and talas, giving each musician many compositions to use as the basis for her own creativity. The most important role of compositions is as a reservoir of knowledge of raga and tala. In the next essay, we shall see how each musician finds expression using compositions as the foundation. And we shall see how improvisational forms and techniques are then built into Karnatik music.

6

Creativity Unbound
Manodharma

The word 'manodharma' has two components to it: mano, meaning 'one's own will', and dharma, which refers to a certain righteousness in the path. This is a challenge not to the music, but to the musician's ego – and how much of it she is willing to give up to let the dharma lead the will. This does not mean that a rule book is controlling the will. There is no rule book, only a depth that every aspect of Karnatik music has. In this depth lies the journey of every raga, tala and composition. All these are like living beings, because of what they have experienced and the way they have transformed. They also carry the bruises of manipulation. Every musician seeks to respect this journey of Karnatik music and take it forward. Dharma here signifies not a controlling force, but the attitude of being respectful yet questioning. In this critical balance, the musician allows Karnatik music to engulf his sense of music. From within this submission is born an expression of creativity that is truly the musician's.

Various improvisational techniques built into the aesthetics of Karnatik music give the musician scope for creative expression.

In this lies the beauty of the form. It enables an interplay between the creative compositions of the vaggeyakara and the inherent creativity of every musician. Compositions give the musician the rubric of raga and tala. The musician then proceeds to internalize the composition, and in so doing, opens up newer raga and tala possibilities. This process can, in turn, lead to fresh compositions that use these very expanded creations of the musical imagination. It is in this interaction that the musical possibilities of raga and tala evolve continuously.

Let us now discuss the aesthetics of the various improvisational methods used in Karnatik music. Improvisational music is what is referred to as manodharma sangita, or the music that issues out of the individual musician's very own and personal musical sensibility. In other words, the music that is generated by the musician's distinctive imagination and creativity. This process is built around the aesthetics of raga, tala and compositions. Using these basic properties of Karnatik music, the musician explores various ways of interpreting and rediscovering Karnatik music as an art music form.

Alapana

In manodharma sangita, the principal vehicle of exploring a raga's identity is the alapana, which in Sanskrit means 'to speak, address, convey, communicate'. In the context of classical music, alapana is the opening of a raga that brings forth all of its facets without the use of other elements, like sahitya or tala. The focus of this exercise is entirely on the exploration of the raga.

How does one explore a raga? We have already discussed what a raga is and the various factors that go into the making of its identity. A musician should have internalized the different facets of a raga before attempting to present an alapana in that raga. The resources needed for internalizing a raga lie, of course, in the numerous compositions that have been created by vaggeyakaras in the raga. In order to present the raga in an alapana, the musician needs clarity regarding the essential svaras, phrases and movements. A similar internalization exists in the mind of the musically attuned listener. In this commonality of cognition between the musician and listener is the raga's identity. It is this internalized rendering of a raga that best reflects what is referred to as the musician's manodharma. So closely integrated is the singer's manodharma with the raga's identity in an alapana that the alapana becomes synonymous with the raga.

But the role of an alapana is not just to establish raga identity. Once the essential phrases have been rendered, the raga has been identified and established. So what more is there to do? How does a musician expand, explore the raga? With the raga identity established, possibilities for creative interpretations within a known phrase or svara begin to develop, and the possibilities for this lie within every phrase and svara. How does this process take shape? This arena of creativity is difficult to describe in objective terms. We need to relate it to the previous discussion on imagination and creativity.

When a raga-identifying svara or phrase is presented, it is at that very moment being received by the musician as the gift of a creative possibility. So it is not just being presented. Once the musician becomes aware of this, small variations start appearing in her renditions. These can be in the form of different gamakas or slight deviations from known phrases. As the musician builds on these possibilities, the gamakas lead to an unknown path. While the path is fascinating and the terrain unknown, it is nonetheless a continuation of the raga's known elements. At simultaneous work in this journey are the musician's intuition and conformity. Every change that the musician makes is intuitively exploring the 'unknown', and at the same time, remains instinctively aware of the raga's 'known' pathway. Without this kind of awareness, the musician will be unable to go along with the phrase. I use the construction 'go along with the phrase' rather than 'develop', because each phrase and svara movement ignites another in a continuous stream, while 'development' suggests a far more consciously constructed change in the phrase. As this stream continues, it leads to newer phrases in the raga that, over a period of time, become part of the raga identity.

A new phrase is one that arises afresh during that journey of the musician, and relates only to that specific exploration, irrespective of whether or not the phrase has ever been rendered before. Every time a phrase is discovered or rediscovered on the journey, it is revealed anew. This is why a raga is a living being, not a static entity.

Every true phrase or svara, as it moves forward, generates the essential 'sound' of the raga – not an isolated decibel unit, but the aural impression of the complete body of the raga's aesthetics. This is established by the known phrases, stress on the appropriate svaras and established interpretations of the svaras. When a creative mind is at work, the expansions of the raga are always linked to this sound. It changes and moves, while remaining rooted in the raga's aesthetic integrity and retaining the identity that makes us relate to it as a specific raga. This concept is at the core of the alapana or any manodharma in Karnatik music.

Another area of the musician's creative journey is along, around and within the spaces between two known phrases. This is a very interesting area of musical endeavour. Earlier, we spoke about known phrases generating phrases unvisited earlier, but here, in the interstices of known phrases, resides extraordinary opportunity for exploration. When a musician moves from one established phrase to another in a raga, the possible ways in which she can connect the two are numerous. There already exist connecting pathways, but the practitioner of art music creates new ones in the course of the journey, generating links beyond the known phraseology of the raga. Here, the musician, through her practice, renders a phrase that she is well aware of and brings instinctively into the stream her own phrase, while moving from one known phrase to another. As this movement occurs, an interesting consequence follows. The aesthetic impact of the preceding known phrase and the anticipated aesthetic of the ensuing known phrase inspires a new phrase linking the two knowns like a bridge, giving the sequence an altogether new unexpected integrity. This is a beautiful occurrence, where the music is already being played in the mind; that is, the sound and form of the two known phrases are already heard before the rendition of the second phrase, generating a third possibility based on them, which appears as a creative outburst linking the two.

In order to expand ragas in their aspect of alapana, musicians also use important and specific svaras as reference points to build ideas. As we know, every raga has certain svaras that are important, which would mean that they are stressed upon within the phrases in the raga. These important svaras also come to be used as elongated pauses. Each raga contains certain svaras that can be used in this manner. The musician can use these pre-positioned svaras as points of reference. Phrases are directed towards these svaras so that they conclude there. Starting with phrases that are of shorter length, the musician can build on every phrase, with each adding to the previous one, but all leading to the reference svara. This method usually leads to either phrases being built in concentric circles around the svara of reference or a linear development leading to that svara.

We need to distinguish here between the creative procedures. The first is creativity that is svara- or phrase-based; the second is the creativity that is born out of connecting two known phrases; the third, creativity is based on using one svara as a reference anchor. While the first two forms of creativity are born out of creative abstraction, the third rests on the pre-existing architecture of the raga. This implies a lack of abstraction in the third method. Creativity that is born out of purely structural rules that are imposed on a raga lack the organic quality of creativity. When a musician is discovering newer interpretations in a svara or phrase, he is being led by what is heard in the phrase. The phrase itself encapsulates the sound of the raga. Similarly, when a phrase is created to connect two established phrases, the aesthetics of the phrases guide the creativity. Here, the creativity is born out of the raga experience, which functions from within the environment or ambience of the raga. Melody generated thus reiterates the aesthetic content of the raga. These two plumes of the creative imagination are caused by this ambience of the raga and not by its structural rules.

But in the third creative procedure, when we build phrases around or leading to a svara, it is usually driven by the raga's svara structure. This form of improvisation is more about permutations and combinations that can lead to a given svara rather than phrase evolution. I am not suggesting that this method precludes the abstractive kind of raga exploration, but the very nature of using a svara and singing phrases leading to it makes the mind think structurally rather than in creative abstraction. The necessity to build towards a svara and continuously increase the length of the phrases requires the musician to concentrate on svara combinations within the raga, rather than the other two kinds of creativity. Even when built in concentric circles, this results in creating svara combinations that would fit into the svara structure of the raga. This conditions how one idea leads to another, as also the svaras that form the phrase combinations.

The alapana, as I said, does not use any sahitya but it is usually rendered with the use of certain other syllabic sounds, including ta, da, ri, na, no. Some musicians use a few more of these. These syllabic sounds are used as supports to help the musician render the alapana. The vowel sounds 'aa' and 'ii' are most commonly heard, though some musicians also employ other sounds, such as the vowel 'uu' and the labial 'mm'. The use of these extended sounds is interspersed with ta, da, ri, na, no. None of these sounds have any linguistic meaning, and every musician uses them in his own way. That said, these sounds contribute a very important aesthetic to the rendition of an alapana. Each of them brings something of its own to the aesthetic form of the rendered phrase. The position of ta, da or ri within a phrase breaks the melodic form of the phrase accordingly. Therefore, if certain syllables are positioned in places they should not be in within a given melodic phrase, the intended aesthetic of the phrase is lost. Even when established phrases of a raga are rendered in an alapana, there are established positions for these syllabic sounds. These are not in the form of one predetermined and fixed path, but as a few possibilities for each phrase that we want to render. When this is changed, the same phrase takes on a wholly different melodic identity. While this change in syllabic position can generate newer ideas for raga exploration, it can also do something else: it can cause a break in the raga's aesthetics. Thus it is imperative that musicians use these syllables with utmost care. The art of using syllables in an alapana rendition is imbibed from listening to the alapanas of great musicians. The positions of sahitya syllables in compositions are indicative of the raga's melodic flow and help the musician to see where the syllables can be used in those phrases. Each vaggeyakara has also reinterpreted the position of the sahitya syllables in common phrases. Appreciating the musical value of these repositionings and internalizing them can open windows into the flexibility inherent within a phrase.

The alapana cannot be an aesthetic form unless there is cohesion within every phrase, between phrases and the larger picture that the alapana is painting. The raga exists in every svara as much as it does in the whole presentation of the raga. The alapana is not a bunch of known phrases around which the musician creates newer phrases, melodic lines. It is the distilled aesthetic experience of the raga in its entirety. Thus the alapana leaves at the end of its rendition a wholesome experience of the raga and of the creative genius of the musician.

This being the objective of the alapana, we need to understand how its presentation unfolds. These vary depending on factors such as the musician's intent – in terms of how she wants to depict the raga, the length of rendition and, most importantly, the nature of the raga itself. Certain ragas provide a larger scope for improvisation, while others much less so.

Ragas are of various types: those that evolved naturally as phrase-based aesthetic creations, theory-based assembled or synthetic linear ragas, synthetic linear ragas with less than seven svaras, synthetic non-linear ragas and ragas adapted from other music traditions.

A word on each of these types of ragas. Ragas that are phrase-based aesthetic creations have evolved by the coming together of musical phrases or melodies. Their unified identity lies in the way the phrases are connected with each other. The nature of these ragas is abstract as their basic 'atom' is the phrase, and not only the svaras they are made of. Synthetic linear ragas evolved purely out of theorists mathematically assembling one variety of each svara in their natural order. The natural order implies that all the seven svaras are present in them. I refer to them as 'linear' due to the fact that they contain all the svaras one after the other. This is an important feature. It is also important that the natural order be maintained in arohana and avarohana. Arohana refers to the ascending set of svaras from madhya sthayi sa to tara sthayi sa and avarohana to the descending set of svaras from the tara sthayi sa to the madhya sthayi sa. Together, they give us the fixed structure of the svaras in synthetic ragas, also known as the 'scale' of the raga. Synthetic linear ragas that do not have all seven svaras are also ragas that have been created by theorists and some vaggeyakaras, but the difference is that, instead of placing these svaras in a linear natural sequence, they have skipped a svara or more in arohana, avarohana or both. Synthetic non-linear ragas have been created by manipulating the sequence of the svaras in arohana, avarohana or both. Apart from having complex svara formations as their scale, these ragas may not have some svaras. I have used the word 'synthetic' for many of the types of ragas because they were artificially created using the theoretical possibilities of manipulating the svaras, their varieties and positions. All synthetic ragas are highly dependent on the arohana and avarohana for their identity. This is not the case with phrase-based ragas. There are also ragas that have been adapted from other musical traditions, such as the Hindustani. A detailed discussion on the origins of these different types of ragas has been taken up in the chapter 'The Raga's Trail'.

Every alapana begins with a phrase that clearly establishes the raga's identity. There cannot be any ambiguity in this. Therefore, phrases that are common to two ragas should not be rendered in the opening. Following this, if the raga has complete scope without any built-in aesthetic restrictions regarding its limits in the three octaves, the musician settles down at the madhya sthayi sa. Then, in an ascending step-by-step method, she proceeds to ascend the octave, stopping at svaras that are important to the raga and using them as long svaras. In this way, at every pause, she explores the musical space or 'region' around the svara that is used as reference. As the musician reaches the tara sthayi sa, a certain momentum is built in the alapana, reaching a crescendo beyond the tara sthayi sa. This is followed by a descent, which is much shorter than the build-up, usually concluding at the madhya sthayi sa or pa, depending on the raga. While this is a general description for the structure of an alapana, in this method, every section has its own form with inbuilt flexibility in terms of how a musician chooses to build on every important svara and region.

After the opening phrases have clearly established the raga and the musician has settled down at madhya sthayi sa, she can then explore the region around the sa, which will also include regions below in mandra sthayi. In Karnatik music, the normal extent of exploration in mandra sthayi usually stops at pa. The phrases in this region in the beginning of an alapana are usually slow-paced, letting both the musician and the listener settle into the raga. After exploring this region, the musician proceeds to the next svara of importance.

It is important to observe how the musician moves from one area to another. The musician needs to first establish the svara and the region. Once that is done, he renders phrases of the raga relevant to this svara and region, allowing creativity to guide the exploration, while keeping in mind that the exploration does not depart too much from the svara used as focus.

When an alapana is developed around a svara, there are two principles to be observed. First, the length of the phrases rendered grows from short to long. Second, the laya of the phrases rendered always moves from slow to fast. As the alapana moves to the tara sthayi, there is a noticeable tendency to increase the number of faster phrases as compared to the madhya sthayi. This leads to a climax beyond the tara sthayi sa. I would refer to this approach as a cyclo-linear development of the raga, as the process moves the alapana in a clear ascending movement, followed by a descending movement across the octaves, with a cyclical build-up of phrases around every important svara.

When I use 'slow' and 'fast', it must be understood that I do so in relative terms and in relation to the overall laya of the alapana. Though an alapana does not have tala, the inbuilt laya in the raga determines the relative speeds of phrases used in the alapana. That laya includes the whole range of speeds of phrases within the raga. In an alapana, phrases that are heavily gamaka-laden, fast-moving phrases with limited gamaka, subtle movements and long sweeps can all be used. But the kind of phrases rendered and the speed of their rendition is determined by the 'sound' of the raga. In ragas that have an unlimited laya range, each alapana has an individual laya based on which faster and slower phrases would be sensed.

Another method of raga alapana, which several musicians of an earlier generation used, has a certain abstraction in its approach. The alapana here is not clearly structured, but almost like strokes on a canvas. The musician begins with an essential phrase of the raga, but then does not build the raga on the basis of its svaras, ascending the octave. In fact, the movement is completely driven by the established phrases within the raga and – unlike the step-by-step method, where the phrases in each region remain specific to that area – the phrases here have greater room for movement. They move across the length and breadth of the raga, from small phrases to larger sweeps. There could be points of clear linear movement even here, but those would be much less than actual phrase elaborations. This method also does not build towards any clear climax. The tara sthayi sections often have faster phrases, but the momentum gained in the step-by-step approach does not clearly happen here. The overall impact of such an abstract approach to alapana is less dramatic, but nonetheless aesthetic. At the same time, if one is to render a long alapana, the former method serves better to explore every region specifically.

The step-by-step alapana approach is logical, systematic and stimulates thought on the origins of the raga. I wonder whether this organized form has something to do with changes in the perception of a raga, more specifically the difference between phrase-based ragas and synthetic ragas. This system seems to work much more in ragas that have evolved from svara structures, than in those that have an organic, abstract evolution. Since in the former, the raga is only a derivative of a possible set of svaras, it is quite easy for the musician to approach it in a linear step-by-step manner. These ragas do not carry too many phrases that govern their identity. Since these ragas have not evolved from the 'phrase atom', vaggeyakaras and musicians have been compelled to create and draw distinction between two synthetic svara-based formations on the basis of artificially created phrase distinction. This means that, while a certain phrase may be appropriate for two synthetic ragas, musicians have chosen to only peg it to one of the two, more for convenience than internal aesthetic identity. Given the svara-based approach in the creation of those ragas, the linear step-by-step alapana works well in them. The lack of clear raga features beyond their established scale allows the musician to develop the raga almost on any svara. At each svara, the musician can stop and render many phrases with the use of svara permutations and combinations. Since the method is systematic, it leads to a structured approach to exploration. However, exploration with subtle variations between phrases does not fall into a structured format, and naturally occurs less in this alapana method.

In the case of organically evolved ragas, there are numerous phrases that carry the raga identity. A step-by-step alapana approach for these ragas could prove problematic. The primary problem is that adopting a linear ascending approach to alapana exploration affects the aesthetic content of the raga, because the phrases have not evolved with the scale of the raga in mind. This also leads to a certain distortion in the raga identity. But a level of standardization has, over time, come to be adopted in the alapana format, whereby most musicians take recourse to the step-by-step approach to raga alapana for almost all ragas. This has led musicians to subconsciously use a scalar approach to alapana even for phrase-based ragas, leading to the loss of many important phrases. They use unnecessary stresses on regions and svaras that are of no relevance to the raga, leading to a loss of aesthetic identity of some ragas. This is one of the major problems we face in Karnatik music today.

The situation created by this standardization needs to be addressed if we want to retain ragas and their aesthetic form. As we have come to accept synthetic scale-based ragas within our raga spectrum, we need to clearly differentiate how we sing alapanas in these ragas as compared to phrase-based ragas. If we do not do so, we might unwittingly destroy many beautiful melodic phrases in the older ragas.

Every alapana, as we have seen, is a combination of abstractive creativity and creative permutations and combinations. The balance between the two has, however, to tilt towards abstractive development, as this keeps the essence of a raga and gives the alapana its specific aesthetic identity. Abstraction is always far more difficult to capture, for when we create an abstractive phrase, we cannot confirm its identity based on its svaras. This has to be determined by its 'sound' within the context of the raga. Svara-based permutations and combinations are identified purely on the svaras that exist in the raga and hence do not carry any aesthetic identity beyond the svaras that they contain. Permutations and combinations help in providing another dimension to the creative possibilities, but they cannot be the basis for raga development. Thus, for an abstractive alapana, synthetic ragas prove difficult for the reason that there are hardly any naturally developed phrase identities that can be used creatively. It is also true that it is in search of these phrase-based identities that some vaggeyakaras and musicians have tried to artificially create such phrases for many scale-based ragas. In spite of this, synthetic ragas have not been conducive to abstractive alapanas.

When a musician wants to render long alapanas, she has to invariably resort to svara permutations and combinations to extend the raga. Phrase-based abstract developments are far more difficult to create, and, after a point, the musician could easily hit a wall. On the other hand, svara combinations are almost mathematical in nature, and the mind can construct them with far more ease. One could ask if a longer alapana is even necessary. Does it enhance the aesthetics of the music if the method impedes the aesthetics of the raga? There is merit in these questions. In fact, I wonder whether we need to look at the alapana more on the basis of its creative input rather than length of rendition. This does not mean that shorter alapanas are better. It just means that we need to revisit the form and structure of the alapana based on the raga chosen.

Niraval

The improvisational technique niraval is unique and valuable, for it uses one creative imagination, that of the vaggeyakara, to kindle another, that of the musician. A musician takes a line from a composition and renders the niraval, repeating it many times over, multiplying exponentially the original line's numerous melodic varieties. While alapana allows a musician to develop a raga directly, niraval uses three important aspects of Karnatik music for its contribution to the creative expression. Raga, tala and sahitya come together in niraval to create melodic and rhythmical variations that enhance the form's interactive aesthetics. The musician can choose any line from any section of the composition for niraval, whether it be the pallavi, anupallavi or charana. Usually, niraval is rendered only in kirtana. However, lines from the pallavi are seldom used. Lines chosen are such that the linguistic meaning is complete and self-contained within the chosen section, so that the repetition reinforces the content. The length of the line can be one avartana or run across multiple avartanas. In many kirtanas, the lines chosen for niraval have become almost standardized, with most musicians choosing the same line. It is a habit of the mind ingrained in both the musician and the listener through sustained repetition. Cognition plays an important role in the choice and appreciation of the niraval, so a musician is tempted to pick the same line for niraval within a composition.

The selection of a line for niraval is not wholly subjective or whimsical. Not all lines in a composition are suitable, linguistically, for niraval. In certain compositions, only a few lines are appropriate; naturally, those are chosen. That said, one needs to ask whether, in art music, it is really necessary to pick a linguistically complete line – as a written sentence would have to be in an essay, for instance. It should be more important to choose a line not so much for what it says linguistically in its sahitya, but what it does, syllabically, in congruence with the melody. It is in the chosen line's close-knit identity with the music that the niraval comes to life. Sometimes the search for a linguistically complete line becomes self-defeating, as it suffers from aesthetic limitations. If the lyrical meaning and melodic form come together within the line chosen, this conflict does not occur. The right lyric–melody knit is crucial, given that the singing of the niraval is completely pivoted on the aesthetic structure of the line, not on its linguistic meaning. By aesthetic form, I mean the relationship between the melody, tala, laya and text.

Once the line is chosen, the exact structure of the line within the tala matrix becomes most important. When sahitya is structured in a tala, the various syllables of the words spread themselves right across the melodic structure of the line. This spread is in relation to the sahitya, tala, laya and, of course, the melody. This melodic structure of the 'niraval line' has been handed down to us through the guru–shishya parampara, and it is important for every musician to respect it. When this line is internalized, the musician knows the aesthetic flow of the line, and that in turn defines the aesthetic structure in his mind. This aesthetic form of the line is important to niraval elaboration. Every syllable of the sahitya is positioned at specific places within the tala as part of the melodic line. The musician must be constantly aware of the interaction between the sahitya, raga and tala as presented in the line. The idea of niraval is to try and use the sahitya and tala relationships to develop melodic variations between the syllabic positions. It is a beautiful method of developing the raga within certain parameters set in the composed line.

The relationship between the sahitya and tala is a very important part of the aesthetic structure of a composition. We have already discussed the importance of alliteration while describing the facets of a composition. Also, the spread of the syllables within a tala emphasizes the melodically essential syllables of the words, thereby creating an important aesthetic impact in the listener's mind. Similarly, as the melody flows along with the syllables of the sahitya within the tala, the melodic line impacts the listener in various ways. This tripartite relationship cannot be ignored even when the musician attempts melodic variations as part of niraval. We should also remember that sangatis in compositions, which are melodic variations, often adhere to this and emphasize the structural beauty of the line.

There are two schools of thought regarding retaining the exact positions of the syllables during niraval. Certain musicians consider the positions of the syllables, and consequently the sahitya within the chosen line, sacrosanct. This would mean that whatever the melodic variation, the syllables of the chosen line must fall at exactly where it does in the composition. Another section believes that there is a certain limited flexibility here, and that the syllables can be moved from their original positions within a permissible range. As such, there is no 'rule' about the extent to which the syllables can be moved, but this moving is based on certain cognitively accepted norms. I am inclined to agree with the second view. This is because, unlike sangatis, niraval techniques are continuously flowing melodic movements, making it difficult to place the syllables in exactly the same position. Doing so would interfere with the melodic flow. In such cases, minor adjustments are permissible for the sake of the raga and melody.

There are many methods of improvising using the niraval technique. Once a line from a composition is chosen, the musician first establishes the melodic and lyrical structure of the line within the tala. This implies not just the position of the syllables, but also the laya that is intrinsic to the line. Once this is established, the musician begins with changes to the melody of the line, which are not at great variance from the composed melody. The duration of the initial niraval is also traditionally limited to one repetition of the line. The variations begin around the areas of flow in the original melody of the line. As the musician builds on the niraval, two or three changes take place. For one, the variations become more and more perceivable, leading to melodic movements that are not in any way connected to the original melody. For another, the range of variations move away from the original composed line and the treatment of the laya within the line undergoes a change. These changes happen as a natural progression of the musician's creative impulses. The number of times a line is repeated within one continuous niraval increases in every subsequent round. After every exploration of niraval, the musician reiterates the original melody of the line.

There are three self-contained ways in which niraval is used as an improvisational tool: free-flowing alapana type, sama-kala or 'tight' type and mel-kala or 'fast' type. Each of these is self-contained, but leads to the subsequent method.

Let me take up the alapana type first. Initially, niraval uses the various continuous phrases from the alapana. This method is free-flowing and is distinctly reminiscent of an alapana, with the musician using many different kinds of phrases in terms of their speed and texture in order to develop melodic variations. These include long sweeps referred to as jarus, very fast phrases called brigas, little filigree-like phrases and phrases with slow gamakas. When these variations are used, tala divisions do not constrict the flow of these phrases. The melodic phrases flow across the divisions of the tala and are anchored only on the basis of the syllabic positions of the sahitya within the tala. This creates a continuous non-rigid aesthetic experience for the listener. Any rigidity that may be perceived is only a result of the intrinsic nature of the melodic phrases, like the brigas, and not due to the divisions within the tala.

While describing laya, I had described the possibility of varying the laya in a tala based on the number of svaras between every beat (kriya). This is used in niraval singing. Three layas are defined: sama-kala, mel-kala and kizh-kala. For example, in adi tala (eight beats) when two svaras are rendered between every kriya, it is referred to as sama-kala. When four svaras are sung, it is called mel-kala and when one svara is rendered, it is referred to as kizh-kala. This would apply to almost all the talas used in Karnatik music. If the nadai, or gati, of the composition were already tisra, khanda, mishra and sankirna, then the natural value of this nadai, that is, 3, 5, 7, 9, would be considered sama-kala and their double mel-kala and their half kizh-kala.

In the case of two talas, namely khanda chapu and mishra chapu, which are unusual talas since the interval between every kriya is not equal, we cannot have a common value between every kriya. Hence the sama-kala would be the basic total value they represent as a tala, that is, five and seven respectively. Kizh-kala would be two-and-a-half and three-and-a-half, and mel-kala ten and fourteen. Both these talas have a unique history and have to be treated differently.

The second improvisational method is the sama-kala niraval. Sama-kala is also the inherent laya in most compositions. While singing sama-kala niraval, stress and emphasis are placed on this inherent laya of the line as composed. Melodic variations in sama-kala niraval in all talas in chaturashra nadai have to emphasize two svaras per kriya (beat). This is a far more rigid exercise than the alapana-based one. While rendering this type of niraval, the laya of the line plays a very important role, as do the exact positions of the syllables within the tala. Both these have to be completely adhered to. In general, this technique employs a melodic variation that has an exact number of svaras within every division of the tala, creating a fixed, rigid movement. For example, in the adi tala (an eight-beat cycle), within every beat the melodic movement has two svaras in it. Along with this, the syllables of the sahitya are rendered exactly at the position where they are situated in the composition. As I have indicated, the idea of sama-kala niraval in mishra chapu and khanda chapu tala will be slightly different.

The third, mel-kala niraval, has melodic variations with

exactly double the number of svaras within every division of the tala as sama-kala niraval. So, in adi tala, the variations will contain four svaras within every division. Mel-kala niraval is very exciting because it creates a climax to the whole form. When mel-kala niraval is rendered, the musician fills the interval between every syllable with a stress on every svara in the melodies being rendered. This makes the movements tight and sharp. The pace of the melodic movements in mel-kala niraval makes retaining the original positions of the syllables that much harder. We do find that musicians take liberties here, especially when connecting the niraval improvisation to the original line, where for the sake of highlighting the end of the line, musicians reposition the syllables. While singing this niraval, musicians tend to vary the syllabic positions slightly in order to give the renditions a certain impact and punch. We notice again that the laya of the niraval starts at slower speeds and slowly increases, ending with mel-kala niraval.

Within the free-flowing alapana form of niraval, many variations to the types of continuous melodic movements can be employed. But neither sama-kala nor mel-kala niraval allow much variability in the kind of movements that can be used, as both need to strictly follow the laya in svara emphasis. In each of these three methods, the niraval is built up from shorter lengths to longer ones – by which I mean that the number of times the line is repeated with melodic variations increases as one progresses.

Not all these techniques are used every time. The laya of the composition and the number of syllables within the line chosen influence the pattern of niraval. If the composition is sung in a faster speed, it makes it difficult for the musician to perform niraval using the alapana style, as this method requires the flexibility to include various continuous melodic movements. Therefore, the musician sings shorter phrases between the syllables and moves into mel-kala niraval very quickly. Similarly, if there are too many words in the chosen line, the lack of space makes niraval very difficult. Again, the casualty is the alapana-style niraval, and the musician renders niraval in mel-kala. Therefore, if a musician is to explore niraval to its fullest extent, it is necessary that the chosen compositional line be in a reasonably slow speed, and not densely populated with sahitya. There is no optimum speed or a prescribed number of lyrics, but this is something that every musician knows based on the methods of niraval exploration that are part of the system.

The Tamil word niraval suggests 'to fill'. As this explanation suggests, the gaps between the various syllables of the words in a line of a composition are filled with melodic variation.

Unfortunately, niraval is one of the most ignored forms of improvisation in Karnatik music. It is used only as a stepping stone to singing kalpanasvaras, as a niraval usually leads to the latter. In actual fact, niraval is an extremely difficult form with many parameters influencing its creation: raga, sahitya, tala and laya. The laya here is in itself complex, since both the laya within the tala and the general laya of the composition itself influence niraval possibilities. To be able to internalize the melodic, rhythmic and lyrical aspects of a line and use the same to create different variations is extremely challenging. This is one of the reasons why most musicians sing only very few variations. The beauty of this form is in the variety one can present, especially in the alapana-style niraval, where almost all the various types of raga phrases used in an alapana can be employed. But the experience is distinct, since the niraval has to be presented within a tala structure and is bound by the syllabic structure of the sahitya. The secret, if one may call it that, lies in the internalization of the fundamental melodic line chosen for niraval. Once this is done, the musician is able to bring together various styles of variations and naturally place them within the tala and sahitya structures. This relationship has to be maintained in order to retain the integrity of the niraval form.

Kalpanasvara

Alapana uses vowel sounds and a few other syllabic sounds to camouflage the existing svaras behind the melodic variations that musicians create. In niraval, musicians use melodic lines from compositions. Kalpanasvara is the only manodharma technique that lets musicians improvise, using svaras in their articulated form. This improvisation is the exclusive province of the musician's imagination – 'kalpana' means imagination. Whether we sing compositions or render an alapana, the basic melodic atoms behind the melodies are svaras. Improvisation in kalpanasvaras allows the musician to go right to the raga's basic melodic atoms and use them to express its essential elements, thereby expanding its horizons. There is a distinct elegance to this manodharma form that comes from its independence. How is it 'independent'? Kalpanasvara does not use an already created melodic line to improvise, but proceeds along the milestones of its own creative exploration. Nevertheless, it is connected to compositional music by the necessity of rendering it in such a manner that every creative exploration has to end at a chosen sahitya in a melodic line. Hence kalpanasvaras are creative renderings of svaras in a given raga, determined by the chosen composition from which a specific sahitya is to be used as the concluding point of each set of kalpanasvaras, which in turn will be rendered as composed by the vaggeyakara. This independence only refers to the way kalpanasvaras are rendered, but does not imply that the ideas for creativity are removed from what the musician receives from learning compositions. Also, this manodharma technique is bound by the tala and laya of the chosen composition.

One of the important aspects of kalpanasvaras is to conclude every round of creative exploration with the svaras at the beginning of a certain sahitya in a given line of a composition. Kalpanasvaras are not usually rendered to a set of syllabic sounds that are linguistically void. It is common practice to choose a sahitya that is the beginning of a line in a composition, though any sahitya at any place in a given composition can be chosen. Once again, the kirtana form is predominantly used for rendering kalpanasvaras. When choosing a certain sahitya, it is important for the musician to understand its exact position within the tala. The sahitya's first syllable is used as the concluding point of the kalpanasvara. So, where this is positioned in the tala is exactly the point where the musician concludes the svaras. She should conclude rendering the chosen sahitya in the same melody as in the composition.

We have seen that kalpanasvaras have to end at a sahitya. What really matters in this context is the melody of the sahitya, which is constant and cannot be changed by the musician. This brings us to the question of how the kalpanasvaras will be connected to the sahitya. Usually, musicians try and conclude the kalpanasvaras on a svara in the raga, closest to the svara on which the melody of the sahitya begins. This helps provide a natural melodic connection to the melody of the sahitya. However, a creative musician can connect to the sahitya of the line from almost anywhere in the raga using beautiful phrases that highlight the raga aesthetics. This requires a great deal of insight into the raga and is governed by the svaras and phrases of the raga.

The sahitya in a composition is in melodic form, a destination that the musician has to reach by his kalpana. In this endeavour, kalpanasvaras proceed to the svara on which the first syllable of the sahitya is seated. And so it follows that in choosing a certain sahitya, the musician also keeps in mind its melody. In the melodic flow of a composition, the syllables of the sahitya move along with the raga melody traversing the identity of the raga. While the raga's important svaras and phrases are highlighted, the melody also moves along the less important svaras within the raga. Sometimes a composition's sahitya can have words beginning at points in the melody where it touches upon svaras of less importance. It would be inadvisable to choose such sahitya as the reference points to render kalpanasvaras, as it would lead to morphing, even altering, the raga's identity.

Though the concluding section of the kalpanasvaras has been stressed upon, true artistry lies in how creatively the musician weaves through the svaras, creating a melodic picture of the raga. When svaras come together as phrases, they are each representative of the raga's aesthetic. The musician tries to go beyond the svaras into the emotive intellectual grandeur of the raga, culminating each exploration at a sahitya, creating continuity between her journey and the composer's melodic creation.

How is a kalpanasvara actually rendered? Once a sahitya from a line in a composition is chosen to render kalpanasvaras, the musician has two paths to take: sama-kala and mel-kala. In terms of laya, it is the same as we discussed earlier for sama-kala niraval. The musician begins by rendering kalpanasvaras that are within a single avartana of the tala, connecting them to the chosen sahitya exactly at the point in the tala structure that has been composed. Each time the musician renders them, she is trying to present different phrases from the raga and allowing for her creativity. Slowly, she increases the length, each kalpanasvara patterns becoming progressively longer before concluding at the sahitya. They cover multiple avartanas, allowing the musician to also explore the raga in svara form across the various octaves. Starting with less than an avartana, the musician extends the length of each exploration to one, two, three and then more avartanas, returning each time to sahitya. The beauty of the sama-kala kalpanasvara is that, since it is slower-paced, it allows the musician to render it with intense focus on the various gamakas of the raga. The movements of the svaras are also delicate. Melodic movements in sama-kala kalpanasvara as in sama-kala niraval have to display the laya strictly. But here, the clear emphasis on the number of svaras between each kriya is far more obvious due to the articulation of the svaras. This means that the number of svaras per beat is fixed. Even if this is true, musicians can present them with a lot of curves without creating a rigid aesthetic in the listener's minds.

Mel-kala kalpanasvara is exactly double the pace of the sama-kala type. Here again, the process of development is similar, with shorter lengths of kalpanasvaras and later increasing the number of avartanas of every attempt at kalpanasvara exploration, steadily building a momentum. But an increase in speed completely changes the aesthetic of the creativity. In the slower speed, with the space available, the musician can focus on the subtle aesthetics and phrases of the raga, making the melodic movements delicate. Mel-kala makes the creative process less focused on delicacy and subtlety, with a great emphasis on tighter, definite, sharp melodic movements. The speed also greatly influences the direction of the creativity. In mel-kala, the creativity veers towards svara permutations and combinations within the raga rather than the phrase-based approach used in sama-kala kalpanasvara. The excitement generated by mel-kala kalpanasvara is naturally far more due to the speed and sharpness than in sama-kala kalpanasvaras.

Connecting the kalpanasvaras to the compositional line is intrinsic to the aesthetic experience. As the sama-kala or mel-kala kalpanasvaras connect to the sahitya, the aesthetic shift from svaras to syllables, combined with the flourish of the musician, generates excitement. There are certain traditionally rendered kalpanasvara–sahitya links consisting of three or five svara patterns, which are fixed by the melodic nature of the raga and the svara of the connecting sahitya. The link is automatically a point of great expectation and, in mel-kala, excitement as well. In mel-kala, the musicians too present this bit with greater emphasis to highlight the connection. The musician must conclude the last svara exactly before the position of the first syllable of the chosen sahitya. This sahitya position, as we know, cannot be altered, and so it takes great precision to conclude the kalpanasvaras exactly where the sahitya begins in the tala.

Though kalpanasvaras conclude exactly at the point where the chosen sahitya begins, there seems to be no connection between that position and the rendition of the kalpanasvaras within the tala. For example, if the sahitya begins at a certain position between two beats, while rendering kalpanasvaras, the musician does not stress this exact position in every avartana of the tala or even between every beat in the tala. This leads me to wonder if there is any relevance to the exact position of the sahitya, except that each round of kalpanasvaras ends there. In an aesthetic sense, the position of the sahitya plays no role in the kalpanasvara exploration except when at the end point. In other words, if another sahitya from the same line – which is at a different position in the tala – is chosen as the point of reference, the musician can still render the same kalpanasvara patterns until the point of connection where it will change. This is a relevant criticism of the kalpanasvara method used in Karnatik music, as it questions the relevance of the sahitya position in the tala and its relationship with the actual creativity of the musician. If in every avartana, the musician was to provide emphasis in his kalpanasvara forays on the exact position of the first syllable of the sahitya within the tala matrix, the musician's creativity will be influenced by this specific focus.

I would also like to ask whether mel-kala kalpanasvara distorts the raga identity. When any form of improvisation shifts the focus of the raga from abstraction to permutations and combinations, the aesthetics of the raga cannot but be affected. In the case of ragas that have evolved as scales, this may not be a problem, but it is one in the case of older phrase-based ragas. In these cases, the musicians have to be far more careful rendering mel-kala svaras, allowing their creativity to guide them towards enhancing the aesthetic form of the raga within its phraseology. This seldom happens, as musicians are driven by the excitement that mel-kala permutations and combinations can create.

Tana

Among all the manodharma techniques, the elusive one is tana, both to the practitioner and the listener. For a practitioner, the concept takes many years to grasp. We are used to improvising without a tala or obvious laya (as in an alapana), or within a tala and laya (niraval and kalpanasvara). The tana is neither here nor there. With its lack of tala, the tana gives a feeling of being rhythmically 'free'. But in its melodic development, the tana is very structured. These two – rhythmic freedom and melodic structure – seem antithetical, but come quite magically together in this unusual and captivating manodharma technique. Tana is generally rendered in madhyama-kala, and is even referred to as 'madhyama-kala'.

In the alapana rendition, there is a free-flowing exploration of the raga. Phrases and patterns are created in a continuous flow, with no rigid structure in their formations. The laya in which various phrases are strung together are also completely flexible. Tana is a free exploration of a raga sans tala, but a clear laya is maintained within it. The tana is structured so as to create emphatic melodic patterns that establish the laya without being contained within a tala structure.

In a chosen raga, the tana is rendered using the syllables aa, nam and ta. This is interpreted as the word 'ananta' meaning 'unending', and some musicians believe that is the reason for the use of these syllables. Between every one of the given syllabic sounds, the musician also clearly emphasizes each svara of the melodic movement – a-a-a-nan-ta-a-a-anan-ta, for instance. Therefore, every movement is definite and clearly establishes the svaras of the melody. The way in which these melodic forms are built is also interesting. They are not textured like raga phrases, but are combinations of svara patterns, in sets of 3, 5, 6, 7, 8, 9 svaras in the chosen raga. That is, every tana pattern will have that many svaras. Typically, once a three-svara melodic pattern is rendered, the musician will create melodic movements with different svaras in the raga using that three-svara pattern. Similarly, if the musician has begun a five-svara pattern, she will develop the same with varying svara combinations. Once a pattern has been exhausted, the musician moves to another pattern.

Evidently, all these patterns are clearly structured, emphatically establishing the svaras and the number structure of the patterns. So the aesthetic experience of a tana, while it does not fit into a tala, is very structural. This means that the pattern is not predictable in terms of where it will begin or conclude within the avartana of the tala structure. Each melodic structure has a fixed number of svaras. These being in continuous motion, they change from one formation to another. The conclusion of each formation is only dependent on the creative journey of the musician. So the musician could either continue until she exhausts the possibilities of one set of tana patterns or shift to another. This flexibility makes it difficult for tana to be contained within a tala. At the same time, instinctively, while rendering or listening to tana, we find ourselves keeping time, which is different from tala, with our feet or hands. This is because one very important aspect of tana is that, though the patterns can be formations of any number of svaras, the whole form still has an underlying chaturashra measure. This basic meter is the matrix on which all the various combinations are placed. It functions only as a basic guide on which patterns are placed, and does not make the tana fit into the tala structure.

A typical tana rendering will begin in a manner similar to the step-by-step method used for alapana. First, an introductory tana will be presented. From the second section, it is developed step-by-step around all the important svaras in the raga, building up to the tara sthayi. One characteristic of the tana is the manner in which every section is concluded. Each section involves tana rendition around a specific svara or region. The conclusion is always a svara formation of 3+3+3+5 (svaras) with a pause, ending on the svara used for the section's tana development.

As with each section, so also with the whole tana, the conclusion has a common structure. This includes certain patterns that are rendered in three places – tara sthayi shadja, madhya sthayi panchama and madhya sthayi shadja – if the raga permits such a formation. This begins with the same structure as mentioned, repeating the structure in all three places. Then the musician goes back to the tara sthayi shadja and renders a diminished structure of the above, repeating the same in the other two places. Once the structure is reduced to its minimum, the musician concludes at the madhya sthayi shadja with the original structure ending on a sustained madhya sthayi sa. The melody of these concluding structures is also almost the same in all the ragas, as long as the aesthetics of the raga permits the usage of those svara patterns.

While rendering tana, some musicians increase their pace as they reach tara sthayi, and others reduce their pace for the final conclusion in madhya sthayi. These are exceptions rather than the rule.

There remain two issues to be discussed pertaining to the practice and the aesthetics of tana. The first is about the tradition of the mrdanga being played while tana is being rendered. One wonders if that is wrong. It is true that I had mentioned the underlying chaturashra, but I have also said that this is only a guide, a base, on which other patterns are placed. There is a great deal of flexibility on how this base chaturashra can be adjusted or even ignored in order to present other patterns. While keeping time with a tana rendering, we will notice that the patterns do not always fall into the chaturashra, that is, the endings of each round do not finish on a beat as they should if they are meant to exactly fit into the meter. These adjustments are as much part of the tana aesthetics as is the underlying chaturashra. If we box tana into a definite chaturashra with a mrdanga accompaniment, we are tampering with the basic aesthetic form of this technique, which allows for a flexible rhythmic base on which structured melodic patterns can be placed. A fixed chaturashra base will constrict the tana's melodics. Enforcement of the strict chaturashra meter will make it imperative that all other melodically created number patterns have to fall on a beat, as that is the only way they will fit into the chaturashra matrix. This destroys the very essence of tana.

Another issue is whether tana can be rendered in all ragas. Traditionally, there were certain ragas – those that come to life when rendered in madhyama-kala – that were specifically used for the rendering of tana. In this laya, these ragas exhibit all the characteristics that define them. The aesthetics of these ragas also allow for creating svara pattern and building on them without affecting their identity. Over the years, this has changed, with great musicians being able to present tana even in ragas that are aesthetically chauka-kala ragas or those that do not come to life when handled as svara patterns. It certainly requires a creative genius to be able to actually present tana in such ragas, but I wonder whether, in doing this, we are not taking something out of the raga. The tana's aesthetics dictate that we create svara patterns in structural forms. In some ragas, like nilambari, this is very difficult, as the very soul of that raga exists in a non-rigid continuous melodic flow. Even so, a great musician can present a wonderful tana in this raga. What does that do to the raga's aesthetic identity? The genius may make it sound wonderful and true to the tana form with an overall feeling of the raga. But if we analyse the way the tana is employed, we will find that in many stages of the tana's progress, the raga's aesthetic identity has been altered.

Musicians should be very careful that tana renditions do not meander into becoming alapanas. Creating rigid melodic patterns in ragas that can be developed within a flexible chaturashra laya structure requires a clear comprehension of the raga and tana form. When musicians are unable to comprehend either, they find an escape in presenting a few structured tana-style formations and tag them to alapana-style melodic movements. This too is a disservice to the aesthetics of the tana.

Viruttam, Shloka and Ugabhoga

These are three names for the same form of improvisation. When the verse is in Sanskrit, it is referred to as a shloka, in Kannada as ugabhoga and in Tamil as viruttam, but they refer to the same aesthetic form. This form of improvisation is very close to alapana. But I am taking it up for separate discussion because of the many characteristics that make it altogether unique. Simply put, this technique is about presenting poetic verse in the free-flowing form of an alapana without tala or a laya matrix.

There are certain important aspects that define this form. Since these verses are rendered in a free-flowing style, it is adaptable to almost any kind and form of poetic verse. Once the verse has been chosen, the musician can identify and select the raga to present it in. Before rendering it in musical form, he should have absorbed the text of the poetry. The musician then begins to render the verse in the chosen raga. Every word in the text has extended syllables and short syllables. A musically 'right' interaction of these two is essential to give the rendering its melodic structure and beauty. The musician has to keep in mind the fact that this piece of verse is being presented melodically, not narratively. Therefore, long melodic movements have to be and will be rendered on longer syllables and, where the syllables are short, melodic movements will also be correspondingly short. Similarly, it is crucial that the melodic variations are rendered along with changes in the grain of the verse. This means that as the musician is saying the syllables of the verse, the melody is also being varied. This is important as it is, technically speaking, possible to recite a full line of verse on one svara and then tag the long melodic variation at the end, using just the last syllable of the rendered verse. This would do injustice to the form. When viruttam is presented, melodic variations occur between every syllable of the verse. The melodic development is very abstract and never follows a step-by-step alapana-style development of the raga. The melody moves right across the different octaves, presenting the raga in many large strokes. The musician can also choose to present the verse in multiple ragas, moving from one to another.

Looking at all these different forms of manodharma sangita, we may wonder whether they leave any room for true creativity at all. Paying heed to the aesthetics of raga, tala, dhatu and matu is not optional; it is an inherent requirement of the genre of classical music. Added to that are the numerous rules built into each of the manodharma techniques. And yet, within this world of rules, there exists a state of endlessly creative possibilities. I use the term 'state' as it is a state of mind, of ideation and of imagination that creates the endlessness of creativity.

Once a musician has truly absorbed the aesthetics that exist in every component of raga, tala, dhatu and matu, all the rules that govern manodharma sangita stop appearing as conditions. They cease to impinge on the musician's conscious mind. Thus unfettered, the musician goes on to create music. Creativity flows unbridled, without any restrictions in the mind. All the rules stay in the subconscious. But they support and guide the musician's journey. They do not impede, inhibit or restrict. These rules become restrictions only when they are not completely interiorized and absorbed as being part of the aesthetics of the music, but treated as external limitations. In essence, the 'rules' are not restrictions but definers of the aesthetics of the music. They do not restrict creativity, only give it a direction. And the truly creative musician will go beyond all expectations. Even though not expressly invoked, 'freedom' has permeated this narrative. It is difficult to describe the freedom as the free musician experiences it. Freedom, in this context, can mean but one thing: the unrestricted creativity that flowers within the world of Karnatik music.

7

The Rendering Unfolds

Is music the proverbial 'whole' made up of different parts? It is not. As in a human being, the whole and its parts in music are a unity, with each part having specific characteristics, functions and a form. Together, they are much more than their sum. The aesthetics of music pervades the totality – the whole as well as its several parts. I use the word 'parts' only for the sake of understanding; these are actually seamless sections of the whole. They are as much the whole as the whole is them.

Thus the interaction between the different parts of a musical form involves the sharing of common aesthetics. The structural elements in the alapana or the kirtana are unique in their construction and purpose, but only within the seamless aesthetics of Karnatik music. Their very structure is designed to drive the purpose of expressing the music's larger aesthetic intent. Their structure shapes the aesthetics they exhibit and their specific focus within the music. The forms and structures of the music carry in them the content of the music.

The question as to which evolved first need not detain us, as the two are inextricable. Form and content were born together and exist together. Form and structure provide content, which are framed by them. All of these elements are determined by the intrinsic – and constantly evolving – aesthetic intent of the music.

The previous essays discussed various specific components of Karnatik music – form, content and their roles within its aesthetic framework – all the while keeping the larger picture and the context in view, namely, the music itself. Here, another perspectival clarity is required: the various components of Karnatik music do not 'come together' to constitute the whole. Rather, the various aspects discussed emanate from the music in order to express its aesthetic intent. From this perspective, music will always be a completely living being that has a purpose and expresses itself in many different ways to achieve it.

What is the Purpose of Music?

For an answer to that question, we need to go back to the description of art music. The aesthetic primacy of raga and tala and their abstraction is the driving force of art music in the universe of the Karnatik system. The music's emotional and intellectual manifestations are connected to these two primary elements of raga and tala and their abstractions. It is important to establish this, since the more common understanding is that the linguistic meaning of the lyrics is an important part of the experience. I will address this view separately, but it is necessary that the various components of the music, including matu and dhatu, be directed towards raga and tala and their abstraction. Every element of Karnatik music uses its specific nature towards this end. Therefore, I would say that the purpose of music is not to present the linguistic meaning of the lyrics, but the aesthetics of Karnatik music.

How is Karnatik music actually presented? Do the different components of the music and the manner in which they are presented serve this aesthetic intent? Our study of compositional types and manodharma techniques in the previous essays focused on how they were presented in practice today. I also critiqued certain presentation forms on whether they undermine raga and tala. To understand this fully, we need a critical assessment of the various aspects of actually presenting Karnatik music. After all, the music is absorbed only on the basis of how it is presented in a concert. A concert can shape the offering of the music.

The word 'concert' has multiple meanings, but is used primarily in the domain of music. Its origins refer to a union. The Italian word 'concertare' or 'to sing in concert' is perhaps derived from the Latin 'concertare' meaning 'to strive', as in concerted effort. These descriptions give us some very important ideas on what is expected of a concert: a concerted effort to strive and create music in unison. We could add here that concerts featuring multiple genres risk this lack of union. But what about music within one genre? Must a concert then be a union of the various musical forms into one composite body, or could the multiple parts or features be presented separately, linked only by the commonality of musical history? Clarity on this is critical to an understanding of the role of a concert within the aesthetics of Karnatik music. But in order to address this question, we need to understand what it means to present Karnatik music as a concert.

The placing of Karnatik music on the platform of a concert, by that very act, influences the music. The process begins with the intent of the performance itself. Is there a conflict between the aesthetics of the concert and that of the music? This may sound like a redundant question, as surely both should be the same. But in reality this is not the case. The very character of a concert requires it to include various internal and external aspects – the ambience, audience and context – which affect the musician's internal perceptions. This can sometimes result in a specific concert turning out to be at cross-purposes with the music's aesthetics and also, more significantly, of becoming a recurring pattern, influencing the music itself. In an ideal situation, everything must submit to the music's aesthetics, but this does not happen.

Let us begin by understanding the role of various musicians at a Karnatik concert. I will look at a vocal concert, as voice is the primary mode of expressing Karnatik music. Instrumentalists too utilize vocal concerts as the basis of their instrument-based interpretation. That said, an instrumental concert has its own aesthetics arising from the instrument and technique.

The Vocalist

In a concert, the vocalist is the pivotal artist and decides the concert's aesthetic direction. The guru–shishya parampara and the artist's own perspective on Karnatik music influence this. The direction reveals itself in the choice of raga, tala, compositions, alapana, niraval, kalpanasvaras and the like, and in how she handles all these aspects. The voice texture is also closely linked to this process. Whether it is the voice that changes the musician's approach or the musical approach that influences the voice cannot be clearly stated. These two aspects work closely together in music.

Since the voice is sensitive to many external influences, it can sound different from day to day – something the musician keeps in mind while presenting a concert. As the primary performer, she decides the compositions to be presented at the concert, the ragas for alapana, the lines chosen for niraval, kalpanasvara and the exact positioning for rhythmic interplay known as the tani avartana. In short, the vocalist has complete control of the concert. Whether these arrangements are decided in advance or in situ depends on the vocalist. Some prepare a list of compositions and alapanas to be presented in advance, but there are those singers who decide the content and the sequence on the stage even as the concert progresses. I am not passing judgement on either approach, as these only indicate the musician's nature, not the quality of the music.

Some may wonder if a lack of advance planning indicates irresponsibility or carelessness. This is not true; by and large, such musicians are very committed and constantly engaged in the music. This gives them the ability and the confidence to make choice-and-sequence decisions during the concert. This exercise of freedom comes from an unroutinized mind and it is in and through that freedom that they chance upon the various colours, tones and shades of their musical imagination. Then, one may wonder if a planned concert can lead to a lack of spontaneity, instinct or improvisation. The musicians who have planned their concerts do so to let their minds soak in the ragas and compositions that they have chosen to present. Through this conscious immersion, they get a sense of stability, not because of the prior planning, but by the premeditated intensity that invests their music with greater depth.

The vocalist's role is to present a concert so that all the essential aspects of Karnatik music are presented, bearing in mind the character of the music itself. This is a serious responsibility. As the person who defines the direction of a concert, every svara she sings influences the other musicians on the stage.

Many accompanists speak of how their own music is a response to that of the vocalist. It is also true that the accompanists inspire the vocalist, but this may not happen unless the vocalist can provide the space needed by other musicians to express themselves to the fullest extent. Every singer's musical training, focus, acumen and voice is different, and this influences the choices she makes. While the proportion in which various aspects are presented varies from musician to musician, as I said before, an honest expression of Karnatik music must necessarily remain true to the aesthetic qualities of the whole and the specific.

Any vocal concert has both melodic and percussion instruments as accompaniment. The former is primarily the violin, and mrdanga provides the percussion accompaniment. These two instruments and the musicians who play them in a vocal concert are called pakkavadya vidvans (the word vidvan coming from 'vidya', learning; musician-scholar), meaning the support-musicians. Sometimes a few more percussion instruments, like the ghata, khanjira and morsing, also form part of the concert. These musicians, providing additional support, are referred to as upa-pakkavadya vidvans. Let us now look at the role of the accompanying musicians in a concert.

The Violinist

Over the last century and half, the violin has come to be the primary melodic accompanying instrument in Karnatik music. In a concert, the violinist probably has the most challenging job. He is not only providing melodic accompaniment to the singer but also expressing his creativity during the manodharma sections. This dual role is all-absorbing and leaves him with no respite.

As a melodic accompanist, the violinist's major contribution to a vocal concert is to support and enhance the melodic experience. The singer, therefore, has the advantage of being helped by the violinist to complete the music's picture. Whether this happens every time or not is a different issue, but it is the intent. 'Shadow' is the most commonly used word to describe the violinist's accompanying role. A person's shadow is slightly behind or ahead and is sometimes larger or smaller, but it is always a reflection of the person. The violinist is exactly that. Often just behind the vocalist, he tries to anticipate what lies ahead in the vocalist's mind; not exactly the music as sung by the vocalist, but its form, very close to the music of the vocalist.

When a composition is rendered, the violinist hugs the coast of the vocalist's rendering. He tries to follow the melodic movements by observing the movements of the singer's lips. Over a period, all musicians learn to connect melodic movements with changes in the movements of the mouth, lips and neck. This helps them intuitively correlate the musical phrases with physical changes, which explains how a violinist can shadow the vocalist within a split second of a musical passage being sung. There will be a small gap between the musical movements of the vocalist and violinist, but with an experienced violinist, this will be negligible. When the accompaniment is extraordinarily good, the audience will believe that there are two voices, so perfect will be the synchronization between the vocalist and violinist. Such a melodic shadowing of the compositions provides a certain depth to the listening experience. Could vocalists and violinists practise together so as to create a unified melodic expression? This is a possibility, but the nature of Karnatik music being spontaneous and based on improvisational abstraction, it necessitates a fresh and unrehearsed frame of mind.

In this duality of textures between the voice and violin, there is a certain enhancement of the melodic lines. It is possible that the violinist may or may not know the composition being rendered, and when that happens, he has to be extremely attentive and use his musical insight and listening powers and stay very close to the vocalist's rendition. If it is a known composition, there is still the possibility of the vocalist's recension, or pathantara, being different, which would mean that the ideal violin accompanist subordinates his knowledge of the composition to follow the vocalist. Both cases require an immense level of attention from the violinist. Any deviant following of the composition will affect the vocal presentation. It takes years of experience to master this technique of accompaniment.

It is in the manodharma exchanges that the violinist's skill and experience shines through. When a vocalist renders an alapana, it is always followed by an elaboration of the same raga on the violin. The accepted practice is that the duration of the violinist's alapana should be about half that of the vocalist. There are no fixed norms about how the alapana is to unfold. This unchartered vista is ideal for creativity, but can also bring problems in its trail. We will discuss this later, when we critically assess a Karnatik music concert.

Apart from presenting their own raga alapana, violinists have another crucial role. They follow the vocalist as she renders the alapana. As the musician renders every phrase, the violinist observes very keenly and at the end of a phrase repeats the last span. What exactly is the 'last span'? It is that last stretch of the phrase which the violinist senses in his musical being as appropriate. An understanding of this is gathered through listening to the great accompanists and also keeping in mind the need of the specific vocalist. Each vocalist may require a shorter or longer section of the rendered phrase to be repeated. The nature of the phrase rendered by the vocalist provides some indication. The sense of appropriateness also changes depending on the length, complexity and gamaka in the rendered phrase. By repeating the last part of a phrase, the violinist is providing a pause for the singer and simultaneously creating the reference point so that she can move to the next phrase. Though the singer renders the original phrase, the repetition by the violinist fixes the melodic movement in the minds of both the vocalist and the audience and, importantly, provides a guide to both on how the next phrase is likely to move. This is where the 'shadow' is slightly ahead, as the violinist is the psychological indicator of what lies ahead.

While playing the role of a shadow during the vocalist's alapana, the violinist's volume level is usually less than that of the voice. But during the repetition of the last section of the phrase, there is a clear increase in volume to establish the aspects mentioned above.

This 'following' is something that can never be taught. This is a technique that every violinist acquires through concert experience. In contrast, the violinist's alapana is a solitary journey. The violinist renders the alapana by himself, with only the tambura providing the shruti. This puts the violinist at a disadvantageous position, as the melodic effect of the combined voice and violin during a vocal alapana is missing during the violinist's alapana. There are clear gaps between the phrases rendered by the violinist since no one is 'following' him. These I mention as disadvantages in terms of the experience that a concert seems to provide. It does not reflect my views on the aesthetics of the music.

When the niraval is presented, after the vocalist's exploration ending at the melodic line, the violinist plays a similar niraval. Once agian, the violinist 'follows' the singer during her niraval explorations and responds immediately with his own niraval. This presents some other challenges. Unlike the alapana, the 'following' here is very similar to the technique used during the rendition of compositions. The difficulty is that even when the violinist is not able to predict the vocalist's exact melodic flow, he has to remain very close to her rendition. There is also the fact that, even while rendering niraval, the vocalist will be enunciating the syllables of the chosen line in specific positions of the tala. The violinist has to sense this. Every lyrical enunciation has to also be closely followed by the violinist with melodic stresses at the syllabic points. If ignored, there will be a certain disconnect between the vocalist's niraval and the violinist's 'following' pattern. The violinist must also be very precise, so as to not overshoot the vocalist, as niraval is strictly bound by the line and tala. If this occurs, it would throw the vocalist completely off balance. The dual role of following the vocalist and rendering his own niraval allows very little time to the violinist to switch between being an accompanist to presenting his own creativity. The vocalist has had the advantage of being able to draw musical resources in silence from the creativity of the violinist. The musical imagination of the violinist and the vocalist remain interlinked because of the tight nature of the exchange between them in the niraval.

During kalpanasvara rendition, each time the vocalist renders kalpanasvaras and ends at the chosen line, the violinist immediately responds creatively with kalpanasvaras. As in niraval, the violinist 'follows' the vocalist and then immediately allows himself the freedom to creatively express his own rendition. While following sama-kala kalpanasvaras, the violinist has to emphasize every svara, just as the vocalist does. This emphasis includes the vocalist's gamaka interpretation. Since every svara is clearly presented, yet flows into the next, if the violinist were to introduce any change to the interpretation while following, it will be clearly highlighted and disturb the aesthetics of the vocalist's creativity. During mel-kala kalpanasvaras, the sheer speed at which these svaras are rendered makes it much harder for the violinist to follow. One may wonder why this is different from mel-kala niraval. The difference is that while in mel-kala niraval, the rigid movements still emphasize exact syllabic positions, here every svara is emphasized by itself.

Both in the case of niraval and kalpanasvaras, a certain highlight is created as the vocalist completes her improvisation and links it to the composed line. The violinist needs to anticipate this link and establish the composed line. At the same time, he should remember that the length of a niraval exploration by the vocalist can be equal to the exact length of the chosen line or multiple variations on the same line that will cover the appropriate number of avartanas. The violinist needs to be aware of this since rushing in to complete what the vocalist intends to continue will affect melodic and rhythmic flow. Similarly, the violinist must be conscious that every kalpanasvara exploration can cover multiple avartanas. Both in the case of niraval and kalpanasvaras, the only accepted norm is that if a vocalist renders a niraval for two avartanas, the violinist also plays for the same length.

The violinist's role during the renditions of tana is very similar to his role during an alapana. The differences lie in the violin technique, which has evolved over the last century, and the method of exchange. Unlike the alapana, where the vocalist usually traverses the raga structure without pause, in the tana the vocalist and the violinist alternate their renditions, pausing at svaras around which each section of the tana is developed.

During the renditions of shlokas or viruttams, the violinist's role is the same as during an alapana. This form combines poetry along with melodic movements in an alapana style. The violin, though, can neither articulate nor mimic the lyrics in a shloka. Considering this, some vocalists do not provide an independent opportunity for violinists in this section.

The Mrdanga Accompanist

The role of the mrdanga in a concert is unique. It goes far beyond maintaining the laya or defining the tala. The mrdanga, as the primary percussion instrument, provides a parallel aesthetic layer to the experience of the concert. The vocalist, having decided the composition's laya, demonstrates the tala and its every anga. Clearly then, that is not the role of the mrdanga artist. The responsibility falling on the mrdanga artist is to adhere to this decision and complement it by maintaining the laya along with the other musicians on stage. The fixing of the laya, or any change in it, is decided by the vocalist, but during the course of a concert, any of the artists can influence its acceleration or deceleration. Determination of laya and adherence to tala, in many ways, is the collective action of all the musicians, as they come together in the flow of music. As the musical presentation develops, sometimes the musicians feel a need for change in the laya or tightening of the tala frame. This is collectively executed without any verbal communication between them. This rapport between the musicians is developed through years of musical relationship and experience.

The idea that the rhythmic support comes exclusively from the mrdanga needs rethinking. The singer provides the visual correlative of the tala with her hands, which defines its structure and determines the laya, thereby establishing the rhythmic framework. Hence, rhythmic definition already exists and is not the contribution of the mrdanga artist.

We have already discussed in detail the interactions between tala, matu and dhatu. We have also observed the way in which this differs from one compositional form to another and even between compositions that are of the same type. Every mrdanga artist must necessarily understand the composition being rendered. In the structure of the tala, matu and dhatu, there are clear definitions, points of emphasis, melodically highlighted areas as well as rest. Varying layas are placed on the basic laya of the composition within the tala framework. This is the complex amalgam of variables that the mrdanga artist deftly draws from. What he then does is give the composition a rhythmic counterpoint to every melodic movement through the varying rhythmic patterns and tonal variations that can be produced on the mrdanga. The idea is not to divert the listeners from the composition, but to enhance its melodic and syllabic elegance.

In a kirtana, when there are multiple sangatis of different speeds and containing free-flowing movement, rigidly defined movements or fast phrases, the mrdanga artist responds differently to each, providing the listener a clear understanding of the sangati movements. Along with this, the mrdanga also gives every melodic movement a rhythmic casing. It sometimes fills the melodic gaps within compositions with rhythmic patterns, which gives that section an emphasis. The mrdanga artist also employs silence to highlight the composition. After continuously playing along with the composition, the mrdanga artist can choose to remain silent for a specific line. This highlights the melody of the line. More than the silence itself, what is significant is the way in which the mrdanga artist re-enters the composition. The re-emergence of the mrdanga sound makes the preceding silence invaluable. In certain sections, the fast phrases of the sangati is accompanied by playing patterns at one speed faster than that of the sangita, thereby creating an illusion of greater speed. For example, if the sangati is in sama-kala, the mrdanga patterns may be in mel-kala. The aesthetics of the mrdanga, together with the knowledge and sensitivity of the artist, gives dhatu and matu, which are also intrinsically rhythmic in form, an interpretation that underlines the movements in a composition.

Each compositional form has very different aesthetics and intent. The aesthetic layers of a tillana are very different from those of a pada, for instance. Well aware of this, the mrdanga artist adjusts his accompanying style accordingly.

Another important function of the mrdanga artist is to clearly accentuate the divisions of a composition, for example, the pallavi, anupallavi, charana. These parts are clearly segmented by a small rhythmic pattern played as the vocalist concludes each segment. This rhythmic pattern concludes either at the sama of the tala, or at the point in the tala where the next segment, like the anupallavi, begins. The mrdanga artist plays a crucial role in giving to the listener a sense of completion to each part of a composition, while also linking it to the one that follows.

While accompanying niraval or kalpanasvara, the mrdanga artist has to follow the techniques used during the rendition of compositions. But along with that, he also has to respond to the creativity of both the vocalist and the violinist, and has a few other specific roles in niraval and kalpanasvara. While niraval is being rendered, the mrdanga artist tries to emphasize the syllabic structure of the chosen line. This is because the syllabic positions are a very important part of the niraval expression itself. Depending on whether the niraval is being presented in an alapana style, sama-kala or mel-kala, the mrdanga artist changes his approach. Within these broad ways of presenting niraval, there are numerous variations, depending on the melodic movements that the singer presents. The laya of these melodic movements are variable and the mrdanga artist, aware of this, responds to these changes, even though the framework of the basic tala and laya is fixed.

During kalpanasvaras, the mrdanga artist is completely following the svara creativity of the musicians. The svaras can be rendered with great definition in the chosen kala, or include pauses, extensions and movements. The mrdanga artist interprets all this. This includes using silence and different tonal and structural patterns to enhance the kalpanasvara presentation. The style of accompanying is different for a sama-kala and a mel-kala kalpanasvara presentation. This is determined by the fact that sama-kala kalpanasvaras are intrinsically focused on the graceful movements in the raga, while mel-kala kalpanasvaras are faster and hence more rigid in style. It is only the mrdanga vidvan who can hold these up in the sharpest relief. During kalpanasvaras and niraval, the mrdanga artist also plays the crucial role of highlighting the musician's re-entry to the composed line. As the singer or violinist finishes each niraval or kalpanasvara turn, the mrdanga artist carefully approaches the place where the improvisation ends and the composed line is being reiterated. Towards the end of the improvisation, there is a clear emphasis that leads to the establishing of the composed line. This support gives definition to the improvisations, and establishes the significance of the chosen melodic line in the minds of the listeners.

Through all this, the mrdanga artist needs to be sensitive to the volume levels of the vocalist and the violinist.

One aspect of mrdanga accompaniment that is usually ignored is the response of the mrdanga artist to the raga of the composition being rendered. Within a concert, the vocalist may demonstrate a certain approach to a particular composition in a raga with a specific emotive content. In understanding the raga and the composition and responding to every musical passage, the mrdanga artist is required to interpret it through the tonal and pattern variations. This would mean that every mrdanga artist should necessarily possess deep knowledge of the melodic aspects of Karnatik music.

Musical accompaniment has no prescribed pathway. This basically means that the art of accompanying is not a composed form. Using the rhythmic patterns and multiple tones, mrdanga artists respond to the melodies being presented. Though this is creative, over a period of time, certain fixed ways of accompanying compositions or accompanying certain popular compositions have emerged. This is due to the impact that these methods have had on the minds of musicians and listeners. However, it is equally true that a good mrdanga artist will be able to present multiple aesthetic methods of accompanying.

Two generic methods of accompanying can be observed. The mrdanga artist can either actually play the melodic and sahitya structure as it is, emphasizing every syllabic position and melodic structure or create a parallel rhythmic web under these two structures. The former is like looking at a relief sculpture that presents various highlights and stories as a complete experience. You see every part of the sculpture: the feeling of movement, emotion and expression is presented as one body. The latter is like viewing an intricately sculpted two-layered roof. Here, the primary roof is the one closer to us. Behind it is another, with space between the two. The sculptor uses the panel behind to provide focus on the one in front. Neither is bare, but carefully sculpted with motifs that do not repeat but serve to magnify the one to the fore. A discerning person will not view these as two different carvings, but as a composite whole. This is very similar to the styles of mrdanga accompaniment. The former is within the melodic expression, the latter is parallel to the melodic expression, and both form the whole. The methods and styles of adopting either of these are numerous, but the broad approaches are the same.

The Rhythmic Interplay

The tani avartana is also very important to the aesthetics of a concert. In presenting a tani avartana, the mrdanga artist provides the concert an expression that is exclusively about the rhythmic sounds and, in the process, creates a section of solo rhythmic abstraction without a constant melodic reference.

The tani avartana extracts the role of rhythm in the concert for a spectacular moment of autonomous display to revert to the balance of the concert's mutuality.

The tani avartana is a segmented presentation of rhythmic variations and mathematical possibilities within a defined tala. Within each segment are further divisions based on the rhythmic patterns and motifs that the mrdanga artist chooses to focus on and develop. Similar to the development of a phrase in a raga alapana, every rhythmic pattern can be expanded into further patterns. This is precisely what the artist does. The tani avartana is played after the presentation of a kirtana to which niraval and kalpanasvaras have been rendered. It is played in reference to the line chosen for niraval and kalpanasvara. Therefore, the tala, laya, the line chosen and the point of reference to which kalpanasvara is rendered are all important to the artist.

When the tani avartana begins, the mrdanga artist first establishes the structure of the tala and the laya within it. This laya is what has been expressed in the specific line chosen for niraval and kalpanasvara. Once this is established, the artist slowly begins to build rhythmic phrases. These are placed on the tala, with the artist exploring the possibilities of these phrases as the tala moves in its known cyclical patterns or avartanas. Each rhythmic phrase evolves according to the artist's creativity, culminating in an emphasis of the sama or the position in the tala that was chosen as the reference point for the kalpanasvara rendition. When the reference point is being reiterated, the artist also employs a defined mathematical form known as a korvai to emphasize the reference point of the tala or the sama as the case may be. Across various patterns and segments, many such korvais are played. The difference between the development of rhythmic phrases, patterns and a korvai lies in the fact that the development of a rhythmic phrase is not fixed by a defined form, but a korvai is defined by a pre-assigned form to which any mathematical pattern has to adhere. Of course, there are variations within the korvai form.

Every segment of a tani avartana itself has many smaller segments that are defined by the mrdanga's rhythmic patterns. Usually, in one of the segments of a tani avartana, the artist creates patterns in a nadai/gati other than the one present in the composition to which it is being played.

The last segment of a tani avartana involves specific mathematical formulations. These comprise the reductive kuraippu, followed by the mohra that clearly embraces the tala structure, establishing its total beat count, linking to a final climactic korvai.

As much as melody and the abstraction of melody are essential in Karnatik music, rhythmic abstraction using tala and laya is no less so. This abstraction is the direction towards which the artist journeys. In this journey, he is constantly sensitive to the raga, tala, composition and the sensibilities of the vocalist and violinist.

The Upa-pakkavadya

The khanjira, ghata and morsing are together known as upa-pakkavadyas, or ancillary instruments. The instruments and the artists playing them are completely different from each other, with each providing a different set of tones and rhythmic patterns to a concert. Their role is to follow the lead of the primary rhythmic support, or the mrdanga artist. However, when the upa-pakkavadya artists accompany the melody without the mrdanga, they have to follow the vocalist or violinist. There are certain norms that the upa-pakkavadya artist follows. During the rendition of kirtanas, the upa-pakkavadya artist joins in during the anupallavi or at the end of the pallavi. The patterns they play are constantly with reference to the patterns being established by the mrdanga artist. There are also times when the upa-pakkavadya artist accompanies parts of the composition on his own. This is usually in the charana. During the niraval and kalpanasvara exchanges between the vocalist and the violinist, usually the vocalist is accompanied by the mrdanga artist and the violinist by the upa-pakkavadya artist. This segregation of their roles gives the presentation a unique textural feel.

The mrdanga artist always begins the tani avartana. After the mrdanga artist finishes every segment, the upa-pakkavadya artist plays his interpretation. If there is more than one upa-pakkavadya artist on the stage, each of them gets an opportunity. The upa-pakkavadya artists do not repeat exactly what the mrdanga artist has presented. They use some basic structures that the mrdanga has played as a reference to create their own ideas of rhythmic patterns or mathematical calculations. The shift to a new rhythmic development in a segment or another nadai/gati is only made by the mrdanga and is followed by the upa-pakkavadya. After presenting clearly segmented sections, we come to the kuraippu in the tani avartana. With the presence of an upa-pakkavadya in a concert, a kuraippu is an exchange between the mrdanga and the upa-pakkavadya. The leader of this exchange is the mrdanga artist. At the end of the kuraippu, the mrdanga and upa-pakkavadya come together, leading to a mohra and a korvai. Choosing the mohra and korvai is the privilege of the mrdanga vidvan.

The role of the upa-pakkavadya artists is a difficult one, as they have to keep in mind the rhythmic ideas of the mrdanga artist during the rendition of compositions, niraval, kalpanasvaras and tani avartana. At the same time, they have to be sensitive to the melodic interpretations of the vocalist and violinist. To be able to keep all this in mind and yet present their own rhythmic contribution to a concert is as challenging as it is admirable.

One may wonder whether beyond the mrdanga, yet another percussion instrument is necessary at all in a concert. This is a valid question, but it is a fact that this addition heightens the tonal and rhythmic patterns in the presentation. They are not only supportive of all the artists, but actually add a certain lustre to the melody and the rhythm in a concert.

We cannot ignore the fact that there is a hierarchy to the roles of the musicians on the stage. The vocalist is the main musician with the most freedom and the prerogative of complete control. The violinist's role depends on the vocalist; he has to be mindful of the vocalist's musical journey in the concert and present his own invaluable creativity from within that mindfulness. The mrdanga artist's rhythmic interpretations draw upon both the vocalist and the violinist. And all three artists in turn influence the upa-pakkavadya artists' role on the stage. Which, of course, takes us back to the English word 'concert' and its allusion to 'concerted' effort.

These observations present an ideal based on what is believed to be not just necessary, but paramount for the Karnatik experience at its fullest. How much of this actually happens? Do the artists' respective roles actually affect the musical aesthetics? Is the hierarchy needed? What defines the hierarchy? These are all important questions.

The Tambura

There is one other musician on stage – the person who plays the tambura. Put simply, the tambura provides the shruti, or tonic, for the artists. It gives the musicians, and therefore the concert as a whole, the tonic cue and reference they require. But the tambura is far more crucial to the aural experience of Karnatik music than that. The musical sound of the tambura is the collective expression of its four strings and provides the concert its aesthetic platform. The tambura, like a musician, contains within it the condensed emotion of its structural and aesthetic integrity. The collective resonance of the four-stringed instrument communicates the emotion of the tambura and imbues the physical site of the concert with its aesthetics. It is in this quality that the musician drowns himself to discover the music. The sound of the tambura is a deeply emotive and aesthetic component of the Karnatik experience.

The intended roles of all the artists in a kutcheri (a music concert – literally a court) are defined by what we have come to expect as a kutcheri. This experience is our representation of Karnatik music. In giving each musician a certain role within the kutcheri, we have also defined what we perceive as Karnatik music itself. This implies that there cannot be a separation between the presentation pattern, the musician's roles and the music's aesthetics. This is the collective experience that we seek. But in order to understand what exactly this collective experience entails, we need now to understand the actual details of the presentation: the kutcheri.

8

The Concert Unravels

In order to understand a Karnatik concert better, we need to study the musical aspects of the concert, its ambience, its svarupa. Let us begin the journey with what we see as we walk into a concert space. From there, we can move on to the experience of a Karnatik concert as it is presented today.

A Karnatik music concert is referred to as a kutcheri, a term that has originated from the Hindi word 'kachehri'. How this word came to be adapted to the Karnatik context is quite fascinating. The word itself means a court, a public office and, by extension, the people assembled in such a place. The association with a court is very clear. It is most likely that this word came to be employed in the Karnatik music world during the Maratha rule in Tanjavur (1676–1800). We know that the courthouse in those times was not a separate or remote precinct. It was the darbar of the king, the hall where he held audience, appeared before his court and subjects and dealt with matters of state. Inevitably, this was where the king made time and space for his subjects and visitors to present their aspirations and concerns to him. It was in this same space that music was presented to the kings. This overlapping of activity is believed to be why a Karnatik music presentation is called a kutcheri. Today, this term brings with it not just its linguistic meaning, but also the cultural context of Karnatik music as we have known it over the last century or so. In it lies the subtext of the concert format, the nature of its audience, its social group and the geographical reference to the southern regions of India.

I will describe the kutcheri as a vocal concert, as Karnatik music accords primacy to the voice. Instrumentalists endeavour to replicate the qualities of the music as expressed by the voice. Their solo presentations too follow the established vocal kutcheri format.

Even before the curtains go up, the tambura can be heard being tuned to the vocalist's shruti. The sounds from other instruments – the violin, mrdanga – also being tuned to the same shruti follow the tambura's invisible lead. As the tambura begins to sound, the performance space reverberates with its collective resonance. When the curtains go up, the vocalist is seated in the middle of the ensemble of musicians. Towards his left is the violinist, and to the right the mrdanga artist. If the mrdanga artist is left-handed, these positions are interchanged. Behind the singer is either one or two artists holding the tambura upright, strumming the four strings, establishing the shruti. This sound is essential for creation of the aesthetic base for the music. There may also be one or two upa-pakkavadya artists seated behind the mrdanga artist and the violinist.

Let us now move to how musicians render the concert. The kutcheri format has been in vogue for about a hundred years. It usually begins with the presentation of the varna. The pallavi, anupallavi and muktayi svara of the varna are rendered in one or two speeds (sama-kala and mel-kala). The varna is considered a warm-up and most musicians believe that it helps the voice gain stability before the more elaborate kirtanas and manodharma aspects. The charana and the ettugada svaras are rendered in slightly faster speed. This is a tempo between sama-kala and mel-kala. The speeds mentioned here are in terms of a generic understanding of slow or fast within Karnatik music, not to the specific laya between the beats. At the end of the varna composition, the voice of the vocalist as well as the hands of the other musicians are ready for far more complex musical renditions. The varna with its raga musicality and its rendition in multiple speeds attunes musicians in the ideal attitude for the kutcheri.

The second composition is the relatively smaller kirtana, in terms of the length of both sahitya and sangatis, and is set to smaller talas or in one kalai of the longer talas. The speed of rendition is madhyama-kala. In Karnatik music, madhyama-kala, as with speeds in general, cannot be defined. This is a cognitive understanding born out of the generally accepted speeds established during a period of time in history. This medium tempo is something between what is accepted as slow and fast.

The vocalist begins to render some mel-kala kalpanasvaras to a chosen line in this kirtana. We have already discussed how the length of each round of kalpanasvaras gradually increases, ending in the rendering of kalpanasvaras across numerous avartanas. The number of rounds of kalpanasvaras rendered is limited. Musicians describe this as a 'crisp' rendition of kalpanasvaras, meaning that it is not elaborate. Before venturing into the first alapana of the concert, the vocalist may render another kirtana sometimes in chowka-kala.

Both musicians and connoisseurs refer to the first piece presented with an alapana, followed by a kirtana in the same raga, as the 'sub-main', the 'main' being one of the pivotal presentations in a kutcheri. Though in general the alapana will be developed step by step, the musician does not spend a very long time at each svara that allows such a pause in the chosen raga. The objective is that the musicians and the audience slowly enter the deeper aspects of the music. This alapana is not exhaustive, yet it must capture the essence of the raga being depicted. The concise alapana serves as an introduction to the idea of an alapana. Brevity marks the rendition of the alapana and the kirtana as the sub-main. An elaborate composition is one that has a grand and intricate structure in terms of melodic movements, sangatis, layering of the melody over the tala, laya variations in the melody and sahitya. The alapana and kirtana that follow comprise a suite. The detailed alapana is generally followed by the elaborate kirtana, while the shorter alapanas are followed by shorter and faster kirtanas. This choice is based on a cognition of alapana and kirtana complexity, and not merely on the length of the alapana.

The kirtana presented as the sub-main is also rendered in madhyama-kala or a slightly slower pace. The musician sometimes renders niraval to a line from this composition. The niraval – like the kalpanasvaras for the first kirtana – is not detailed. Also, since the composition is itself rendered in madhyama-kala, the movement of the melody is naturally fast. This leads to the sahitya being quite tightly packed, thereby influencing the niraval possibilities. In general, musicians opt for mel-kala niraval with very little alapana-style niraval and absolutely no sama-kala niraval. The niraval is followed by the rendition of kalpanasvaras. Here, for the first time, the musician presents kalpanasvaras in both kalas (sama and mel). This exploration is more detailed than the one presented for the first kirtana, but not exhaustive. An exhaustive rendition would be that which pushes the musician's creative instinct to its furthest horizon. The sub-main usually presents the alapana, niraval and kalpanasvaras together for the first time in a kutcheri with restrained creativity. This restraint is a result of the fact that a Karnatik kutcheri is focused on two major pieces known as the 'main' and the ragam–tanam–pallavi, abbreviated with typical Tamil-English flair to RTP. The choice of kirtanas, ragas and manodharma contribute to this centralized nature of the kutcheri. Until the main, there is a slow but steady increase in musical complexity.

The next piece has a curious colloquial reference. It is a short kirtana – known as a 'filler' – rendered in madhyama-kala or even faster. As the term suggests, this kirtana does not serve any specific aesthetic purpose, but provides relief between the 'sub-main' and the 'main' and gives a certain momentum to the concert. Not venturing into manodharma aspects, the filler's flight remains easy and brief.

The 'main' is exactly what its name implies; the most important presentation in the concert. It consists of an alapana, kirtana, niraval and kalpanasvara. In this presentation, the alapana explores the possibility of the raga. The alapana rendition uses the step-by-step method, wherein the musician ascends the octave, stopping at important svaras and exploring the musical space around them. This is followed by the violinist presenting her own alapana in the same raga, also following the step-by-step approach. The violinist must, however, limit the duration of her alapana to about half of that of the vocalist. Then a grand kirtana makes its appearance.

Choosing a line which is not too crowded by sahitya, the musician presents every method of rendering a niraval. This is followed by a detailed presentation of kalpanasvaras in both kalas. After multiple rounds of kalpanasvaras between the vocalist and the violinist in the mel-kala, they render the kuraippu. The kuraippu is borrowed from the mathematical reduction played by the percussion artists in a tani avartana, which I have touched upon in the previous chapter. The kuraippu is a way of rendering kalpanasvaras as continuous exchanges between the vocalist and violinist, but slowly reducing the length of their specific turns in every exchange. This reduction will be in sync with the length of the tala. For example, if the tala is adi tala (eight-beat cycle), the first exchange could be one avartana (eight beats) long, then four beats, then two beats. The kuraippu could of course begin with two avartanas, which would begin the reduction at sixteen beats (8x2). This reduction structure is exactly the same as the one followed by percussionists during the tani avartana. Once the reduction ends, the vocalist continues rendering kalpanasvaras, leading to a crescendo, connecting to the line chosen for the kalpanasvaras. I must mention here that sometimes vocalists and violinists also present a korvai as the percussion artists do in the tani avartana. The korvai is rendered as a finale in the kalpanasvaras. Obviously, in the vocalist–violinist exchange, the kuraippu and korvai are rendered not in terms of rhythmic syllables, but in the form of svaras.

At the end of an expansive kalpanasvara for the main, the percussion artists present the tani avartana. When they finish, the same line chosen for niraval and kalpanasvaras in the 'main' is repeated to signal the link between the tani avartana and the kirtana.

Following the main, the musicians may render another 'filler'. This is again a relief between the main and the next presentation, which is the most elaborate manodharma presentation in a kutcheri: RTP. This is a composite presentation that consists of an elaborate alapana, tana, niraval and kalpanasvaras with the focus remaining on truly manodharma sangita. The raga here refers to the alapana, tana to tana, and pallavi to a single-line composition set to the raga in which the alapana and tana are rendered. One is not to confuse this pallavi with the pallavi that is a part of compositional forms. This pallavi is usually of the length of one avartana containing sahitya spread over the tala in a manner that provides ample scope for niraval. Apart from the fact that it has all the main manodharma aspects of Karnatik music presented together, the RTP has some features that distinguish it.

The alapana rendition as part of the RTP sometimes features in the vocalist's presentation of it as two or more distinct sections. Instead of the vocalist's detailed alapana, followed by the violinist's, in the RTP, the vocalist completes one stage, then the violinist responds with her alapana, concluding at the same svara as the vocalist. This is structured in such a manner that the alapana progresses from the lower to the upper octave. The final stage is when the alapana is brought to a conclusion. Sometimes the alapana is presented in four stages.

The matu and dhatu of the pallavi are also closely linked. The structures in pallavis are often complex in terms of the extensions given to each syllable and even include clear arithmetic forms within the melodic structure. The sahitya is simple, but most musicians believe that, linguistically, the pallavi sahitya must contain a verb that connects the adjectives. The lyrical content is again usually devotional or religious, but there are some pallavis that deal with society and love.

The pallavi is divided into two clear parts on the basis of the tala structure. Therefore, the first section (purvanga) ends with the completion of the first anga of the tala, and the uttaranga commences after that first anga. The purvanga and the uttaranga are also melodically divided with a pause. The point where the purvanga ends is called the arudi or muktayi. The melodic pause is an extension of the arudi. After the melodic pause, the uttaranga is rendered, leading back to the beginning of the pallavi. Unlike kirtanas, where the lines begin close to sama (the beginning of the tala), the pallavis can begin anywhere in the tala, making their structure even more complex.

The tala and laya for pallavis are similar to those in compositions. But only in pallavis do we see artists employing talas rendered in four kalai (naalu kalai) or more. Usually, compositions are in not more than two kalai (rendu kalai). Similarly, compositions only use chaturashra or tisra nadai, but pallavis are composed in khanda, mishra or sankirna nadai.

During the rendition of the pallavi, the vocalist and the violinist also include some specific mathematical presentations unique to RTP. In simple terms, every pallavi is composed in one speed (kala). Here I am referring to the specific laya between every beat (kizh, sama, mel), and not generic sense of speed (chauka, madhyama, durita). The musician first renders the pallavi as it is and then in different speeds, keeping the structural form of the line intact. For example, if a pallavi is of a single avartana length in adi tala, with two svaras per beat, sama-kala, the musician will try and render it at a slower speed (that is, one svara per beat), kizh-kala, and a faster pace (four svaras per beat), mel-kala. The varying of speed entails varying the length of every syllable in the pallavi to match it. This may seem effortlessly simple, but the relationship between the sahitya spread and the consciously altered laya has to be maintained with exacting attention to detail. The inclusion of mathematical presentations in the RTP has evolved over the last century, with musicians attempting variations to this idea.

During the renditions of niraval in a pallavi, some musicians believe that there can be absolutely no alterations to the syllabic positions in the tala. This is possibly due to the fact that when the pallavi line is rendered in other speeds, the lengths and position of the syllables have to change in proportion to the speed. A contrary view is that there can be a little flexibility. There is also a view that when niraval is rendered in kirtanas, the meaning of the sahitya has a far more important role than when compared to the niraval in pallavis. These are all perceptions of musicians.

There has been a development over the last century in the rendering of kalpanasvaras in pallavis. Musicians render the kalpanasvaras in other ragas as well, each time returning to the pallavi line and rendering it in the raga being sung, but keeping the structure of the pallavi intact. An unusual method, because in kirtanas, kalpanasvaras are rendered only in the raga of the kirtana. Thus, the raga chosen for the kalpanasvaras changes the melody of the pallavi. This is rendered as an exchange between the vocalist and the violinist, which brings ragamalika svaras or a svara medley into action.

At the conclusion of the kalpanasvaras, percussion artists sometimes present another short tani avartana.

The post-RTP compositions are known as tukkadas. That word, drawn from Hindi, indicates that these compositions are not the main part of the kutcheri. Tukkada literally means 'a piece' or 'a bit' and also suggests a certain lack of importance. Simple compositions are presented after the RTP sans any manodharma. This segment of the concert is expected to provide the audience with a less intensive melodic experience. While presenting the compositions in this section, musicians focus more on the lyrical meaning rather than melodic or rhythmic abstraction. Poetry that was not originally part of the Karnatik music repertoire is presented, including verses from the tiruppugazh and the poetry of various saints. Often, the ragas include those prevalent in Hindustani music. At the same time, it is quite interesting that the pada is always rendered in this section of the kutcheri. The pada is certainly an elaborate and complex compositional form, yet finds place here. The javali is also presented as part of tukkadas, as are the shloka or viruttam, with the lyrical emotion taking precedence over raga emotion. Patriotic and romantic songs are also included in this section. Over the last century, many other compositional types, like bhajans and abhangs, have found way into the repertoire of the Karnatik musician and are presented as part of the tukkada segment in a kutcheri.

The penultimate piece of a kutcheri is the tillana. The tillana is rendered in madhyama-kala and gives the concert a rhythmic conclusion. It also provides a 'high' for the audience as it prepares to leave. The percussion artists present this exciting finish with a great deal of verve and energy. Invoking the Divine, the mangalam concludes the kutcheri.

There are certain other ideas that have also come to be accepted both by musicians and connoisseurs as part of the kutcheri experience. The madhyama-kala is accepted as the most appropriate speed for a successful kutcheri. Chauka-kala kirtana presentations are fewer in general, though there are a few musicians who have rendered predominantly chauka-kala in a kutcheri. Musicians also feel the necessity to present a variety of ragas – ragas with different types of svaras and thus very different collective sounds. Similarly, audiences seem to want variety in tala, vaggeyakara and languages.

All these elements, considered crucial to the success of a concert, both in the eyes of the musician and the connoisseur, have been constructed over the last hundred years.

Solo instrumentalists playing the vina, flute and violin also present Karnatik kutcheris. While each instrument contributes to the music with its own instrumental aesthetics, the kutcheri as such is almost completely structured on the basis of the vocal kutcheri. The presentation of compositions and improvisation by instrumentalists reflect the accepted pattern set by the vocalists.

By and large, musicians have configured their musical priorities to fit into this established pattern. The effect of this presentation format on the aesthetics of Karnatik music has unfortunately not been adequately analysed or discussed seriously by musicians or musicologists. While I have touched upon some important aspects of the format, we still need to critique certain practices that affect the aesthetics of our music.

9

The Karnatik Concert Today
A Critique

view the performance format of Karnatik music as a presentation technique. The musical form and its presentation are closely knit. So, to understand the nature of the form, it is important that we look at the presentation itself. But first, we must recognize an essential fact: the aesthetics of Karnatik music did not begin with an end in view – let alone something so transitory as performance. This does not mean that Karnatik music was not presented in public in the past: it was, but primarily as part of the continuing evolution of its aesthetic identity.

All music has an inner force of emotions. But art music does something with that force that is unique. It creates from its gifts of melody and rhythm the purest abstraction. Karnatik music exists within a certain socio-political environment, and in the course of bringing it into the realm of performance, inevitably certain changes will occur. Over a period of time, the essential qualities of the music may yield ground to its audience and the prevailing listener environment due to social changes, or those that take place within the community of musicians. This can result in a situation where the format compromises the aesthetics to satisfy performance needs. This is the situation we face in Karnatik music today.

The Intent and Direction of a Kutcheri

Let us investigate the situation more closely by asking a fundamental question: is the kutcheri as a whole an integrated aesthetic experience? Or is every item presented in it an individual aesthetic experience? If the latter, we would have to take every item within a kutcheri as aesthetically defined only by itself. We would further infer that a kutcheri is the cumulative aesthetic experience of its individual items and that no overall aesthetic intent governs it.

As presented today, it seems that there are only very superficial connections between each item, which includes the choice of ragas, talas, laya, vaggeyakaras and languages. I say this not as a critique of the format; the question at this stage is whether the kutcheri as a whole needs to have an aesthetic intent and direction. I believe it should, and that the aesthetic intent of a kutcheri should be the fundamental abstractive power of music, not themes or other externals.

Tamil-speaking connoisseurs of Karnatik music use the expression 'kalai kattaradu' (establishing a certain charm) when discussing momentum in a kutcheri. By 'momentum', they mean a certain pace or tempo and the excitement of speed that a concert generates within the first half-hour. It could be argued that as a mere charm that sounds an auspicious note, this initial raciness is transient and therefore unimportant. A close observation of how this term is applied to concerts shows that it is directly connected to the laya of the initial compositions.

This feeling is the contribution of either the madhyama-kala and/or durita-kala, both working through the time-tested mechanism of listener habituation. We seem to want a certain acceleration within a certain range. This makes us feel that the kutcheri has got off to a good start and has excited us enough to listen to the rest of it. But like all performance-related conditioning, I believe that it is the musician who conditions the audience and not the other way round. This has restricted both musicians and connoisseurs from offering and accepting a serious aesthetic presentation in the early stages of the kutcheri.

The first varna is treated as a warm-up piece. The first kirtana is rendered in madhyama-kala with some kalpanasvaras. A kutcheri's initial parts are structured in this fashion to lead into the more serious part: first, the 'main' and second, the RTP. I believe that every art music presentation is deserving and worthy of equal receptiveness. Therefore, the question that needs to be asked is: do we need to build the kutcheri towards just those two presentations, or move beyond them to something greater, more complete? This question should not be taken to imply that musicians working within the two-module format undervalue the other parts of a kutcheri. They do not, but they do tend to focus more on the main and the RTP.

Even though a musician may engage earnestly with every composition, the overall aesthetic intent can still go missing. It is unfortunate that more consideration is given to the kutcheri format than to the possibilities of raga and tala. This means that musicians sacrifice manodharma opportunities in other kirtanas. If this method can be dismantled and reworked, every piece can be presented with extensive manodharma and even in chauka-kala – from the very first piece onwards. This will have the effect of reducing the number of compositions, but it will give to every item the serious treatment it deserves. The sense of kalai kattaradu, both for the musician and the connoisseur, must stem from the musical quality of every piece, and not from this warped sense of momentum.

As explained in the previous chapter, the kutcheri format usually includes a few kirtanas before the main piece and a number of post-RTP compositions. Therefore, a concert of about two-and-a-half hours can have ten to fifteen compositions. This focuses the Karnatik concert on presenting kirtanas, rather than exploring the inherent abstraction.

The kirtanas themselves are, undeniably, important aesthetic creations, but they need to be presented in a manner that enables them to be used as a vehicle for improvisation through the vehicles of matu, dhatu and other techniques. Instead, compositions are usually just presented one after the other. We must pause to ask here: are we meant to just reel off compositions in rapid-fire sequence, or are we meant also to unveil their inherent beauty? The answer, to my mind, is clear. In doing justice to the variety of compositions, we must view them as beautiful aesthetic creations that capture our attention only to set it free in the musical imaginations of the Great Beyond.

The life breath of a composition lies not in its lyrical content, but in the interplay of matu and dhatu within the tala. Every composer has created such art pieces. These pieces must inspire us, as musicians, to explore ideas. I feel that every composition presented in the main section of a concert – until the RTP – must have some type of manodharma. This is, in my opinion, a true tribute to the vaggeyakara. In such a rendering, each creation of art offers every musician the opportunity to perceive and present a new perspective to raga and tala. Compositions that do not inspire this perspective should be considered unfit for Karnatik music.

With the number of kirtanas being presented in them, many concerts today resemble Namasankirtana sessions. This devalues the very essence of Karnatik concert's aesthetic. Since we have allowed a plethora of kirtanas to be presented in a kutcheri, musicians who have not developed their manodharma have perpetuated the limitations of the stereotypical kutcheri. Indeed, all they need to do is present a smattering of manodharma and a number of other compositions. This blurs the very intent of

Karnatik music. If the manodharma techniques are considered to be only supplemental to kirtanas, they run the risk of being treated not as creative improvisations, which they are, but as practised and repetitious presentations. This has become the prevalent practice in Karnatik music today. By allowing the number of kirtanas in a concert to increase, we have abetted in the degeneration of Karnatik music.

The Compositional Forms of Karnatik Music

Karnatik art music has about seven compositional forms, but the kutcheri primarily presents kirtanas. The kirtana is accepted as sophisticated in terms of how the matu and dhatu combine in perfect balance. This observation is especially true of many compositions by the musical Trinity. This is the argument advanced for why the kirtana dominates the kutcheri.

The presumption that a perfect balance is required between matu and dhatu is open to question. In Karnatik music, the matu is part of the dhatu vehicle, not the other way around. Furthermore, since Karnatik music is about raga and tala, even other compositional forms that may not give importance to matu need to be treated with the same amount of consideration. The tana varna, for example, is treated as a warm-up piece in a concert, but is actually an art music composition of the greatest musical value. The sahitya in it is minimal, but the way in which it is used to link together complex melodies is, in musical terms, quite simply exquisite. This fact is ignored due to our preoccupation – bordering on obsession – with the content of sahitya.

Many varnas too are far more complete art pieces than the kirtanas we present. The varna as an aesthetic creation can be presented in any section of the main part of the concert and should be presented with alapana, niraval and kalpanasvara. We do not realize that presenting a varna with niraval offers musicians a huge opportunity because the number of syllables in a line is much less, thus allowing for a great deal of scope to expand the niraval technique. At the same time, the format of the varna gives the niraval itself a very different aesthetic. I must add that even the pada varna can be used as an important art music presentation.

I am also intrigued by the positioning accorded to the important musical form, the pada, in a kutcheri. The pada is like a carving with filigree work all over. It is a complex and grand expression of raga, but it does not find a place in the main section of a concert. The only reason I can think of for this is that the erotic content of a pada's lyrics makes the puritan uncomfortable about presenting them in the main segment and using them for manodharma, especially niraval, as this could mean repeating a line of erotic poetry. Some scholars have associated this lowered status of the pada in the modern kutcheri format to the decline in the devadasi's standing as an artist. Traditionally, the devadasi community was the repository of the padas. Interestingly, the pada varna and the pada are very important compositional forms used in Bharatanatyam. These perspectives were influenced by the social context in which these forms developed – a matter that I will address in some detail in another essay. Like the varna, the pada deserves to be treated as a serious compositional form. The same can be said about the svarajati of the first type. I have also wondered why kutcheris do not use other forms of compositions, like jatisvara (also used in Bharatanatyam) that reflect the essential qualities of art music.

The Order of Presentation

The idea of presenting compositional forms strictly in one specific order and no other – beginning with a varna, a mid-section (the most important one) with only kirtanas and a later section with pada, javali and tillana – does not in any way contribute to the aesthetics of Karnatik music. If anything, it narrows the sweep of the music. As long as a compositional form is contributing to the aesthetics of art music, it deserves to be treated as one. This would mean that the compositional content of a concert can alter every time, as long as the constant focus on the aesthetic intent of abstracting raga and tala is maintained. This will give every concert a unique flavour in its compositional content, yet retain the integrity.

KIRTANAS AS FILLERS

While describing the kutcheri format, I had spoken of some kirtanas presented as 'fillers'. I must say it gives me no pleasure to use that unattractive description, but I see no other way of describing a musical entity that is wedged between two serious renderings. The logic seems to be that we need to present some shorter compositions in between so that the audience and the musician can relax mentally before getting ready for the next serious art piece exploration. Do we really need to present such compositions? What aesthetic contribution does that kirtana make to the music when presented as a filler?

Art music concerts need to be intense and focused. They are not the musical equivalent of a blockbuster film. I am not devaluing the blockbuster film, merely placing both forms in their respective realms. If we understand this, both as musicians and listeners, we would not seek a filler in a concert. Some may say that presenting a kirtana as a filler does not mean disrespect to the kirtana or the kutcheri as such. But as a matter of fact it does, because every musician and member of the audience knows that the musical intensity of a filler is necessarily less than the alapana or the composition that precedes or follows it. Moreover, these fillers are often presented in a faster speed, which is chosen because the previous and next serious kirtana presentations, in which manodharma is included, are relatively slower. Compositions sung at a faster speed cannot but reduce the scope for manodharma. This again reflects a trivializing attitude towards these compositions.

The argument that we need something lighter between the presentation of two art pieces is specious. In no other form of art music are there concerts sprinkled with light numbers serving as relaxants. Every kirtana – small or large, complex or simple – needs to be presented with equal seriousness of intent. If the composition does not provide the aesthetic content to be part of Karnatik music, we must be bold enough to exclude it.

Having already critiqued manodharma techniques, the method of presenting them within the currently accepted kutcheri format brings to light another set of critical issues that need to be discussed.

ALAPANA

The alapana is presented before a kirtana, rendered by the vocalist and followed by the violinist. Then the violinist presents an independent alapana of the same raga.

Does the violinist need to shadow the vocalist? Does this really enhance the aesthetics of the alapana, or are we conditioned to believe that it does? This question becomes particularly relevant when we consider that, as listeners, we do not have an issue with listening to a violin alapana without a following, or even when the main performer is a flautist or a vina artist. Why then does a vocalist need a violinist following her alapana phrases?

I see no reason why it is needed at all. The gaps present between phrases may, in fact, contribute to absorbing the rendered phrase without the violinist's reiteration. It is also almost impossible for the violinist to reproduce the exact phrase rendered by the vocalist. An attempt to do so sometimes leads to a change in the melodic content. If the change is distinct, it will register in the audience's mind, of course, but even a small change, whether or not perceivable to the listener, affects the creative flow of the vocalist. The parallel flow of two manodharmas is not in the interest of either musician. One may argue that, instead of being hindered, the vocalist could in fact be inspired by this change.

But we should remind ourselves that the vocalist's alapana at mid-performance is not an occasion for the lending or borrowing of inspiration. It is the vocalist's sole privilege and prerogative. The alapana is purely the vocalist's personal expression, which needs to be experienced in its complete, composite form without alterations from anyone else. In some cases of extremely insensitive violinists, the whole phrase rendered by the vocalist is changed or even ignored, and the violinist plays something altogether different. Unfortunately, as audiences, we have reached a point of such imperviousness that this too is accepted as part of the presentation. We are oblivious to the problems it creates to the aesthetic experience. There are very few violinists who can actually reproduce the vocalist's phrases almost exactly as rendered.

There are, as we have seen, two alapanas that are presented before a composition: one by the vocalist and the other by the violinist. Are the two connected? Should they be connected? These are two very important questions if we are to understand the aesthetics of alapana presentation in a kutcheri. The instinctive reaction would be to say that they are connected, as they are both rendering the same raga. But does that define connectedness?

Each alapana is a composite presentation, with melodic lines driven by the emotional abstraction of the raga. This would mean that every alapana is not just the raga, but also a creation from the raga. When two such alapanas are presented with very different points of imaginative origination and intent, their so-called connection becomes obscure, even non-existent. The two alapanas are individual melodic identities that reflect very different ideas of the ragas. In such a situation, why present two alapanas? If the violinist can direct his alapana towards the intent experienced in the vocalist's alapana, then this form of presentation can, in theory, work. In reality, however, this rarely happens. When we hear two alapanas, we actually experience two different melodic forms one after another. The other serious problem is that the alapana rendered by the violinist can and often does impair the aesthetic edifice built by the vocalist. There are great exceptions among violinists who so interiorize the vocalist's manobhava as to not only follow it with self-effacing yet skilful fidelity, but even anticipate it. However, these rare exceptions do not prove the rule. It would be better if the vocalist presents an independent alapana of a raga, and the violinist presents an alapana of another raga in the course of the kutcheri.

The inherent possibility of a conflict in the two alapanas also leads us to question the connection between the alapana and the kirtana presented. There are many views to this. Some scholars believe that the alapana must reflect the melodic interpretation of the raga as encapsulated in the chosen kirtana. Others think that not only should the alapana reflect the melodic approach of the kirtana, but also the larger perspective of the vaggeyakara towards the raga. Some argue that the kirtana needs to be chosen before the rendition of the alapana. Others believe that the alapana must be the driving force in deciding the kirtana, which would mean that the kirtana is selected after the rendition of the alapana. In either case, if there is a conflict between the aesthetic intent of the alapana of the vocalist and that of the violinist, the link between the alapana and the kirtana that we seek is completely broken. Some may say that there need not be any connection between the alapana and the kirtana, in which case why even present them together? These are all serious questions regarding the aesthetics of an alapana that require introspection.

Does the alapana need to be presented only as preface to a kirtana? An alapana is a complete, stand-alone composite raga exploration. It represents a manodharma form that is not connected in its presentation to any composed form. The connection lies in the ideas that the musician draws from various compositions. The alapana itself completes the idea of the chosen raga in its presentation, which in turn contains various types of movements, pauses, ranges and speeds. Taking this view, I believe that an alapana can stand by itself as a singular presentation sans a kirtana in the same raga to follow. This also relieves the alapana of the necessity of being connected aesthetically to a kirtana.

At an experiential level, after rendering an alapana, I have often felt that I had finished singing all that I could present of the raga on the day, making the presentation of a composition after the alapana redundant for me. It is even worse when vocalists feel compelled to render niraval and kalpanasvara for the kirtana, making the whole experience laboured.

NIRAVAL

This is an ignored manodharma technique in the kutcheri format. Almost always, the niraval is presented as a small exercise before the musician moves into rendering kalpanasvaras. The various methods and styles in which a niraval can be rendered are unexplored, causing it to sound almost like the sangatis, which are part of the kirtana. There are two issues to discuss in this context. Does niraval rendition always need to cover all the various techniques? This question is especially relevant when niraval is presented for the main piece. As this is the focus kirtana – irrespective of whether the raga, kirtana melody, laya and style suit a certain approach to niraval – many musicians feel compelled to render it. Once again, I must bring up the matter of aesthetic intent. There are many situations where the flow of the compositions demands that mel-kala niraval is not rendered, but kutcheri format compulsions make us act otherwise. Lines chosen for niraval and the styles of rendering should be dictated by the aesthetics of the composition, rather than the kutcheri format or the position of this piece within the format.

The violinist's method of playing niraval also needs scrutiny. When violinists render the niraval, more often than not, the position of the various syllables within the chosen line are not emphasized. This means that the violinist only presents melodic lines in the raga without any actual connection to the aesthetic construction. This destroys the basic framework of the niraval form. This problem becomes even more accentuated when mel-kala niraval is rendered. When the movements are rigid, emphasizing every svara behind the melodic movement, it ends up sounding more like mel-kala kalpanasvaras, rather than mel-kala niraval. It follows then that the mel-kala kalpanasvaras presented later in the same compositions sound repetitive.

KALPANASVARA

In the context of a kutcheri, the climax is achieved during the rendition of the mel-kala kalpanasvara. The speed and flurry of svaras in a continuous string creates a huge impact on the audience, often leading to explosive applause. Joining in this musical high is voluble percussion support. This aspect of kalpanasvara singing has, over time, affected the basic aesthetic elements of the form. Kalpanasvaras must be guided by the aesthetics of the raga, svara enunciation, tala, laya and the point in the composition to which they are dovetailed. But in the context of a kutcheri, the influence is primarily the permutations and combinations possible from the bare svaras of the raga and the excitement they can consequently generate. This is specific to mel-kala kalpanasvara. The other fallout of this effect is that sama-kala kalpanasvaras are given very little importance, in spite of the space they provide for expression of the various manifestations of the raga's svaras.

Another feature of kalpanasvara rendition over the last half a century of kutcheri music is the complex mathematical structures presented in the form. While this definitely has its appeal, the hijacking of the aesthetic beauty of kalpanasvaras and the overuse of mathematical calculations has resulted in raga aesthetics being treated with scant respect. Many of these calculations are pre-planned and hence, to some extent, rehearsed. This is alright if they enhance the kalpanasvara form and provide a new aesthetic dimension to this manodharma technique. Unfortunately, we have now reached a stage where free-flowing kalpanasvara renditions have been almost replaced by pre-planned mathematical combinations. This has also, lamentably, facilitated musicians who have not mastered the art of improvisational kalpanasvara rendition, and instead resort to presenting rehearsed mathematical calculations in the garb of kalpanasvaras.

TANA

The issues relating to 'following' that were discussed in the context of alapanas are applicable here as well. There is also the question of whether tana can be presented as an individual piece, without being connected to the RTP or even the alapana. The tana is rendered after the alapana, because in a way it is an aesthetic flow between a manodharma form that is sans rhythm to a semi-rhythmic form, leading to the pallavi which is structured in tala. Yet, the tana by itself is a complete form and does not need to be presented before a pallavi or after an alapana. By itself, it can present a unique perspective to the raga through its rhythmic melodic lines, which are not contained within a tala structure, and leave the audience with a specific aesthetic experience. There are also many compositions that display a gait that suits the rendition of the tana, rather than an alapana, before they are presented. The aesthetic connectivity in form is what ought to be considered here.

Percussion

Another dramatic change over the last century is the way percussion techniques have come to influence a kutcheri. Recordings of concerts from around the 1940s help us to trace these changes. Some of the older percussion styles, though seemingly simplistic, were clearly based on the compositions themselves and manodharma, or to put it another way, on the aesthetics that governed the music. Over the last century, we see the evolution of percussion styles based on personal technique, dexterity and intelligence, without reference to the aesthetics of the music being presented by the vocalist or violinist. When this happens, the music is viewed from the percussive perspective. To clarify, the percussion perspective is not the same as the tala or laya perspective. Music is built on raga and tala and this is applicable to all musicians, whether vocal, instrumental or accompanying. But when a percussive view is taken of the music being rendered or heard, it is the individual's style and technique that takes centre stage. The focus is on enhancing the artist's own dexterity, mathematical patterns and, importantly, presence. This has far-reaching effects on the aesthetics of the music, which ends up taking a back seat. In many cases, we find that the melodic elements of the music, whether compositional or improvisational, are only used as references to the expression of the percussionist. This dominance affects the aesthetics of the music. I am using the word 'aesthetics' here as a technical term, not as a preference. This development of percussive style also springs from a core focus on the performance format and its intended effect.

THE MRDANGA

The dominance of the mrdanga in a kutcheri has changed the laya of the selected compositions. We find that it is not the aesthetic form of the composition that has influenced the choice of laya. Instead, the accompaniment techniques that have been established by mrdanga artists have conditioned us to present certain compositions in certain speeds. In the long run, this has changed the melodic experience of the composition.

Another interesting development is the addition of sangatis in kirtanas on the basis of percussion patterns rather than matu and dhatu. Similarly, niraval and kalpanasvara aesthetics have been influenced by mrdanga techniques.

The dominance of mathematical calculations in the presentation of kalpanasvaras is a direct influence of the percussionists. Vocalists and violinists today employ extremely complicated mathematical melodic presentations. These ideas are born out of the mathematical presentations of the percussionists, and have changed the experience of kalpanasvaras.

Interestingly, it has also influenced the method in which alapanas are rendered. This is a subtle point, where the alapana phrases today are not just melodic phrases of the raga as perceived by the vocalist, but formed as specific patterns with a certain number of svaras that are built upon regularly. It is a technique that could cause the alapana to lose its natural flow, and become a contrived construction of patterns, leading to a loss of abstraction. In some cases, it leads to phrases that alter the aesthetics of the raga. Also, when this pattern is overdone, the phraseological connections inherent in the raga are lost. The alapana then begins to resemble a rockery of svara structures.

These basic questions and issues are not about enjoyment, but the effect that alterations can have on the aesthetics of manodharma techniques. We know that aesthetics is part of a continuum through which the various aspects of music have got their identity and intent within the spectrum of Karnatik music. While mrdanga accompaniment would naturally influence the melodic and rhythmic content, it has to come from a position of respect to the aesthetic identity of the music. Regrettably, these influences have come from the standpoint of the kutcheri presentation rather than the music – a fact that has had a far-reaching effect on Karnatik music.

THE TANI AVARTANA

The word 'tani' is derived from Tamil to indicate singular and distinctive qualities, rather than separate or exclusive. This meaning is important to bear in mind for reasons I shall presently go into.

The tani avartana has also fallen into a certain template due to the pressure of expectations from a performance. There is almost a fixed method of developing the tani avartana now. The reason for this is that a certain excitement is felt to be a necessary part of the tani. Therefore, it is driven towards the final climax, to lead back to the kirtana. The 'tani' consists of numerous self-contained sections that are gradually built on for the final effect. The problem with this approach is that the tani avartana structure is also not based on the aesthetics of the music. As melody gives pause to its stream, the tani avartana should draw from the emotions shaped by laya and tala and dazzle us with the magic of percussion. As the tani climaxes, melody returns unobtrusively to where it left. Thus is the concert's musical continuity enriched and maintained.

Today, the tani is not so much an integrated part of the whole presentation, as it is a way to achieve a conditioned end-of-thrill. Every emotion that the tani avartana evokes must, ideally, be internally induced. A sense of excitement ought to be a result of a seriously developed pattern. A musical high can be achieved by the sheer investment of the musician towards the expression of the underlying aesthetic beauty of his presentation. The musician is as much in a state of wonder at the creation as is the audience. In a tani avartana, this wonderment can be of its mathematics, the patterns of rhythms, tonal variations and the construction of the tani. None of this is independent of the musicality of the concert and the specific composition. The intention in the musician's mind is not the end result of excitement, but the very rhythmic form in which he is engaged. But today, percussion musicians have a predetermined attitude to what needs to be induced in the minds of the listener.

Of course, this is true not just of tani avartana, but most aspects of kutcheris.

What is the exact connection between the tani avartana and the composition to which it is dovetailed? There are musicians who suggest that the tani avartana is an extension of the kirtana. What this means in terms of aesthetics is not very clear. If it is an extension, is the connection emotional, constructional or laya-related? Emotionally, the connection is only to the tonality of the initial section of the tani avartana. If the composition were to be sung with a great deal of vigour, the tani would begin with a strong tonality. In the case of a tender handling by the vocalist, the tani avartana would begin with soft, deft touches. But this too disappears very fast. By the time the second section of the tani is reached, there is no emotional connection. Even this so-called emotional connection is superficial, and does not address the idea of emotional connectivity that goes beyond tonality towards rhythmic constructions that can abstractively emote. In terms of construction or laya, the tani avartana does not reflect the kirtana of the chosen line. Even if it does, it is only for the first few moments. Soon, the tani avartana only relates to the tala and nothing more. Therefore, tani avartanas for two different adi tala (two kalai) compositions rendered in a similar laya can be exactly the same. The complex laya relationship that exists within every kirtana and the chosen line that connects the tani avartana are not always part of the tani avartana explorations as they should be. This raises a question: what is the relationship between the tani avartana and the kirtana, or the specific line? Maybe there needs to be no connectivity, and the tani can not only be presented as an independent piece, but actually stand alone and have its own identity that can yet be connected to the overall abstractive aesthetic of the concert. But if it is connected to a composition, one needs to inquire into what sense of connectivity we seek.

If the tani avartana was focused on using its various components to enhance every rhythmic movement within the framework and to explore possibilities as an end in itself, the experience would be very different. The format of the tani will then automatically be dynamic, because the chosen kirtana and even the raga will influence its texture. In this approach, every rhythmic and mathematical pattern will be explored. This may or may not result in a climax, but it will ensure that every tani avartana contributes a different aesthetic relevance in a kutcheri. Excitement must be the result of a pursuit of the aesthetics of the form rather than appreciation for the presentation. My critique of the tani avartana admits of exceptions, but they are exactly that – exceptions.

Tukkadas and 'Lighter' Compositions

The post-tani avartana section of a kutcheri today consists of various types of compositions collectively described as 'tukkadas' – javalis, tiruppugazhs, abhangs, bhajans and so on – that have been part of different musical traditions from across India. What is the real role of such a segment? Musicians and connoisseurs feel that after a concert of over two hours, it is time for 'lighter' compositions towards the end. The word 'lighter' indicates that these items will not be heavy in manodharma and will be in ragas that are not heavy on gamakas, especially the weighty kampita gamaka. The underlying assumption is that the audience needs to go back home relaxed.

Quite simply, I am not convinced. Traditionally, the pada, which is an intricate compositional form, was also part of this section, indicating that serious musical creations used to be part of this segment. Increasingly, though, the pada is rarely presented in kutcheris. I think rendering a variety of compositions, including the so-called lighter art music pieces, is fine as long as we are willing to treat each one as 'equal music'. But many of these compositions are not art pieces, thus leading to a serious conflict between the aesthetic of Karnatik music and the impact that a kutcheri is currently expected to have.

Do non-art pieces have a role to play in a kutcheri? Many believe that by excluding such musical creations we are only cosseting the art form. But their inclusion does not add to the musical value of the concert. The melodic beauty of many of these compositions is not in question, but that cannot be reason enough for their inclusion. Any musical piece that is part of a Karnatik kutcheri must possess the qualities of a pure art piece, where qualities of raga and tala have gone beyond lyrical content, beautiful melody and a fixed tala structure. It may not be easy to understand this, and indeed one may wonder if this is not true of all compositions. But the fact is that certain compositions are not embedded with the textural layering of a pure art piece. It is only the pure art creations that can open avenues of natural abstraction in the minds of the listeners and the musician. The other compositions tend to result in creating experiences of lilt rather than melody, and the tinsel of sound rather than the gold of aesthetic abstraction. Linguistic meaning, temporal nostalgia and religious construction merely flirt with art music.

An art music presentation has no room for light miscellanies. Hence, the choice of these end-of-concert compositions must be more judicious than it is today. A Karnatik kutcheri by its nature must have an intensity. To tinker with it at any stage of the concert is not in order. A change in mindset is necessary for the kutcheri to remain relevant to the aesthetics of the form. The notion that the audience cannot be taxed mentally towards the end of a kutcheri speaks of a certain casualness towards this section of a concert. It also underestimates the propensity of the audience for musical experiences of a 'serious' kind. A kutcheri is not a variety entertainment show or a circus presentation, where you need to experience the frown of the lion and the snigger of the clown.

Over the years, the length of the tukkada section of the concert has also increased. As most of the compositions presented relate to everyone at a linguistic and personally emotive level, musicians have taken advantage of this. Musicians use a pleasing tukkada section to erase a poor interpretation or failure to realize pure art. The result has been a manifold increase in the focus on 'light' tukkadas.

Audience Appreciation

The audience appreciation of Karnatik music is also an important part of the concert. While it is easy for musicians to blame the audience for many of the issues generated from the kutcheri, the real problems lie with the perception of the musician community. What the audience expects and is conditioned to expect is based on what has been presented to it as Karnatik music. The present template is our success formula. Skills are enhanced and techniques developed that lead to satisfying our perception of the kutcheri – a perception that comes from a performance perspective rather than a musical perspective. Breaking away from this will not only deepen our understanding of the music as musicians and audiences, but will also change our perception of musicianship.

Back to the Kutcheri

It is imperative for us to question our notions of a kutcheri and our motives when performing. The applause is a performing musician's bane. It is a drug, and an addictive one. Through years of performance, musicians have mastered the art of generating applause. In fact, we have trained and retrained the audience in this direction. We need to realign our priorities and give the audiences better experiences of Karnatik music. Every element of the music that is aligned to generate the required applause must be re-examined. Alapana style, kirtana renditions, niraval, kalpanasvaras and tani avartana should not be governed by how they can elicit applause from an audience. Applause or any other form of appreciation must be generated by the stature of the music. It will come as a result of the musical form rather than performance manipulation. A musician who experiences this understands it. Musicians may react by saying that they are always singing ragas and kirtanas. Yest, they are, but I am speaking not of habitual practice, but introspective practice.

Such introspection must generate in us an urge to understand why Karnatik music is where it is today. This is not to throw away the past or accept it in toto. We have to realize that, in Karnatik music, we have been given a unique art music form.

To be true to it, we must transcend personal predispositions and social preconditions.

It would be unfair to say that the kutcheri does not represent Karnatik music. It does to an extent, but over the years the kutcheri has altered the aesthetics of many components within the Karnatik idiom. Today, the music does not represent itself; the kutcheri represents it. By 'today', I mean the last hundred years or so. What we experience today is not isolated from the past. The present kutcheri format is about a hundred years old. The performance of Karnatik music in the context of organizations, ticketed audiences and the rest is very closely linked to the way the presentation format has evolved during this era.

It is necessary for us to revisit the kutcheri format, the way manodharma is understood and treated, the way the various aspects of the music are presented and, importantly, the attitude of musicians towards music and performance. The observations in these pages may lead some to ask: are these not minor issues? If one is to analyse them and the deep repercussions they have on Karnatik music, one will realize that they are not cosmetic problems. This reassessment I seek may result in Karnatik music being presented in different formats. But such change must originate from an internalization of the music's aesthetics, not a search for novelty. Only then can we make our meaningful contribution to Karnatik music's evolving aesthetics.

10

Voicing the Note

The human voice is a beautiful contrivance. As with the eyes, it expresses the innermost emotions and thoughts of the human being. The very tone of a person's voice can tell you a lot about him. You do not need to see the person and he need not be near you, yet you understand from his voice more than just the linguistic meaning of his words or the sound that you hear.

Sound as music, by its nature, can only be experienced, not seen or held – it is an intangible. In this intangible, almost mystic nature of the voice's beautiful progeny, music, lies its capacity to abstract its own meaning from life. This is very different from visual abstraction. You can stand in front of a painting or sculpture for a long time and let your eyes constantly receive the painting.

Music, and the perception of abstraction in it, does not work that way. A line of music once sung is gone, but is still alive in your mind. The faculty of hearing completes its work very quickly. The voice is both a natural instrument and the vehicle of this abstraction. There is no external transfer of the mind's abstraction, neither does the music emanate from an external source. This gives the voice a personal nature that makes it different from any instrument. This may be the reason why, in India's artistic traditions, the voice has been regarded as music's prime vehicle.

The musician or the listener never sees the physical seat of this instrument, the voice box. All one sees is the movement of the lips, mouth and tongue. Yet, the music that is born from it conveys an emotion that rings true in the listener's or musician's own being. While music from the voice is very intimate, it does not speak automatically to everyone.

Awareness of the Voice

One has to become aware of the voice, not only in a technical sense, but intimately – the sort of intimacy we have with a plant that we nurture. We do not just water the plant and watch the flowers bloom. There is something more: an emotional relationship, even if the reciprocity which that expression implies is not evident. What is it that gives us this feeling? It is a deep sense of awareness of the plant and, through that, ourselves. This awareness makes us spend that extra second with the plant, to watch and experience. This is the kind of relationship that we need with the voice.

We don't just train it, we actually listen to it: the sounds, movements, emotions that it conveys. This awareness is about knowing oneself through the voice.

In music, awareness comes with listening; it is something we need to develop. I would like to differentiate the act of hearing from listening. Listening contains the awareness of what is being conveyed. Meaning lies not only in the words. As we listen to our voice, like with the plant, we become aware of the meaning behind every musical sound, every movement, every pause and every breath. This opens us to the world of pure music. This music is in every person and we understand it only if we understand our voice, the 'first messenger'.

Training the Voice

The voice needs to be trained not only to produce musical sound, but also musical emotion. Conversely, training for a student of vocal music is not only about the music, but also about developing the voice so that it can be the right sort of vessel.

First, the shruti of the voice has to be determined. This is gauged by listening to the student sing, rather than a specific technical analysis. The pitch, tone and texture of the voice as it moves across the different octaves give a good teacher a way of determining the ideal shruti for the student.

Most students start learning Karnatik music early (between the ages of seven and ten). In general, the shruti of a young student would be about 5 or 5½ (G or G#). To clarify, these are exact pitch positions that have been identified. One of these pitches is chosen as tonic for the singer. The choice of the pitch indicates the exact position of the madhya sthayi sa (tonic). The sa would be at G if that were the shruti.

The major 'voice difference' between boys and girls is that a boy's voice changes, or breaks, once he attains puberty. This is a crucial period in the life of a young student. In simple terms, the pitch of the voice lowers (usually settling around 1½ or 2 which is C# or D) and the texture changes. During this process, the boy loses control over his voice, often going out of pitch, cracking, all of which makes singing very difficult. Even in boys who do not sing, these changes are audible. But they are much more evident and critical for a person who is learning to sing.

During this transition period – which could last anywhere from a year to a few years – the student has to be extremely careful about the kind and extent of practice. He must maintain a delicate balance between the right practice techniques and the right amount of rest. If the individual's training has been good, the shruti will remain the same for a couple of decades or more. While girls do not go through this breaking of the voice, all musicians, irrespective of gender, need to lower their shruti between the age of forty-five and fifty as a natural result of ageing.

Training the voice to cover a minimum of 2½ octaves, which includes one octave in the madhya sthayi and half an octave each in the lower or mandara sthayi and higher or tara sthayi, is important. While singing, the voice must sound as one continuous form in all octaves. The voice may change in texture as the musician moves across octaves, but it is essential that this is seamless, giving the voice completeness. The voice must be able to render all the gamakas and phrases that are essential to convey the aesthetics of Karnatik music. The training involves practising specific exercises.

There are two parts to any voice training: that of the individual and the music. It is essential that every individual understands his own voice as much as the music. Such an understanding will instinctively give him techniques to keep the voice healthy and still produce the aesthetics needed for the music. But it is also true that all voices may not have the same felicity, pliability or speed. This reiterates why the musician must understand her own voice. It is only through such understanding that she will be able to use the strengths of her voice to present Karnatik music in a personalized way. Every voice is naturally different and with the help of musical training comes into its own. In this process, the guru's role in guiding students through the various stages and giving them a perspective towards understanding their own voice cannot be undervalued.

Training the voice is as much about flexibility and ease as it is about being able to produce the aesthetics that drive Karnatik music. It is crucial that every teacher and student arrives at this cognition. The varying texture and volume of every voice gives each musician a different aesthetic expression special to his own music. The voice, when directed towards Karnatik music must be driven towards the Karnatik 'sound' – its body of aesthetics, which contains the complex manifestations of the svara, raga, syllables and the demands of tala and laya. If this is not fulfilled, the training of the voice serves no purpose. Simultaneously, the student and guru must keep in mind the nature of the individual's voice and focus on increasing its potential.

The use of the voice in Karnatik music is both musical and syllabic. In fact, the uses are a unity. When a musical sound is produced with lyrics, the pronunciation is not an independent poetic identity, but a form of the music. The way the same words are pronounced may often vary. This does not mean that the sahitya is being mispronounced, but that the musical intonation is modifying the poetic sound. The moment we try to pronounce the words exactly as we would in a non-musical form, we notice that there is a certain harshness in the sound of the music. This is the product of a disconnect between the music and the poetry. While melody is prime in Karnatik music, sahitya is not secondary to it, but very much a part and parcel of it.

Sahitya as a part of music is a completely different entity from sahitya as only poetry. We should also keep in mind that the vaggeyakara conceived of sahitya as being part of a musical expression. This establishes again the fact that matu and dhatu are one inseparable creation. The musician's voice has to translate this into music.

Although every voice is an individual identity, it is necessary to use certain common ways of employing the voice in order to express the aesthetics of Karnatik music. A phrase which gurus commonly use while addressing students is 'sing with an open mouth'. This is often misunderstood to mean shouting, whereas what is intended is that the vocalist must open his mouth wide to allow the sound of the voice full rein. The reason for this advice is that the habit of using the voice in a stifled fashion could lead to strain – quite apart from what that might do to the music! In the initial years of singing, the student may sound a little loud, but that is fine. Subtlety and modulation can be developed over time.

However, if the basic sound release is not appropriate, the singer may never achieve the full potential of his voice. For a person to sing comfortably, the voice, mouth and tongue are not the only parts that need to work harmoniously. Vocalization in music involves the diaphragm, chest, lungs, shoulders, spine, head and neck. Actually, the whole body sings, not just the voice. This understanding brings about not only a completely different perspective to voice training but also to the music. Total involvement – both physical and mental – is required for music. The physical act of singing cannot be separated from the stimuli that inspire music. Every musician has to be mentally free, you could even say 'empty'. Empty is not a negative word; it describes a state of mind without any pressures or pre-existing notions. When the musician sings with this free mind, every musical phrase becomes a discovery, to be shared in a state of sublime rapture. In this journey, the voice will be relaxed and every trigger from the mind will be expressed comfortably, weaving beautiful musical motifs.

Breathing and the Voice

Breathing is the life of music. Most people discuss breathing only in terms of holding one's breath and learning where to breathe in music. In life, breathing is an involuntary action influenced by the state of our mind. Thoughts trigger reactions in the body, including the motion and extent of our breath. We clearly notice changes in our breathing patterns based on these stimuli. Anger, excitement and fear all change our breathing, and the source for these changes is the mind. In a state of complete silence, our breath is not noticeable; it blends with the silence.

A state of silence is not inaction or passivity. This discussion centres on the quality of the action – of involved action. This is a natural state, not forced by external or internal pressures. The whole self contributes to the act involved. That is how the action of breathing ought to function during singing. Our breath is part of the music. The melody flows with the breath and the tone of our voice changes according to the needs of the music. Breathing patterns influence the texture required in our voice. When the mind is completely immersed in the creation of music, the mind, voice and breath are in unison. This is when breathing becomes the music. Many voice-related issues can be handled by dealing with an individual's breathing. In order to do this, one has to work with the mind and make the individual aware of his breathing, thereby bringing the individual to a state where the mind is clear of everything else. This internalization leads to an open mind, translating its state into the voice and music.

The act of breathing requires the diaphragm, chest and lungs to regulate breath appropriately. While singing, breathing patterns contribute immensely to enunciation, pronunciation and musical aesthetics. To get the right musical intonation, one must be able to alter the breathing style naturally, in order to achieve the needed musical sound. This is usually imbibed directly from the guru. As a result, when the guru has bad vocalization, the student imbibes that as well. In these cases, the students need to spend time in understanding their own voice, and expression and take corrective measures to let the voice flower.

For beautiful music, one needs to learn the act of breathing, yet forget about breathing. The Sanskrit word 'prana' most beautifully embodies the idea of breath, as the spirit of life.

Experiencing One's Voice

As the voice moves through various octaves (lower to higher), a singer will feel as if the sound source within her is moving from the chest to the top of the head. This description is experiential, rather than technical, but it is not a false feeling, as it is associated with the movement of the voice-related apparatus. It is also true that the texture of the voice changes. In a great singing voice, the textural changes are seamless. A singer must also be aware that the texture that she herself hears while singing is very different from what is heard by the receiver. This difference is because we also hear and feel our own voice from inside our body, not just through our ears. The voice texture heard when the sound seems to come from the chest or even the back of the head/ neck is what we call 'heavy'. The texture heard when we feel that the voice comes from the top of the head is what we refer to as 'false voice'. There is nothing false about that voice – singers use various voice mechanisms that are naturally at our disposal. All musicians, including Karnatik vocalists, use the false voice. But in Karnatik music, the aesthetics demands a vocal texture that is closer to heavy.

There is definitely a shade of false voice when Karnatik musicians sing at the higher octaves, but much less than what is heard from, for instance, singers of film music. This is purely a demand of the idiom and its aesthetics. It is also interesting that the terms light and heavy, which describe physical experiences, are used for a purely acoustic experience. These words indicate what we feel when we hear these voices. They are also indicators that the aesthetic experience of Karnatik music is 'heavy'.

Music and the voice are inseparable. True enough. But was the voice created only so that human being could sing or, for that matter, speak? This question has been raised by many scholars. Some feel that the voice is there because singing is as natural as speaking. Be that as it may, to me, the voice was created for expression. Expression by itself entails more than words and their meaning. It includes every sound that the voice can produce to convey experience, emotion, thought, understanding and idea. Within this, art music is the most creative form of aural sound. The vehicle for these expressions is the intimate voice, and in this connectivity exists the world of voice. The voice is Karnatik music. This intrinsic relationship is why every musician – not just the vocalist – must learn to sing. In singing, the musician discovers music, voice and, with utter clarity, the person within.

11

A Matter of Style

The word 'bani' is integral to the vocabulary of Karnatik music. Connoisseurs can easily identify musicians by their bani in concerts.

What is bani? The word, derived from the Sanskrit, literally means 'voice'. But in its application, it refers to a school of musical training and presentation that developed through years of practice and refining, a school that has a 'voice' of its own, a musical idiom that can be called its very own. Unfortunately, bani does not have an equivalent in English, nothing that captures the complete sense of the word.

A phrase often used to describe or explain bani is 'style': a specific musician's style that is followed by his or her students and other musicians. Even connoisseurs and musicians do not look for a larger meaning for bani. That being the case, every evolved musician – that is, one who expresses the individual self through music – may be said to represent a bani. At the same time, not all individual styles are relatable to a bani. To put it plainly, bani is a distinct style, but the word is not used for all distinct styles. In this unconscious discrimination, we are qualifying the idea of bani. So is there something more than style in a bani?

In Karnatik music, style refers to the musician's individual expression of music. This includes vocalization or playing technique, musical intonations, style of rendering compositions and improvisation, the method of presenting kutcheri, as also raga and tala interpretations. A critical element in all this is the training and the influences that a musician has internalized while acquiring this musicianship.

When a student begins her musical journey, the guru's influence determines her music. The student's view of the musical world is based on what is taught, imbibed and experienced with the guru. At this stage, the student is not in a position to look beyond. I would even say that it is essential that she does not. In this initial single-stimulus journey, the student acquires a keen sense of musical aesthetics from the guru. This is necessary, so that the mind can develop the ability to later receive other stimuli and build on this foundation.

An important note here. In the past, most gurus did not permit their students to listen to concerts of other musicians. While this has often been interpreted as a sign of rivalry and control, the practice could well have had a deeper significance. It is not possible for any student of music to understand numerous styles within the context of their own unless they have come to terms with the one in which they are being trained. Multiple signals from various musicians, if they come prematurely, can lead to a great deal of confusion in a student's mind. This is similar to what we face in society today; we are surrounded by so many stimuli that it is impossible to distinguish one from the other. And so it is that we think of both a person standing on his head for twenty-four hours and a rendition of raga bhairavi by a vidvan as 'awesome'. Until the student's music has reached a point where technique and musical quality have become a part of his person, he struggles with the onslaught of varied stimuli.

When the student starts listening to other musicians as well, changes occur in the dynamics of learning. First, by listening to a large number of musicians, the student is exposed to a melange of styles and approaches to Karnatik music. Soon, she begins to acquire likes and dislikes of her own. Certain styles are more appealing, the techniques of certain musicians are captivating. Slowly but steadily, the individual's new selectiveness rigidifies. The process of acquiring musical preferences is consolidated by other influences coming in along the way and impacting her listening culture. A new sensibility begins to be moulded through her fresh relationship with the 'other' styles she has come to admire. She starts making associations between them and thereby evolves a unique perception: one that is rooted in what was taught by the guru and is also being shaped by the interaction of the styles that are now capturing the mind.

Around this time, the student may take her first steps into the sphere of performance. Once this occurs, her whole idea of Karnatik music is completely transformed. The experience of performing gives rise to perspectives of presentation that she never would have thought about earlier. Getting up on the stage and communicating musical ideas to the audience is a new experience for her. How does musical thought translate into musical action? Dealing with this challenge hones the young musician's sensibilities. At the same time, the musician is also interacting constantly with her contemporaries. Musical thoughts and ideas are being exchanged, likes and dislikes are discussed, conditioning is questioned and even challenged. Peer influence and interactions play an important role in shaping musical ideas, and also contribute to the development of a performing artist.

In this process of evolving as a musician, let us not forget, the individual is also evolving as a human being. She gains a certain self-assurance and a clear sense of identity. This new-found assurance then reveals itself through her music. In the process, the various stimuli that were once external influences get internalized to become part of her musical expression and an integral part of what is now clearly discernable as her personality.

This hypothesis of an individual's very singular evolution can be challenged because in every style it is possible to detect the influence of another musician. To outward appearances, this contrary view seems to have merit. But what this overlooks is that when a certain phrase or approach, externally identifiable as an influence, enters a truly evolving musician's style, it does not remain independent of the individual's musical sensibility. It blends into the musician's larger representation. Because the derivation is so overt as to draw attention to itself, we may not notice that blending. In all distinct styles, external influences become integral to the individual and are not aesthetically what they were before this metamorphosis. Once this occurs, it is the unique musical expression of a musician who, as a musician and a human being, is also evolving.

Style and Musical Manner

At this point, we must differentiate style from manner and mannerisms. This is a very real danger, as individual mannerisms are part of the music. Mannerisms are guided not by musical expression, but by the individual's physical expression, such as gesticulation, facial expression or even unusual ways of intonation. Though all this is part of the individual's music, it needs to be separated from musical style, which is a much deeper phenomenon and relates to a critical understanding of kirtana renditions, gamaka usage, interpretations and manodharma With many musicians imitating mannerisms in the belief that they are following a certain style, it becomes important to understand what constitutes style. It is a much larger phenomenon than manner, which is merely a way of doing things, or mannerisms, which are only quirks or individual traits.

Beyond what is learnt from the guru and the understanding

that comes from listening, a certain instinct propels a musician's quest. Learning techniques, acquiring skill development and understanding musical parameters are necessary requirements of the art. Each musician has different ways of absorbing these. With some, it is a subconscious assimilation that cannot be articulated. With others, it is a clear and conscious part of their music. In both cases, the musician evolves without really contributing to the canvas of musical thought in a conscious manner.

The Musician and Identity

In the next stage of musical development, an 'aware' musician tries to give style and thought to his identity. It is important to understand that this is a retrospective act. Musical instinct and gathered knowledge integrate through experience into a mature style. The musician now seeks to base her knowledge on this established identity, and begins to deconstruct every part of her music, questioning the aesthetic content and trying to layer thought within the musical expression. This does not mean that there is an attempt to straitjacket or rationalize things, though that may happen in some cases. Mostly, it is an attempt to establish a thought process that covers the individual's entire expression. The musician seeks to clothe her aesthetic thought with his style. This happens only when the musician introspects on her music, from which will emerge clarity about various aspects of the music. With a deepening of the musician's inquiries in this direction, her music acquires a certain special clarity, which is the result of a completeness acquired from a conscious linking of various musical aspects.

In this process, the musician may completely change previously held positions on music, including those received from the guru.

The musician, therefore, comes to hold and subscribe to a conscious body of thought that defines every musical action. It evolves from an understanding of the music learnt from the guru, the internalizing of other influences and finally a reinterpretation of the music received within the self. The musician is aware of this reinterpretation, even though it may have happened as a natural process of evolution. I have described this process in a linear fashion, but in its totality it is actually a constant, with the musician evolving within that constant, and many of the stages that I have described overlapping. As this process reaches completion, the musician comes to possess not only a style, but also a clear understanding of the music, which in turn is expressed with clarity in his presentation.

The Transference of Musical Experience

When this state is reached, the musician may feel naturally inclined to transfer this collective experience – both the music and the thought underlying it – to other individuals. This also leads students of music to seek out such musicians. In this process of sharing and searching, the musician's style broadens into a larger methodology. This must not be construed as music losing its quality of art, because the school of thought itself is built on the artistic quality of the music. The process of musical thought, instead of binding the music, ought to mantle it.

I spoke of a certain 'completion'. But there is more. When students start learning from this 'complete' musician, the teacher sees that the process of teaching itself further refines his own understanding of music. If the students have an inquiring disposition, their questions can lead the teacher to reinvent the music every time. Depending on his skills, insights and abilities, each student hears every line of music differently. This also requires of the teacher that he should understand the student's perspective and so reinterpret the music that, when rendered, it remains the same. This gives further definition to the thought that captures the music.

It is through such a process that a musician's individual style becomes a bani. The recognition comes not only from the musician, but also from the transfer of that school of thought to students. We also find that almost any musician can absorb musical ideas from a bani, irrespective of whether they have been learnt directly from an exemplar of the bani or one removed, this easy transferability being a result of the clarity in the music.

Bani, therefore, is a school of thought, much like philosophical thought. Both are born from natural perceptions, learning and assimilation through deep introspection. Once established, these thoughts are imbibed by students, followed by some and emulated by many – but always with the knowledge that a bani is not a destination, but a musical state.

12

Studying the Song

In the world of the arts, there has long existed a divide between artists and academics. Both deal with the same art, but find themselves unable to communicate with each other. This divide seems to me to be essentially an issue of mental attitudes, restricting the free flow of ideas between the two.

Artists have their own perceptions about the role of art, while academics are bound by the structures, rules and the dynamics of their specialization, which is founded on 'reason'. And yet, in a very real sense, both are interdependent and interlinked, though unable to quite appreciate this because of their myopic involvement with their own activity. I will address these issues in the specific context of Karnatik music.

Music, Its Practice and Its Study

To most Karnatik musicians, music is an experience that has been defined by what they create within the unique format of the kutcheri. The truth of the art lies in this experience of music, for without it there is no art. Musicians also distinguish between music rendered and experienced during practice or in private sessions and those presented in a kutcheri for an audience. From this, the musician establishes that, for a kutcheri, the artist must cultivate a way of providing a sensory experience to others, quite apart from himself.

Experience is purely the result of an interaction between an object, event or stimulus (temporal and illusionary) and a human being, and is personal to every individual. But we do hear people talk about trans-sensory experiences. I am not sure these really exist. What they may be referring to are transpersonal experiences – being transported to a realm beyond themselves. This would mean that though the experience does not relate to the individual's own personal feelings, yet a powerful experience has been felt through the sensory world. I use the term 'sensory' to refer to that which is experienced. It follows that in life one need not place sensory experiences at the lowest level of the hierarchy of experience. The way and the manner in which we sense make for the unique experiences in music.

A musician should contribute something new and distinct to the human experience. Therefore, the musician is one who gives a world of new meaning to emotions. He brings into reality the world of the imagination. The shared experience of music is necessarily an emotive one, both for the creator and the listener. Therefore, an alapana is not just about svaras, phrases and form, or a kirtana about raga, tala, language and linguistic meaning; it is about the emotion that permeates all these. This is why abstraction is the essence of Karnatik music.

I have already stated my views on emotion in art music. Even for one religiously inclined, there is a difference in the experience of a recitation of a religious verse and a kirtana with religious content. This is due to the emotional experience of music, irrespective of how the musician or listener engages with it. The role of emotion in music is clearly beyond doubt or debate. Irrespective of how a musician views the idea of art or emotion, she knows that the listener is touched by the experiential quality of music.

What about musicians who are deemed intellectual? The word 'intellectual' when prefixed to music can be extremely deceptive. When we use this term, we seem to refer to a level of perceived complexity or intricacy. This is usually linked to the kind of ragas rendered, the difficulty or rarity of phrases in known ragas, or 'mathematical' presentations. We have boxed the idea of an intellectually charged musical creation or rendition into these baskets. The idea of intellectual music, as I see it, is both wider and deeper. I see intellectualism in music as an action of serious thought; in other words, of intellection. However – and this is the crux – it does not imply a lack of emotion. On the contrary, it carries, through the very act of intellection, and through a conscious intellectual choice, an emotional charge with it. Intellectual music is one that has, through a process of willed intellection, placed emotion, or bhava, at its very core. The senses, physical as they are, are as inextricably connected to the mind as mental processes. There is such a thing as emoted thought that is born out of one's senses, either due to a personal or dispassionate experience. The love I feel for an individual is different from the love I have for Picasso's art. Both are love, but the experience of love is different.

When emotions are the driving force for a musician, the thought transforms into experience, becoming an emoted thought. I see this as true intellectualism. The receiver does not realize the deeply introspected nature of the creation as it is emotively appealing. The emotional appeal of music also camouflages the level of difficulty of the musical creation. This is the genius of great musicians.

A closer scrutiny of many musicians who are labelled intellectual reveals that their music relates to people at the level of emotions no less than at the level of the intellect. Musicians of the most highly intellectual kind layer these complexities with emotion; it is through this vehicle that the music speaks. Their communication is both internal and external. Those who present music purely as an exercise within given parameters and constructions are not musicians. Their creations reveal that the rules of the music are being followed, that they have studied a great deal and they are technically accurate. Yet, this is not music. Even the most intelligent musician touches the listener only through emotion.

That emotional experience of music is the result of expression, which in turn arises from the musician's inner urge to give life to an idea. The idea is the imagined, and art is the created. Reason, cause, logic and rationality do not exist here. When asked about technique, structure and framework, the musician's response is that these are only the instruments of creation. These instruments are necessities, but not the defining factors in the creation of art. After mastering the skills of Karnatik music, the musician seeks to develop an individual expression, and in so doing shapes the music. In their pursuit of such expression, some musicians may feel that any change in form and aesthetics is permissible if it enables creativity. This is when serious problems begin to appear in their idea of Karnatik music.

The idea of aesthetics is very simple for such musicians: it is what I like. My conditioning, environment and developed sense of Karnatik music influence what I like. But at the level of personal preferences, there is no room for discussion or deliberation. Sadly, this is how most musicians deal with aesthetics. Without serious questioning, our understanding of the art remains highly limited.

Today, Karnatik musicians derive their sense of music primarily from their guru, the experience of listening to musicians live and from the recordings of past musicians. The guru is the greatest influence and an important one. Musical learning is both actual singing and subconscious absorption. Not only does a transfer of musical knowledge take place, but the seeds of perspectives get sown in this process. Along with this exists the influence of listening.

The past we are discussing is already bound by what we can describe as kutcheri music. Therefore, the music and the musician are perceived as inseparable from the idea of a kutcheri. Even today, when musicians discuss music, the role of the kutcheri hovers over such conversations. The other factor is that in Indian traditional learning, the guru is venerated to the point of being deified. Every word uttered by him is sacrosanct, and questioning is rare. By questioning I do not mean plain querying, but interrogating the whole subject after much introspection for a deeply grounded understanding. The problem is that all thoughts are circumscribed by the kutcheri and the guru. As long as they remain within that sphere, true questioning is impossible. The possibility of going beyond these spheres rarely arises in the musician's mind. While the oral tradition is a beautiful feature of our music and needs to be respected, we need to accept that it is not necessarily perfect. Errors of omission and commission have been committed through the ages. But it is difficult to recognize this as a problem because our perceptions of the ideal are stuck in this conditioned world.

Similarly, our perspective of listening to Karnatik music is completely conditioned and limited by the last century. Even when we think we are discussing the music of the previous centuries, we are actually talking about what has been heard in kutcheris over the last century. This flaws our understanding of Karnatik music, which is spread over a larger canvas. We are only discussing conventions as practised by musicians within the kutcheri context. Though there is great ambiguity in sifting convention from tradition, we accept all of it as tradition. This view clouds and constricts our vision of the music. A contrary error would lead some to negate the past without inquiry, imagining that it is in their power to create an alternative sound.

Every musician is responsible for the nature of Karnatik music that she presents. But assuming that responsibility would require the musician to traverse the path of a researcher or musicologist. The fact is that this is not an option, but a necessity. As I see it, in order to understand why Karnatik music exists with a certain form, structure and aesthetic, we need to step back from our conditioned environment. This will give musicians a sense of the pervading aesthetic, which is not personal but all-encompassing. An aesthetic flows through time. And time, or what we know as history, is not perfect either, with many of its links broken or missing. But unless we give ourselves a chance to apprehend the evolution of the music, we will not be true to Karnatik music.

Every musician must take a serious analytical journey in Karnatik music. The analysis must include a study of oral and literary traditions, which must be placed in the context of social and cultural history. Karnatik music is not only about music; it is also about painting, dance, sculpture, poetry, politics, caste hierarchy, religious practices and social reorganization. Through such a study, the musician will be able to sieve through the past and the present, and unravel the quality of the music. This is not the dry journey that musicians might believe it to be, but as challenging and revealing as every svara that a musician practises. It is important that this journey is taken not to reinforce the existing concepts that the musician believes in, but with the realization that it may result in a complete reorientation of the idea of Karnatik music. The musician must be willing to internalize what is revealed in that search. This is neither a journey of negation nor acceptance, but one of realization. Yes, the prospect is daunting, but the process is necessary if we are to feel the ground on which we stand as Karnatik musicians.

The musicologist is on the other side of the same page. To the musicologist, the story of Karnatik music is one of textual tradition, with oral tradition being the practical manifestation of the music. The musicologist constantly wants to tally one with the other. This results in discrepancies the musicologist dismisses as errors. The basis for this judgement is the textual reference that suits her perception. Therefore, we find that just as the musician is conditioned by oral and listening traditions, the musicologist is conditioned by a selective reading of musical history. The conditioning that occurs through imbibing her mentor's ideas and methodology too plays a crucial role in how the musicologist sifts history. These factors predispose the musicologist to arrive at conclusions about what is right or wrong, acceptable or unacceptable. This not only narrows down the idea of Karnatik music but also dangerously negates oral practices that may be as much a part of the continuum. Therefore, in thought and action, the musician and the musicologist are only mirrors of each other.

The general musicological view of Karnatik music, unfortunately, desiccates it, removing the essence of art from it. When emotion and experience are removed from music, it ceases to be art. Somewhere, in the pursuit of rationality and reason, most musicologists have lost the plot. The reason for the existence of art music is the music itself, not logic.

What we must seek is to comprehend the beauty in the creation of art. This includes the acceptance of infraction, which is not a mistake, but an abstractive tool used creatively by the musician. Nuance is problematic because it is not black or white. This would mean that the conditioned musicologist could break free.

The biggest problem with musicologists is that they study Karnatik music as a science. In fact, over the last hundred years, even musicians have referred to it as science. There cannot be a greater fallacy. Science tries to understand the functioning of Nature through observation and analysis, and creates frameworks to explain its functioning. This includes the study of sound, light and so on. Similarly, academics try to frame generic rules and conditions for music and its components based on observation and analysis. Every human action is connected to science, as it is within the realm of existence. This does not make every action of the human being an action of science. It is within the body of scientific work only to the extent that all life is based on scientific frameworks. This does not make it science. Science exists in Karnatik music as much as in anything else. If the expression of a musician's creativity means that the scientific frameworks of Karnatik music have to be bent, so be it. The aesthetics of Karnatik music are within scientific analysis, but cannot be confined to it. Quite simply, musical abstraction allows these frameworks to be dismantled. The aesthetic of Karnatik music, as much as it can be analysed through a scientific perspective, has defied scientific generalizations. This is due to the interaction of the elements of its aesthetics with the artist's endeavour to abstract the emotional world through music. The intent of the musical form supersedes everything else. We also have to take into account the natural course of Karnatik music's journey through the centuries. The changes in this journey cannot always be explained in scientific terms. Practices change as culture evolves. Musicologists have to develop an openness to change both in the past and present, and to the fact that it may not fall into accepted scientific musical outlines. What the musicologist does not realize is that, even when the change seems unscientific, it is guided by a sense of tradition.

For instance, when musicological constructs are built based on the frequency of repetition – a scientific approach – they are flawed. Art is not made up of probability rules, because each art expression is an entire form on its own. When generalizations about musical practice are drawn from isolated samples, practices that fall outside those sampling also get inaccurately branded by the same assumptions. This causes as much damage to the aesthetics of Karnatik music as the actions of a musician who lacks an understanding of musical tradition. Compositional structures are analysed based on the general conditions thrust upon them. For example, musicologists will often say that a pallavi of a kirtana cannot have three avartanas. The fact that most compositions do not have such a structure does not make such a construction wrong. The idea of wrong and right cannot be framed and thrust upon art creations. Instead, the inquiry must be an analysis of that particular kirtana to see if it reveals the aesthetics that are at the basis of the kirtana and the aesthetics of Karnatik music as a whole. This must take into account oral and textual history, the past and the present, without predispositions.

The intent of art music is to create a world that gives us a dispassionate idea of emotion. In the search to create this experience, the musician has developed ways and means to achieve that abstraction. With the serious musician, this will not damage the aesthetics, but give it a different dimension. It will be an extension of the collective historical aesthetics – even if it does not fall into the framework that the musicologist tries to create.

There are serious lacunae in the understanding of textual tradition. In their quest to create generic rules for musical content and action, most musicologists conveniently use only textual content that supports their perception. In Karnatik music, we saw the result of this kind of application when the modern melakarta system was adopted. Let me illustrate with an example.

Musicology has influenced the perception of so many older ragas, like yadukula kambhoji, by placing them into the melakarta system, the established raga classification system described in detail in the chapter 'The Raga's Trail'. Similarly, synthetic ragas like dharmavati have been accepted though they do not contain the aesthetic features of a raga. Both are the result of flawed musicological and musical practice. This is not a comment on the beauty of the melodies of either of these ragas, but on the aesthetics of yadukula kambhoji, dharmavati and the idea of a raga.

In creating such systems, scholars have clearly displayed the need to construct raga notions born out of scientific classification, rather than natural melodic evolution. It is important for musicians also to accept that even some of our greatest composers – Tyagaraja and Muttusvami Dikshitar – had a role in establishing this, using these systems for their compositions. The advantage of such systems is that they feed into the very psyche of the musicologist's need for simple recognizable mechanisms to classify music. Therefore, most musicological studies have been limited in their perspective of musical history. If one were to try and understand older textual references, it would be difficult to find this kind of raga classification. Scholars have tried to record practices, and for a long time they took into account the fact that musical practice was an art and not a science and therefore cannot be limited. The few musicologists who travelled this open-minded path viewed Karnatik music as an art.

Essentially, textual history has been selectively used to propagate a scientific sense in Karnatik music. Music practice has followed this tradition, and therefore most musicologists have established and fed into this flawed perception of history. This has seriously affected the aesthetic content of music.

There are similar issues with compositional history too. Compositions have been reframed by musicians on the basis of scientific reorganizations that musicologists have propounded. This has led to serious loss of melodic content in numerous compositions.

Musicologists also interpret the idea of intellectual music in a certain fashion. Musicians who follow all the rules and regulations prescribed in textbooks are considered intellectual. The musicologist does not care whether the musician is creating an object of art. This is shocking, because any study of art music must recognize its real intent. The musicologist who approaches Karnatik music from an art music perspective is rare to find.

As much as musicologists have narrowed the history of Karnatik music, they have also tried to reinterpret ancient musical history to corroborate current practices. This has not only given Karnatik music an artificial ancient historical context but also tried to create logic to current practice. Right through musicological history, the same terms have come to be employed multiple times, but the inferences underlying these terms have varied widely depending on the music they are applied to. This inconvenient fact has been conveniently ignored, and Karnatik music made to look like some anthropological entity of a strictly linear disposition.

Linearity is also closely linked to the scientific tradition. A results in B and B results in C; therefore, C comes from A. But art history is largely organic and lateral. Here are a few examples of such theories. Some musicologists claim that the improvisational form tana came from thaya. Thaya was part of the chaturdandi system of art music. When one studies the two forms, it is difficult to see the connection. How are such conclusions arrived at? Similarly, musicologists will justify the current artificial raga classification (the melakarta system) of janya and janaka by stating that these terms are found in the thirteenth-century treatise *Sangita Ratnakara*. They completely miss the point that the music mentioned in that treatise and the context of its use are very different. Similarly, the simhanandana tala of 128 beats is mentioned in the same treatise. The fact that the tala is found even now does not mean that it is the same. A tala is not just about total number of beats; it is a concept of time measure, where every internal division and its duration integrate. Therefore, even if simhanandana tala has 128 beats today, it is not the same tala as described in the *Sangita Ratnakara*. Concepts and terms have been drawn from different musical traditions, resulting in Karnatik music as it is today, but trying to make direct connections to an ancient past would lead to a wrong sense of history. The use of a term at different times in history does not mean there is a direct musical connection.

A change in the musicologists' approach to music is necessary if Karnatik music is to be researched seriously. It is imperative that the musicologist realizes that musical study is not about propounding general notions based on empirical data. Her study must go into the deeper question of aesthetics, keeping in mind that Karnatik music is a collective aesthetic form that has structures and components, all achieving a similar abstractive goal. In the journey of the music, linear connections are very difficult to find, but concrete perceptions can be drawn based on textual cross-referencing, along with an understanding of the cultural and social influences of each period.

Every raga, tala or compositional form has a history of aesthetics. It is in the unravelling of this history that we can find the roots of the aesthetics we know today. Some of this study may defy logic, but we need to accept that too as part of the aesthetics. At the same time, we must be aware of tendentious interventions by both musicologists and musicians leading to skewed interpretations. This can be detected if we use more than one source for our understanding. I suppose what I am trying to say is simply this: there are frameworks in every aspect of Karnatik music, but they are not a result of logic. They are a product of the aesthetic intent of the music.

Every musicologist must closely follow oral tradition. As much as it is varied and filled with unaccountable changes, there is a certain sanctity to learning in the traditional schools of the guru–shishya parampara. They have retained the spirit of their lineage. An analysis of many of these oral traditions will corroborate and amplify textual tradition. When a conflict is found between the two, one must be very sensitive to both traditions and attempt an understanding of whether there could have been errors on either side. It is important for the musicologist to accept that, in Karnatik music history, answers may not always be found, but that too is a part of history.

One argument that I have heard from some musicologists is that, since they have learnt to sing or play an instrument, they have a practitioner's understanding of music deepened by scholarship. I am not entirely convinced by this. The learning of music definitely gives a musicologist personal experience of Karnatik music, but this may not change anything in their perception as musicologists. It is not only knowledge of music, but the attitude that informs it that affects perception.

Ultimately, both the musician and the musicologist must seek the same: an understanding of the aesthetics of the music. In this search, the musician must be willing to give up personal notions and conditioning and look beyond his practice. The musicologist needs to seriously reorient her view of music and approach musical tradition as an art. Both will face situations of conflict, with some being totally irreconcilable. This does not mean history is wrong, or that the current practice is wrong. It only gives each one of them another layer to break through. Over a period of time, clarity will emerge from both their journeys. From that clarity, we can retrieve the real sense of Karnatik music. One may say there is no single answer. True – but there is something intrinsic in every aspect of music that has survived through time. This is the real music. It is when one gains this sense – both as a musician and a musicologist – that one asks the important questions about music as we see it today, questions that can preserve the music and also let it move in a direction that protects its continuum.

Book 2

The Context

'The music of life is in danger of being lost
in the music of the voice.'
– Mohandas Karamchand Gandhi

13

A Song in the Dance

The idiom of Karnatik music or its elements have historically been used in other singing traditions, such as Namasankirtana, artistic traditions like Bhagavata Mela, and dance forms like Kathakali, Mohiniyattam, Kuchipudi and most significantly Bharatanatyam. Music runs through all these as a connecting thread. At the same time, the degrees to which various aspects of Karnatik music have been utilized, either in their entirety or in a modified form, vary according to the demands of their aesthetic. For example, the music in Kathakali, called sopana, uses some Karnatik ragas, but in conjunction with the region's own deep-rooted instruments and musical practices, giving it a distinct character. The music in Bharatanatyam, however, has remained closer to Karnatik music. In that sense, sopana is more distinct from the art music form than the music in Bharatanatyam.

While it is true that elements of Karnatik music are partly or wholly employed in all these art forms, I would not agree with the music aficionado who might say that, at one level, both are Karnatik music.

When used in other art forms, Karnatik music undergoes a very important change. This extraordinary transformation is not

in the raga and tala, but in the very purpose of the music. As art
music, Karnatik music creates at a subliminal level an environment
within which it is self-contained. The musician and the discerning
listener are also contained within it. Each individual engages with
the music in his own personal manner and, in doing so, derives
satisfaction on many planes. The music's own aesthetics do not
seek such satisfaction. Similarly, there is no necessity for any other
form of artistic expression to substantiate the experience of the
self-contained environment of Karnatik music.

When the music becomes part of another form, it reorients its
artistic purpose. Karnatik music in Bhagavata Mela is part of the
aesthetics that govern that form. In that environment, the music
moulds itself to allow Bhagavata Mela to achieve the aesthetic
intent of that form. The music then is no longer a separate
element. By meshing into Bhagavata Mela, it ceases to be art
music. Its intent is no longer abstractive in the sense of pure art;
in fact, it relinquishes its own aesthetic intent. This might seem
like a change in the inner urge of the music alone, but everything,
including the melodic or rhythmic content, transforms.

The very elements of Karnatik music take on a different
meaning in their new environment. 'Meaning' here should be
understood as 'that conveyed by musical expression', rather
than in the textual sense. Such meaning depends on the context
of presentation, the other elements being expressed and the
overriding aesthetic identity and intent. The meaning that raga
kedaragaula brings to Bhagavata Mela is different from that
conveyed in Mohiniyattam, though it may be recognized as such
in both. Yet, the meaning is moulded by the aesthetic context
that governs the two different forms. Therefore, all kedaragaulas
are not the same. Is this differentiation purely intellectual? If that
were the case, the raga in two contexts – Bhagavata Mela and
Mohiniyattam – would have a similar aesthetic impact on us, the
receivers. But we know this does not happen. Even if the general
emotional import of the sequences is similar, the effect of the

raga is distinct in each instance. Hence, even when it is revealing similar melodic lines, kedaragaula is different in each of these cases, as well as from its existence within the art music context.

A melodic line exists not in a conceptual form, but an acoustic one. Only when it is heard is it music. At a conceptual level, it is a possibility, but it takes on a different identity once it becomes music. Therefore, when sung or rendered, the idea that 'was' undergoes changes to become the raga it 'is'. This happens due to many variables, including the musician's skill, thought, emotive expression, interpretation and, importantly, its intent within the larger context of the art presentation. Once this is recognized, we will hear it not just at the academic level of being the same in all cases, but at the aesthetic level of being different in each art form. Then, the same kedaragaula melodic line will not only be unique in aesthetic context, but also as an acoustic experience.

In the process, kedaragaula first sheds its art music identity, then within each art form takes on another identity that enhances the aesthetics of that form. Every aspect within an art form is thus webbed with another to achieve a certain aesthetic intent.

This understanding is very important in order to perceive music, when it moves into another art form, doing so not as an addition to the tradition of other performing arts, but as an integral aesthetic element in it. Karnatik music, in such a situation, is not used in the other art form as a borrowing; it is a part of the form and inseparable from it. Just as abhinaya (articulation of emotions using facial expressions and the limbs) is part of Bharatanatyam, Karnatik music is part of it too. The notion that Bharatanatyam is presented using Karnatik music must change if the experience of the dance form is to be complete for both the dancer and the music connoisseur. Often, the dance aficionado sees good music as a necessity for the dance, but the music lover does not even see the dance. In both cases, the root of the problem is with how music is perceived within the context of dance.

This leads to the question: when removed from the art music

sphere, is it still Karnatik music? There is no easy answer. Before I address this issue, we need to understand where the identity of the music lies. Is aesthetics created by the form and content, or is it driven by intent? The identity of Karnatik music is rooted in both. That all facets of the music come together in a certain fashion is a result of the urge to achieve the intent. If the intent is missing, raga, tala and manodharma will not blend together in a specific manner to create the Karnatik art music form. The word 'specific' is critical for our understanding. When a kirtana is composed, the vaggeyakara is conscious of the way raga, tala, laya and sahitya come together. His sense of beauty lies in the intent as he visualizes the artistic intent of the creation as a whole. What the creator considers beautiful is the abstracted idea, but that exists only because of the kirtana. They are inseparable.

We must at the same time view music from purely an acoustic point of view. Karnatik music has a clear identity in the 'sound' that embodies all aspects of the music. But when its elements become part of other art forms, we come across an interesting challenge. At one level, we hear the same sound in the music during a Bharatanatyam recital. The acoustic sound we hear from the singer and the mrdanga player seems to be the same as in a Karnatik music presentation. We say that the sound seems to be the same, yet we are aware that it is not an art music presentation. Where does this awareness come from?

It comes from the altered intent, which also results in specific changes to the way each aesthetic element interacts with the other – and that in turn changes the aesthetic experience of the music. We need to recognize that the singer's musical expression and that of the mrdanga artist are unique to Bharatanatyam. There are also other additions to the Bharatanatyam experience as a whole, including the use of cymbals, which contribute vitally to the form's acoustic dimension. Interestingly, when I said that the sound was the same, most readers would have agreed. But the sound of the cymbals and that of the dancer's feet too are part of the acoustic experience in Bharatanatyam. The acoustic experience in Bharatanatyam is an independent experience to Karnatik music. Our conditioned listening to Karnatik music as an art music form causes us to tune out these elements.

So we now have a clear answer: when the context and intent of Karnatik music is changed, it immediately stops being art music.

Bharatanatyam and Karnatik music have lived and breathed the same traditions through the ages of their evolution. They have been practised and developed by similar communities. Most regions that patronized Karnatik music also patronized Bharatanatyam (though this name is a twentieth-century creation). With such a connected history, it is only natural to discuss the two forms together. But having said that, it is true that these art forms are aesthetically distinct. They exist individually and even have very unique sets of people who appreciate them. It is quite interesting that dance aficionados are often a completely different set from the music connoisseurs – possibly because the aesthetic experience of each cultivates very different kinds of audiences. Though both art forms evolved like conjoined twins, the perception of music in dance is that of a provider or base. Everyone accepts that dance cannot exist without music, but also needs to understand that the music in dance does not have an independent identity removed from the dance.

While discussing the various aspects of Karnatik music that live as part of Bharatanatyam, we must be clear that 'Karnatik music', there, does not refer to the art music presentation.

Musicians for Bharatanatyam train in Karnatik music in exactly the same way as kutcheri musicians. They could have chosen to become kutcheri musicians, but opted to be a part of dance. In making this choice, they need to develop a different understanding of music. The vocalist who sings for Bharatanatyam cannot view herself as providing melodic or lyrical content for dance. In the context of dance, the music has to be viewed as being the dance itself. The music is not being danced to. The music is the dance and the dance is the music. In this environment, none of the musicians in Bharatanatyam is separate from each other's expression. They function as parts of an aesthetic whole and, in doing so, relate internally with each other. The mrdanga artist is part of every melodic and dance movement. He is not adding to the movement; the movement itself exists as a collective form with the mrdanga in the experience. This is true of all the musicians, including especially the nattuvanar, the anchor who brings together melody, rhythm and expression in perfect unison. All this with a pair of cymbals in his hands.

I would like to use the pada varna to try and describe how a vocalist is part of the Bharatanatyam experience. The pada varna is the central presentation in a Bharatanatyam recital. In presenting it, the dancer builds a superstructure around the melodic, rhythmic and lyrical content of the varna. The dancer's vision expands the pada varna to a multilayered presentation that uses all the elements of dance to bring to life his creative world.

When a pada varna is presented, the vocalist renders every melodic line as an expression of dance. In this, the musician can be said to be 'in dance' and the dancer 'in song'. The dancer builds upon every line in a varna to convey the linguistic meaning. This is only the first step. From here, he develops different interpretations. The literal meaning moves to the emotional, philosophical and mythological. Every musician needs to be part of the changes in the dancer's journey.

How does the musician participate? The dancer's method of extrapolating layers of meaning from a line of composition is referred to as sanchari. The dancer uses abhinaya to create the sanchari. When this happens, the musician, we are told, can render a niraval: a word one associates with a kutcheri. But the niraval rendered here is very different from that in a kutcheri. Here it is not independent. It is part of the sanchari, and needs to melodically convey that which the sanchari conveys visually.

A single sanchari can have multiple meanings. The melodic movements need to convey the essence of every sanchari. A mere repetition of the line for sanchari, with different melodic ideas, does not mean that the music and dance are functioning as one. The singer responds to the dancer's eyes, feet, body, expression and every gesture. This also means that the singer must understand the meaning of every abhinaya in the dance. Only when all this comes together do the dancer and the musician become part of the same art creation. Many kutcheri musicians do not realize the nuances involved and think that it is physically exhausting, as each line has to be repeated numerous times. This, of course, requires rehearsals with the dancer. In reality, music in dance is a complex and sensitive presentation.

It is a curious fact that most modern compositional forms that we consider part of Karnatik music came from the dance traditions of south India, including the pada varna, svarajati, tillana, pada and javali. Some forms that were created to be presented as dance came into the sphere of art music performance. Even the kirtana style established by Tyagaraja, Muttusvami Dikshitar and Shyama Shastri may have been influenced by the pada form. Today, these kirtanas have been adapted into Bharatanatyam. This exchange between Bharatanatyam and Karnatik music has been constant; each has influenced and contributed to the aesthetic development of the other.

There is a need to draw a distinction in aesthetics between compositions that were devised for dance and those for art music. This difference permeates everything from the compositional structure, melodic movement, rhythmic accent, lyrical content and flow. When a work is composed for dance, its intent is to fulfil Bharatanatyam as an art form. The abstraction in Bharatanatyam is of a different nature from that of art music, and hence the music will be built differently. The vaggeyakara who composed for Bharatanatyam saw the music as dance. He needed to be able to visualize Bharatanatyam in the composition. Such a composition naturally integrates into the dance repertoire. When a composition is meant to be presented only as art music, its focus is purely on melodic and rhythmic abstraction. Its inclusion in Bharatanatyam will thus need a conscious effort from the dancer. The aesthetic experience of Bharatanatyam reveals the varying intent in both these compositions.

The dancer is as aware and sensitive to the compositional structure as the musician is in a kutcheri. Each Bharatanatyam-related compositional form has a unique melodic and visual manifestation. The aesthetic experience from a pada varna is completely different from that of a pada. This is due to the compositional aesthetics that the vaggeyakara has seen as necessary in order to create varied visual aesthetics through the dance. Melodic presentation too will be different, based on the composition's form and content, which dictate the dance. Aware of this, the dancers create distinct interpretations for every compositional form. Even within the same compositional type, the interaction between the matu and dhatu changes the dance interpretation.

Right through the presentation, musicians have to be in sync with the dancer's aesthetics. Apart from sanchari, even the rendition of the compositional lines – whether in a tillana or javali – is related to the Bharatanatyam aesthetic. This can be tonal, relating to the volume, lyrical emphasis and melodic emphasis. There is not a single moment in the presentation where the music is independent of the dance.

Over the last few decades, there have been interesting exchanges between Bharatanatyam and Karnatik art music. Traditionally, compositions for dance were distinct from compositions used in kutcheris; but this distinction is no longer clear. In this context, two forms come specifically into discussion: the tillana and pada varna. The tillana – though it was a Bharatanatyam-related compositional form – was brought into the art music fold. Many of the tillanas composed by the vaggeyakaras of the nineteenth and early twentieth centuries became very popular in both Bharatanatyam and kutcheri presentations and, over a period of time, came to be integral to both. In the latter part of the last century, some vaggeyakaras reinterpreted the tillana, whereby it has acquired a distinct art form related to music and shed some of its traditional form. This can be sensed in the melodic lines. These vaggeyakaras have also included unique mathematical motifs, which are purely melodic creations. In this form, the tillana is a very different composition. It is not visualized for Bharatanatyam, but as Karnatik art music. These tillanas too are now part of the Bharatanatyam repertoire, where their essentially art music persona changed into tillana in the dance form. There is no right or wrong in the use of these compositions by Bharatanatyam dancers, but one needs to ask if this disturbs the aesthetics of the compositional form of the tillana within dance, or whether it adds a new dimension. This is equally true in the case of pada varnas.

When an art music creation, like a kirtana, is adapted into Bharatanatyam, the form faces a difficulty. The composition should not be altered, so what has to and does change is the focus on sahitya. But here too there is a challenge: every syllable being melodically manifested, the sahitya is not always heard as complete words. The positions of the syllables cannot be altered, as that would change the melodic line, completely deconstructing the composition. The melodic movements of a purely art music composition are not always suited for Bharatanatyam. Issues like these create a situation of conflict in the process of adaptation. Does this lead to a change in the aesthetics of Bharatanatyam? This is a question that only dancers can answer. What is imperative is that the adapted composition must make it possible for the dancer to visually and emotionally abstract its content, which includes matu and dhatu. The composition must, in its created structure, be adaptable into the aesthetic identity of Bharatanatyam. When presented as Bharatanatyam, the intent of these compositions is automatically transformed.

When a musical composition meant for dance is brought into Karnatik music, one immediate change that occurs is that melodic and rhythmic abstraction become paramount. The text is not changed or altered, but the musician uses the composite identity of the text and melody as part of her musical exploration. The composition remains the same, but is reinterpreted to be absorbed into art music. I must stress that this can only happen if the composition possesses the musicality for this and the musician is sensitive to the nuances of the transfer from dance. In the absence of this, it remains only as a composition in the fringe.

The immediate question is whether any composition from any form of music can be adapted into Bharatanatyam. The answer is no, it cannot. When we use the phrase 'aesthetics of Bharatanatyam', the music in the dance is as much part of that discussion as the dance. In Bharatanatyam, the elements of Karnatik music are deeply rooted and contribute to its unique identity. As in Karnatik music, change has taken place in Bharatanatyam as well, but there is a clear continuum to be seen in certain essentials that have remained firmly in place in the dance. Karnatik music, with its intent merged in that of the dance, is located within these essentials.

The mrdanga artist's role in Bharatanatyam is unique. He needs to be acutely aware of the dancer, vocalist and nattuvanar – in other words, of the dance, music and rhythm. In linking all these, he brings together a single aesthetic synchronization of the presentation. In a Karnatik kutcheri, the mrdanga artist is responding to the composition's matu and dhatu, tala, laya and the manodharma of the melodic artists. In Bharatanatyam, his role is a little more complex. When the dancer is presenting pure abstract movements (nrtta), the rhythmic structures presented by the dancer's foot movements are reproduced on the mrdanga. Along with the footwork, nrtta involves the movement of the other parts of the body as well. The mrdanga artist provides definition and stability to all the complexities of the footwork. During the presentation of abhinaya, the mrdanga artist provides crucial highlights to the dancer's expressions and gestures. These highlights are presented through tonal variations, short bursts of patterns and even through spells of silence and modulation of volume. To the viewer, this adds to the experience of the emotions that the dancer is conveying. When the dancer presents compositional lines as they are, in a matter-of-fact manner, the mrdanga artist frames the melodic line while fixing the laya.

But right through the dance performance, the mrdanga artist is also relating to the vocalist. When a compositional line is presented without elaboration by the dancer, the mrdanga artist must make sure that his technique of playing is in unison with the melodic structure of the line. He cannot sacrifice this for the dancer. This means that the artist has to find a way of giving simultaneous support to both the dancer and the vocalist. During sanchari, when the dancer uses abhinaya to elaborate the line, the mrdanga artist is also aware of the vocalist's melodic variations even as he is reacting to the dancer. The vocalist, as we know, is also connected to the dancer. The mrdanga artist creates in real time emotive layers to both the music and the dance. When pure abhinaya pieces like padas are presented, the mrdanga artist has to be aware that these compositions are melodically extremely intricate, yet support the dancer's abhinaya. This is a fine balance, which ensures that the music and dance become one.

The nattuvanar is like the conductor of the presentation. He controls the laya. In this role, the nattuvanar is the conduit between the dancer, vocalist and mrdanga artist. This means that the mrdanga artist has to be in synchronization with the nattuvanar. During nrtta presentations, the nattuvanar recites the jatis (pronounced without an elongated 'a') within the framework of which dance movements are embedded. The nattuvanar uses cymbals to mirror the exact foot movements that are built into the jatis, but are not the same. This implies that there is complete coordination between the mrdanga artist, nattuvanar and the dancer.

Originally, all the nrtta-related jatis were composed by the nattuvanars, who came from traditional dance and music families. Unfortunately, over the last century, we have lost almost all the renowned nattuvanars with their children moving on to other work. The rhythmic structures composed by these nattuvanars were guided by the aesthetics of Bharatanatyam and not by kutcheri-derived mathematical structures. But they were perfect in another sense. The nattuvanars, who had imbibed the aesthetics of both Karnatik music and Bharatanatyam, were guided by the aesthetic expression of Bharatanatyam when they composed jatis. When presented, they revealed the dance in all its visual fluency. These jatis were very different from those that were part of the mrdanga repertoire in Kutcheri music – a difference evident in both form and content.

The non-availability today of traditional nattuvanars has made the mrdanga artists indispensable. Today, many of them compose the jatis for nrtta. When, in times past, these mrdanga artists were themselves immersed in the dance tradition, they followed the principles of the nattuvanars. But over the last two decades, a number of kutcheri-playing mrdanga artists have come to accompany Bharatanatyam dancers. When these artists compose jatis, there is a discernible difference. Kutcheri-based mathematics can and should be adopted within the dance aesthetic as long as it does not negatively influence the dance form. However, most of the time, the highly arithmetical approach to jati structures does impede the aesthetic content of the dance. This being the case, we need introspection on whether the very structures of these nrtta forms have changed, thereby influencing the presentation of nrtta in Bharatanatyam.

I have not discussed the role of the violinist, vina or flute artist in Bharatanatyam, as they only provide melodic support to the vocalist. They also provide alapana leads before each presentation and melodic interludes during sanchari.

Karnatik music within Bharatanatyam belongs to the dance form. It is important to treat it as a part of the whole if we want to appreciate the true beauty of Bharatanatyam. Karnatik musicians, on their part, have not realized that the Bharatanatyam aesthetic is a discovery they need to make in order to understand the fullness of their own art. The historical interrelationship between the two art forms cannot be ignored and is something the musician needs to experience. They must feel the other manifestation of Karnatik music within Bharatanatyam, and through this open their eyes to its captivating fluidity.

14

A Distant Cousin

The Karnatik and Hindustani music traditions have an intertwined history.

Both trace their roots to the same treatises on ancient music. Works like *Natya Shastra* (between the second centuries BC and AD), *Brhaddeshi* (AD 9) and *Sangita Ratnakara* (AD 12) are often quoted while describing the antiquity of Karnatik and Hindustani music. In the south, we have Tamil works, like *Silappadigaram* (AD 2) and *Pancha Marabu* that give us a great deal of information on the music prevalent in that area.

Though their seeds can be traced to ancient music systems, Karnatik and Hindustani music are not a continuation of a common body of music practised in ancient times. It is true, of course, that there are terms and ideas that are common to both. But through the ages, all of these terms have been used and understood in completely different ways, based on the musical context of the region and the times. Therefore, while a word that is used today may be traced to ancient treatises, it is quite likely to have meant something else in its cradle years. Any discussion of the two classical music systems of India must begin with an acceptance of this concept – and furthermore must acknowledge that it is quite possible that the musical link we seem to take for granted and seek does not in actual fact exist. Both traditions are the product of an intricate maze of influences and creativity from various parts of the country and the world.

Over the last 500 years, musicologists have only complicated our understanding by seeking this connectivity. They have quoted from texts of ancient music even when it was very clear that the music they were writing about had no connection with that music of the old. This has been an act of reverence to tradition, not accuracy. However, the citing of ancient authority has certainly invested their treatises with a certain venerable validity. This method, still used by many scholars, continues to cloud our understanding of both systems. Clarity emerges only when we engage directly with the ancient treatises and understand the music that they refer to, that is, when we see the fallacy of referring to Karnatik or Hindustani music as continuations of 2,000-year-old traditions. There is much yet to be understood about the ancient systems of music, and more clarity may emerge with serious comparative studies of ancient Indian musical traditions and those of the Greek and Roman cultures, with their known trade connections to India and rich cultural history. Research into the Indian ties of both these civilizations may provide us with many important missing links.

A study of the evolution of both systems shows that they arrived at their present form based on ideas of raga and tala over the last 500 years, with independent identities that gave each a captivating quality. Beyond form, content and performance traditions, they differ in the 'sound' that permeates their music. Just one line of the music of either – irrespective of the kind of improvisation or composition – will immediately establish an identity. Karnatik and Hindustani music are art music traditions, and all that has been discussed in the previous essays on the guiding force of art music holds good for both music systems. Having said that, we should bear in mind the fact that though their intent is the same, each has found different paths for the fulfilment of their musical quest, which is not separate from the music itself.

In this context, it is necessary to address a naïve – yet commonly held – perception: that India had one classical music system, which split into two after the Mughal invasion. 'Hindustani music' itself is a generic term that includes forms such as Dhrupad, Khyal, and Thumri. Dhrupad is considered the oldest among these, and is said to be the oldest living classical music form in India. Some musicians who believe in the theory of the 'split' even say that it is of an era that predates the split of Indian music into two distinct systems. While the antiquity of Dhrupad is true, the theory that it is the oldest system or of some kind of a split from which the two systems emerged is rather simplistic. The subcontinent was culturally diverse even in ancient times, as is evident from a study of painting, sculpture, architecture and dance. It is queer then that we think there was one classical system that was the root of both Karnatik and Hindustani music. Musical treatises, depictions in art and references in poetry indicate that there were many musical systems in different parts of the subcontinent. It is also evident that they were constantly interacting with each other. This was happening even before the Mughal era. Both the Hindustani and Karnatik systems evolved out of multicultural exchanges. There is no doubt that Dhrupad was a prominent classical form in the courts of the Mughals before the clear dominance of Khyal during the later Mughal rule, although Khyal may have had its origin much earlier. But there were other influences from various traditions that gave shape to the forms of music we celebrate today. These were varied and intricate cultural and social influences. Some of the commonalities that we may see in Karnatik and Dhrupad are a result of these multi-regional shared influences.

In the south, Karnatik music, as we see it today, emerged from the late eighteenth century as a result of a continuous period of change that predates the Mughals. The evolution of both systems was at once complex and organic. The influx of travellers and communities from different regions who intermingled and settled down in various parts of the subcontinent, bringing with them their cultural tradition, shaped both musical forms. This is evident from the way Karnatik music drew from scholars and musicians who were Tamil-, Marathi-, Kannada- and Telugu-speaking. Some practical methodologies may have come to it from courts in the north, while textual references can go as far up as Kashmir. This constant exchange of ideas, art forms and social customs raised a two-chambered basket of musical creativity. It is from the confluence of circumstances that these two beautiful art music systems in India have emerged.

A notion held by many Karnatik musicians and scholars is that theirs is the older tradition and resembles the ancient music much more than Hindustani music does, because the south was not directly influenced by the Mughals. Karnatik musicians will claim that Karnatik music has retained in its aesthetics an 'Indianness'. This viewpoint harks to a non-Islamic musical authenticity. I am afraid I just cannot subscribe to it. How much of an influence Islamic cultural traditions and Mughal rule had on the development of music in the south is not yet clear. But it cannot be doubted that they did influence the music. Gopalanayaka who is said to have been part of the court of Alauddin Khilji (1296–1316), is considered one of the founders of the chaturdandi tradition practised in the Tanjavur courts in the seventeenth century. Scholars from the south, such as Pandarika Vitthala (sixteenth century), travelled to other courts in the north. One scholar made out a strong case to say that the melakarta system used in Karnatik music may have Islamic, Persian and Turkish origins. The tambura, so indispensible to Karnatik music itself, may well have been a Persian import. The name 'tambura' is of course known to be of Persian origin. The use of certain terms in compositions and the adaptation of ragas from different regions clearly indicate that the south may not have been as insulated as it is believed to have been. Methods and forms appreciated and interiorized in the aesthetic sensibilities of musicians and scholars could not but have surfaced.

But the more serious question is: what is Indian? This needs serious reflection and reconsideration. Cultural changes are not about 'insiders' and 'outsiders', as such distinctions do not exist within the osmosis in society. These are dangerous political and religious positions and should not be imposed on history, let alone art and its study. Treatises reveal that there was a constant exchange of ideas between different regions, making prior antiquity or authenticity a moot point. Karnatik music itself was greatly influenced by the traditions of many regions, which are known today as Tamil Nadu, Karnataka, Maharashtra, Andhra Pradesh and Kerala. All musical impulses from society are multi-stranded and hence do not belong to only one place or region. We can separate the strands and look for the source, but there is truly no beginning. What we identify is only the obvious place of its recognizable emergence or practice. Karnatik music is not music of ancient India retained through generations. It is a new idea born from the integrated assimilation of various cultural connections.

We do not know what influences the Portuguese or the French brought with them. We do know the British have influenced Karnatik music. Their influence was not only in the introduction of the violin and in the attempts to create a notating system, but most significantly in generating studies into the theoretical basis of Indian classical music in the modern era. With this historical knowledge, it becomes clear that Karnatik music has been influenced, just as Hindustani music has been, by our own indigenous traditions and also by other cultures. These facts seriously dent our idea of the antiquity and presumed authenticity of Karnatik music.

With this short background placing both systems in a certain historical context, I would like to address some misconceptions about Karnatik music held by connoisseurs of Hindustani music.

Curiously, these are also to be found in connoisseurs of Karnatik music. It is necessary to discuss these issues, as they continue to impede listener appreciation.

These may be described as follows:

- Karnatik vocalists have a very poor sense of shruti.
- Karnatik musicians lack 'voice culture'.
- There are too many compositions in a Karnatik kutcheri, leaving very little time for manodharma.
- Karnatik alapanas are too short to delve deep into the raga.
- Karnatik music is too percussion-oriented.

I will now address each of these notions individually.

Karnatik Vocalists Have a Very Poor Sense of Shruti

This is probably the most oft-repeated criticism. The criticism is that during the rendition of melodic phrases – both in manodharma and within compositions – Karnatik musicians err in two ways. First, in their chosen shruti, svaras are not rendered in their svara positions. Even with the tambura being played in the background, Karnatik musicians are not in sync with the shruti. Second, while rendering the sa (tonic) or the pa, which is often sung sans gamaka, they are not in pitch. This basically means that Karnatik musicians sing 'off key' or 'out of shruti'. There is some truth in this, but more importantly, there is a fundamental misconception. Let us deal with the misconception first. Karnatik music, as we know, is very expressive and each svara has many different expressions due to the gamaka possibilities. Among all the gamakas, one gamaka, kampita, epitomizes the Karnatik sound. The unique feature of this specific gamaka is that, during its movement in the raga, often the svara does not fix itself or remain close to its fixed pitch position (the svara's pitch position without any movement). It exists somewhere in between, in a state of flux – and it is in that state that the svara's identity lies.

To the untrained listener, this movement would seem 'out of shruti', because it is not giving her the acoustic sound of any of the svaras as fixed pitch positions in the raga. This can give rise to an uncomfortable feeling, since one will hear the sa and pa from the tambura, and due to the harmonics generated by the four strings, certain other fixed svara positions will also be heard. Against this background, these gamakas will seem out of shruti. Actually that is not so. Each of these kampita gamakas has a very clear area of operation. This important aesthetic feature of Karnatik music has been lost sight of by the Hindustani misconception.

The other 'off key' sense is felt when a moving svara – rendered especially with kampita gamaka – connects to another svara, which in that specific melodic context is rendered as a fixed pitch position. Sometimes, after the rendition of a svara with kampita gamaka, the svara is left hanging between fixed svara positions. This hanging position is felt as a sound and not placed as a point. Moving from this state of flux to another svara's fixed position is a conscious journey of melody and not a wandering of the lost.

In Hindustani music, though every svara is expressive, they are often very close to the fixed pitch position. The svara movements with gamakas (as used in Hindustani music) touch upon a fixed pitch position of a svara. This makes for a very different listening experience. When the svara movements are closer to the fixed pitch position, they would seem more in shruti than when they are not. The moving from one fixed pitch position of a svara to the fixed pitch position of another svara is naturally easier on the ear. This is why there is this huge difference in the listening experience, and also what gives rise to the 'off key' misconception.

The expressive nature of Karnatik music makes the music much harder on the untrained ear. It is not an error of the music, but a specific and complex feature. To train one's ear for appreciating this kind of melodic movement requires de-training in conditioned listening.

While I defend Karnatik musicians and point to aesthetics as being an important reason for this feeling, let me also say that Karnatik musicians are part authors of this problem. During the description of a kutcheri, I referred to the sound of the tambura permeating the space of the performance before the curtains went up. This is what should happen, but does not always. The Karnatik musician generally gives scant importance to the sound of the shruti emanating from the tambura, and is least concerned whether or not it is heard in the space of performance. When the tambura is not heard, the audience is unable to absorb the shruti – this means that its sense of the musician's shruti too will be susceptible to error.

The use of the electronic tambura poses another serious problem. Acousticians say that the tambura is a flawed instrument as it does not sound the exact harmonics that it, scientifically speaking, should, once the four strings are tuned. While this may be true in a very strict technological sense, a musician's concern is not the mathematical perfection of the tambura, but its acoustic perfection. Through years of training, every practised musician can tune the tambura to the perfection required by the human ear. This is the perfection we seek. When the tambura is not able to do this, when it is not tuned and used thus, the shortcoming adds to the sense of shruti imperfection.

One may go on to ask if the electronic tambura, which can be scientifically tuned, satisfies the human sense of tune. The answer is that it does not. Why? One answer may be that the digitization of sound in the electronic tambura changes the manner in which the human ear hears it. This again distorts the human sense of shruti – including, of course, the musician's. A simple experiment of asking a musician to sing for about half an hour with an electronic tambura, and immediately thereafter with an ordinary tambura will demonstrate the difference between the two. The use of the electronic tambura in the training, practising and performing stages has worked to the detriment of shruti. All this has consolidated the misconception about Karnatik music going 'off key'.

Karnatik Musicians Lack 'Voice Culture'

This has been a critique from inside the system rather than outside. There has been a constant comparison of the voice training of Karnatik vocalists vis-à-vis Hindustani vocalists. In my essay on the voice, I discussed two aspects of it: the individual and the music. Only an understanding of both can bring the best out in a voice. Voice culture is not a generic system that is applicable to every individual and every music. Depending on the music being practised, each student needs to be viewed specifically. It is completely erroneous to think that Karnatik music does not have an adequate voice-training system. If we were to analyse the training methods in place, we would see that every aspect of voice culture is inbuilt. If in the process of learning, a Karnatik music student spends enough time on the various exercises and learning processes for the nurturing of the voice, this 'lack' will not arise. All this is not to create a generic 'pretty' voice, but a Karnatik voice. These lessons are built around svara exercises, practice of vocal sounds, breathing, enunciation and pitch training – methods that have been touched upon in the chapter on voice.

At the same time, I need to acknowledge that many teachers have ignored the training systems that are meant to develop their students' voices. This decline of voice-related training has affected numerous aspects of the music: voice throw, intonations, pronunciation, flexibility, fidelity, shruti perfection and tone. This has affected the quality of music as much as it has their voices. Today, we have extremely talented vocalists who have serious issues with their voice. The careless approach to training has also affected their shruti sense – this is not a problem of the system, but of the practitioners, including performers, teachers and students. If the Karnatik community as a whole were to address this issue, it would be quite easily corrected.

The right path to Karnatik voice culture has been shown by the masters, such as M.S. Subbulakshmi (1916–2004), D.K. Pattammal (1919–2009), T. Brinda (1912–96), K.V. Narayanaswamy (1923–2002) and T.V. Sankaranarayanan (b. 1945), who have all sung with a perfect sense of shruti and lovely use of the voice. Voice culture and shruti sense are inherent in Karnatik music, and it is up to the practitioners to dispel the misconception that it is not.

There Are Too Many Compositions in a Karnatik Kutcheri, Leaving Very Little Time for Manodharma

We shall discuss the issue of manodharma independently, but this criticism I completely accept. Karnatik kutcheris have, over the last century, become more about a series of compositions, dominated by the kirtanas, with a sampling of the various manodharma presentations, which has laid the ground for this criticism.

One may argue that this observation comes from the Hindustani music connoisseur, since Hindustani music does not have the kind of compositions that Karnatik music does. As true as that may be, it still does not mean that Karnatik concerts can be a series of compositions. A true celebration of a composition is when it allows every musician a window into the improvisational world. It is this opportunity that our great composers have given us. Why then are we not using it? I do not think we need to look at a Hindustani type of a concert, but we do need to respect every composition as a possibility for improvisation given to us by musical geniuses and use our faculties to explore them. This change in focus is important to retain the creativity in Karnatik music. The kutcheri must strike a balance between compositional music and improvisational music. Today, we lean heavily on the composition side. Fewer compositions in a concert result in better art music. Ultimately, whether it is Karnatik or Hindustani, the quality of the music rests with the musicians.

Karnatik Alapanas Are Too Short to Delve Deep into the Raga

Does a long or detailed alapana mean that the essence of the raga has been unveiled? This is a question that every Hindustani musician needs to introspect about. We have all heard alapanas, where even after half an hour, the raga has not opened itself. This can happen to any musician. All I am trying to say is that the length of the alapana is not a barometer of its quality. It is its 'depth', an elusive yet specific quality, that gives the discerning listener an insight into the raga. A single musical phrase rendered 'right' can reveal depth in a manner that no length can do. Long or short has nothing to do with the quality of the alapana.

'Short' is a sense of time and not a specific unit of time. The idea of short within Karnatik music itself varies between each raga. The nature of the raga and the scope for improvisation that its melodies give a musician define how long or short the alapana for a raga ought to be. A short alapana is necessary if the raga itself does not provide for much improvisation. Then why render alapana in this raga? The rendering of an alapana is a way of exploring the free-flowing improvisational possibilities of the raga, and not necessarily exploring the extent to which a raga can be explored. With the former as the reason, every raga has its own sphere of possibilities, and it takes but the journey of the musician to explore it.

What about a short alapana of a raga that offers immense improvisational scope? This is tricky. I have heard many musicians say that, after a few phrases, they had reached a certain sense of completeness beyond which they did not feel like exploring it further. This moment, an epiphanic moment, is reached in a burst of objective emotion. Once it is revealed, any further improvisation becomes irrelevant. This is possible and I see it as an important part of the alapana experience.

The shorter alapana ought not be an escape route for the

musician's inadequacy. In this sense, I completely agree with the criticism. When the short alapana is the result of a fulfilment, the listener will also experience the sense of depth. In the other case, both will be missing.

The longer alapanas are usually rendered before the 'main' and for the ragam–tanam–pallavi, even though they may not be as long as the Hindustani alapanas. But the Hindustani musician and connoisseur does not seem to recognize the longer Karnatik alapana. The general laya in a Karnatik alapana is faster than in Hindustani music, which also gives an impression of a shorter or compressed time frame. Also the compositions presented after the alapana are sometimes so complex and intricate that the Hindustani listener forgets the length and intensity of the alapana that had gone before it. In a Karnatik kutcheri, the musicians try to render an alapana for a duration that seems appropriate to the length and form of the composition. This means that there will be alapanas of varied lengths.

I do not believe that the length of an alapana is a way to gauge the quality of manodharma. It is the intensity and dedication involved in the improvisation that determines its quality. Unfortunately, it is also a fact that the increase in the number of compositions in a kutcheri has affected detail in alapanas. This has led to shorter, convenient alapanas by ill-equipped musicians – another factor that might be responsible for this skewed perception of alapanas in Karnatik music.

Karnatik Music Is Too Percussion-oriented

As with the other criticisms, there is some truth and some error to this perception. The idea of a tala and the way it is treated in both systems is completely different. Let us take a tala of twelve beats, which is common to both but is differently subdivided in each system. More than the difference in their subdivisions, it is when this tala becomes part of a melodic composition that we feel the divergence in aesthetics. Though within a subdivided tala, the melodic composition in Hindustani music considers the whole twelve-beat tala as one unit – a continuous rythmo-melodic construct, which means that if the melody begins at the first beat, the point of stress in the tala usually comes only after the completion of the twelve beats. Between them, the tala appears like an undivided unit, though it is actually divided. It is within this sense of melody that Hindustani music compositions are created. I am specifically referring to Khyal here. Sometimes there are extremely slow compositions, but even there, the melodic movements flow without accents on every beat until the completion of the melodic line, which is always constructed to emphasize the first beat of the tala cycle (the sam in Hindustani music, sama in the Karnatik tradition). The melodic line can also extend to two tala cycles. In the absence of obvious melodic accents within the tala, the tabla artist has to keep the flow of the tala constant and make sure that the accent on the sam is clear. Thus the total unit form of the tala is maintained. The tabla artist's method of accompaniment is within the flow of the tala without emphasizing the divisions within and flowing along with the melody. When this happens, the tala is a continuous flow without sharp cuts. The resultant feeling is of a smooth melodic movement with the tala, and of the tabla artist residing in the background, appearing to emphasize only the sam. The extension of this tala feeling is found even in the treatment of tala during the tabla solo, where the rhythmic structures are whole forms of varied patterns culminating in an emphatic sam.

The Karnatik experience is the exact opposite. A tala of twelve beats – divided in a certain way (5+2+5) – is regarded as a whole of the specific division. The compositions clearly display the division in their melodic structure. The melodic flow in the tala is such that, in multiple places, the syllabic and melodic form is emphasized. The melodic nature of Karnatik music, with its heavy usage of gamaka, also creates these points of melodic accent. This aesthetic makes it a necessity that every beat in a tala be a clear division. We should also not forget that, unlike in Khyal music, the tala in Karnatik music is physically expressed, with the musician displaying every beat. This makes tala a very clear part of the aesthetic experience. In this aesthetic, every beat is distinct and the exact way the tala is divided is as visible as it is audible. To an unfamiliar listener, this experience can seem rigid, tight and sharp. These clear demarcations are an integral part of the melody. They are not looked upon as stops in the melodic flow. This is critical. To an ear unfamiliar with this music, the tala beats, melodic emphasis and syllabic stress within the clearly divided tala would feel like multiple interruptions in the melodic flow. But that is not the case. It is just that the idea of continuous melodic flow in Karnatik music is different from that of Hindustani music.

Due to this emphasis on the tala divisions and form, the mrdanga accompaniment is far sharper than the tabla in Hindustani music. To the mrdanga artist, every melodic and syllabic stress is as important as the total flow of the melody. The mrdanga artist creates rhythmic patterns within each avartana, emphasizing the melodic structure and the tala's internal divisions. The result of such an approach is that the melody feels divided to one used to Hindustani music. This approach to the tala is also seen in the tani avartana, where every beat and part of the tala is used for rhythmic patterns and mathematical calculations. In fact, the whole system of mathematical calculations that have evolved in Karnatik music is a result of this use of tala – not as a whole but as a divided whole.

There is always a 'but' after all this. The divided-whole approach to tala has resulted in mrdanga artists developing accompanying techniques purely on the framework of the tala, rather than the melody. I have already dealt with some of these issues in the essay critiquing the kutcheri. The altered approach of mrdanga artists has affected the melodic flow of compositions and compositional manodharma. That distortion has even led to the mrdanga dictating the manodharma. Similarly, when the technique of highlighting every part of a melodic line is taken to an extreme, the melodic line gets overtaken, overwhelmed and overpowered by the rhythmic sound. The volume level of the mrdanga has also increased, making the music sound even more percussive. This is not a critique of the method of accompanying, because at one level it is necessary and is a part of the Karnatik aesthetic form. But anything being presented as part of an aesthetic needs to have an element of restraint in order to retain the integrity of the music as a whole. When this is lost, the aesthetics loses its sheen.

There are two sides to every story, including the criticisms of Karnatik music by Hindustani musicians and connoisseurs. There are similarly numerous criticisms about Hindustani music from the Karnatik community. Both can be countered, sometimes convincingly, at others times not. As we have seen, it is a combination of a lack of awareness from the connoisseur and some amount of carelessness within the musician community that leads to such misconceptions. Every lover of aesthetics will need to make a conscious effort to leave the conditioned mind behind so as to be able to enter the world of another art form. It is better to not listen than to listen in a prejudiced manner. This effort is necessary for every Hindustani musician and connoisseur who truly wants to appreciate the aesthetics of Karnatik music. Comparisons are a waste of time, as each form gives us a different experience. At the same time, if a certain criticism is valid, it is the responsibility of the musical community to take it seriously. Karnatik musicians need to reflect and introspect on this.

15

The Melting Pot

We live in an era of access. It does not matter where we are, we can smell the fragrance of violets from Mayfair and the scent of the jasmine from Mylapore. This is a gift of the modern times, no doubt, and connects us with life elsewhere on the planet. However, this access has also changed the texture of our experience of the world around us.

A violet is not just a flower; its life is closely knit with the soil, seasons, bees and the people of England. When experienced in its natural setting, it is a violet. We see it not just for what it is, but for how and why it is what it is. We are sensitive to its entire being. When the violet arrives in Mumbai, it is still a flower. We do see the colours, shapes and perhaps catch some of its fragrance, but can the living being that it was in its own home hope to be recreated here?

Can the violet become part of another environment? Grow there, share its life with the people there, absorb that soil, wind, rain, dew and sun? We see that, in a manner of speaking, it can. It can come to life as a creation within the new context. But will it be or, indeed, can it be the same violet as the one in England? The answer is yes and no. The physical qualities may be the same, but the different soil, bees and the people who nurture it have made it part of another existence. I do not speak scientifically here, but about how we experience the flower.

A flower plucked from our garden is also distanced from its self. Most of us would agree that the beauty of a flower is far more enveloping when it is part of its holder, nature, than when seen in a vase. But by virtue of sharing the same environment as the flower in the vase, our mind can visualize it beyond. This awareness makes our relationship with the garden flower distinctly different from that of the airlifted violet.

Environmentalists could argue that introducing some plants from another ecology may threaten indigenous flora. Their misgiving points to the importance of the natural home for nature's creations. This view does not challenge the diversity beyond, rather it brings attention to the diversity within. This is as much an aesthetic thought, as it is ecological.

Fusion is a fascinating word. It is derived from the word 'fusio' meaning 'to melt' – the union of diverse elements using heat. The word also indicates a state of fluidity. In music too, fusion suggests the melting together of elements of music. Here, the heat source is the action that initiates this melting, leading to the evolution of a cohesive musical idea. The melting of musical elements as a result of active minds leads to the emergence of a new idea, form, interpretation. Once the fluidity that results from the fusion has settled down, we have a new and different entity. The melting, therefore, leads to a combined solidified state. In this state, the music is a different entity.

I am specifically avoiding the use of the term 'mixing' here. Mixing means the putting together of different elements, but does not denote fusing with one another. When something melts, there is a certain surrender to the other. Surrender is not subordination. It is a giving up of individual identity. When the elements are mixed, their identities are clearly retained in the combination. In melting, this would not be the case. Fusion in music results from the melting of an idea or ideas within a new framework, settling down to reveal an independent musical expression.

Melting in music is beautiful indeed, because it describes not only the evolving of music but also the response to it. When elements of music melt, there is no conflict; there is instead a transformation of identity. One that is complete on its own. This new form need not relate to its source. Similarly, when a discerning listener is immersed in music, the mind of the individual also melts into the music. In this state, there is a sense of fusion in the emergence of a different consciousness as a result of the fusing of the minds of the musicians and the connoisseur.

As an idea, every musical system contains fusion. Every aspect of a musical idiom has to be fused with the other for the music to have a singular identity. It is the aesthetics of the music, including its past and present journey, which guides the fusion of its elements. Like every other musical tradition, Karnatik music is fused into one distinct entity, which encompasses every aspect of it, including compositional and improvisational music.

There are many instances of fusion in Karnatik music, ranging from instruments used to the ragas and compositional forms that are being infused into the music's evolving idiom.

The violin is one of the most magnificent examples of fusion. While we are not very clear about the Roman or Portuguese influence on south Indian music, we can be very sure that the inclusion of violin into the Karnatik fold was a direct result of British influence. Visually, the violins used in Karnatik music and Western classical music look exactly the same, in terms of size, shape, bridge, strings, pegs and bow. That is because they are the same. Most professional violinists playing Karnatik music use a European violin. But beyond this, everything about it, including the music it produces, is different. The type of strings used, the tuning, the position in which it is held, the techniques of playing and finally the music that emanates are all Karnatik. The violin is completely fused with the sound of Karnatik music. This is, therefore, no longer a Western classical violin; it is a Karnatik violin. The instrument is only a piece of carved wood until a human being plays it. The relationship between the instrument and the instrumentalist defines it. The music being played is the essence of the instrument. The fusion of the violin into Karnatik music is built on this relationship between the instrument, the instrumentalist and the music.

Karnatik music has for long adapted Indian and folk traditions. That music fused into Karnatik music, thereby discovering a Karnatik sound for itself. The agent who brought about this process of fusion and discovery is the musician. Again, driven by the aesthetics of the music, these ragas came to be an integral part of the Karnatik raga spectrum. Similarly, compositional forms from other musical traditions have also been infused into Karnatik music. The tillana was assimilated from Hindustani music as an idea of a melodic compositional form made up only of rhythmic syllables instead of sahitya. This form evolved using the inherent jati patterns from the south Indian rhythmic and dance traditions. Over the last century, the tillana has developed many avatars, all within Karnatik music. This is fusion of a compositional type.

All the above examples, one may argue, refer only to the fusion of one instrument, raga or compositional form with an existent musical system. There is only one fused element that is melting into the musical system. This is partially true, but one has to recognize that when this fusion occurs, the musical system changes its aesthetics to accept the new entrant. In embracing a raga that has melted into Karnatik music, the music gains a new dimension and in doing so reinvents itself.

Jugalbandi is a word often used for musical presentations that involve both Karnatik and Hindustani musicians, but is not restricted to this interpretation. It can include presentations by two musicians from the same genre of music too. Jugalbandi literally means a conjoint bond, the coming together of two in one. The confluence one seeks is the coming together of musical ideas, which connect with both the musicians and the music they represent. The connection is in the bond that one experiences. Jugalbandis bring different musical interpretations or forms together to consciously seek points of connection. These intersections are used for exploring music, keeping in mind each musician's tradition, which naturally leads to diversions from common motifs.

When two artists from the same musical system come together, the search is to find points of commonality and present diverse perspectives to similar musical content. The artists are constantly responding to each other's music, resulting in exchanges displaying their distinctive interpretations. There is also some mixture of styles. The musicians' broad sense of beauty is similar as the aesthetics of their music is common. This kind of jugalbandi is natural, as it does not require any change in the musical framework. The musicians respond to the other's music based on their own bani and style, and the identity of both the musicians and their music is clearly maintained.

When a jugalbandi involves Karnatik and Hindustani musicians, it becomes complex. Here the aesthetics of each musical form creates clear frameworks for the musical expression of both musicians. Keeping these aesthetics intact yet finding common ground with the other musician is an onerous task. There is a commonality between both systems, but the interpretations of these common aspects are so diverse that bringing them together is very difficult. What happens in such jugalbandis is that, except for the choice of raga or tala, the music remains largely separate. The conjoint nature is achieved only in the connection of the basic raga or tala. Raga may be the same at a very basic level, but its identity within each system is what truly defines it. A jugalbandi highlights these aspects, while reminding us of historical sharing.

The musical connections established in such jugalbandis are confined to the given performance. The joint performance's aesthetic intent also becomes difficult to define. How do two musicians find common space when the aesthetics of their individual traditions move them very differently? The ideal way would be not to seek commonality beyond the basic aspects of tala and raga. Keeping this intact, the musicians should present their musical form to the best of their abilities. What the audience receives is a clear representation of how the two systems with similar building blocks have created very individual ideas of beauty. This may not, therefore, be a jugalbandi as the name suggests, but could be a worthwhile experience all the same. Concordance brings the musicians together, but music keeps them independent.

When Karnatik-Hindustani jugalbandis try to go beyond and seek stylistic and aesthetic commonality, they become slanted affairs. The presentation moves largely into one genre. This defeats the very objective of confluence. As far as the melody is concerned, Karnatik musicians try to render ragas with a Hindustani slant, while the Hindustani musician tries to remain true to his tradition. In the case of percussion, often all percussionists end up following the Karnatik tradition. This destroys the aesthetics of both systems. When musicians try to imitate the other, they will not be able to express the music truly because their aesthetic sensibilities lie within their own music. This makes the attempt seem more like a poor imitation rather than an interpretation. The result is an evening of aesthetic confusion. The musicians' appeal remains divided, as does the audience's receptivity, but aesthetic discernment is abandoned comprehensively by both.

In the contemporary use of fusion, there is the coming together of two independent musical systems or ideas to create a 'new' identity. When musicians come together with their musical knowledge and skills they hope to create a new musical idea, another sense of beauty, evolving from the existing forms. This evolution of a new paradigm, concept and sound is extremely difficult as it involves shedding some and retaining other musical ideas of each system involved. It also requires a degree of deconstruction of the music, which hopefully leads to a radically different construction.

Is this possible? If so, does fusion music achieve this today?

I would like to address this whole issue from the angle of Karnatik music and how musicians have sought to use its elements in the context of fusion music There are many hurdles in such an endeavour, and addressing them will give us an idea of what has been happening in the world of Karnatik fusion music.

Why would a musician within the Karnatik tradition seek to explore fusion using Karnatik music? The intent behind any action is crucial to the direction in which it leads the person. Some answers from musicians are:

- 'To explore beyond Karnatik music'
- 'To remove the barriers imposed by the music'
- 'To expand the listenership of Karnatik music'
- 'To showcase the universality of Karnatik music'

All these answers indicate that Karnatik music is restrictive, but can be adapted to any musical context, that this will result in a greater appreciation of Karnatik music. The artists seek to break the shackles of Karnatik music but use its universal adaptability to contribute to the music. This whole cycle of thought is flawed.

'To Explore Beyond Karnatik Music'

As an idea, this is fine, but why does it have to involve Karnatik music? Every musician can learn and absorb various musical systems of the world. This does not require a manipulation of the aesthetic environment of Karnatik music. Musicians must understand that their attempt to increase their range of musical abilities must not be at the expense of Karnatik music. Every music must be given the treatment that its history and aesthetics demand, irrespective of the musician's need to explore other systems. Karnatik music gives you a musical vision, but does not allow us to misuse its beauty to advance our personal yearning. We need to respect the music, yet use its vision to look outside if we so seek.

'To Remove the Barriers Imposed by the Music'

Once someone views the aesthetic framework of a music system as a restriction, there is a serious problem of understanding. The restrictions are not 'stop signs'; they are signposts of the music. They guide a musician by giving him a direction that retains the integrity of Karnatik music. A musician who views these as restrictions has not internalized the aesthetics of the music to feel the absolute freedom of exploration, with these signposts playing only the role of indicators. The moment these are removed, the music loses its identity. Karnatik music is as much in the signposts as in what is between them. They are not restrictions; how then can there be a need to remove them? Once the musician completely immerses his mind in the all-encompassing aesthetics of the music, it will become clear that these perceived restrictions in fact contribute to the evolution and expansion of the music. Karnatik music is suffocating only for those who do not live within it, and use its aesthetic elements as mere tools.

'To Expand the Listenership of Karnatik Music'

The listenership of an art music form cannot be compared to that of any other form of music. The involvement in Karnatik music requires of the listener a certain serious level of engagement. This makes it necessary for the listener to have a certain level of understanding. The number of people who can be involved in Karnatik music – or indeed any art music – cannot compare to the numbers of listeners for a popular music form, which do not require the same level of study and engagement. When we say that we want to 'expand the listenership of Karnatik music', we are also saying that, in order to do so, we need to change its aesthetic form. The change may include simplifying some aspects or using other instruments from popular music. Is this an appropriate way of approaching the issue of listenership? I believe that education in the intricacies of Karnatik music from a very young age will help cultivate a young audience for it. This will not only create a healthy audience in terms of numbers, but also in their awareness of the music.

It is believed that listeners of fusion will be able to gradually understand the intricacies of Karnatik music. Many people will say that this is how they developed an interest in Karnatik music. What this hides is that many of them have a lopsided idea of the music – the result of a lack of understanding of its aesthetic structure. Dangerously, many fusion musicians carry traits from that music back into their Karnatik music, thereby altering its aesthetics. Karnatik music then sounds increasingly like popular music, losing the complex structure and content that is part of its nature. The attitude of these musicians is altered because of the belief they imbibe that manipulating the core of Karnatik music is part of making it more accessible.

Karnatik music is accessible for those who seek it. Our role as musicians and educators is to give every individual an equal opportunity to learn. We should retain the aesthetics of the music and present it in all its honesty to let people appreciate it. The notion that the listenership of Karnatik music can be expanded only by using the altered elements of fusion music is presumptuous, even preposterous.

'To Showcase the Universality of Karnatik Music'

No musical form is universal. No doubt Karnatik music empowers the musician to understand different musical environments. This does not imply that Karnatik music is universal. Every art music form gives musicians the ability to recognize the aesthetic structures that constitute music in any form. With vision, it is possible for musicians to use these skills to interpret all forms of music. In presenting Karnatik music as universally adaptable, we also believe its nature needs to be changed. Once we alter its nature, though, what remains is no longer Karnatik music. No art music form is a loose collection of elements that come together. Karnatik music is a tightly packed entity, held together by a vital core.

All the notions discussed here are geared towards one specific action: convenient changes being made to Karnatik music. It becomes a set of musical ideas that can be manipulated to produce a more popular sound and presentation.

The intent driving any journey towards a possible fusion of musical ideas must be based purely on music. A musician who is seriously engaged with Karnatik music but open to other forms may be able to carry the sound of the music into a different context. When the trigger for fusion is pure musical quest, what emerges is special. The musician is not merely taking aspects of the music to present a new formation, but is able to internalize the elements in such a manner that one musical idea effortlessly melts into the other. The intent here is the musical journey of this seeker of aesthetics. The musician is not seeking to create a new form of music for her own sake, but her creative impulses are being driven in that direction based on serious involvement in the music. This, I must say, is extremely rare and difficult, which is why we don't find new genres of music emerging very often.

For true fusion, the Karnatik musician must first immerse herself in the music. She would then respect the intent of the music and recognize that there is nothing frivolous or superficial about it, nothing that can be glossed over as irrelevant. She would have practical knowledge backed by theoretical understanding, and the highest order of skill levels. She would also understand the social and cultural context of the music. When such a musician is involved in fusion music, the work can acquire the value of a new contribution.

The Karnatik musicians involved in attempts at fusion must also have a good understanding of the forms of music they are involving with. It cannot be a case of 'I bring this music and you bring that'. Fusion is neither a barter nor a negotiation. The musicians attempting it must be equipped to intuitively recognize the possibilities that can transform into fusion – and that is possible only if they have a clear understanding of all the different musical ideas that are part of the creation.

Fusion with this level of commitment results in a fluid flow of various ideas into each other. The musician in such a situation is not only aware that this path will take him towards another musical form, but is also aware that he will be moving away from Karnatik music. The new musical idea evolves over a period of time, with the musicians seriously engaged in the activity of giving shape to a music that is inspired by Karnatik music but is not Karnatik music. It is not a form derived by altering some elements of Karnatik music, but rather from a different aesthetic sound that the musicians discover in their journey. The element of Karnatik music and the other forms that may be a part of this discovery are incidental to the actual experience of the sound. This expression 'sound', which I have used multiple times, is what gives unity to any musical system.

The world of fusion today is very different. Karnatik musicians are part of fusion bands along with artists who play Western instruments or African and Middle Eastern percussion instruments. They sometimes present Karnatik compositions with Western harmony arrangements or background scores. The rhythmic section is also enhanced by other types of drums that impose a completely unrelated style of accompaniment on the compositional aesthetic. The composition, however, is rendered as it is in Karnatik music. The musicians say that this is a way of retaining the 'Karnatik element'. A composition is not just the pallavi, anupallavi, charana composed in a raga and tala by a vaggeyakara. It is the aesthetics of the complete melodic and rhythmic flow. Any addition to the composition can destroy it – an idea that, despite its simplicity, appears to be difficult to grasp.

Some musicians compose special pieces for fusion. These are generally in scale-based ragas, which are used as svara combinations that the musicians render. Many of these bands also have a guitar player to contribute to the melodic variation. In such cases, the term 'composition' is used in the most frivolous sense. A composition must have an intention behind its creation, form and content. It cannot just copy elements from different compositional forms of various musical systems. A composition can exist only if the intent of the music exists. Almost no fusion band really understands the intent of the music they are creating. They want to create a popular sound using elements from Karnatik music as a base. There is no serious musical insight in any of the efforts.

A worrisome trend is that many of those engaged in fusion experiments are very young Karnatik musicians who are yet to understand the depth of the music. Their Karnatik music acumen is superficial. Such experiments affect their Karnatik music talent, blunting their development as serious art musicians. Some musicians involved in such efforts display their capacity to adapt to any kind of music, using their training as Karnatik musicians. Clearly, these are supremely skilled musicians, but that sort of proficiency is one baby step in the understanding of music. If his approach to music itself is limited to skill, that is the only facet that the musician can bring to the new situation as well.

Fusion music today is neither a single system of music nor a collection of systems or concrete ideas. It is anything that does not sound like one specific established genre, yet has recognizable aspects of the original music. When we have such a loose idea of fusion, is any serious work possible? The word 'experiment', which is so often used in the context of fusion music itself, undermines the very idea. Fusion music cannot be chanced upon. Fusion happens with a conscious, serious and aware mind. The problem is that the fusion bands' understanding is limited to the elements they mix, not fuse. There is a lack of continuity in ideation. The aesthetics of all music – popular, folk or art – have evolved to give it clear definition. This takes a very long time and occurs over generations and cannot happen unless it is driven by intention.

I must return to the violet. The emergence of modern fusion music, as understood today, is a manifestation of our avariciousness, our craving to be able to do anything and experience everything, with no respect for context. We do not see the intensity of that which is within. It is only a realization of what is within that will give us true insight into what exists beyond.

16

The Sound of Cinema

So embedded are song and dance in the world of Indian cinema that they have come to define it to the world. This is not a contemporary phenomenon. Music was interwoven with our dramatic arts even before cinema made its appearance. In theatre, traditionally, dialogue was a coin of which one side was spoken and the other sung. The idea was to heighten human situations, giving them powerful emotional undertones. Tunes played on instruments and songs with lyrics, often containing profound messages, plotted the twists and turns in the narrative, and most likely the performance would conclude with a powerful musical denouement. The musical ensemble in Indian theatre was not an appendage, but an integral part of the cast.

When the medium of cinema, specifically talkies, came into being, it was but natural that actors and their audiences would consider the movies an extension of theatre into a new and fascinating medium. Actors transposed their skills and audiences their expectations of theatre seamlessly from the stage to the screen. Though the craft was different, the idea was the same.

But what was the kind of music to be used in this new medium? That was a period – we are talking about the 1930s –

when Madras had already come to be the hub for Karnatik music and, as the most important city in the south, became the obvious host for Tamil cinema. Incidentally, the evolutionary pattern of Tamil cinema is applicable to Kannada, Telugu and Malayalam cinema too, with some qualifications.

Karnatik music and folk songs were the dominant musical sounds of the time. Traditional theatrical presentations like Yakshagana and Bhagavata Mela used elements from Karnatik music, as did traditional dance forms. At the same time, storytelling traditions like Harikatha were widely popular, especially among the Brahmin community. Most Harikatha exponents were trained Karnatik musicians who used numerous kirtanas and shlokas in their presentation.

The theatrical traditions that were not connected to Karnatik music do not seem to have played a significant role in cinema music, most likely because the cinema establishment was dominated by upper castes in the initial years. It is clear that at least the socially dominant theatre traditions in those days, especially during the early twentieth century, used Karnatik music as their primary melodic source. So almost every actor had to have a fairly good training in Karnatik music. Every actor gave voice to the songs used during dramatic situations. South Indian talkies were thus born in a musically suffused environment.

Much of the music used in early cinema was structured on Karnatik music. Ragas, talas and compositional structures were all borrowed from this art form with such fidelity that if the same compositions were rendered outside of the cinema context, they could be seen as pure art music compositions. The brilliant Karnatik music composer Papanasam Sivan (1890–1973) was also a pioneer in cinema music. His music in films was primarily Karnatik in content, yet focused on the story. Many Karnatik musicians, like G.N. Balasubramaniam (1910–65), M.S. Subbulakshmi and Musiri Subramania Iyer (1899–1975), acted in movies.

Since the music was so Karnatik in texture, the musicians had to have more than a passing acquaintance with it; they had, in fact, to be accomplished musicians. This was a time when musical skills, not acting ability, determined the choice of the actors, even determined their success. Other composers who were trained in Karnatik music, although they were not 'mainstream' Karnatik musicians, and made significant contributions to film music were S.V. Venkatraman, C.R. Subbaraman, S.N. Subbiah Naidu and G. Ramanathan. Many movies were based on mythological and religious themes with social issues being a subplot. Karnatik music being deeply embedded in mythology and religion, the movies got their musical content handed on a platter. Music was so important in the movies that sometimes there could be as many as forty songs. Interestingly, in a reverse flow, many of the songs composed for films in the Karnatik mould later found their way into kutcheris.

Many actors also entered the movies from the world of theatre. Though these actors too may have trained in Karnatik music, they brought with them a distinctly different musical flavour. Singer-actors of this era included M.K. Tyagaraja Bhagavatar, N.S. Krishnan, P.U. Chinnappa and T.R. Mahalingam (not to be confused with the famous Karnatik flautist of the same name).

This differentiation in the expressions of the two groups is important. As times changed, so did the music of the cinema. The non-Karnatik expression evolved into a distinct cinema music expression.

Cinema Music and Social Change

Interestingly, in many movies, both the language used and the music seemed to imply a social distinction. The actors who played characters from the higher social strata invariably spoke in a more literary script, while the common man spoke in casual, colloquial language. In music too this differentiation was evident. The songs sung by royalty or higher castes were closer to the Karnatik idiom, while the music of the commoner was closer to folk music. This phenomenon is important because, in my opinion, it influenced the democratization of cinema music, drawing it away from Karnatik music.

After the initial years of a completely music-based cinema experience, the medium diversified in many directions. Technological changes made it possible for an actor to be selected on the basis of his acting ability rather than musical skills. This is when music came to be associated with a word it had never known before: playback. Singers and musicians were specifically employed to provide the much-needed music through this playback. Music was recorded in a studio and the actors only had to lip-sync to the track. This immediately improved the skill and quality of acting and many leading actors such as Sivaji Ganesan and M.G. Ramachandran, with no known singing talent, entered cinema. Even during this period, 'classically' trained musicians like Ghantasala, Sirgazhi Govindarajan, T.M. Soundarrajan, P. Leela and M.L. Vasanthakumari were part of the cinema world, but as playback singers. But this too was to change very soon.

South Indian film music began to be influenced by many musical forms from across the country and around the world, like Hindi film music, Ghazals and popular music from the West. The influence of Hindi film music was a major factor, as some of the Western influences came via Bombay. All this naturally reduced the 'Karnatik' elements in south Indian film music.

By the 1950s, cinema was the most popular entertainment in the country, cutting across all class and economic divisions. The 1950s and the 1960s were also turbulent times, especially in Tamil Nadu. The political sphere had changed due to the social revolutions that questioned social norms and the dominance of the brahmin community. This had serious implications in the world of cinema as well. The most popular form of entertainment could not but be seen as a handy tool for political and social change. Actors and scriptwriters joined political parties and their enormous popularity proved advantageous to the latter.

The stories changed, with social and political themes dominating cinema. All of this also changed the nature of the music required in films. It began to move away from the upper-class-dominated Karnatik music influence. Caste equations within the cinema world were changing simultaneously. During this period, there were a number of film music composers who were truly in the transition phase between film music that was heavy with the Karnatik influence and one that was unique in its sound. While K.V. Mahadevan, a leading composer, was deeply influenced by Karnatik music, composers like the brilliant duo M.S. Viswanathan and T.K. Ramamurthi were clearly moving away. But even during this phase, the music of films based on mythology remained under the influence of Karnatik music. This is true even today, although there are not very many such films made any more. I am not aware of any religious or mythological film in south India that is completely devoid of a Karnatik influence. This has serious religious, cultural and social overtones, which are not within the purview of this essay.

Viewing these developments against the backdrop of the obvious exclusivity established in the kind of music and language used in the early days of cinema music, one can see why a gradual movement away from the Karnatik idiom was inevitable.

At the same time, it is important to understand that cinema music did not evolve as one specific musical form. Nor was it necessary, given that film music responds to movements in the plot. Stories and contexts too change with the times, which means that the music is not required to retain a specific form. This dynamism makes it imperative for film music to embrace newer technologies and influences from across the globe in the search for the most beautiful aural pairing with the visual.

As a result, the nature of singers and composers also changed. Gradually, they were not necessarily trained in Karnatik music.

People with a natural bent for music, and capable of absorbing musical ideas from the many impulses and developments around them, became singers and composers in the film world. Some came from folk music backgrounds and evolved into versatile musicians after entering the film world. They were not classically trained like the Karnatik musicians of the 1940s and 1950s. This does not imply that their music was any less wonderful. It only shows that cinema music was moving further away from the Karnatik idiom.

The Ilayaraja Phenomenon

The advent of Ilayaraja in the mid-1970s is another interesting phenomenon in the complex relationship south Indian cine music shares with Karnatik art music. Initially, he was considered to be a musician who brought folk music into south Indian films, but with his understanding of Western classical and popular music, he changed the very arrangement of music and the role of musical instruments in films. During his time, electronic sounds were given form and shape.

What makes Ilayaraja an interesting personality from the position of Karnatik music is the way he composed many tunes based on Karnatik ragas and juxtaposed them with complex harmonies. Examples of such melodies include 'Poonkadhave' (*Nizhalgal*, 1980), 'Kundhalile' (*Balanagamma*, 1982) and 'Anandaragam' (*Pannir Pushpangal*, 1981). This was something that had never been tried at this level in Indian film music. Though composers like M.S. Viswanathan and T.K. Ramamurthi had used Karnatik ragas as the basis for melodies in the new film music context of the 1960s, their instrumentation did not have this Western classical approach. Ilayaraja was largely successful in this bringing together of unconnected elements from different musical traditions.

The Rahman Effect

The post-Ilayaraja era was, and is, dominated by A.R. Rahman. The first major change that Rahman brought to film music was the quality of the sound that one heard, irrespective of whether it was a voice or an instrument. His arrival coincided with major leaps in technology, which made it possible to completely transform the way cinema music was produced and experienced. I do not want to discuss his music, as it is beyond the scope of this essay, but the Rahman effect continues to dominate not just south Indian film music, but Indian cinema.

Despite all this, elements of Karnatik music have appeared throughout the history of south Indian film music and continue to do so. Rahman and his successors have at times used Karnatik ragas as superficial sources for melodies.

Here, a small note on Malayalam film music is necessary for its distinct connection with Karnatik music almost until very recently. It is interesting that even as music in the Tamil, Telugu and Kannada film industries changed in similar ways, the Malayalam industry stayed rooted to its Karnatik moorings. The way Karnatik elements were being interpreted in Malayalam film music changed, but the dominance of the Karnatik sound did not.

The Rise of Cine-Karnatik

It is not my intention to provide a historical summary of the south Indian cinema industry, but, as a musician, to track the journey of Karnatik music through its many frames.

Where Karnatik music remains a source of inspiration to Tamil cinema, even if at a many-times-removed distance, I am interested in certain perceptual overlaps and actions over the last two or three decades. These, I believe, have influenced Karnatik music, the musicians and the listener.

Of particular interest are two films, released within a few years of each other, that specifically dealt with Karnatik music. The first was *Shankarabharanam* (Telugu, 1979), which was also released in multiple languages and went on to become very successful. The music director was the legendary K.V. Mahadevan. This film is considered to have revived a huge interest in Karnatik music outside its stronghold. A number of Telugu films that followed in *Shankarabharanam*'s wake used many Karnatik music elements.

How 'Karnatik' was the music in the movie? This is a question that could have been, and I have no doubt was, asked of *Shankarabharanam*. It appears like a redundant question, because the music of a film, even if it is named after a raga, need not be completely true to the Karnatik. But as it happened, the theme demanded an honest depiction of a Karnatik musician. While the melodies were largely based on Karnatik ragas and talas, none of the playback singers were Karnatik musicians. This gave the melodies a distinctive cine-Karnatik feel.

This sense of Karnatik music existed even earlier in cinema music, but came into sharp relief in this film about a Karnatik musician. An idea of Karnatik music, which is not art music in its true sense but nonetheless has a perceptible connection to it, had now been clearly established in cinema.

How do I explain this? Extremely difficult as it is, I will try. Just as we have a speaking accent depending on our language and the locality we live in, every musical form has a singing accent. This is defined by the aesthetics of the music.

A generic term used for Karnatik music is 'heavy'. A sense of weightiness is associated with it. This comes for the method of vocalization, emphasis, pronunciation and in the essential nature of the melodic movements. Now, this heaviness is sought to be diluted in what I call cine-Karnatik.

Karnatik music, we should note, requires a kind of guttural emphasis when certain phrases are sung, giving them definition and stability. This is usually done away with or cushioned in cinema. The general use of the voice is very different in light music, where 'softness' and 'pleasantness' are considered important, especially in 'melodious' songs. If we put all this together, we have the sound of cine-Karnatik music. I am deliberately not using the phrase 'quasi-Karnatik' because 'quasi' has a pejorative connotation, like 'pseudo' does, and I do not want to be negative here. But recognizing this is essential to an understanding of what Karnatik music 'sound' means to a film music aficionado.

Every Karnatik music student hears film music and can be an active participant in its appreciation. This has led to a certain spillover of the cine-Karnatik sense into the art music form. While such an influence may not be intentional, it has definitely made its presence felt. Some may feel that this is part of the form's musical evolution. I do not agree. We have to analyse every influence in the context of what the music itself is, where it comes from and what it means. I believe cine-Karnatik fails this test and, hence, is not part of Karnatik music's development process. The internal aesthetics of the music are disturbed when its sound is altered on the basis of an external influence. We need to analyse Karnatik music in the context of its existent expression and see if the influencing cinema has a place under its sun or not. A blind acceptance of any influence as being part of a larger process of evolutionary change is unacceptable, as it defies the basic nature and dynamics of Karnatik music.

The second film in this discussion is *Sindhu Bhairavi* (Tamil, 1985). This hugely successful film used predominantly Karnatik music elements – once again, the story was about a Karnatik musician. The composer, the inimitable Ilayaraja, used a Tyagaraja composition, 'Mari mari ninne', in raga saramati. This was an interesting situation, as Tyagaraja had composed it in raga kambhoji and, more importantly, there was an oral version of the song available. So, if Ilayaraja had wanted to, he could have used 'Mari mari ninne' as rendered in Karnatik music. Why he did not do so, I do not know. Maybe he felt that the meaning of the lyrics and the context of the film demanded another raga and melody? Only he knows and only he can tell.

But we can and must ask: what does this transposition of a composition from its parent raga onto another actually do to the kirtana? A great deal, actually. The essence of its being disintegrates. This is not to say that the film version of the kirtana was not beautiful. I am examining what the film version did to the integrity of the kirtana. As I said, the film song destroyed it. To me, the film version was unacceptable.

What was more interesting was the lack of reaction from the Karnatik music community. This lethargy was evidence of both a fear of the popular and, more significantly, a certain lack of confidence in the music itself. I for one wish questions had been raised, not because a particular film's use of a Tyagaraja kirtana would have been brought under the scanner, but because it could have led to a serious questioning of the veracity of changes that are made to compositions – not by film music directors, but by Karnatik musicians themselves. Essentially, Illayaraja was not doing something that Karnatik musicians had not done themselves.

This film also brought up another debate, again based on the same kirtana. In the movie, a member of the singer's audience asks him why he sings only in languages that the Tamil people do not understand. She comes up on stage and, in fact, renders a Tamil song in the same raga, complete with kalpanasvaras. This leads, in the film, to the musician going on to include a number of Tamil compositions in his recitals. That scene brought back the debate of the early twentieth century on the issue of language in music. It was clear also that no one had understood the role of language in art music beyond the confines of lyrical understanding. The fact that those beyond the Karnatik environment were discussing the issue of language in Karnatik music was most fascinating. It was a rare opportunity to understand the general perception of a complex issue. It emerged that even within the world of Karnatik music, language and its lyrical import was a strongly held idea, and this had been communicated to the world outside. As a community, we believed and still believe that when a musician renders a Tyagaraja kirtana, he must emote the word meanings of the compositions. This lack of a larger perspective – a matter I have delved into at length in a separate chapter – persists both within and outside the Karnatik music world and will probably never die.

Ilayaraja did something more. He consciously ventured into another territory: Karnatik music itself. Taking on the role of a vaggeyakara, no less, he invented scales and composed in the kirtana format. This, in my opinion, was an unfortunate venture by the great film musician – unfortunate for him and Karnatik music. Neither the ragas nor the compositions hold up as composite Karnatik music creations. But it would be wrong to critique only Ilayaraja, as he merely reflected the superficial understanding of Karnatik music that the music community itself had by then accepted. A raga was only a scale, which could be manipulated. A composition was a mix of lyrics, tala and raga. This rather immature and simplistic understanding of Karnatik music led to all musicians feeling that it could be easily handled, as Ilayaraja did. Although his compositions have not yet been accepted into Karnatik art music, the phenomenon deserves discussion. It reveals in Ilayaraja a certain understanding of raga that is a creation of Karnatik musicians.

Another phenomenon that started in the 1980s deserves mention. This is the popular series of lectures and programmes to cull out ragas used in films and then connect them to Karnatik compositions. What is important to remember is that the moment a raga is taken out of the Karnatik music context, it is not a Karnatik raga any longer. The melodies in various other art forms, including cinema, use the melodies of the raga to create a composition within another artistic identity.

Sadly, this is not the general perception. Most people believe that a raga is only about scales. A scale is the lowest common denominator, which is what film composers use along with certain phrases that they are familiar with. A raga does not end here. But no film music composer needs to justify a raga's identity in films. He need not be true to the idea of any raga. The film music composer needs only to be true to the context of the film. It is the Karnatik music community that seems to seek legitimacy through making serious raga associations with the film world. But these presentations devalue Karnatik music more than anything else. Film composers are not Karnatik composers and do not seek to be. To them, Karnatik music is as much a source for ideas as is jazz, Sufi, pop or Arabic music. Each of these will be used if the cinema demands it.

There are those who argue that this drawing of parallels is a way of bringing people into the Karnatik fold. For a long time, I thought there might be a point to this. But after thinking deeply on the matter, I disagree. When people come into the Karnatik fold through these lectures that connect film songs to ragas, their understanding is totally clouded. The ideas sown by such a first exposure remain through their Karnatik music experience, even if they don't realize it themselves.

But does not the understanding change once they are involved with Karnatik music? In most cases, I am afraid not. The baggage remains at a subconscious level and influences the way these individuals receive Karnatik music. The more people we have with such an approach to Karnatik music, the more we create an unaware audience. Many would argue against this viewpoint. They would say that their window to Karnatik music was, in fact, film music. My problem is not with a person who listens to film music and is exposed to Karnatik music elements, thus leading him to explore the art form. My problem is with Karnatik musicians themselves speaking about elements in film music as being similar to Karnatik music itself. This correlation is dangerous. In making these literal comparisons, Karnatik musicians are blurring ideas of Karnatik music and disfiguring the thoughts of the new entrants.

Given the popularity of film music, the Karnatik music community probably feels a need to rival it. This is not only unnecessary but also leads to a deconstruction of the Karnatik edifice. We must first accept the inherent nature of every musical form, which ultimately defines its musical access. I stress musical access, and not social or economic access. Once we respect the aesthetics of a music and its demands on all concerned, it will determine how the music is positioned among the musically inclined. Our approach to making it accessible will be completely different. Karnatik music must reach more people, but not at the cost of a dilution of its form.

Film music is popular and there is nothing wrong with that. Karnatik music is not in competition with film music. Everything in life has a specific place based on what it is and not what we seek it to be. What we need are programmes that educate people about Karnatik music as it is, that reach out to the youth and adults, that cut across various social and economic groups. This is the responsibility of every musician, impresario and listener. Among the thousands that we reach, only a few hundred may engage with the art music in the long run. There is no blame in this; it is the nature of Karnatik music. An acceptance of the music and its aesthetics has to be the bedrock of any activity that aims at letting more people know about Karnatik music. Neither film music nor fusion contribute to Karnatik music. You contribute by being in Karnatik music as a musician or listener.

The Scene Ahead

Over the last decade and a half, Karnatik musicians have made a comeback of sorts as playback singers. This has given rise to questions of whether this has affected their Karnatik music and whether there is anything wrong, in principle, with singing in films. To the answer that this is not a new phenomenon, people argue that in the past the music was more 'Karnatik' in nature.

True, but the fact remains that when they sang in films, every Karnatik musician knew that it was about the film. The cinema music in south India today is not as Karnatik as it once was, but this does not mean that a classically trained musician is incapable of adapting to the needs of film music.

Classical training provides a musician with the outlook to understand music of various genres. It equips her with the ability to adapt to the needs of other musical forms. This does not mean that rendering a film song is easy. In fact, it is a completely different technique and requires a great deal of skill and feeling to achieve the desired effect. Karnatik musicians who sing in films need to develop separate film-music-related skills in order to be successful playback singers. This needs to be lauded, not critiqued. If a musician is well entrenched in the Karnatik idiom, rendering another genre should not affect her Karnatik flavour. The problem arises, as in fusion music, when musicians whose Karnatik sensibilities are yet to mature venture into film music. In such cases, their nascent sense of Karnatik music is altered and this is reflected in their rendition of the art music.

Karnatik musicians who are also established playback singers do, however, make another kind of contribution to Karnatik music, and it is an important one. They bring listeners of film music into a kutcheri just by their presence in both worlds. A person who may never have entered a kutcheri otherwise, comes only because the musician's name touches a chord. It opens up the possibility of a new listener emerging. But I strongly disagree with Karnatik playback singers who claim that, by singing raga-based melodies in films, they are introducing the larger public to Karnatik music. It is their sheer presence in both fields that, in fact, contributes to this larger awareness. We cannot ignore the number of new listeners who have entered the Karnatik world due to their love for a K.J. Yesudas (b. 1940) or a P. Unnikrishnan (b. 1966), who have both straddled the two worlds. It is important for such musicians to clearly demarcate the two areas of music so that both the audience and they themselves realize that there is a necessary insulation of each.

Those listeners who naturally flow into Karnatik music from film music, either because of familiar names or out of curiosity from having heard Karnatik elements in film music, may grow into serious Karnatik music rasikas. That would be a natural process and must not be tampered with.

'But music is universal' is an oft-heard refrain that is interpreted to mean that all music is the same. Music is the same in a basic way in that it is about groups of sounds that provide an aesthetic effect. Once the word 'aesthetic' is used, we need to move into realms of form, content and intent – all within a sociocultural context. Music as an idea is universal, but how each individual relates to it is not. There will be group cultures in all this, but that still does not indicate universality. Every musical form is unique and needs to be appreciated clearly within its context. A foreigner who tries to learn Karnatik music is not only learning the music, but also its culture. This social context determines the level of engagement that the individual can have with the music. Therefore, music is an idea, but is also a specific contextual experience. In that specific experience, it is not universal and we should not seek universality there. The fact is that this psychological need to seek universality is a major issue today. Since a form like Karnatik music is not popular music, there is a feeling of being a minority, which in turn leads to the various issues discussed here.

Karnatik music has to be accepted for what it is in a musical sense. At the same time, its socio-economic baggage has to be shed, so that more people can develop a serious relationship with it.

Karnatik music has and will always be a serious influence in south Indian film music. But this has to be viewed exactly for what it is: a source for musical ideas. Karnatik music itself does not exist in a film form, but only as itself. Efforts to increase awareness of the music must not look for vehicles outside of itself.

It is important for Karnatik musicians to realize that these issues with perception are not a result of external misunderstanding. These are born out of our own carelessness. What is needed is introspection on how we perceive and present Karnatik music. This is what determines the view of the rest of the world.

17

Meaning the Word

The amorphous nature of the music's building blocks and the complex formations within their conceptualization make it vital that we grasp how those aesthetic blocks function. Of course, any form of music can be 'enjoyed' without an understanding of its statics or dynamics. But the totality of the constituent musical elements requires that we know its meaning. To this end, one must discover and understand the meaning of 'meaning'.

Every individual compartmentalizes musical understanding into two broad categories. One deals with understanding aspects like raga, tala, composition, improvisation, presentation, style and the rest. The other is the language it uses, exploring the use of the words and their linguistic meaning. For new listeners, these present two different sets of challenges. The former is a problem of aesthetic engagement and the latter a problem of linguistic innocence.

In a form like Karnatik music, it seems necessary to understand the lyrical meaning of the words, considering that compositions today constitute over 50 per cent of a kutcheri. Compositions are rendered in Sanskrit, Telugu, Tamil, Kannada and sometimes in Malayalam, though other languages do feature in the tukkada section. It is also true that in almost every other art form that uses words we seek linguistic meaning. It is but natural that we look for a similar understanding in Karnatik music. It is not only the listener who feels this imperative, but also musicians. Vocalists talk about the need to understand the meaning of the kirtanas in order to convey emotion. Even in the case of instrumentalists it is said that such understanding is necessary to translate meaning into melody and then transfer the meaning into their playing. Seeking linguistic meaning has, therefore, been accepted as a requirement. As an extension of this thought, when a Telugu musician sings a Tyagaraja kirtana or a Tamil musician renders a Tamil kirtana, the audience expects to experience a higher emotive quality in the music.

But the question that begs asking is whether Karnatik music as a form needs to convey lyrical meaning at all. Every musical form has its own journey, which can be traced back sociologically or musicologically. Despite socio-political pressures, musical forms retain within their core certain basic tenets that guide their evolution – a fact that can be grasped only from a dispassionate perspective. As we revisit the idea of language within Karnatik music, we will journey through musicological, sociological and historical realms.

Let us begin exploring the relevance of meaning in the lyrics used in Karnatik music with the word 'meaning' itself. It is a beautiful word that carries within it the essential truth of our lives. We can trace its origin to the German 'meinen', or 'to think'. In its noun form 'meaning' denotes 'that which is in the minds or thoughts' with regard to the signification of things and words, the sense in them, their purpose and their intent. But we do use the word to signify more than its linguistic sense. For instance, when we wonder: 'what is the meaning of life?' There is something even more important that we do not go into: the question of whether language can convey more than the meaning of its words. This is not about the linguistic understanding or emotional reaction to the word 'meaning'. Meaning beyond meaning-in-language provides us an experience that removes language from its own conditioning. The Sanskrit 'manas' and its closeness to 'meinen' is significant. The manas is mind, heart, understanding, intelligence and that which seeks meaning. It is this unified field of intangible experiences that we use to draw out the abstract identity of Karnatik music's 'meaning'. A great deal of imagination, creativity, discrimination and reflection on aesthetics has given life to language in Karnatik music, where the meaning of a sound includes but goes beyond the word.

The Karnatik music community as a whole would take the stand that it is impossible for the musician to render compositions emotively without understanding the lyrics. The thinking is that melodic movements are given emotional charge on the basis of the sahitya. Musicians use the terms sahitya bhava and sangita bhava. The former denotes the emotions of the sahitya and the latter those conveyed through the melody. What is sought is the unified experience of both. To me, this is a rather naïve understanding of a composition and needs to be addressed if we are to perceive a composition as a true art object rather than a lyrical messenger. The current position does not consider the overall intent of Karnatik music and whether such an understanding of sahitya fits into what we intend to experience in this art form. If this question were to be asked, we would most likely find that this search for literary meaning is meaningless.

I have already discussed the role of the syllabic form within a musical composition. But we need to revisit that idea in the context of this discussion. Every syllable – whether or not it has linguistic meaning – is part of a musical unit. For instance, if a syllable like 'shra' is rendered multiple times and on a different svara each time, then aesthetically each shra is an individual unit within the melodic identity of the composition. Just because I am articulating the sound shra, one cannot ignore the tone, texture and melody that encapsulates the syllable. As a singular unit, each shra evokes different emotive responses. Each of these units contributes to the aesthetics of the specific melodic line and to the larger melodic experience of the composition as a whole. This 'syllabo-melodic' (if I may call it that) aesthetic experience is purely a creation of musical sound.

But does this 'sound' have any meaning? If the understanding is purely linguistic, none of these syllabo-melodics has any meaning. In the world of linguistics, it is only when syllables come together to create words that they acquire cognitive meaning. But in many musical forms, and certainly in Karnatik music, the opposite is true. Melodic movements that articulate these syllables do so by creating individual musical identities for the syllables. The word syllables move not syllabo-linguistically but syllabo-melodically, investing every syllable with an aesthetic meaning so that the 'words' come together, though not as linguistic forms. If we are to extend the understanding of meaning beyond language, every such musical syllable has a meaning of its own. That meaning is the charge that this combination of melody and syllable creates. Each syllabic unit is charged by its melodic presence and, together with all the other syllabic units that connect the strings of melody, creates a unified aesthetic identity.

In this musical experience, language is important only as sound, not linguistically. The experience itself is the result of two processes combining: word syntaxes that put syllabic sounds together and raga aesthetics that create the melodic stream on which the syllables flow. Every syllable in its articulation provides melody with a stability and shape. In fact, the musically determined positioning of these syllables within a melodic movement is what gives the melody its structure – not their values as words in language. The beauty of poetic construction is reinvented within the musical context. The poetics within Karnatik music has been studied, but the syllabo-melodic relationship and its impact on music have not been fully understood. The syllables do not only interact closely with the music individually but also in combinations that enhance the compositional experience. This is an aesthetic connection bound by context and experience. The whole syllabo-melodic creation conveys the essence of the melody and raga within its constructed tala matrix. It is in this essence that the meaning of the composition lies.

When poetic expression is in musical form, every syllable transforms into a melodic unit. It follows then that its sound becomes a melodic sound. In this existence, it needs to negotiate the requirements of the melody, raga and tala. Such a melodic unit becomes distinct from the non-musical recitation of the poem. Every musician learns a composition as a musical creation. This entails manoeuvring the sahitya to suit the requirements of melody. The method of articulating the syllables constituting the sahitya can, and does, change in accordance with the requirements of the melodic movement. These subtle changes are closely related to the melodic flow, while remaining true to the sounds that the terraced palate of the human mouth is capable of. It does not mean that the sahitya can be mispronounced or ignored. Instead, the syllables will be given a specific melody-related identity. In such a form, the syllables will continue to be recognizable as syllables, yet also emerge clearly as melodic entities. Therefore, when I talk about syllabic meaning in art music, I am not ignoring the role of the sahitya in music or the necessity for clear articulation. All I am saying is that it has to be conceived of as a musical form, not a poetic form. Otherwise, the perceived disconnect between melody and language will persist.

The Sense and the Sound

The ideas of matu and dhatu have evolved together and developed a relationship that helps define the position of a syllable of text in a melodic phrase. There is also the fact that the sound combinations of each language bring a different quality to the aesthetic structure. Sometimes these can become impediments to the melodic movements of the raga, which creates a conflict of aesthetics. Certain movements do not flow easily with some sound combinations in some languages. This can cause a change in the melodic stress and in the gamakas and even affect the musical articulation of the syllable itself. My observations are conditioned by the fact that I have listened to Karnatik music in but a few languages. I am aware that royal composers in the Tanjavur court used Marathi. There is always a possibility that another language can be used and another aesthetic created from its sound. This new language would, in that event, have to be infused with the Karnatik aesthetic and given its own melodic sound.

I suggest here that the linguistic meaning of the words becomes secondary, if not actually redundant, in Karnatik music, with the aesthetic form taking precedence.

The question then is: does not the understanding of the sahitya provide the musician and the listener with an important emotional experience?

This is an important question and needs to be asked. The words have meaning, the meaning has context and the understanding of this relationship has emotion. Should we ignore this? There is no denying that the understanding of the lyrics creates a serious emotional impact on the musician. Every word has emotional connotations for an individual within a social context. Understanding the lyrics would normally be considered important for contextualizing the composition and providing it with the necessary emotional input. The problem is what this does to the music. Does it add to the aesthetics of Karnatik music or diminish its experiential quality? I pose this question here philosophically, not emotionally.

It could be said that understanding the emotion that words generate would naturally transfer the necessary quality to the melody. I believe this is incorrect. The musician does transfer his intention of conveying the meaning into the composition's musical aspects, but this transfer comes as an extra expression in the rendering. Most significantly, a musician's preoccupation with configuring the music with the sahitya leads to an important realignment of the musician's priorities within the composition. The melodic, rhythmic developments then come to be viewed only from the paradigm of how they convey the meaning. The whole composition comes to be pivoted on the sahitya.

How faithful would this be to the intent of Karnatik music? The musician's artistic investment must be towards the aesthetics that govern the composition. In my interpretation, this aesthetic does not include the word's literal meaning. It is a stance derived from the simple logic that, in Karnatik music, a composition's aesthetic unit is such that all its constituents complement each other – raga, tala, matu and dhatu function as a unified expression, in which none of the components take individual ownership of the aesthetic import. But the moment we start viewing the composition from the perspective of meaning, the whole composition becomes a manifestation of only linguistic meaning. This deconstructs the composition.

Within Karnatik music, a composition is an abstract aesthetic that is essentially a creation of its musical intent. I would contend that the lyrical focus transforms an abstract exploration into a literal interpretation. In doing so, it devalues the aesthetic power of the composition. This literality of understanding makes the whole composition a prisoner of sahitya. Matu, dhatu and tala working together get attention only to the extent that they are serving a linguistic purpose. These abstract units then lose the identity created from their musical form, and the musician expresses every melodic motif as an extension of or an appendage to the lyrical meaning and not as a distinct melodic import. And that is when the music, regretfully, ceases to be art music. The shift in focus from melodic to lyrical meaning deeply affects the compositional experience for the listener. In my world of meaning, 'Kamakshi' is a melodic and not a lexical concept.

When listeners come with the mindset of understanding

sahitya in order to connect with Karnatik music, they make the same mistake as the musician in not allowing the art object to create the magic. The listener is only listening to poetry in the garb of music. Although this can be a deeply moving experience, it prevents the listener from connecting emotionally to the abstraction. The music they are listening to becomes religious, social or political music.

I am not devaluing the experience that sahitya-oriented music can generate, but I am definitely questioning the necessity for such an experience within Karnatik music. Such an orientation is necessary in a bhajan or in a Harikatha, where linguistic meaning is crucial to the overall aesthetic experience. I am conscious of the fact that kirtanas can be rendered in the bhajan or Harikatha format, where the melodic variations are minimal and the lyrical articulation is closer to the actual words. But then the kirtanas concerned have donned a distinctly different style for the purpose at hand.

The challenge of distancing ourselves from the lyrical content of compositions leads us to the question of why at all great composers created such beautiful compositions that convey so much philosophical, social and religious thought? Why should we seek to keep a distance from the literalism of the sahitya when the composer has invested the compositions with linguistic meaning? Does this not do disservice to composition?

Bicameral Genius

In answering this question we need to ponder the role of the composer or vaggeyakara. Vac (word) + geya (singer) + kara (person). Did the vaggeyakara intend to use the composition as a tool to convey his ideas on religion, faith, life and society? If that were not the case, would he not have used linguistically void texts for his compositions? I would suggest that this is a simplistic line of thinking. We cannot afford to forget that the vaggeyakara is not a poet, nor a versifier or a 'songster', but a multifaceted creative personality well aware of the cognitive impact of language, syntax and its close relationship with musical movement. Every vaggeyakara has explored, expanded, innovated and designed musical movements that are closely associated with this understanding. Also built into this is a poetic structuring that has been incorporated and reinterpreted into musical forms. It is important to note that even compositions with linguistically void texts do not use arbitrary syllables or gibberish, but use either the verbal syllabic forms of rhythmic sounds or the svaras themselves as text. In both cases, there exists an important cognitive relationship between the syllabic sounds and the musician and even the discerning listener.

Let us return again to the fact that Karnatik music has numerous compositional forms that have a great deal of sahitya. It is true that our point of reference for compositions is the kirtana form – specifically, the three vaggeyakaras who have shaped modern Karnatik music and are celebrated as 'the musical trinity': Tyagaraja, Muttusvami Dikshitar and Shyama Shastri. Before we discuss the idea of textual and musical meaning in relation to the trinity, let me place them historically within the art music context.

From available manuscripts and treatises, it seems that art music was practised as prescribed in the chaturdandi musical tradition around 150 years before the trinity. This tradition was brought to the Tanjavur area during the reign of the Nayaks appointed by the Vijayanagara empire in Tanjavur, Madurai and Gingee. During this period, scholars and musicians wrote numerous treatises on art music. I have dwelt on the historical detail in an earlier essay, but in this context it would suffice to say that this tradition included primarily two compositional forms, prabandha and gita, and two improvisational forms, alapa and thaya.

Art music in its essential being, as a form complete and contained in itself, embodied this tradition. At the same time, we also know that padas and kirtanas were being rendered within the contexts of ritual, dance and religious music. We are aware too that theatrical and operatic compositions for Yakshagana, Kuravanji, Bhagavata Mela were being composed in the same areas and not at very far-removed times. It is also interesting that the same vaggeyakara was at times composing for various art forms. This meant that musicians were negotiating different musical forms using the same ideas of raga and tala. Masters of their compositional tradition that they were, they were versatile and skilled at adaptation. The idea of using the same musical tenets for different artistic forms could be why Karnatik music absorbed many compositional forms into its identity. The idea of art music, which only included prabandha and gita, changed to encompassing compositional forms that the same musicians were arranging for ritual, devotional and dance music.

The musical trinity emerged after this period. It is to their credit that they transformed the kirtana into a complex art music creation. The earlier kirtanas of Annamacharya (1424–1503), Purandaradasa (1484–1564) and many other composers leant towards devotional music rather than art music. But I must concede that since we have lost the dhatu for all their compositions, this observation is based purely on the lyrical structuring and contemporary musical interpretation that they lend themselves to. In order to differentiate between the kirtana in art music and the kirtana in devotional music, some scholars refer to the former as krti, although this practice does not seem to have any musicological basis.

Against this background, we need to critically understand what the kirtanas of the trinity contain. Were they composing them as art music forms, or purely as bhakti music? As in the case of vaggeyakaras before them, the trinity used their music to compose for different artistic contexts, though they were musicians of primarily art music. An analysis of their compositions leads one to the conclusion that they primarily created art objects. A look at the language, syllabic form and musical structuring of many of their compositions reveals a level of artistic abstraction that is a feature only of art music.

Tyagaraja's compositions lyrically are simple, even colloquial. He used language dexterously to reveal the composition's melodic charge and not for linguistic effect. The lyrical content in Tyagaraja's compositions is earnest and diverse, including appeals to the lord, descriptions of the lord, comments on social practices and philosophical ideas. But what Tyagaraja's kirtana construction reveals most strikingly is his serious approach to raga and melodic development. He has created numerous compositions in a single raga, with each revealing a completely new melodic approach to it. This would only be possible if he was creating art music compositions. If his main object was to convey devotional meaning through the lyrics, he would have probably used repetitive melodic themes for all the compositions in the raga to make the composition more accessible to people.

Shyama Shastri's lyrics are, in fact, repetitive in nature. Almost all his compositions are appeals to the goddess. Considering this emotive lyrical content, one would expect the rhythmic formations to be simple so that they do not impede the emotional value. But that is not what Shyama Shastri has done. He has used rhythmic motifs within the melodic movements, juxtaposed the laya flow of the melody with that of the tala and created emphasis at unusual points within the tala. This suggests a focus on the matu–dhatu relationship with varied rhythmic possibilities within various talas.

Muttusvami Dikshitar's compositions are linguistically far more stylized. In content they are primarily descriptions of the various deities, temples and rituals, but include his learning as a Shrividya upasaka. A mode of worship of the Supreme Being, Shrividya upasana visualizes it in its feminine form, as the mother goddess. But the compositional structures of Dikshitar's creations point to a clear musical focus in the close relationship he has built between syllables, melody, laya and tala. All this indicates a detail that can only be oriented towards an art music experience. The interplay he created using syllabo-melodic identities shows that this was a composer who was doing much more than describing the divine. His approach to melodic movement in a kirtana displays a slow and expansive raga development. Added to this are his innovations with regard to the kirtana format and changes in laya within the composition.

It is also true that Tyagaraja seems to have created new ragas, and Dikshitar gave life to a completely new raga classification system initiated by the seventeenth-century musicologist Venkatamakhin. I would also like to point out that Shyama Shastri has revealed his serious art music orientation by primarily using only those ragas that were traditionally in practice and accepted in older theoretical texts. This presents us a musician's clear musicological and historical perspective. At the same time, we know that Shyama Shastri created a new raga, chintamani. These and other indicators tell us that these compositions were far more than bhakti creations. They were serious art music pieces.

An analysis of many of the trinity's compositions reveals that they were clearly exposing musicians to melodic possibilities in each raga and providing creative inputs for their own explorations. Also, the very structure of such compositions enables improvisational possibilities, providing gateways for musicians.

All three are inextricably associated with piety, devotion and religiosity. Their compositions have given succour to the worshipful and faith to the prayerful. But taking a wholly dispassionate view of their work in its totality – ideational, aesthetic, technical – I would say this: irrespective of the votive divinity being sung to, each of the three musical geniuses have in common another 'divinity' – one that is the essence of art music, which for want of a more effective phrase I will describe as the fulfilment of a quest for the purest musical abstraction.

None of this means that other composers before or after the trinity were not art musicians. I have centred the discussion around these three for two primary reasons. First, Karnatik music today is dominated by their compositions and, second, the musician community at large finds it very difficult to comprehend their compositions purely as art music pieces – something that needs correction.

So we return to our question: do we ignore the meaning of the sahitya?

The sahitya conveys the outlook of the composers. What else would it convey? Any vaggeyakara would necessarily provide sahitya that expressed his impressions, aspirations, disappointments and inclinations. The religiously charged environment of the period and their own households naturally led the trinity to express their religious, philosophical and moral opinions. This does not mean that they intended to make a massive religious impact on society through these compositions or initiate new religious trends. If that were the case, they would have created simple compositions in familiar ragas, melodies and talas that everyone could repeat. They were geniuses who created musical masterpieces, which contained their beliefs and used sahitya as a musical idea. The meaning of the sahitya was not the focus of the compositions. It was merely the natural input from the experience of each unique human being. These observations on the trinity have been made after an intertextual analysis of the older pathantaras (rendering variations) of their compositions.

But here lies an irony and a problem. We idolized the trinity, converting major musicians into minor deities. And thus arose a problem – one created by musicians. Because we eulogized the trinity, we lost the capacity to critically analyse their various compositions and separate their art music pieces from the others. Like musicians before and after the trinity, vaggeyakaras have always used their music to create compositions for various art forms. To give a modern example, Dr M. Balamuralikrishna has created art music compositions, Bharatanatyam, operatic and devotional compositions. We cannot use the same lens to see all of these. Within its own art form, each composition has a very different intent.

Not recognizing this is the mistake we have committed with the trinity – and since then, we have extended it to all composers that came before and after. For example, it is clear that the utsava sampradaya kirtanas of Tyagaraja or the nottusvara sahityas of Dikshitar were not art music pieces. But the fact that they have been absorbed into the Karnatik music repertoire creates a serious issue. Utsava sampradaya kirtanas are devotional compositions with simple structuring and repetitive melodic motifs. They do not have the qualities that would lead to abstracting emotion from their musical identity. The compositions are part of bhakti music. But having placed them beside art music compositions, we begin to look for 'meaning' in the bhakti sense in the latter as well. This blurs any critical differentiation between the two. I believe that the utsava sampradaya compositions do not have a place within Karnatik art music.

Muttusvami Dikshitar's nottusvaras were created out of Western band music tunes and are definitely not serious art music creations. They are only appropriate for teaching children. The unfortunate presence of these compositions within the Karnatik music environment has confused our own understanding of composition. These vaggeyakaras had different sides to them and used their genius to express each facet of their creativity in unique ways. This was why Tyagaraja could create a complex kirtana form, a simple utsava sampradaya composition and a musical opera in *Nauka Charitramu*. They were not intended to be treated in the same way. Shyama Shastri seems to have been the only one among the three who did not compose anything but art music. I strongly believe that the art music compositions of the trinity, or indeed any other composer, must be treated as art music and not anything else. At the same time, compositions that do not posses the quality to abstract as an art music piece should not be used within Karnatik music. This abstractive quality is the reason why Karnatik music was able to absorb into itself numerous compositional forms like the varna and pada from the dance repertoire and yet retain its core art music nature. If the possibility for abstraction does not exist in a certain composition, it is not an art music piece.

There is another aspect to the whole issue of meaning: the interpretations of musicians. We know that musicians have added sangatis over generations. Such additions have been not only on the basis of the melodic motif of the line but also the lyrical content. This means that musicians have reinterpreted the melodic line on the basis of its lyrical meaning, even if the melody of the line as received through the guru–shishya parampara was different. I have heard musicians say, 'Tyagaraja would not have composed it this way, as the meaning is not conveyed.' Leaving aside my position on the role of textual meaning, what is lost in this reinterpretation is the value of the contexts of time and space for the understanding of meaning and melody. Ignoring this context, musicians have added sangatis, assigning an emotional quality to each one. They link every sangati to a change in the emotional tone of the same line, thereby equating musical development to lyrical emotional development. These ideas only confuse listeners by presenting them with a non-musical reason to listen to the composition.

Musicians also change the melodic stress of lines in compositions based on the logic that words have to be articulated as intact, unbroken words to express meaning, often adversely impacting the raga and composition. A melodic line may be such that the musician needs to take a breath, thereby splitting the word into two. This greatly discomfits musicians or connoisseurs who seek word meaning. They fail to register that the split, in fact, correctly provides an emphasis on the prasa structure of the composition, which makes the breath imperative. Similarly, a syllabic stress in a composition also needs to be formulated on the basis of melodic structuring and alliteration. We should also ensure that an artificial break, made in order to articulate a complete sahitya, does not impede the melodic flow of the compositional line or its connection with the next. If we can negotiate all these requirements, it is fine to present complete words, but a musician must not sacrifice the aesthetic creation for word correctness. Unfortunately, with the focus on word meaning, all the other relationships between matu and dhatu are being ignored, thereby affecting the melodic structure of compositions.

This focus on sahitya and its meaning has, over the years, led to numerous lecture demonstrations and panel discussions on the spiritual, philosophical and religious content of vaggeyakaras. Interpretations, mystic correlations, tantrik adaptations have all been called upon to prove that sahitya meaning is indispensable in Karnatik music. While all these ideas received from these composers may be true, we need to look at them as the thoughts of individuals who were primarily engaged in the task of creating great art music pieces. In that process, it was but natural that they poured into their compositions deeply felt thoughts and ideas. But we will do well to note that many of these interpretations are our creation. Because of the borrowings from the Hindu religious registers, it is possible to seek correlations between most aspects of sahitya and Hindu beliefs and practices. Looking at the number of discussions that are held on the religious or devotional thoughts of our vaggeyakaras, I have often wondered why we do not seek lecture demonstrations and intense discussions on the literal lyrical meaning of the erotic poetry of the pada or javali, though we have accepted them musically within Karnatik music. We also do not expect musicians to truly emote the literal word meaning of a javali. Their overt sexuality makes us uncomfortable. These aspects are all closely linked to a discussion on religion in Karnatik music, which we shall take up separately. Yet the fact that we are willing to ignore the idea of lyrical meaning for certain compositions but seek them for others is significant. These discussions are loaded with religious and caste issue subtexts, as also the culture of taboos within the Karnatik music fraternity.

Musicians have, over the years, tuned a number of poetic works and brought them into Karnatik music. While some have been created as art music pieces and presented with the seriousness of abstraction, many have only been brought in as devotional pieces. The result is that understanding of lyrical meaning has come to be imperative for both musician and listener. The proliferation of such music sends out confusing signals to listeners. The confusion actually exists within the mind of the Karnatik musician, as he is not able to reconcile in his mind the dichotomy that exists between the various art music compositions, improvisational forms and their intent with devotional and nationalistic pieces and their focus.

Verse and Obverse

No discussion on the role of meaning, melody and sahitya in Karnatik music can be complete without a reference to the serious debate that took place in the early twentieth century with the development of the Tamil Isai movement (Isai is the Tamil word for music). Though these debates had much to do with caste-related issues, here I will only discuss some of the language-related points that were brought out. In the context of the Karnatik music, which was finding its new home in the urban setting of Madras, the dominant brahmin community created a concert format and performance structure built around the music of the trinity. They also established the Madras Music Academy in order to provide what they considered order, system, structure and proper direction to Karnatik music. This is a clear case of trying to create a 'classical' identity for Karnatik music. I have, in the previous essays on aesthetic and musicological aspects, questioned these very systems that were set in place. The compositions that dominated were those of the trinity, who composed predominantly in Sanskrit and Telugu, and so these languages became the alternating lingua franca of Karnatik music. The reasons for this can be provided in anthropological, sociological and musical terms. But many compositions, especially those of Tyagaraja, came into the modern Karnatik music presentation due to the influence of numerous Harikatha exponents in the later part of the nineteenth century and early part of the twentieth century. Many great Harikatha exponents and Karnatik musicians belonged to the Tyagaraja shishya parampara. In view of this development in the 1930s, the non-brahmin higher castes, led by prominent chettiars and mudaliars began the Tamil Isai movement with the sole objective of creating a parallel 'classical' identity for Karnatik music that was based on Tamil compositions. The seeds for this tree of dissent were probably sown earlier with the rapid changes caused by religious, social and nationalistic movements of the late nineteenth century. Yet this rupture is an important reference point in the discussion on the role of language in music.

The position of the Tamil Isai movement was that Tamil must be the language for Karnatik music, because the music itself belonged to the 'real' Tamils, from whom the brahmins had usurped the music. The Tamil Isai movement stressed that Karnatik music must have a Tamil identity. The Music Academy and its prominent members, including the future Union finance minister T.T. Krishnamachari (1899–1974), tried to debate this aesthetically by saying that only the music mattered (art music) and the word did not. But this was not a pure aesthetic argument as it was made out to be, and hence was flawed. The anti-Tamil Isai lobby pointed out that Sanskrit and Telugu were far more musical languages than Tamil. They even felt that if a composer of Tyagaraja's quality was to compose in Tamil, those compositions could be accepted, but for the sake of language 'cheap' tunes cannot be used in Karnatik music. They ignored or did not value Tamil compositions, which had always existed and did not openly explore the possibility of reviving or reconstructing older Tamil compositions. These were not considered fit for their 'classical' sense. This was a classist statement, which eulogized Sanskrit because it was the 'classical language', accepted Telugu as it had been the 'state' language in Tanjavur for over 300 years and, of course, since Tyagaraja and Shyama Shastri had used it. The deification of Tyagaraja made it impossible for the establishment to critique his compositions on an aesthetic basis.

It is evident then that they were not making just an aesthetic argument. If that were the case, they would have critically analysed the trinity and also accepted Tamil art music. The tertiary status that Tamil was assigned was the result of the Aryan–Dravidian divide that prevailed in society. Some even thought that the whole Tamil Isai movement had more to do with politics than art. A purely aesthetic idea would have included Tamil into the Karnatik fold and accepted that every language can provide its own aesthetic quality based on its inherent structure. But this would demolish the religious and sanctified ideas that the establishment wanted to hold on to vis-à-vis the music and its past.

The weakness of the Tamil Isai argument was that most of its votaries saw the issue as purely one of discrimination against the mother tongue. The Tamil Isai Conference in 1941 had a set of interesting resolutions. It demanded that songs in kutcheris be predominantly in Tamil and other languages be used minimally. It asked for Tamil songs to be given preference in the education system of Karnatik music. There was a request to Karnatik music lovers to give a preference to Tamil compositions and to the radio to provide a similar preferential treatment. This clearly shows that they were only interested in the language. Men of eminence such as Coimbatore industrialist and the first Union finance minister R.K. Shanmukham Chetty (1892–1953) made it clear that they were only interested in meaning, in textually generated emotion, and stressed the fact that an emotional response to music cannot be achieved in a language that was not understood. Music, they argued, had only one purpose: to convey lyrical meaning. Though written some twenty years before the Tamil Isai conference resolutions, the essay 'Sangita Vishayam' by the brilliant poet and nationalist visionary Subrahmanya Bharati (1882–1921) anticipated many of its preoccupations and concerns. In the essay, he asked for more Tamil compositions in Karnatik music so that people could understand the lyrics. But Bharati being Bharati, he also went on to severely criticize Karnatik musicians for not concentrating on the correct pronunciation of the sahitya in Tyagaraja kirtanas. He accused them of not emoting 'rasas' in the compositions. This only further establishes the fact that the issues of language, meaning and emotion had been brewing for a long time before they erupted with the Tamil Isai movement in the 1940s.

The dominance of language and meaning in the Tamil Isai movement stifled its opportunity for a great musical intervention. Most of the votaries of this movement conceded the brilliance of Tyagaraja, but used that to argue that if Tyagaraja composed in his mother tongue should not the Tamilian be doing so too?

A most interesting and sociologically revealing consequence ensued. Even while demanding a Tamil Karnatik identity, the Tamil Isai movement never faulted the lyrics for their religiosity, nor demanded a secularization of their content. The movement was well positioned to have done so, for those positions were very much part of the then burgeoning Dravidian protest movement. So the devotional content was never a problem; after all, the Tamil Isai movement drew its inspiration from Tamil hymns such as the Tevarams. Not surprisingly, the flag-bearers of Tamil Isai were criticized by the rationalist 'Periyar' E.V. Ramasami Naicker (1879–1973), who felt that the movement was falling into the same religious trap as laid by the brahmins, albeit in Tamil. Even with the caste divide, which was part of the language debate, it was interesting that influential and opinion-setting brahmins like

'Kalki' Krishnamurthi (1899–1954) and 'Tiger' Varadachariar (1876–1950) were part of the movement.

Though it has become a milestone in the region's socio-cultural history, the movement had but little success. The reason for this was its inability to view Karnatik music sans linguistic meaning. Had the Tamil Isai movement looked at Tamil as a purely aesthetic phenomenon that provided the Karnatik form a unique sound, it would have led to the opening of a new chapter. With that position, the Tamil Isai movement could have embraced other languages, while insisting that Tamil too be included. Due to the lack of an art music vision, the Tamil Isai movement was not able to create a parallel idea of Karnatik music. It was more about Tamil than about Isai. Though some individuals, like Kalki, did express the view that the movement was about reviving lost Tamil compositions and presenting them in Karnatik concerts, the movement's mindset remained self-defeatingly centred on 'discrimination'. But the complex socio-political environment polarized both sides of the discourse. What we saw in the process is the seeking of a modern classical identity rather than an art music identity, which I contend already existed as a collective among the various musicians and dancers that practised Karnatik music in courts and temples. The issue of the Tamil Isai movement then was a sociological, rather than aesthetic, one.

While this is only a short encapsulation of the various arguments that existed in the 1930s and 1940s, the fact that I would like to highlight is that neither side was able to distance itself from the idea of linguistic meaning. Both the Music Academy and the Tamil Isai movement were trapped in similar mindsets. While the Academy, under the argument of aesthetics, placed Telugu and Sanskrit on a pedestal and has always favoured the propagation of 'meaning' in compositions, the Tamil Isai movement got stuck in language-pride rhetoric. These failures are probably why we continue to debate the role of language and meaning in Karnatik music. Similar positions are today held by musicians and audiences who are Kannada-speaking or Telugu-speaking. The upshot is a linguistically fractured Karnatik music community.

It is quite possible that all this is but a reflection of language-related socio-political changes that India went through. Nevertheless, language remains an impediment to the inclusiveness of Karnatik music within the art music context. Some may believe that I am propagating the idea of getting rid of sahitya from Karnatik music. I am, in fact, indicating the opposite. I hope we can see sahitya, a beautiful creation of sound, as part of the abstraction of music. There, inseparable from the music, it plays its own unique role in the creation of rare beauty. I seek the experiencing of this beauty, this abstract idea, this vital creation of the human mind.

18

The Shrine and the Song

The music and the culture we are dealing with are Indian in origin – and I am writing about these in English. It makes sense, therefore, to look into the etymology of some of the words I will use in this essay. While some words hold identical meanings for all individuals (for example, action words), words signifying emotion, indeed emotion itself, rarely mean the same to everyone. Besides, when we deal with feelings and emotions, words usually fail us. It is not easy to translate 'that which is felt' into a communicative form – language.

So it is that every emotion-related or feeling-related word expresses a different idea for each user. But the ones that interest me are not those of feeling or action; they are the indefinable words that betoken the many forms of 'trust'. Due to this mystical quality and their close relationship with our emotions, these words of trust have and will remain ideationally unique to every individual. To add to the complexity of the situation, every culture too looks upon these words through different lenses. It is in this socio-individual relationship that these words, as well as the images and ideas within them come alive and influence our inner life.

A word that could evoke trust in its most intense form is 'god'. The origin of this word has been widely debated, but one of the hypotheses is that it comes from the German 'guth', and that is about as much as we know. Most dictionaries describe it to mean a superhuman force, an object of worship, the Supreme Being in monotheist faiths, the Creator or even just an idol. Through these different interpretations, we gather that god is a powerful entity, the originator of life, an object of worship as an idol or an idea. This very understanding puts the concept of god beyond the realm of normal life, an object of utter wonder – a sense born out of the feeling that god does not and need not obey the rules of nature, indeed that god controls its very existence. God created this realm, yet is beyond it.

Connected to this idea is a closely related one – divine. This is derived from the Latin 'divinus', which is traceable to the 'divus', both meaning godlike. We cannot but notice that the Sanskrit 'div', meaning to be bright or to shine, is the root from which is derived, among other words, deva (celestial, heavenly). *The Concise Oxford Dictionary of English Etymology* expresses the meaning of divine as 'belonging to or proceeding from a god, holy, excellent in the highest degree'. It not only signifies god or godliness, but also qualifies the attributes of god and hence is descriptive of god's nature. We establish our rules of engagement with that omnipresence through religion.

Derived from the Latin 'religio', meaning binding or obligation, 'religion' is also closely linked with the Latin 'lagire' (the root of 'ligature'), which again means something that binds. In these descriptions of bond and binding, there is an indication of a fastening, a joining, but no suggestion that this is forced nor of any tension in this bond. That nuance is important. The etymology of the word suggests that religion is a belief or emotion generated by the sense of something higher than oneself; an unseen control.

There is no gainsaying that even within the Indian ethos

words like god, divine and religion have very varied meanings and spiritual or philosophical connotations. But in their most universal application within the Indian context, the core emotion and associations around 'god', 'divine' and 'religion' are not at any fundamental variance from those of other cultures.

For me, the relevance and allure of these three words lie in the fact that they are representative of humankind's search for existential answers. This is also true of Hindu philosophical interpretations. Advaita looks at man and the idea of god to be one, dvaita demarcates a clear separation, while vishishtadvaita is a nuance between the two. But the objectification of god as a distinct entity is inbuilt. Thus is created the idea of god, the divine. With that comes the bond, the binding that man creates with god – a willing surrender. This surrender is devotion, reverence, loyalty, worship, service and attachment. The Sanskrit word 'bhakti' encapsulates this relationship.

This brings me, as a Karnatik musician whose training, repertory and musical practice have necessarily included music saturated in bhakti, face-to-face with a certain reckoning. The idea of religion is a strong emotion. It is, equally, a strong presence. Removing oneself from its material, social and cultural presence would be difficult for anyone; for a Karnatik musician it is almost impossible.

Do I, as a musician, want to do that? Yes, I do. That notion is not about being atheistic, rather about trying to experience life without the manifestations of religiosity or the constructed presence of a godhead. The power of religion is so strong that once we place an experience under its umbrella, everything else becomes submissive to it. If one is able to move into a space without a religious identity, it is quite possible that all the other elements that constitute the experience come to life in a way that never existed before. This is what I seek in Karnatik music. You could even say I seek bhakti, but to the aesthetics of the music and not to the names of the Hindu gods and goddesses.

I find myself devoted, intensely devoted, without even realizing that I am so devoted and certainly without thinking of bhakti or devotion when I am singing. But if I were to ask myself 'devoted to what?', I must pause and reflect. And in so doing I can see that my devotion is drawn to the soul of the music that has been given to me, and not to the names or images of deities. They are there, very much so, but they flux into the energy that overtakes and overwhelms me when I am one with my music. The song, the singer and that which is being sung to become one, which is when all weighty and ponderous constructs of the human mind, like religion and gods and goddesses, become extraneous to it.

The Theology and Pantheology of Karnatik Music

Rama, Krishna, Govinda, Shiva, Srinivasa, Kamakshi, Muruga – anyone who has heard Karnatik music has probably heard them all within the context of the compositions, pallavis, shlokas and viruttams rendered in a kutcheri. The pantheon of Hindu gods and goddesses, their stories, myths and temples predominate a standard repertory of what is rendered in a kutcheri. Even when the verses rendered are erotic, they are often connected to Hindu gods or to the concept of atma and paramatma. It is an accepted fact that Karnatik music sahitya is dominated by Hindu religious content. The musicians and the audience are used to this and, in fact, derive a great deal of pride in the divinity of the music. This divinity is not just an abstract idea of sound (nada), but is truly present in every composition rendered in the lyrics.

Such being the all-pervading presence of Hindu religiosity in Karnatik music, religion cannot be treated as just another aspect of the music. It is, in fact, the first thing that would strike a new listener. Audiences experience the presence of the gods, musicians speak about their own piety and it is in this mutual acknowledgement of their religious and spiritual moorings, that Karnatik music revels. This is the 'umbrella' that I spoke about.

Within this thought process, we tend to construct the aesthetic content. To be sure, there are some moments when religiousness may not appear – during alapanas, tana, kalpanasvaras or during mathematical melodic renditions. But even in those, the musician and the audience may be carrying over the content of the composition into the manodharmic sphere. An example would be a survey of the lines in kirtanas used for niraval. Though the religious content cannot be avoided, the lines in most cases would have the name of a deity or a reference to a strong religious or spiritual idea. There may be other lines that are aesthetically far more evocative, but are lyrically insignificant or problematic due to their construction. They are not chosen due to the overlapping problems of meaning and religion. During almost every part of the Karnatik experience, Hindu gods and goddesses and the myths associated with them hover above us. In their compositions, vaggeyakaras delineate different equations with the divine, which acquire their own nomenclatures: friend, parent, lover, child. Their beauty, valour and other attributes get described. Also presented are detailed descriptions of places of worship, ritual and practice, and thoughts on the various philosophies in Hinduism. Even comments on social practices are placed within the religious context. There are very few compositions that are non-Hindu, so I will not take those up for discussion here.

If the musical community believed, as I do, that lyrical content had no place in the search for meaning in Karnatik music, this essay would be redundant. The Karnatik music community would collectively transcend linguistic meaning, and it would not matter if the sahitya was on gods, nature, life or human relationships. But the fact is that this is not a generally accepted point of view, making this exegesis worthwhile.

The Karnatik music community at large works within the religious context. Kutcheris in temples are not looked upon as art music presentations, but as devotional offerings. Musicians have traditionally been advised not to present padas or javalis that are erotic in content within temples. When such pieces have been brought into the sanitized realm of religious bhakti, their presence within the temple walls makes everyone uncomfortable. Ironically, the devadasi sang and danced these very padas in the same temples in times past. Recordings are produced based on religious themes; lectures and talks are given on the deep philosophical and ritualistic meanings of the compositions. Hindu religiosity constantly makes its presence felt. In the world as we know it, people are by and large conditioned by religion. With the Karnatik music community being primarily Hindu, it is hardly surprising that the associations with these gods and goddesses hold the field.

I will be the first to concede that, in spite of my views on the relative unimportance of textual meaning in art music, certain names of gods and adjectives touch a deep chord in me. This cannot and need not be avoided. But at the same time, the issue of religion in Karnatik music needs to be addressed because we need to understand the relationship between religion, spirituality, Karnatik music and ourselves. I also believe that, in due course, we should see if it is possible to engage with Karnatik music without the religion factor, at least in its overt and overbearingly obtrusive manifestations. I move in this direction, as I believe religiosity narrows our vision of experience.

Is Karnatik music inherently religious?

To answer that, I must ask whether Karnatik music was intended to be religious. It is not possible to respond in 'yes' or 'no' terms to this. Karnatik music was not one single initiative that started like some association or a movement, but an aesthetic impulse that acquired shape and definition and then, through shared experiences and cognitive energies among master artists, developed a set of coda over a period of time.

But clearly its journey included a relationship with temples and their associated rituals. This is where we need to look beyond the function and the practice of the music. We need to recognize the brilliance of musicians whose genius was logistically linked to religious sites, but was aesthetically free to and did indeed travel beyond the precincts of the temple where they practised their art. In this complex formation lies the answer to the question about the intent of Karnatik music. My point of view on this subject is not atheistic but aesthetic. Many of the issues discussed with regard to meaning are applicable to religious content in Karnatik music and therefore I will not repeat myself.

Now to pose another related question: what happens when the thought in the musician's mind is the music's religious content?

This is not an academic question, but is about a very real situation. Most Karnatik musicians in the past and many in the present hail from conservative families, more often than not of brahmin descent. They believe strongly in religion and ritual. This automatically makes their relationship with Karnatik music religious. In this situation, the lyrics rendered further entrench their already conditioned minds in religious belief, leading many musicians to feel, believe and then propound the belief that they are conveying the philosophical and religious meaning of the vaggeyakara to the audience. Many kirtanas are rendered with deep feeling and focus on the names of the deities and the vaggeyakara's yearning for these gods.

In doing so, is the kirtana's aesthetic make-up influenced? As much as the musicians are engrossed in the music, the focus is driven by textual meaning as they understand it and their own associations with the words being sung. Lines in the compositions are rendered with a clear emphasis on those words that create a religious – if not devotional – emotion both for the musician and the listener. These lines are even repeated to constantly emphasize the same emotion. In the process, the musician's thoughts veer away from the musical structuring.

As with every argument, there is a counter-argument to this: the vaggeyakaras, who knew their bhakti but were extraordinarily skilled in musical movement, would have made sure that the melodic flow was such that these parts of the devotional sahitya were focused upon. The point is theoretically well taken, but does not pass the test in its application. In many cases, the lines that extract religious fervour are, in fact, redesigned by musicians to provide this experience. Just like the rendition of lines in a kirtana is reconfigured to ensure word meaning, repetitions and word-splitting highlight the names of gods and goddesses and descriptive adjectives. Musicians consciously make these changes in order to generate a religious emotion in the audience. This is actually an exercise in emotional manipulation, but the psychological conditioning of both the artists and audiences makes it inevitable.

A similar 'technique' is adopted to stimulate nationalistic ardour by highlighting the patriotic content in some compositions, but since there are not many of those in a kutcheri, the dexterousness does not become as much of a departure. Obviously, this manipulative technique is meant well, but the point is that it changes the composition's aesthetic experience and leads to a departure from Karnatik music's intent. In Namasankirtana, the same technique of religious emphasis is used, but in that context, it is both felicitous and necessary.

When a composition is presented in Karnatik music, its very presence must inspire the musician to abstraction. The discerning listener too must submit herself to the seamless aesthetic construction of the composer. Instead, when just about everyone receives the composition as a religious presentation, every other aesthetic is seen as an instrument for enhancing or accentuating or, in one way or another, subserving the religious experience. Divinity becomes the rendering's principal inspiration. This limits the melodic and rhythmic possibilities, as the musician is conscious that his creativity must not undermine the emotional quality of the religious content. In this trap, the musician ignores or is unable to see the creative opportunities that the compositions present.

How is such a Karnatik concert different from Namasankirtana? It is the essence of manodharma and compositional music that gives character to Karnatik music. If this essence is reconfigured, Karnatik music loses its reason for existence.

There are times when the musician manages to leave behind all religious baggage. This happens because of laya. During mel-kala niraval or kalpanasvara, the speed of rendition makes the musician momentarily forget the religious content, even if he had been engrossed in it only moments earlier. This shift happens not because of a sudden realization of aesthetic intent, but courtesy the other trap of modern Karnatik music: the kutcheri. In the need for applause and a performance 'high', the musician jettisons religious orientations. The result? Both the religious and the aesthetic intent get sacrificed at the altar of a 'successful performance'.

One reason for the increase in the compositional content in a kutcheri is this obsession with religion. Many compositions – especially those of Tyagaraja – entered the modern kutcheri via Harikatha, where they were already popular. When presented in the kutcheri, musicians and listeners could relate to these compositions soulfully. This approach spread to all compositions. Many Harikatha exponents were serious scholars, gurus, vaggeyakaras and even kutcheri musicians. This mutuality reinforced the religiosity of the music community. The increased presentation of these compositions in kutcheris consolidated the misplaced religious focus of Karnatik music in concerts. This is a development that I believe has seriously undermined the music's abstractive qualities. A composition is chosen less for its aesthetic content than for the religious emotion it engenders or the philosophy it expounds. This has of late led to a further deterioration. As long as the names of gods and goddesses and descriptions are evocatively vouchsafed within a composition, and the melody allows this emotion to be transferred, musicians do not mind overlooking compositional aesthetics. This can leave a kutcheri looking like an evangelical congregation.

The tukkada section of a concert is probably the most affected by religiosity. The nature of this section within the concert format leaves it open to the inclusion of several devotional compositions. With the audience for Karnatik music concerts being primarily Hindu, the tukkada section has come to define the whole kutcheri experience. A majority of the audience even waits for this section. Many even say that though they do not understand the music, they still enjoy the tukkadas; the melodies are simple and they highlight devotion. Though there could be musical reasons for the increasing importance of this section, I believe that religiosity is the driving force behind this trend. Musicians too reason that since many in the audience do not understand the nuances of Karnatik music, they need to compensate them with this devotional content.

Having discussed the composer's and the singer's roles, let us turn to that of the listeners. It is the received wisdom that the Karnatik music audience is deeply religious and that its belief system must be satiated by Karnatik music concerts. The audience does not realize that the tukkada section is scant compensation for what it is missing out on by its lack of understanding. Attending a Karnatik music concert is essentially about serious engagement and not entertainment. As far as I can see, the devotional focus within a kutcheri panders to religious entertainment. The musician knows that by satisfying the religious and devotional needs of the majority of the audience, a concert can be moved up from an average rating to that of a successful one. Therefore, neither the musician nor the listener wants this to change. In maintaining the status quo, they are both caging Karnatik music in religion.

The listener has, in many ways, been trained into believing in the divinity of Karnatik music. This divinity is of a very literal kind. Often, even discerning listeners tell a musician that they actually 'saw' the deity she was singing about. This experience may have been true for them even if the musician had not focused on the devotional content of the lyrics. The listener – like the musician – comes with his religious predispositions, and more importantly, expects the concert to deliver a devotional experience, if not a catharsis. The expectation from a concert then becomes religious, rather than musical. The listener wants to be satisfied by the musician devotionally rather than aesthetically. This is where the problem exists; everything else is then seen with reference to that expectation of a particular sentiment and only that.

Devotion in Karnatik Music

A discussion on religion in Karnatik music necessarily leads to the debate about bhava, or the emotional aspect. As much as bhava is a generic idea, it is constantly related to the devotional requirement that we have imposed upon a kutcheri. This is the practitioner's doing. A musician cannot emote unless he or she feels the divinity and thereafter transfers it to the audience. I believe this discourse undervalues the idea of bhava, which is inherently sublime – one that cannot be trapped by literality. It exists in our very experience of life. Abstract music generates bhava in the most profound sense, without having to refer to any direct associations to god. In thrusting this experience into the box of religiosity, we have only reduced the intensity of the experience that art music can offer.

The alapana holds the key to what I am trying to explain. When an alapana, bereft of any lyrics and therefore the names of the gods and goddesses, is rendered, it has no religious or philosophical content. And yet it is profoundly moving. It is possible, of course, that if the kirtana that follows the alapana has a melodic motif with a strong religious connotation, then the musician can give it an anticipatory highlighting in the alapana, thereby setting a religious tone in advance. That said, the fact remains that most alapanas are either independent or only melodically connected to the ensuing kirtana. An alapana without any religious reference can leave an indefinable, unquantifiable emotional impact on everyone. This is the quality of emotion that art music can create. The same can be sought within a composition only if we can shed our religious carry-overs.

But was Karnatik music not born out of temple music? Is it not both natural and crucial that we emphasize the religiosity within?

Music seems to have evolved from humanity's search for that which lies beyond the realm of understanding. Therefore, the very existence of music can be related to god. But this is only part of the story. Almost all musical forms have their source in a religious environment, but some clearly and quickly moved beyond that setting into social music, political music and, most significantly, art music. Therefore, it would be incorrect to categorize any music as religious based on its historical antecedents. Even so, the history of music in south India presents a problem. Due to the overwhelming number of compositions having religious texts and given the fact that bhakti music has a long history, it is natural for us to see Karnatik music as an extension of the bhakti movement. This position negates the fact that the idea of art music existed right from ancient times. Whether it was the gandharva music of the *Natya Shastra* and *Dattilam* (pre-fourth century), the later deshi music developments (sixth to twelfth century) or the chaturdandi music (sixteenth and seventeenth centuries), all regarded art music as integral to the development of musical forms in India. Bhakti music used the musical aspects of art music to propagate religion. Whether the human impulse of devotion is anterior to the human instinct for music is debatable, but that music is older than musical devotion is not to be doubted. Bhakti music used art music's resources that pre-existed it. In so doing, bhakti music gave back to art music many important facets. This give and take between different art forms was natural and the evolution of each was due to this open receiving and giving. Yet, even while absorbing ideas, each retained the intrinsic intent of their form.

Bhakti music gave the kirtana format to Karnatik music. But in receiving this gift, art music practitioners reinvented the idea within the matrices of Karnatik music. Even concepts of tala were adopted from devotional music, but that did not make Karnatik music devotional. It was still art music, with its own distinct intent. Its content remained deeply influenced, as it could not but have been, by the hold of the idea of god over the popular imagination. Likewise, the power of the temple and its links with the ruling class influenced the lyrical content of music that was associated with these two dominating institutions. Even so, we cannot limit the role of the vaggeyakaras to that of mere propagators of religion. As discussed in the essay on meaning, the aesthetics of compositions and the music concepts that we have been handed down are clear proof of its unique status.

Karnatik music is a result of multiple streams of practices. This includes temple music practised by the nagasvara vidvans, the music and dance of the devadasis and the music of brahmin scholar musicians and vaggeyakaras. I believe that the art music identity was established by the seamless exchange of music between these communities. The devadasis and nagasvara vidvans often trained under brahmin scholar musicians and vaggeyakaras, who in turn learnt a great deal from these two communities. Thus evolved the Karnatik aesthetics.

We know all this from the details of the lives of many musicians, dancers and rulers over the last 400 years. Scholars formulated musical theories based on these various practices. It is also important to understand that though the nagasvara vidvans practised the music as ritual music, it is very evident from what they are said to have rendered that their music went far beyond ritual. Even until the early part of the twentieth century, they were playing uninterrupted alapanas, compositions such as mallaris, rakti melam and pallavis, all of which were part of temple practices and yet, aesthetically, retained the identity of art music.

When ragas were aligned to suit the time of the day, artists were abstracting them in alapana or other manodharmic forms to respond to and create the mood for that diurnal, crepuscular or nocturnal hour. This had everything to do with the abstractive resources and possibilities of art music. It is evidence of how it is possible for an artist to conform to a social context of practice, yet take the music innovatively beyond that context. And that seems to have been exactly what the nagasvara vidvans did. They were essentially creating abstractive art objects, but within the ritualistic context. In so doing, they were actually removed – or, to be more accurate, they distanced themselves – from the ritualistic intent of their music.

Similarly, with the devadasis, though many of their musical and Sadir presentations were, choreographically speaking, directed towards the deity and to the satisfaction of 'his' requirements, aesthetically speaking, they found opportunities within the ritualistic practices to go beyond them. They could explore a pada for a long period of time, even though they presented it as part of a ritual. Whether the musicians and dancers were part of the temple or court environment, their training was very similar, leading us to believe that the art music existence of Karnatik music is not a modern construction, but part of a traditional flow. Given the depth of their engagement with the music, it is only reasonable to expect that the devadasis felt the abstractive power of art and its self-contained end.

The vaggeyakaras too, although their works centred on the divine, went beyond their religious inclinations to create art objects. Some of their compositions were even in praise of their patron, but that did not stop them from being beautiful art music compositions. This is also true of the devadasis who performed in courts. Brahmin musicians also took part in pallavi contests in the courts, which were clear examples of art music presentations.

All these groups collectively pushed beyond their socio-political environment and carried forward the already extant idea of art music. At this juncture, we must recognize that many Shiva temples also had the institution of the odhuvars. These were non-priestly and therefore non-brahmin exponents of tevaram (shaivite religious hymns) rendered at the threshold of the shrine. Vaishnavite temples had arayars, who were brahmins rendering divyaprabandhams (vaishnavite religious hymns), illustrated by abhinaya. But these two were never included within the art music world, even though they may have used many of the same ragas and talas. In this differentiation also lies a clue to why music practised by the devadasis, nagasvara vidvans and the brahmin musicians was not devotional music in the same sense as that of the odhuvars or arayars. The training method for odhuvars and arayars was also not the same as that of nagasvara vidvans, devadasis or the brahmin musicians. This music was organized and practised in a way that went far beyond devotion directed towards the deity. Art music is not a recent creation; it only came to be reinterpreted in modern times within the urban setting. The interpretation was social rather than aesthetic, and aimed at creating a 'classical' tag.

The modern 'classical' idea of Karnatik music can be traced to the brahmin community in Madras. These were times of the nationalist movement, with the royalty and even small zamindars losing their power. As a result, patronage of the arts had disappeared. The move to Madras necessitated a new kind of patronage – organizational – with the paying public as the audience. In this environment, the dominant brahmin community took it upon itself to create a modern narrative for Karnatik music. While creating this story, the community formulated a music that was in sync with its own understanding of Hinduism, morality and faith. The musical trinity were all made out to be divine personalities and the religiosity of the Harikatha storytellers was built in. Existent ideas of nada, nadabrahma, music as a vehicle to salvation, the power of chanting the lord's name (similar to gospel music and qawwali) were all extrapolated from religion, philosophy and the kirtanas themselves. These were included as the intent of Karnatik music.

It is, therefore, no accident that kirtanas became the dominant compositional form within the modern kutcheri. I am not discounting the tremendous musical value of many kirtanas, but their religious content was crucial in giving them this dominance. This positioning of religion within Karnatik music changed the nature of the music's intent, performance, structure and practice. Though there have been artists over the last century who went beyond this bondage musically, they too continued to articulate the same interpretation of music. This is why Karnatik music has continuously included devotional pieces of music with absolutely no art music qualities.

The Karnatik Faith

To me, the understanding of Karnatik music as religious appears to be extremely superficial. Practitioners of the art who lived and breathed the music in the temples and courts themselves have given us music that is more than just religious devotion. The religiosity of the music comes from the context of its development, which suffuse the content of its lyrics. The music itself, though, is beyond religion. In traditional society, many forms of music – religious, art, social – existed together and borrowed from each other, but all the practitioners clearly knew the intent of each form.

Even in the rendition of pallavis and shlokas/viruttams, the religious connections are unavoidable. In fact, most musicians would emphasize the need to convey the meaning of the text through musical articulation. This is viewed as the emotional value of rendering them. In pallavis, though the role of the line is purely for improvisation, the content again tends to be religious. But in the structure and rendition of some pallavis, the mathematical possibilities and manodharma techniques make it imperative for the musician to go beyond the religious content. Some of these ideas may have actually come from the nagasvara vidvans. In instances like these, Karnatik music does shed its religious pressure, but by and large, we see pallavis rendered like single-line kirtanas with a complete focus on the sahitya.

In this discussion, the role of instrumental music becomes important. Though one would say that, in instrumental music, religion does not have a place and consequently the intent of art music as an abstractive form is emphasized, I beg to disagree. It is a fact that every instrumentalist knows the compositions, and whether or not he bears the textual meaning in mind while playing solo, he does associate them with the religiosity inherent in the form. Some instrumentalists have tried to say that traditional lyrical compositions need not be part of their repertoire and have, therefore, created forms that are 'purely' instrumental. While I cannot fault this as a creative thought, the problem is that they are unable to create an abstract idea of instrumental music and present music based purely on their virtuosity.

Their urge to create new instrumental forms displays an inability to think of the composition itself as being profoundly abstractive – as more than what it lyrically conveys. In the case of Karnatik music, our understanding of meaning is religious, devotional and oriented towards Hindu thought. I discuss this aspect here rather than in the essay on meaning because instrumentalists too feel very strongly the impact of religion within them, even though they may not necessarily dwell on the meaning of the words. Even vocalists who do not mull over the literal meaning of the words feel the religion through the names of the gods and goddesses and the descriptive words used in the kirtanas. This is a conditioned imperative.

Will the rendition of non-religious sahitya help change perceptions? I have often wondered about this, and have even rendered compositions that are generic in nature with the specific intention of creating non-religious content. While I do not believe that word meaning matters, there is no denying that it does for most, and so I felt that this logical and major experiment ought to be attempted. But then I had misgivings: in trying to remove a certain conditioning, will I be creating another? This is something I need to seriously consider. Maybe this exploration is important in order to provide lyrical alternatives, but it should not hold us captive. We have to move beyond any kind of bondage to the sahitya's lyrical meaning that limits our vision of the music. My direction of travel is to see in sahitya the beauty of sound that has a musical identity within the Karnatik form. The nature of the lyrics must not be guided by the religious or non-religious content, but by one's devotion to art music.

Just as it is possible for an art musician of the highest calibre to render a full concert where at the heart of his rendering is the religious thought underlying the lyrics, it should be possible for another art musician of the same calibre to offer a full concert in which the power of his musical abstraction proceeds with no assistance from words with linguistic meaning. Complimented by his instrumental accompanists and the wordless magic of the alapana, kalpanasvaras, tana and the tani, he should be able to transport his audience to musical fulfilment. I pose this hypothetical horizon not to undermine, much less negate, the syllabo-melodic content of art music, but merely to untwist the two strands and hold them apart for detached contemplation.

Within the modern world, the Hindu religious content raises an important question. Can an atheist or a non-Hindu be a Karnatik musician?

The environment that pervades Karnatik music makes it very difficult for an atheist to function within its world. There may be a few, but they will find it very difficult to come out in the open and articulate an atheistic narrative for Karnatik music. They will silently pamper the religious responses to their music and encourage devotional and philosophical expressions. I am not finding fault, but highlighting the difficulty for them to be who they are within this world. The musical fraternity at large does not feel it necessary to give Karnatik music, especially its compositional forms, a purely aesthetic thought.

What about practitioners of other religions? Among the nagasvara community there were not a few Muslim families that mastered this art form. Most of them flourished in what is now Andhra Pradesh and a few still live alongside the most conservative Hindu communities of Srirangam in Tamil Nadu. My admiration for these people is immense, as they have been able to negotiate two very opposing ideas, but there is a nuance. They have had to, perhaps willingly, accept the Hindu pantheon within their world. You will find their homes adorned with pictures of Hindu deities and their immense respect for Hindu gods and goddesses even when their religious practices are Islamic. This is a credit to their ability to straddle two worlds. But they cannot display apathy for Hinduism and be accepted as musicians by the Karnatik world.

Should we not be able to disassociate musicians' personal religious beliefs from their music? I believe we should, but cannot due to our understanding of Karnatik music. Within the Karnatik community it is a matter of great pride that these Muslim musicians apply vibhuti and kumkumam on their foreheads and accept Hinduism – a rather narrow-minded perspective to both art and religion. While there may be those who feel differently within the Karnatik community, this is without a doubt the dominant position.

Theism or atheism is not the point of this discussion. It is quite simply this: if any of these stances affect our surrender to the form of music itself, those need to be given serious thought. In this essay, I have intentionally not used the term 'secular' as the word today presupposes the presence of its opposite, namely religious belief, as a counterpoint. Besides, that word has a political connotation. I have no fight with religion itself, which is an emotion born from the human being's faith in living. Religion breathes, grows, sheds, flowers and can become the protector of belief in life. But this very idea can and has been transformed to swallow all that it protects. The secular person does not question this loss, but accepts it. I am not willing to do the same. My faith is not religion; it lies in the aesthetic of art music, in my trust that art music is a living being, in my faith in its abstraction and emotionality, its non-articulated existence and in its meaning beyond meaning. I exist within this deep bhakti for Karnatik music.

19

A Man's World

Does it matter whether I am a man or a woman in the world of Karnatik music? Should it matter? These are some of the questions that come to mind as I struggle with this essay.

The role of women as musicians, perceptions about them and the idea of what 'women's Karnatik music' is have been a part of Karnatik music's sociological discourse. In the ideal world, music must supersede everything else, and all that matters is the precious quality of the emotions abstracted by the musician. How then does it matter whether the musician is male or female?

But it is a fact, as regrettable as it is true, that even in the elevated and elevating world of Karnatik music, gender has mattered. Worse, it still does. After all, the same social conditioning dominates the mind of the musician as it does the minds of politicians, businessmen or sportsmen. But the difference is that in Karnatik music the imprint of social history fell not just on the artists, but on the art itself.

Scholars have written about the history of women in Karnatik music, and so I need not go into the details here. But I will not be able to address the serious problem of male chauvinism among musicians without discussing the social changes that have taken place over the last 150 years and the impact of some important women on the music.

From the late 1800s, with changes in political structures and in social mores, many changes came about in the world of Karnatik music. A beautiful collective of musicians and dancers functioning in differentiated yet connected environments was destroyed. The devadasi, the nagasvara vidvans, the brahmin musicians and vaggeyakaras of the courts, the scholars and even the saintly musicians, all created art music and breathed it into the world in which they functioned. They were distinct, each of them, but they were not isolated from each other. The music was still the same. Today we call it Karnatik music. I would like to use this as a unifying term, and not as a description of the modern kutcheri.

A slow but sustained withdrawal of patronage by debilitated royal houses and temples was followed by the legislative glare on devadasi practices over a fifteen-year period from the early 1930s, ending in the final abolishing of the devadasi system in 1947. In fact, even by the turn of the century, many devadasis were living in penury, exploited by men. This precipitated a movement towards urban spaces, putting Karnatik music in a state of turmoil. The art form needed to reinvent its status within society – a process also influenced by the nationalist movement and the resultant search for a contemporary self-identity that was still proud of its cultural antiquity.

This new situation was quickly recognized and capitalized upon by the powerful class in Madras, which was predominantly brahmin. We can debate on whether this was right or wrong, but its reality cannot be ignored. The brahmins were the dominant community in terms of economic strength, social clout and political power. They were joined by some rich merchants and lawyers from the chettiar or vellalar communities, though later they were to oppose brahmin domination through the Tamil Isai movement. With large-scale relocations and changes in patronage,

Karnatik music could not remain unaffected. A foundationally determining process of reshaping Karnatik music took place, in which, alongside modernization, there also came about a certain sanctification of the art form. The brahmin-orchestrated sanctification was considered necessary to rid dance and even music of its devadasi history. This revisionism gave the music and its practitioners access to a moral high ground: it was not some tawdry act by sex workers, but a divine act practised by saintly figures and respectable personalities. The modernization lay in creating a Western systems-based education, codification and presentation for the music. Together, these efforts bestowed 'classical' status on the art music form.

These developments directly impacted the devadasis – who were the only women through history to practise Karnatik music and Sadir (later Bharatanatyam) – and their position as artistic treasure houses of south Indian culture. The issue of caste, which is so intertwined with this discussion, I will address in the essay that follows. By the early twentieth century, the two new contexts of modernization and sanctification had succeeded in marginalizing them. They sought to create a modern re-justification for themselves by releasing gramophone records of their music, acting in movies and trying to fit their unhindered musical sensibility into the kutcheri. But in the newly sanctified world of the kutcheri, most of them were unable to find a permanent space that their art required. How could they? The modern kutcheri context needed, after all, a 'clean' image. Also, the musical requirements of the kutcheri were such that the devadasi music by itself was not considered enough to represent kutcheri music. This meant that musically too the idea of 'Karnatik' was narrowing down. At the same time, the kutcheri space was not sanctified enough yet for women from 'respectable households' – brahmins and the other higher castes – to perform in public.

One significant exception of a woman ascending the public dais was the Harikatha exponent, Saraswati Bai (1892–1974).

Born into an orthodox brahmin household, Saraswati Bai came to be so popular that she threatened the dominance of the male brahmin bhagavatars (title for one who gives discourse on music). This even led the men to make sure that she did not receive the coveted Sangita Kalanidhi title given by the Music Academy. But behind the fact of brahmin women not being permitted to be kutcheri musicians there lies more than just the 'stigma' attached to devadasis. The fact is that we were a highly and uncompromisingly patriarchal society and the equal presence of women in the arts, especially within a modern social environment, was just not acceptable. I believe that this, regrettably, continues to be the case..

Dhanammal of the Celestial Vina

I mentioned the exceptional case of Saraswati Bai. There was another legendary figure, but she was not from the brahmin community. Male musicians and their patrons were happy to acknowledge the musicality of the great devadasi, Vina Dhanammal (1867–1938). They flocked to her Friday musical renderings. However, even with her, the descriptions that they gave to her music – pristine, subtle, soft, old – revealed responses other than the obvious admiration. They showed certain perceptions that, even if they were true, spoke of their bias. Terms like 'subtle' and 'soft' indicated that her music, highly pleasing as it was, was suitable for a salon. But was her music considered appropriate for the larger stage or the man's world? No, it was not. By then, Karnatik music had acquired a robust masculine identity. Typecasting her music as 'pristine' and 'old' was an indication that it was some sort of a museum piece, quaint and not quite contemporary at a time when Karnatik music was being refashioned for the new world. People marvelled at her music. They learnt numerous compositions from her with great love and admiration, but when it came to the kutcheri, she was a non-person, even though she did manage to perform in the sabhas (organizations promoting the arts through sponsored concerts) a few times. In later years (between the 1950s and the 1980s), her granddaughters, T. Brinda and T. Mukta, who did sing in sabhas were much respected by musicians. But they too were not quite accepted as leading kutcheri musicians. They still represented the music of olden times. Modern kutcheri music, by the 1940s, had redefined Karnatik music.

At this point, it is pertinent to recognize that beyond the first-generation urban devadasi musicians – of whom T. Brinda, T. Mukta (1914–2007), M.S. Subbulakshmi and M.L. Vasanthakumari (1928–90) were prime examples – the generations that followed have not given us even one prominent woman musician from this traditional community of artists. This is both a gender and a caste issue, a gender deprivation and a class loss. I must unequivocally state that the almost voyeuristic practice of romanticizing the devadasis must stop. But their artistic legacy has to be excavated from the debris of their history.

Subrahmanya Bharati Makes His Point

The challenges faced by some women pioneers in Harikatha and Karnatik music, such as Saraswati Bai, Bangalore Nagaratnammal (1878–1952) and M.S. Subbulakshmi, were numerous. It was also a time for much discussion and debate on these issues. In his essay 'Sangita Vishayam' (Issues in Music), Subrahmanya Bharati (1882–1921) differentiates between the devadasi and the 'kudumba penn' (family girl/woman). While discussing the good qualities of some current musicians, he mentions that they are both male and female (infer devadasi). Further on, he says, 'Let us move from classical vidvans to people who sing in a natural way.' In this section, he deals specifically with the 'kudumba penn' who renders social songs and some kirtanas. He demands of the kudumba penn that she learns Karnatik music in the proper way so that it improves society's sensitivity to music. He writes about improving their 'laya unarchi' (sense of laya) through formal training. This was considered lacking in women. Bharati says that people ask, 'Are these women dasis? Are they going to render kutcheris? Why do they need to sing with the correct laya and tala?' He then goes on to point out that training in tala and all aspects of music is necessary, so that the music is beautiful, and that if we stop women from singing, life itself would collapse. This is progressive indeed, but in his answer there is no mention of the possibility that the 'kudumba penn' could also become a kutcheri musician. It is very clear that, ahead of his times as he is, Subrahmanya Bharati is conforming to the sharp distinction drawn in his times between the 'kudumba penn' and the devadasi.

Bangalore Nagaratnammal's Intervention

There was also a general fear that women who wanted to learn music may need to go to teachers belonging to 'non-respectable' backgrounds. As early as 1904, Umayalpuram Natesha Ayyar had established a Karnatik music school in Madras, in which many girls from prominent brahmin households were enrolled. What does this show? That these households wanted their girls to learn Karnatik music, but under brahmin auspices. At the same time, this learning was not to be used on the performing stage. All this stigma was debilitating for women artists of the time. It was in this climate that Bangalore Nagaratnammal, of devadasi descent from Mysore with a distinguished concert reputation, built the Tyagaraja Samadhi at Tiruvaiyyaru – the temple town on the banks of the Kaveri, – and installed the Tyagaraja 'idol' in it. She thereby created an important place for musicians to congregate and pay homage to the great composer. Incredibly, senior male musicians refused to accompany her in a concert at that venue. This was no ordinary insult. Nagaratnammal responded by conducting an all-female musical homage to Tyagaraja. The numerous historical anecdotes and quotes available from this period only further establish the difficulty that women had in finding a space, and a respectable one at that. It was from this world that the woman kutcheri musician had to rise. She battled, and continues to battle, many of the old prejudices that have reincarnated themselves for a new age.

Two Harbingers of Change

Before I move on to the issues that women face in the contemporary context, I would like to outline the musical careers of M.S. Subbulakshmi and D.K. Pattammal (1919–2009). A study of their lives is important, not for the purposes of comparison, but as examples of women from two different communities who had to invent a different image of themselves to be accepted among men. I will not go into their life stories in great detail, but cull out essential indicators from their lives.

Subbulakshmi was born to a devadasi mother, Madurai Shanmukhavadivu (1889–1962), herself a vina artist. Subbulakshmi's life changed with the move to Madras and her marriage to T. Sadasivam, a brahmin who was already married and a father of two daughters. Sadasivam was a freedom fighter and very well connected in political and business circles. In this new house, Subbulakshmi became 'MS'. She was already well known, in fact almost a celebrity, because she had acted in a successful Tamil film, *Sevasadanam* (1938), based on Munshi Premchand's 1919 Hindi novel *Bazar-e-Husn* (The Market of Beauty or Red-Light District), which dealt boldly with the subject of domestic abuse and prostitution. But with her marriage came an impulse to refashion a new identity. The first thing that Sadasivam figured was that MS must shed her devadasi history, while keeping her filmic persona intact. She effected this change deftly, both on-screen and off-screen. In most of her post-marriage films, she donned the suitably sanctified mantles of Narada, Mira and other Hindu mythological characters. Given her musical genius and extraordinary personal charisma, MS thereby established a divinity that lives until today. At the same time, Sadasivam also installed her on the kutcheri stage, where he utilized her gift for rapturous invocation to make her the very epitome of bhakti. MS became the vehicle for every great saint that had ever lived and, in her music, was found the true sense of Hindu devotion. In this process, she became the classic brahmin woman. She also became the inspiration for 'respectable' women to become musicians. I am not considering here the question of whether or not she did this willingly, but that transformation was the reality of her life.

MS's transformation has an interesting musical subtext. Devadasi women were respected for their musicality, but were never considered good enough for the rigours of the modern kutcheri. What was considered rigorous included complex mathematics, ragam–tanam–pallavis, aggressive singing and the rest. Men were considered strong singers with a robust interpretation of the music, and so the 'tough' or strenuous aspects of music were their domain. The women were supposed to personify the feminine side of music; therefore, their music was about elegance, beauty and tenderness. It is important to note that this was part of the sanctification process, wherein a cultivated demureness both in the singer and the song was essential. It was conveniently forgotten that not very much earlier devadasis rendered the music that was now considered a male preserve.

Contrary to received wisdom, though, M.S. Subbulakshmi was not just capable of presenting the 'tough' aspects, but actually did present them. In numerous concerts, she rendered complex pallavis, sang rare and difficult compositions and presented all the 'male' aspects of the music with striking effect. Why is it that no one remembers this? Now, that is the interesting twist. In the need to transform herself from an alluring devadasi musician to a respectable brahmin musician, MS immersed herself in bhakti. She did this by focusing on the religious aspects of the lyrics, including compositions of numerous saints from all over the country, rendering shlokas and bhajans. A dasi became Mira. Since neither her bhakti nor her srngara music was part of what was perceived as serious and rigorous, her Karnatik musicality was undervalued. Ultimately, who vanishes and who abides? Neither, really. But a great musician lost out on both counts, for neither part presented her in the truest light of Karnatik music.

Kutcheri music as presented by men was what was perceived as real, and this included much more than the padas and javalis of the devadasi, which came to be considered exquisite music to be rendered in private or in the later part of the kutcheri. The bhakti music of MS was beautiful, uplifting, unforgettable, but it was still not regarded as serious music, as it represented only the devotional music of the pious and the devout. The fact that there was another 'MS music' that was capable of being, and did indeed become, serious with all the rigour of art music has been lost to the legend of the 'divine MS'. I regard this as a great loss. The Karnatik world that men had built denied her the musicianship that lesser men could aspire to. MS had to find her space within this order and manoeuvre within it. She and her husband may have been intensely committed to bhakti music, but the actual positioning of MS and her social transformation was the work of men in society, especially those constructing the modern Karnatik story.

D.K. Pattammal, on the other hand, was a brahmin from Kanchipuram. Her mother had learnt music, but never performed, because upper-caste women were not allowed to do so. Women from brahmin houses only sang devotional songs during religious occasions within the household. DKP, as she came to be known, showed great talent and learnt from numerous teachers and emerged as a champion of Karnatik music. She was also very involved in the freedom movement and rendered numerous patriotic songs in films and released records. In a way, she was the 'family girl' Subrahmanya Bharati had spoken of, out in the public arena. The most common quotes about her are that she was 'the first brahmin woman musician to perform in public' and that she was 'the woman first to render complex ragam–tanam–pallavis in kutcheris'. In proclaiming her to be the first brahmin woman in the kutcheri environment, the brahmin men succeeded in further isolating traditional woman musicians. There is a nuance to be noted here. By proclaiming that DKP was the first woman to render RTP, they were placing the capacity of the brahmin woman musician above that of the devadasi, a wholly inaccurate position. RTPs were very much part of the repertoire of distinguished devadasis like Coimbatore Thayi and Bangalore Nagaratnammal. And therefore the compliment paid to Pattammal was less of a tribute to her than yet another expression of an attitude towards devadasis. These men must also have thought that her presence could serve as an incentive to more brahmin women taking to music. They were also making the point that presentations such as RTPs were the domain of men, but if the brahmin woman could present them, may be she could find acceptance in that world.

Ironically, there were many men in the Karnatik world whose music did not fulfil these demands imposed on the women. DKP's music was called 'man's music' and the brahmin woman was accommodated in the kutcheri world, but many male musicians would not accompany her. Only those who did not find a footing in the male world would do so. When Palghat Mani Iyer (1912–81) accompanied her and, much later, M.L. Vasanthakumari on the mrdanga, it was a gracious personal gesture rather than a conceptual acceptance of women as important musicians. This meant that DKP's kutcheris had to be attractive enough with just her name on the invitation. She could not depend on the names of her accompanists to attract more people. For instance, people attending a concert by Semmangudi Srinivasier (1908–2003) would also be interested in hearing him accompanied on the violin by Rajamanikkam Pillai (1898–1970) and on the mrdanga by Pazhani Subramania Pillai (1908–62). The misogyny inherent in our culture and the baggage of a belief in the 'impurity' of devadasi women led to a subconscious belief that women who performed on stage were of loose morals. A similar attitude persists towards film actresses even today.

Pattammal built her whole musical image around the belief that her music could be as rigorous as that of the men. Her image was contained in an identifiably male musicality as much as MS's was in bhakti. Through her life, Pattammal was known for very tough singing, rendering difficult pallavis and rare Dikshitar compositions. Even though she was brahmin, her music was never associated with bhakti. Though the brahmin community made a clear effort to drench Karnatik music in the bhakti of the composers and the piety of the musicians, yet that identity would not by itself have been enough for a woman from the community. She could not predominantly be a singer of padas and javalis, as that would have affected the sanctity of her brahmin identity. She had to establish herself as a brilliant technician with a collection of rare and difficult compositions and not a woman rendering kirtanas for the elevation of her household. An additional dimension of Pattammal lay in her identification with nationalist ardour. This was most powerfully expressed in her spirited renderings of Subrahmanya Bharati's patriotic songs. And just as it used be said of MS that she was Mira herself, people saw in Pattammal, none other than Bharati himself. All the masculinity of India's svadeshi spirit shot through her patriotic songs. Nothing could have been more conducive to the patronizing of Pattammal by male brahmins, many of whom were ardent nationalists and freedom fighters. Pattammal's music was 'man's music' and her voice, the courageous spirit of the men.

When we reflect upon the lives of MS and DKP, we find a devadasi who through her music became the epitome of a brahmin housewife – pious, divine, with all the qualities of a woman of high culture. The other was a brahmin woman who concluded her life as the epitome of a serious Karnatik musician and an icon for nationalism. Yet she was never accepted as an equal of male musicians. No one sought the classical housewife in her. They became two sides of the same coin minted in the foundry of male, brahmin domination. Men manipulated the space for women in Karnatik music and saw to it that they remained a notch below their own kind.

The Scene Today

What then of the present? Many of the prejudices that existed then continue to persist and male musicians still give multiple reasons to justify their stance. Many male violinists and mrdanga artists are reluctant to accompany women, or are willing to do so only after they themselves attain a certain stature in the eyes of other male musicians, organizers and the audience and have, so to say, nothing to lose by accompanying women singers.

In the two decades between the 1970s and 1990s, the Karnatik music scene changed dramatically, with the number of women vocalists far exceeding that of male musicians. I believe this was the main reason that the chauvinistic men changed from toeing a hard line towards women to an opportunistic one. Over the last century, musicians could take great pride in claiming that they have never accompanied women. Some of them even looked down upon those of their colleagues that did. The latter were seen as having 'stooped' to accompanying women since they were not good enough to accompany male musicians. The tendency to not play for women, or a preference for accompanying men, persists. It is not as overt as it once was, but the attitude is alive and even encouraged by many leading musicians.

I am deeply interested in the reasoning behind this stance, and will now question the veracity of the claims.

For a long time, male accompanists have used the excuse that the shruti (pitch) of women vocalists is high; usually between 5 and 6, i.e. G or A. It is said that at these shrutis, the violin and mrdanga sound unpleasant and that accompaniment becomes difficult. True, when the mrdanga's shruti is higher, the sound becomes more metallic. In the violin's case too the tone becomes sharper, and more crucially, even a minor slip is utterly obvious. At certain shrutis, the instruments have a rounded sound due to a certain balance that occurs between the sharp and the base tones. These shrutis are the ones usually used by male musicians.

Having offered that background, let me now explain why this reason holds no water. First, in the good old days when there were no microphones, men also sang at the same high pitch. Second, even now, these musicians accompany solo instrumentalists who play at higher shrutis. If pitch was the issue, many mrdanga artists and violinists should have refused to accompany such solo instrumentalists. I have not heard complaints in those cases. How does accompanying a woman singing at the higher pitches become difficult then? That excuse is clearly untenable. Similarly, there have been rare cases of male musicians singing at extremely low shrutis, as famously with M.D. Ramanathan (1923–84). In these shrutis, the mrdanga's tone is completely lost and the violin loses its tonal fluidity, but I am not aware of anyone refusing to accompany such musicians because the shruti was too low.

The other idea that needs to be addressed is that a certain fixed shruti is the ideal timbre for an instrument. There is nothing wrong with the tone of an instrument at any pitch. It is the nature of the instrument that determines its timbre at different shrutis. The attitude that only certain timbres are pleasing is a conditioning resulting from the dominance of male vocalists over the last fifty years. The advent of the microphone and the resultant lowering of the men's pitch changed the texture of male music completely. Their voices came closer to the natural speaking voice of the mature man. This decreased volume levels, but increased the base tones in the voice, immediately affecting the music and its experience. It also changed the tonal quality of the violin and the mrdanga and the acoustic experience of the instruments was reframed. This is the sound that is now expected of male musicians. Over the years, solo instrumentalists have also lowered their shruti to conform to a modern sense of 'ideal pitch'. In this new world of the Karnatik sound, the women who sing in the higher pitches are a minority.

To return to my earlier point, instruments do not really have an ideal pitch; this idea is based on habituation and comfort alone. There may be certain technical challenges to playing at the higher pitches, but the search must not be for the least challenging shruti. Instead, there ought to be an attempt to embrace the sound and the acoustic impact of melody in different shrutis. The timbre of the instruments in a higher shruti is what it should be and has its own beauty. But this also means that the musician needs to make necessary adjustments while being fully aware of the music's aesthetics. The method of playing must factor in the pitch at which the instrument is being played. If serious thought is given to such factors, the issue of the instrument sounding worse or better at a specific shruti will not arise.

Added to this is the oft-heard comment from mrdanga artists that while playing for most women, they cannot play with complete freedom and that their accompanying style is restricted. This is attributed to the soft, delicate, non-aggressive nature of women's music. It is completely wrong to make general observations about women's music. There are male vocalists whose music is far more delicate than that of robust women musicians. At the root of this comment, though, is the idea of 'freedom' and 'unrestricted accompanying style'. Mrdanga artists associate these concepts with being able to use loud strokes, fast patterns and mathematical calculations. But is not this image of freedom itself restrictive? I would even say that this interpretation of freedom is unsuitable for Karnatik music itself. This does not mean that mrdanga artists must not employ the above techniques; they should, whenever necessary. Ironically, many mrdanga artists have become prisoners of their freedom. They have lost track of the music, and their accompaniment becomes obtrusive, whether they are accompanying men or women.

Even if there were any truth in the belief that the music of women vocalists is more delicate, I see no problem. This delicacy is not a restriction, but another kind of opportunity in freedom that the mrdanga artists need to explore. You cannot impose your ideas of freedom on the melody of Karnatik music. It must also be said that those same mrdanga artists would accompany vina and violin soloists deftly, never complaining about the lack of freedom. Yet another reason why this criticism is not valid.

Then there is the complaint that most women musicians are weak in tala, making it very difficult for the mrdanga artists to play complicated mathematical structures. This, as we all know, is untrue. There are many women vocalists whose tala definition is far superior to that of their male colleagues. Yes, there are women vocalists who are weak in tala, but then so are some men vocalists. This comment applies to musicians in general, not to women. I feel both these arguments are connected to the thought that women's music was about presenting padas, javalis and kirtanas, and not for the serious, tough aspects of the music. Hard-core Karnatik music is considered an aggressive male musical expression. All sexist notions.

Yet another complaint from accompanists is: 'We don't get the "status" if we accompany women.' By 'status', they mean individual recognition and respect as great artists. Further elaboration will include the statement that the women hog all the attention. It will surprise no one that the reference here is only to the woman's appearance: her looks, clothes, jewellery and so on – not her musicality. The implicit suggestion is that most people do not come to women's concerts for musical reasons and that 'real' music can be heard only in concerts of male vocalists. In an age where even male musicians dress in great style, this excuse is irrelevant. Should we not then say that men too do not sing real music any more?

Status and recognition for the accompanist has nothing to do with whether the vocalist is male or female. It is the quality and adaptability of their own music that leads to recognition. Accompanists only hide behind these excuses to avoid accompanying women.

Then there are those who accompany women vocalists until they get to a certain point in their career, have gained enough concert experience and are recognized by the aficionados (read powerful male vocalists). This is treated almost like a graduation. The fact that it was the women who gave them opportunities, experience, sometimes even taught them the nuances of kutcheri art, made them financially stable and brought them to a point where the 'men' noticed them is forgotten. The woman's usefulness is over, a reflection of how men treat women in other contexts too.

One important reason that pushes accompanists to take such decisions is not known to most people, because it is in the realm of private conversations. There were and are male vocalists who either make it a condition that male accompanists stop accompanying women, or at least actively encourage them to stop. These vocalists are usually in the forefront of their field and wield a great deal of influence. They make no secret of the fact that they would prefer it if their accompanists did not accompany women. Some have even boycotted accompanists who did.

But this comes back to bite many chauvinist musicians when their daughters enter the concert arena. At this point, those very people seek the support of male accompanists. For their own daughters, they ask for the support of male musicians. For themselves, though, they demand musicians who have stopped playing for women.

While these observations are mainly about violinists and

mrdanga artists, similar attitudes are also prevalent among upa-pakkavadya artists. They can be uncomfortable with the idea of being 'second' to a woman. This is not a feeling they can express publicly in today's world, and hence they think up many excuses.

Similarly, many male vocalists do not perform with female accompanists. They may do so during the early stages of their professional life before they reach a certain stage of popularity. Like the accompanists, after a certain point in their career, they decide they will only have men on stage. There are absolutely no musical reasons for such decisions. Vocalists may not actually articulate this, but a careful observation of their choices will reveal this deep-seated prejudice. Some vocalists will say that there are not many good violinists among women. An assessment of quality is individualistic in that every vocalist has a different expectation of the violinist, and that makes the point non-debatable. But take the case of violinists; it is apparent that there are women who are of the same calibre as many popular male violinists. We cannot but believe that they are subject to chauvinism.

There have been very few women mrdanga artists in the history of kutcheri music. The mrdanga is considered a male instrument since it requires a great deal of physical strength to play and master it. This is, of course, the traditional view. The few women mrdanga artists in the past found it impossible to break the male stranglehold over the field. There are a few young women who play the mrdanga now and we will have to wait and watch what happens. Similarly, among upa-pakkavadya artists, there have been some women, but they all speak of great conflict with the male mrdanga artists. I know of cases where women ghata artists have been rejected at the last moment only because the mrdanga artist refused to play along with the woman. These discriminatory actions have all gone unquestioned.

Male vocalists are wary of a situation where they might be overshadowed by a woman. They are happy about a battle among men, but with a woman, the fear – and shame – of failure is higher. 'What will other men think?' Vocalists in general are egoistic and like to dominate the concert and their accompanists. This tendency becomes further accentuated when women accompanists are involved.

Chauvinism in the Karnatik world gives the young male vocalist a distinct advantage over the female, especially when young musicians are trying to find their way in the field. Once a talented male newcomer is spotted, male accompanists descend upon him. He is the next catch who can be used to further their concert needs. They are eager to secure their hold over the next generation of male vocalists.

I must state that many of these accompanists are great musicians and I am not at any point questioning their artistic abilities. In fact, my point is that their musical greatness helps these young men. They encourage the youngster, offer to accompany him at important occasions and even call organizers and ask them to feature him so they can accompany him. This gives the young man's career a fillip. He may be extremely talented, but the fact that great accompanists are playing with him draws a larger audience to his concert. Given the higher visibility, eventually, if he is a good artist, the climb is quick. That is, of course, a wonderful thing, but the problem is that a young girl with equal talent never gets this support. She has to struggle through the various grades with good accompanists of her own generation, or maybe one generation her senior. Her rise is much slower. How is this fair? If these senior musicians were truly interested in supporting talent, it should not matter whether the youngster is male or female.

A silent and unquestioning player in all this is the organizer – invariably male – who accedes to the male vocalist's request that only male accompanists be fixed for his concert and accommodates the powerful male accompanist by confirming that he will be featured only with a male vocalist. Organizers will even go to the extent of changing accompanists to comply with the men's demands. They say that often these are requests from powerful and popular musicians and they have no choice. With this attitude, no social injustice can be questioned. One has to stand up for some basic principles in life and until the organizers wake up, they are party to this unfairness. Organizers must take a strong stance and when asked to make changes on the basis of gender, they must refuse. Only such a collective voice can change attitudes, not of this generation perhaps, but at least the next one.

Alongside this criticism is another inexplicable phenomenon. Many popular and powerful women musicians prefer to have men as accompanists rather than women. Men always point to this when the issue of chauvinism is raised. Like the chauvinistic male vocalists, they perform with women accompanists for a certain period, after which they prefer male accompanists. I do not think women vocalists actually refuse to perform with female accompanists, but they definitely prefer male accompanists. For a long time I was unable to understand the reason for such an attitude. I was quite disbelieving when told that this was because of logistical difficulties during journeys, as women are asked to share rooms limiting privacy, or even that two women cannot work together harmoniously. These were the usual clichés attached to women spouted by men.

But I have since come to see that in any society, the behaviour of the dominant is always the norm. It is but natural that the powerful female wants to imitate the behaviour of her male counterpart. The vocalist is the leader of the stage and dominates the proceedings. When the men have only male accompanists, it is only natural that the women adopt a similar attitude, so that they are on par with men in all respects. An important aspect of this is that it provides women with control over men who usually outnumber them on stage. This is a position of great power and women celebrate it. Now a woman is not only behaving like the socially dominant gender, but also controlling him. If there is another woman on stage, it brings the vocalist's status down as she is not imitating the behaviour of the dominant male and may also have to share the sense of power with the other woman.

It has happened that senior male accompanists suddenly decide to accompany women. Normally one should welcome such a decision, but I stop to wonder: what made them change their mind? There is usually a purely financial motive behind it. In most cases, their concert opportunities with men have diminished, and so they are now willing to accompany women. Others have done so after receiving the awards and titles that they feared they would be denied if they had accompanied women all along. The sad fact remains that women musicians have, without batting an eyelid, accommodated these accompanists. I vehemently disagree with the reason given in these cases – the quality of their music – as it devalues the contribution that her regular accompanist has made to her career. He is made to look like a fool and his concert opportunities stolen by another because of the recognition and respect the 'senior' commands in spite of his discriminatory actions.

I have never come across a male or female vocalist or accompanist who has stated that he or she will only accompany women or men who are not chauvinistic. I have often hoped that a few brilliant, popular and in-demand musicians would make such a proclamation – if only to create an awareness about this serious issue in the world of Karnatik music.

Of course, there are many musicians who do not subscribe to a gender-skewed view of the world of Karnatik music, but sadly there are many more that do. The larger issue is that nobody, including the open-minded, is willing to address this problem. The most disturbing fact is that few women musicians write or talk openly about the issue. One may wonder if the new generation is different. I am not sure that it is. We have all hoped things would change, but not much has. The percentage of those who accompany women has gone up, but that appears to be due to an increase in the absolute number of musicians. Today, musicians are more secretive about their attitudes and provide other reasons for refusing concerts with women, but many continue to harbour such sexist attitudes. This is true even of musicians who accompany women for now. This has to change. In the Karnatik world, music is the only governing principle and gender discrimination has no place. Let everyone have their own sense of quality and live by that, but let it not be based on an individual's gender.

The Female Voice Register

None of what I have said so far negates the fact that the female voice has an identity of its own. It contains a spectrum of musical expressions that are distinct from the male. By this, I am only referring to the quality of the voice. I refuse to typecast either with adjectives of a generalized nature, but accept that the physiological nature of a male and a female voice registers differently with the listener. Given that there are two different sets of voices that present Karnatik music, it is natural that the form's aesthetics develops two sets of impressions. The aesthetics of the music is the same, but a discerning listener gets a very different experience from the male and female voices. This is the beautiful nature of creation.

20

An Unequal Music

Amusician's primary concern has to be and is the music. No surprises there. But does that justify the bypassing of life's rhythms? It should not. And yet it does. Absorbed in their musicality, many artists neglect to recognize the serious social issues that press upon us every day. But these do need addressing, not avoidance, even in our role as musicians.

Karnatik music exists within a social consciousness after all. As a Karnatik musician with a circle of friends from other walks of life, I have been able to view the functioning of my musical world through their eyes. This has given me an altogether different perspective. I have valued the chance to view this art form, so to say, from the outside. The result has been a vital exercise in self-education. My own evolving perspectives on the social dimensions of the practice of Karnatik music are, therefore, based on personal experiences, private conversations, my study of our socio-political history and my understanding of what is and what could have been. In this essay, I will look at the position of caste within the Karnatik community and use history as a reference towards understanding the present.

Caste, as all of us know, is a socio-hierarchical norm that has been part of Indian society from time immemorial. It could not but have influenced Karnatik music, its social identity, the thought processes and behaviour of its practitioners and patrons. And numerous scholars who have known this to be the case have dealt in detail with the caste-related changes that occurred in the social identity of Karnatik music. In this essay, as in the ones on women and language, my focus will be on the last 150 years, which have directly impacted kutcheri music. I am also focusing on the Tamil-speaking regions around Tanjavur and the then young city of Madras, as these were the regions where kutcheri music evolved. From the advent of the kutcheri till today, Karnatik music has been dominated by the brahmin community, both in the practice of the art and in audience composition. In the previous few essays, we discussed the issues of religion, language and gender, but all of those discussions are incomplete without a dialogue on caste. These four social aspects of our music – religion, language, gender and caste – together form a complex, composite narrative. Though I have disaggregated them in my approach, they can and must be read together.

Caste and the Kutcheri

The term kutcheri has come to define Karnatik music. From an identity based on musical intent and form, the phrase 'Karnatik music' now directly invokes the performance, or the kutcheri – a word that has many implied meanings. The kutcheri is about much more than a stage and audience. It reflects a community, its taste, attitude, a social class, including of course, the performing class itself. We experience the music within these various defining elements. Even as I say this, I must clarify that, for the real aesthete immersed in the sound of Karnatik music, all these identifications dissolve. But that cannot be an excuse for ignoring the social or political underpinnings and implications of the music. Both – the 'pure' musical rapture and its complex hinterland – are keenly experienced as a living reality. And the relationship between the two is also, needless to say, most real. The musician, the discerning listener and the aficionado must investigate these. It is in this context that I am exploring the idea of caste in Karnatik music.

The paradigm of the 'kutcheri' largely ignores an important art music community: that of the nagasvara vidvans. While it is true that these hugely gifted artists tried to, and are still trying to, embrace the kutcheri, the truth is that when I think of the various articulations of the kutcheri, I never see an image of a nagasvara in it. I can imagine various artists and their instruments – vocalists, violinists, vina, mrdanga, ghata, kanjira, the tamburas – on the stage, but never the nagasvara. This may just be me, but I need to ask, why? Though Karnatik music is a vocal form, I still recognize subconsciously an instrumental identity for it. And yet, on that platform, a nagasvara vidvan does not find a seat. I know, from the music and the stories I have heard that Karnatik music as it is practised today has drawn a great deal of inspiration from them. I adore the music of T.N. Rajaratnam Pillai (1898–1956), the nagasvara giant who transformed both the instrument and its practice. When I think of alapana, the nagasvara comes to my mind. But when I think of Karnatik music or kutcheri, the nagasvara is not in my consciousness. I say this with great sadness. The reason for this lies in the social realignments that we discussed in the essays on the role of language, religion and women in south India between the latter part of the nineteenth century and early twentieth century.

With the erosion of royal patronage, the temple losing its centrality in cultural life, the crumbling of the devadasi's artistic identity, urbanization and the brahmin's need for a sanctification of musical practice, the nagasvara and tavil vidvans, who were the greatest practitioners of art music, were left with nowhere to go. They were still playing in the scattered temples of the countryside, but power had moved almost exclusively to Madras, where the Karnatik form was being given a modern hospitality. The power of this new identity was such that it was to become the only identity. To the discriminating and perceptive kutcheri musician, the music of the nagasvara vidvans continued to be a source of great inspiration, but what typified Karnatik music was their music. Was this a musically arrived position? No. Behind this dichotomy lay a deep sense of caste and class superiority. In this, the Karnatik musician believed that his was the real representation of the music and included all its essential elements in the most exquisite balance. The Karnatik musicians' collective approach to the nagasvara vidvan at the time can be paraphrased like this: 'The music of the nagasvara vidvan is full of manodharma and inspirational, but it is not the complete form. It is only one part of what the music should be. What it should be is being created by the modern vidvans.' This attitude could not but affect the nagasvara vidvan's musical self-esteem, leading to some of them incorporating more kirtanas into their performances – a victory of conformism.

Before I come to a discussion of that position, a brief examination of that fascinating and gifted community would be in order.

The description 'nagasvara, nattuvanar and the devadasi community' represented a collectivity of musicians and dancers such as perhaps was not to be found in any other music tradition. Operationally, they formed two groups, the periya melam (literally, large drum, where 'drum' is used to mean 'ensemble') and the chinna melam (literally, small drum). The periya melam included instruments other then the nagasvara, such as the tavil, otthu (a piped drone, later replaced by the shruti box) and tala cymbals. The chinna melam musicians, who were part of the devadasi ensemble, included the nattuvanar (who directed a dance ensemble, and was generally the teacher), mrdanga vidvan, mukha vina vidvan, flute vidvan and a person playing the tutti (a bagpipe-shaped drone instrument). Later, instruments such as the clarinet and flute permanently replaced the mukha vina, while the tambura replaced the tutti. Scholars have various explanations for why the names periya melam and chinna melam are used. Some propose that this indicated a hierarchy, while others suggest that the periya melam refers to the larger nagasvara, while the chinna melam refers to the smaller mukha vina.

These artists were not, as a social group, identified with any specific caste. The periya melam ensemble were also known as melakarars or nayanakarars, among other names in different parts of south India. Then in the early twentieth century, to give themselves official legitimacy and social dignity, the whole artistic community of nagasvara vidvans, tavil vidvans, nattuvanars and musicians of devadasi parenthood in the Tamil region began to formally call themselves the isai vellalars (literally, music cultivators, the vellala being a cultivating community). Through the official announcement of a caste status, the isai vellalars entered the architecture of Hindu caste structure. In a highly discriminatory and stratified society that was moving into a new social idiom, this was a natural aspiration for the group to harbour. Isai meaning music, no less, and the vellala being a dominant caste group controlling, with the brahmins, the economy of most Tamil villages, the isai vellalars now found for themselves a place under a common sun. Their vision of self-esteem was that an 'official notification' would end the ambiguity about their status, which included a hypothesis of these outstanding musicians' ambattan (barber) origins.

But let us return to the story of the kutcheri and the nagasvara vidvan. By the early part of the twentieth century, the brahmins in Madras and those moving to the city began creating the modern kutcheri. This created a systematized idea of Karnatik music with only a grudging space left for the devadasi or the nagasvara artists. As I have asserted before, the art music form of Karnatik music was not a creation of the urban brahmin elite of Madras. It was created much earlier in the confluence of the various communities that practised the art within the courts and temples and this included the isai vellalars and the brahmin musicians. The social or religious context of their work was not a deterrent to the art music intent driving the music in both. But modern practitioners were reinterpreting Karnatik music, boxing it into a single kutcheri narrative.

However, a new stage for performance alone was not good enough for the modern idea of classical music. The brahmins were creating a 'pure' form of Karnatik music within which the isai vellalars found it very difficult to create their own identity. Until then, they were respected Karnatik musicians practising the art within their own social space. Now they had to accept and submit to this new narrative. The single-point kutcheri constricted the idea of art music and, in doing so, eliminated all contexts that existed beyond this space. Due to his caste and the ritualistic context of his music, the nagasvara vidvan was not considered an important part of this modern kutcheri. In fact, he was not required. But what of his music? Was that also redundant in this new space? No, that was needed. It was used by the brahmins within the kutcheri context, but in a way that led to both his music and his artistic space being taken away from him. And so it came to pass that if the nagasvara vidvans wanted to become part of this kutcheri community, they had to force their way into its closely guarded precincts. They tried very hard to do this, but except for a few isai vellalars who by their sheer musical genius did succeed, most were left out. Sadly, they were left out not for musical reasons, but social reasons that had by then been injected into the music itself. A mediocre brahmin Karnatik musician could find his voice in the modern narrative, but an average nagasvara vidvan had no place.

I mentioned that a few isai vellalars did manage to enter the kutcheri space. Rajaratnam Pillai was probably the most prominent of them. But even the geniuses had to fight for equal rights. The equality they sought was only plain old 'respect' –

respect for their music, identity, history and contribution. But what they received were concessions and patronizing exceptions for the specially gifted. Had this not been the case, we would have had numerous nagasvara vidvans in the kutcheri world today. Instrumental music itself may be said to be struggling today to find an identity of its own within Karnatik music, but unlike the nagasvara, it is at least accorded respect.

I have heard the social conduct of the nagasvara vidvan described in singularly disparaging terms by brahmin commentators. 'Unacceptable' is a word that is regularly flung around, with insinuations of 'alcoholism' and 'promiscuity'. These are reprehensible generalizations about a community.

Needless to say, 'high-caste' non-brahmins did not appear to have objected to such generalizations. They too, after all, were seeking to be in the same social 'jury' as the brahmins. We all know that many brahmin musicians were 'promiscuous' and 'alcoholic'. Their promiscuity, though, was celebrated as a symbol of masculinity, and their alcoholism as that of disturbed genius. I am not passing a moral judgement here, but merely asking why the same indulgent yardstick was not applied to nagasvara vidvans who were promiscuous or fond of a drink? All this is discussed among musicians in private conversations and is part of the folklore of Karnatik music.

Denying the Undeniable

Modern scholars have faulted traditional commentators, scholars, musicians and musicologists for not including in the history of Karnatik music the fact that many brahmin musicians learnt from the devadasis and nagasvara vidvans, just as the latter did from the former. To me, it seems only logical that an exchange of music must have occurred between all the communities. It also seems that musical wisdom, intelligence and experience was heard, shared, exchanged and absorbed between the devadasis, nattuvanars, nagasvara vidvans, tavil vidvans and brahmin musicians quite freely. We know for a fact that Muttusvami Dikshitar had prominent students who belonged to the isai vellalar community, though he would have not known them by that politically correct title.

There is a view that many compositions attributed to brahmin musicians were actually creations of the nattuvanars, who were the gurus of the devadasis and anchored the chinna melam. It might sound like a truism when I say that we must accept the musical integrity of musicians as musicians, with no reference to their community. But the problem is that Karnatik musicians, connoisseurs, chroniclers live in the story of modern Karnatik music, which continues to be a prisoner of the 'with' or 'against' brahmins debate. In this fallacious and distracting dichotomy, the music is lost.

In the course of this essay, I am making certain considered observations about brahmin musicians' attitudes and approaches to the isai vellalar community. But in all this, I mean no disrespect to their musical contribution. I would, for instance, never suggest that much of what is accepted as their compositional contribution was actually stolen from the devadasis and nattuvanars. All the same, it is important that we take on board certain undeniable facts from our complex social history. The pre-kutcheri world of Karnatik music existed in a society full of social discrimination, but communities interacted creatively in the context of art music collaborations. So where is the scope for surprise that a major composer learnt music from a nagasvara vidvan, nattuvanar or devadasi with whom he shared the same musical space? It is sad that the modern kutcheri rose out of and lives within one community alone, and is unable to recreate the composite environment that prevailed earlier. This is an injustice that needs addressing. We cannot belittle the contribution of the brahmins while regretting the discrimination that led to the disappearance of isai vellalar musicians.

During the early part of the twentieth century, there were some great violin and mrdanga vidvans from the isai vellalar community and other non-brahmin groups. They were all respected and accepted as musical giants within the kutcheri narrative. These were musicians who embraced an instrument that was within the modern idea of Karnatik music and the kutcheri framework. These musicians are still considered all-time greats. Yet, even during their reign, some jarring notes could be seen. There were unwritten caste norms that both the isai vellalars and the brahmins seem to have observed. I am told that when honours were given on stage to a set of mixed-caste recipients, the brahmins were to receive them first. So ingrained was the caste structure that, when it came to awards, recognition and respect, they were first in line, which seriously dented the opportunities and the status of the isai vellalars who were trying to gain a foothold in kutcheri music.

At the same time, from many a beautiful recounting that is part of the Karnatik psyche, we know that once the music began, nothing else mattered. Many brahmin vocalists, in fact, leant on these isai vellalar accompanists to bolster their popularity. Therefore, while adjudging brahmin musicians of that period and later, one has to keep in mind the fact that under the spell of the Karnatik experience at full flow, enlightened practitioners among them spontaneously accepted the greatness of their isai vellalar contemporaries.

Isai Vellalar Guru, Brahmin Shishya

Even during the period that led to the consolidation of the kutcheri culture, isai vellalar musicians also had brahmin disciples. Conversations about these relationships are extremely interesting. We hear about the love showered on these students and even special treatment given to them with regard to their piety and ritualistic practices. But the music lessons were no less intense. All the brahmin students had to go through rigorous training in the same manner as the other students. There was no compromise when it came to music. Similarly, many brahmin gurus had isai vellalar students. Tirukkodikaval Krishna Ayyar (1857–1913) and his shishya Rajaratnam Pillai are a famous example. Karnatik music had it in its DNA, if one may so put it, the capacity to render the castes of its musicians irrelevant. When music took over, caste ceased to matter.

One question pertaining to the studentship of great non-brahmin artists has bothered me. Why have the star disciples of these musicians been mainly brahmins and not people from their own community? Did the control systems in brahmin hands turn it to its own purpose? Was it a case of the gurus themselves giving their brahmin students a preferential status? I have no clear answer to this. But I can comment on the result of what happened. With the nationalist movement and the various caste identities emerging as distinct social and power groups, people supported individuals from their own community. When many non-brahmin musicians nurtured brahmin students, there were very few non-brahmins in the next generation of musicians, a further monopolization of the music by the brahmins.

Caste and the Mrdanga

The mrdanga too has a history of caste discrimination. For long, playing the mrdanga was mainly associated with the chinna mela vidvans and other isai vellalars. The mrdanga was also closely linked with the tavil tradition. Brahmin mrdanga vidvans were more involved in teaching or playing for Namasankirtana and Harikatha. In fact, one can separate the two main styles of mrdanga playing on the basis of caste. While the Pudukkottai school came from the isai vellalar community, with a great deal of tavil influence, the Tanjavur school was influenced by the kirtana traditions of the Marathas, especially by Narayanasvami

Appa (late nineteenth century) and Tukaram Appa (1860–1900), incidentally both non-brahmins. It is also interesting to note that the dholak vidvan Nannu Mian (late nineteenth century), a Muslim, seems to have influenced this style. But from the twentieth century on, the Tanjavur mrdanga style became synonymous with its brahmin practitioners.

For long, the art of mrdanga was the forte of the isai vellalars. Then came Palghat Mani Iyer (1912–81), and everything changed. It was after he appeared that brahmins took control of the mrdanga field as well. To believe that strong community support did not play a crucial role in Iyer's ascendancy to the crown would be rather naive. Pazhani Subrahmanya Pillai (1908–62) and Ramanathapuram C.S. Murugabhoopathy (1914–98) are two names that are always mentioned along with Palghat Mani Iyer, yet it is Iyer alone that is placed on a pedestal. This is not on purely musical or scholarship grounds. The relationship between Pazhani and Mani Iyer has been described in detail by many musicians. Stories of mutual respect and admiration are part of our folklore. But along with this musical bonhomie there existed a social inequity.

Mani Iyer conquered the non-brahmin world of the mrdanga with support from his own community. Caste superiority added to his confidence and domination. He was a genius, with a sound and impact that was unparalleled, but he was a brahmin who was bearding the isai vellalar lion in its own den. This was important for the brahmin community that was then in the process of taking complete control of Karnatik music. So far, the brahmin mrdanga vidvans had never been considered at par with the non-brahmin ones – neither as mathematically sharp, nor as physically strong as the isai vellalar. The isai vellalar community too believed in the superiority of its own skills. All of this collapsed with Palghat Mani Iyer. He was, therefore, feted as the greatest, as Nandi himself (the lord of the mrdanga). Pazhani or Murugabhoopathy were never referred to as Nandi, nor was the kanjira vidvan

Dakshinamurti Pillai (1876–1937), for whom Mani Iyer had great respect. The isai vellalar community is said to have resisted the Mani Iyer invasion, but ultimately succumbed to a great musician backed by a dominant community.

The one domain within the kutcheri that they dominated had now been taken over. Once Palghat Mani Iyer made his breakthrough, the floodgates opened and there was no stopping the brahmin monopoly over the mrdanga. Among the many greats are T.K. Murthy (b. 1924), Palghat Raghu (1928–2009), Vellore Ramabhadran (1929–2012), Umayalpuram K. Sivaraman (b. 1935) and Karaikudi R. Mani (b. 1945). Pazhani Subrahmanya Pillai had numerous non-brahmin students, but then his most important disciple turned out to be a brahmin, Trichy Sankaran (b. 1942). With brahmins controlling the violin and the mrdanga, their domination of Karnatik music was complete.

Caste and the Vocalists

In the pre-kutcheri days, devadasis were the primary non-brahmin vocalists, but they were not accepted into the kutcheri format both because of their occupational history and gender. There were only a few non-brahmin male vocalists who made a name for themselves. Chittur Subrahmanya Pillai (1898–1975) was one such. He was a Telugu-speaking Naidu from the artistic class, but changed his last name to Pillai since he was a disciple of the legendary isai vellalar, Kanchipuram Naina Pillai (1889–1934).

Many of the vocalists at that time were brahmins and belonged to the Tyagaraja shishya parampara. The new Karnatik kutcheri music was flooded with musicians from the Harikatha traditions or those under its influence. The format thus embraced the compositions of the trinity, which these artists were already familiar with. With the foregrounding of piety, sanctity and religiosity, the brahmin musicians were an ideal fit. Many isai vellalars were also storehouses of the compositions of the trinity, but that did not allow them access to the new stage. Musicians like Chittur Subrahmanya Pillai were successful and had many disciples, but neither he nor any other non-brahmin vocalist is spoken of in the same breath as a Chembai Vaidyanatha Bhagavatar (1895–1974) and Ariyakudi Ramanuja Iyengar (1890–1967). Madurai Somasundaram (1919–89), a disciple of Chittur Subrahmanya Pillai, was never accepted as a 'pure' Karnatik musician. While his great manodharma was praised and many brahmin musicians accompanied him, he was accused of pandering to populist demands. Needless to say, this treatment was never meted out to brahmin musicians who did exactly the same.

It is important to note here that the kutcheri aesthetic was an urban creation. The brahmins were the first off the block with it, and everyone else was left behind. Many did not even know how to adjust to these rapid changes. The non-brahmins had to be content with the small space made available to them. It is patent that the vocalist's position from the beginning of the modern kutcheri was monopolized by brahmins.

The Counter-narrative

As we can see, the kutcheri stage – vocalists, pakkavadya and upa-pakkavadya artists (though I have not specifically written about them here) – became synonymous with brahmins. The nagasvara artists were confined to religious and social events, while the devadasi with her wealth of music soon disappeared. The nattuvanars became teachers of Bharatanatyam to predominantly brahmin girl students. One of the few devadasi families that was able to create a niche for itself was that of Vina Dhanammal (1867–1938). However, she was treated by the brahmin modernists as a storehouse of a bygone, exclusive music which did not seem to have a contemporary place, unless it was reinterpreted by the very same brahmins. Was this by plan or an accident? The truth, as in most cases, probably lies somewhere in between. Along with the fact that the brahmins were the dominant caste trying to create a new narrative for the music, there were also various dynamic changes in the political and social scene of the time. These too had a role in cementing the brahmin identity of Karnatik art music.

The struggle for a Tamil identity was closely linked to caste equations. Brahmins lived by the Vedas and Sanskrit texts, non-brahmins lived by various Tamil religious texts, including the Tevarams, and so caste and language were intertwined in this battle. With the creation of the kutcheri based purely on the music of the trinity (all three brahmins, of course) in Sanskrit and Telugu, and the parallel marginalization of the isai vellalars from the Karnatik story, an existing social divide deepened. The Tamil Isai movement was, in many ways, a result of this.

Ironically, the musicians who attended the Tamil Isai Conference in 1941 included senior brahmins, such as Tiger Varadachariar (1876–1950), Papanasam Sivan (1890–1973) and Musiri Subramania Iyer (1899–1975). They believed in the importance of language.

I only wish the Tamil Isai movement's approach had been the far more egalitarian art music perspective. This would have led to a parallel idea of classical Karnatik music, putting monopoly in the dock and spurring an interest among the non-brahmin community, even reviving the nagasvara and devadasi Karnatik musical traditions within the modern context. Unfortunately, even the supporters of the Tamil Isai movement did not recognize the criticality of the devadasis and the nagasvara vidvans to the kutcheri narrative. The socio-political situation too would have made it difficult for them to take such a stance openly. The nagasvara vidvans were not even part of the discussion there, because they were instrumentalists and meant little to the language-obsessed Tamil Isai battle. The movement, therefore, did not succeed in de-monopolizing Karnatik music. The Tamil Isai conferences that followed were dominated by the very same brahmin musicians. All other voices disappeared into oblivion.

From the 1930s, the Tamil-speaking regions of the Madras Presidency came under the influence of E.V. Ramasami Naicker (1879–1973), who created and led the self-respect and Dravidian movements, which had a specific anti-brahmin focus. He firmly believed that the brahmin community had monopolized the bureaucratic, economic and cultural spheres of life. An atheist himself, Naicker pointed to the fact that the brahmin community's historical control was closely linked to caste structures that had religious sanction. The temple was seen as the fiefdom of the brahmins. This was an important movement in the social history of south India and, I believe, a necessary social awakening. This social turmoil had a serious impact on Karnatik music, the musicians and the space of its existence. Unfortunately, it did not lead to a more egalitarian Karnatik music environment, instead spurring it to become even more insular. Over a period of time, the influence of the brahmins over social, political and religious institutions waned, culminating in the final takeover of temples by the government in Tamil Nadu.

The reduced influence of brahmin in temples did not benefit their most eloquent community: the nagasvara vidvans. The government, which took over the control of the temples, hardly contributed to the development of quality nagasvara or tavil vidvans. The end result has been tragic – lack of support for those Karnatik musicians who once breathed musical life into the temple and society.

Similarly, by the early twentieth century, devadasis were being seen by the men of the time as only prostitutes to exploit. What was needed was a social context that preserved the art of the devadasis, while putting an end to the social exploitation of women from that class. The solution sought destroyed the whole edifice without rescuing its art, and perhaps without erasing the stigma. Due to the tunnel vision of the reformers, the arts of the devadasi and her tradition were destroyed.

Let us return now to the beginning of the end of brahmin domination over the political, commercial and intellectual life in the Madras Presidency, and later Tamil Nadu. Centuries-old monopolies were drawing to a close, by reason of political awakenings and state-orchestrated reform. Facing this threat, the brahmins, or at least a section of them, found an island of ownership in the performing arts, specifically Karnatik music and Bharatanatyam. This field, they believed, they held the title to, ignoring those they regarded as unimportant and neutralizing those they saw as threats. It was, literally, the last bastion. The brahmins moved Karnatik music from village to town, from town to city, from temple to hall, from hall to bigger hall. In the place of a temple quadrangle, they created the platform of the kutcheri, and in place of the durbar, a 'sabha'. There were now modernized institutions and standardized education. They urbanized what was rural and globalized what was urban.

This is only a description of what I imagine was the inner force that gave energy to the brahmin community, a force that with some changes imposed by time, exists to date.

The Decline of the Temple

Once the non-brahmin majority took control of politics in the areas formerly comprising the Madras Presidency, the temple's cultural role in society began to fade. This was markedly so in what is now Tamil Nadu. The temple priest was still brahmin, as this was important to even many non-brahmin communities. By the 1970s, all of Bharatanatyam and Karnatik music was seen as belonging to the brahmins, and hence considered unnecessary or even inappropriate within the temple. This seriously impacted the audience composition of Karnatik music. Using the temple as the cultural hub was not so much for the artists as for the audience. The temple is a non-sectarian precinct. In spite of social and caste discrimination, most sections of society barring a few could enter the temple, with or without restrictions. Even those who were not allowed inside were part of the listening public during the nagasvara processions when the idol was taken around the temple. When a concert took place in a temple, the audience was diverse. People from various castes attended the concert or passed by it. Right from their childhood, men and women heard the sounds of the music. All this led to a cross-community absorption of Karnatik music. We have all heard stories about how everyone from a rickshaw puller to the brahmin living around the temple came just to hear Madurai Mani Iyer sing there, or a Rajaratnam Pillai or Palghat Mani Iyer play. All this was possible only in the environment of the temple. Even those who did not come in heard the music on the streets outside and carried the aesthetics away to their homes. Thus developed a natural interest in Karnatik music, simply because the music reached everyone.

We must pause here to consider the example of Kerala. It is the one state in the south where cultural programmes are still an integral part of temple festivals. Kathakali, Bharatanatyam, Ganamela (light music), Karnatik kutcheris, panchavadya performances, Krishnattam and other art forms are all presented within the temple premises. The temples in Kerala reverberate with music, dance and theatre. They serve society not just as a place of worship but also as cultural hubs. These events happen all over the state, even in the smallest towns and villages, which leads to a great deal of exposure among diverse groups in society. Consequently, the aesthetics of Karnatik music reach a cross section of the population. In Kerala, the temple has retained its role as a cultural centre.

That this is no longer the case in Tamil Nadu has led today to the disappearing of Karnatik music from the open arenas. Technically, anyone can attend a kutcheri, but the hangover of caste and the formalization of music inhibit many from entering.

Quite unlike a temple, where the sounds of music waft out into the settlement around it.

If rescuing Karnatik music from the artistic domination of the brahmins was a policy objective, the best way of implementing it would have been to embrace Karnatik music and Bharatanatyam and make their teaching, learning, practice and performing accessible to larger and larger sections of society. I am of the opinion that, instead of condemning all that was brahmin as unnecessary, society should have taken ownership of the arts. Karnatik music deserved to be taught to all and heard by all. Unfortunately, and perhaps understandably, the major battle was fought on linguistic grounds and not on the enfranchisement of kutcheri music.

The advent of cinema further reduced the draw of these art forms. Even though cinema too was dominated by the brahmins and the upper-class vellalars, it became an equalizer and even a socio-political tool. As a useful tool for change, cinema became the cultural entrepôt for Tamil society. Karnatik music lived and lives primarily in the sabhas, practised and heard principally by brahmins. These sabhas today take the form of corporate events. Similar models have sprung up all over the world, but they are all still brahmin-dominated.

I have been frankly critical of the role of the brahminism in the life story of Karnatik art music. But I would like to acknowledge the tremendous support that individuals from the community have given to this art form. Over the last century, many men and women have provided wonderful platforms for performance, education and advancement of Karnatik music. It is only because of their passion that many of us today are musicians and can discuss the various aspects of the music. Therefore, to talk only about the social impact of caste-based artistic positions, but not recognize the contributions of the 'holding' community would be a travesty of the truth.

Before we discuss the reality of today, we should recognize that the practice of Karnatik music was never egalitarian. Over the last 500 years, it has been 'held' only between a few communities. These artist communities and families practised in courts and temples. They held the music very close and, though others had the opportunity to hear the music at the temples, they never seem to have been part of its artistic world. This was classist too. The devadasi was a well-respected artist, as were the nattuvanars, nagasvara vidvans and brahmin musicians. Karnatik music was theirs to own. The importance of the court and the king in both the temple and governance cannot be ignored. So the music was always part of an elitist narrative in its practice, even if the role of the temple made access to the performance more egalitarian than it is today. In the history of Karnatik music, very few musicians have emerged from caste groups other than the ones mentioned here. In a way, the modern capture of this music by the brahmins is only a continuation of the dominance of one of the artistic classes. From a group of artistic communities, the political and social changes of the last 150 years have made the music the heirloom of one community alone.

Many may argue with my assertion that Karnatik music was more accessible due to its presence in the temple. They would say that, after all, the advent of new audio technologies in the early twentieth century must have helped extend its reach far more than any 'temple access' could ever have hoped to. True, gramophone records and especially the radio were important tools for disseminating music. We also know that many devadasis made recordings for record companies, as did many brahmin musicians and nagasvara vidvans. Would this not have increased the listenership of Karnatik music and broken its caste barriers? Yes, but before these modernizing developments, it was primarily the temple that provided people of various caste groups an exposure to Karnatik music. Therefore, the gramophone records and the radio were naturally catering to this established audience, not creating new listeners. Once this generation of listeners passed on, things changed rapidly. As generations passed, it was only the brahmins who were engaging with Karnatik music at the sabhas. Slowly but steadily, society at large lost its living contact with Karnatik music.

Meanwhile, cinema was gaining great significance in the social, political and cultural spheres. In a way, the cinema theatre replaced temples as a place of art where everyone could come. This also nibbled into what could have been important Karnatik audiences cultivating a taste for an invaluable art form.

I have tried to bring out a few important aspects of the role caste has played in Karnatik music over the past century. This essay does not hope to paint a comprehensive picture, but merely record a set of observations. Beyond this historical perspective, what really matters is the present state of affairs and what can be done now.

Almost 95 per cent of the musicians and audiences who engage in Karnatik music today are brahmins. There is no question in my mind that this has to change. Why? Do Christians not go to hear hymns, Muslims flock to qawwalis, Hindus to Namasankirtanas? Is there not a certain clear 'type' that goes to listen to jazz? What then is wrong with brahmins dominating an art form they have grown up with generation after generation? As logical as that argument sounds, it is utterly specious. Karnatik music is not brahmin music, neither is it Sanskrit music, nor male music. These prefixes have to be shed if we are to understand the music. There is no denying the fact that Karnatik music is a rare art music form that requires serious commitment. But that does not mean that only the formally educated or an 'aware' class (infer brahmins) can appreciate it. In today's environment, if brahmins constitute the bulk of the audience, it is only because this music has been heard in their households and a culture of appreciation has developed in them over the past century.

Karnatik music is an art form that is meant for all and must be heard by everyone. Access to it should not be restricted to those who wish to own it, or by reformers who have tried to legislate it into history as an article of antiquity. The music may not be an easy master, but it is not elitist. We have made it elitist. The elitism exists not in the music, but in its practice in society.

Schools that cater to various economic sections of society must be used as a platform to sensitize the young to the magic of Karnatik music. It is my experience that any child can become curious about the music. It is up to us to provide them with an opportunity to experience it. We cannot force everyone to appreciate Karnatik music, as the very form of art music is a challenge. But we can and should make it available for everyone to listen to. If just one out of a thousand students is moved by the music, that is an important beginning. What we need is not a conversion programme, but an awakening.

Similarly, it is important to revive the temple as a cultural hub. Let all those who come to the temple, irrespective of their caste or creed, have the opportunity to hear this music. Here, we would only be returning to the temple that which has in a unique manner belonged to it. I envisage a society that will naturally appreciate the sound of Karnatik music, whether or not every individual becomes a connoisseur. One may argue that by encouraging concerts in temples we are making the music religious. I wish to clarify that when I speak of the temple, I am not referring to its shrine. South Indian temples have varied spaces, from which no individual or community is kept away, including, needless to say, the agnostic and the atheist. As much as the shrine inclines the devotee to religion, these spaces, which are creations of art, incline the visitor towards an admiration, even a passionate admiration of the arts. They are historically artistic spaces, not just religious, and we need to utilize and celebrate them as such.

In fact, I would say that we should make the temple an artistic space that draws people of every other religion and those of no religion. This would lead to a transformation beyond music. I have had the privilege of meeting Muslims and Christians in Kerala whose exposure to Karnatik music was through temples. We also find Christian priests utilizing Karnatik music to embed hymnal lyrics in. This has helped me look afresh at the intersections where religion and art meet. All this calls for many changes in our idea of religion and art. I have raised, in my essay on religion, the question of whether lyrics that are non-religious or even on other religions will help make the music inclusive. I was not sure, and I am not now. Nevertheless, it cannot be wrong for Karnatik music to widen its register for faith traditions that are not dyed-in-the-text Hindu. This could, in fact, transition towards something that goes even further – a deepening of understanding musical texts beyond linguistic meaning. Such inclusiveness need not be seen as being at cross-purposes with the revival of Karnatik music in temples. Discussions and explorations in both are important for the larger change we seek. My own position is that the lyrical content is not paramount, but I am forced to rethink my approach when attempting a solution to this problem.

There is also a need for a change in the mindset of the government's attitude to Karnatik music, especially in Tamil Nadu. The attachment to language is still so high that they are unable to discuss Karnatik music beyond the Tamil aspect. No doubt similar mindsets exist elsewhere too. Government music schools and universities teach a history and musicology of Karnatik music that is completely unconnected to its practice. Terms and ideas of Tamil musicological history are forced upon ideas that are often Telugu or Sanskrit in origin. Tamil, Sanskrit and Telugu terms, expressions and concepts need to be amalgamated. Only then will the student of music in a government music college or university be in touch with today's reality. I am particularly interested in government art institutions, because this is where the maximum number of non-brahmin students are admitted. This makes it imperative that the selection process for teachers at these colleges must be only on the basis of quality and commitment. Similarly, private teachers and music schools must participate actively in this social re-engineering of Karnatik music. As with most traditional art forms, it is the private teachers who nurture a lot of talent. Therefore, they must be welcoming to students from all sections of society, and be the catalysts for social change. Only collective action by the best musicians, along with government-driven reform, can change the caste biases and injustices that are an embarrassing backdrop to Karnatik music today.

Brahmin-driven sanctification has played a largely negative role in the past. But I believe brahmins have a self-transforming, positive role to play in the future. Why? For the simple reason that their presence is real, as the undisputed (albeit self-created) repositories of this art. The enfranchisement of Karnatik music as an art form with the widest possible appeal must come to be their vision too. Karnatik music, after all, does not wear the sacred thread.

Crucial to all this, is the revival of the nagasvara as an important kutcheri instrument. Even now, only the isai vellalars have mastery over the nagasvara and tavil. These artists survive by playing during temple festivals and at marriages. This must change. We need to provide financial security to the nagasvara and tavil vidvans at large through providing access to diverse artistic space. Sabhas, recordings, international tours, corporate festivals and weddings are part of the professional world of the Karnatik musician. Welcoming nagasvara and tavil vidvans into this world will also lead to the constant interaction between the brahmin and isai vellalar groups, something that existed and flourished in the past. Maybe some of them will take to vocal, violin and other instruments, and some brahmins will take up the nagasvara. Breaking these barriers are in our hands, and unless we make a sincere attempt, nothing will come of it.

I have spoken of beginning with the traditional art communities, but we need to go beyond. It would be marvellous to one day see a Dalit perform regularly at the Madras Music Academy and receive the Sangita Kalanidhi title, with the audience being utterly impervious to his caste, but wholly attuned to his music. Until now, even the presence of isai vellalars at the Academy has been nothing more than tokenism. I will never forget the comments made about a few isai vellalar musicians receiving the Sangita Kalanidhi: 'They were given the title on the basis of the caste quota system.' The word 'snide' must have been created for that comment. These were great musicians who deserved the award every bit as much as anyone before them. There should be soon a point when the world of art music wills its artists and its rasikas not from their social addresses, but their aesthetic directions.

Individual musicians too need to do more. Unless they take social responsibility for the imbalanced demographic profile of the artists, they are only feeding the exclusivist attitude of Karnatik music. Musicians must encourage and teach students from other social groups and castes. This is a form of affirmative action that is needed if we want to make a serious change within the community. A few students tutored by the best musicians and teachers will go a long way in changing the social make-up and the perception of Karnatik music.

There is no doubt in my mind that every time I meet a non-brahmin Karnatik musician (the few that there are), I sense the deep hurt within. They have been treated shabbily over the years and still carry the bruises. Those who have tried making a name for themselves over the last few decades will reveal in private that it was their caste that stopped them from achieving greatness as Karnatik musicians. I have to agree with them. Many accompanists, who were and are wonderful musicians, have moved to Bharatanatyam, as they have been unable to break through in kutcheri music. The sabhas also have an important role to play in bringing about this change. They must actively encourage musicians from various caste groups.

Among all these problems that exist, there are positives in the form of musicians from various religions and castes, such as

Sheik Chinna Moulana, K.J. Yesudas, Neyyattinkara Vasudevan (1940–2008) and P. Unnikrishnan, who are household names beyond religious or caste barriers. But they are exceptions. There have also been some changes in the listenership in cities where patronage has widened to other castes and the sponsorship group has also widened. These are slow but sure signs of change. Kerala is still an exception to a lot of my observations in this essay due to the social structures of the state.

This essay has centred around Madras (now Chennai) and Tamil Nadu. Chennai was and is the fulcrum of Karnatik music, and hence dominates the narrative. People from other cities may object, but it is a fact that other cities and states have often followed Chennai's lead in Karnatik music and in the social aspects around it. This essay can be easily read as being anti-brahmin, but I am neither pro nor anti any caste. I am implacably against the caste system itself. I have only made observations based on the changes that took place over the last century and expressed my thoughts on them.

At the heart of all this is my belief that there is no place for caste, religion, gender or language discrimination in Karnatik music. Looking at all these social segregations that the development of Karnatik music has created, especially over the last 150 years, I stress the need to understand aesthetics as an objective idea. Serious engagement with the music requires us to receive Karnatik music as a form of abstractive emotion, shorn of all literality.

Like any art form, Karnatik music will have to battle social identities, but as long as we search for this identity outside the form itself, we will never be able to embrace all of society. While many art music systems of the world are elitist in terms of the social class that listens to it, ours is elitist on the basis of caste. The art and its health should be the focus of our thoughts. One may ask that when Karnatik music has its audience, sponsors and musicians, why should one worry about whether it is present across social groups. It is important then to remember that the art will be enriched if it is practised and listened to by audiences with similar aesthetic moorings but diverse backgrounds. We have some proof of this in all the music that we have received from the devadasis, nattuvanars and nagasvara and tavil vidvans.

The basis for Karnatik music is its aesthetic intent, and that is non-discriminatory. Its power lies in its capacity to lead a truly engaged, discerning connoisseur beyond all literal aspects. Art music can take every individual into a sphere of experiential emotion that need not be attached to any event and person. It belongs to everyone who is willing to take the music within. This is not intellectualism, but pure experientialism.

21

The World So Wide

Over the last three decades, Karnatik music has truly become a global art music form. While its listenership is still largely limited to the south Indian Brahmin community, it is still a fact that people living in different parts of the world also listen to it. This is the result of two things: a gradual movement of people from south India to various parts of the world and the steady development of ethno-musicological studies in the West over the last century. Interactions between musicians practising different genres too have grown in number and intensity. These are not necessarily independent developments, but they have all been strong bridges linking, each in its own manner, Karnatik music with the wider world.

In establishing its international pan-cultural presence, we must note, Karnatik music has lagged behind Hindustani music. There are various reasons for this. To begin with, we must acknowledge that the form itself is definitely a little more difficult to internalize. The Hindustani 'sound' is more accessible to the untrained ear. But it could also be that its practitioners and their sociocultural psyche also contributed to the form's 'stay indoors' nature. South Indian brahmins in general were not adventurous explorers of alien environments. Srinivasa Ramanujan, the great mathematician, who lived tenuously and uneasily in Cambridge, but doing wonders with his intellect, is a prime example. What was true of this community in general was equally true of the Karnatik music 'greats' and their followers. Their ritualistic, God-fearing, self-esteeming mentality kept them strong and secure within the Karnatik music world that they had created for themselves in the early twentieth century. There was no compulsion, nor any desire, to look for newer pastures. It is also probably true that the religious nature and the brahminical focus of Karnatik music created a belief within the community that this music was not really meant for all. The sharp attention on its predominantly devotional sahitya, its meaning and piety all contribute to making Karnatik music a lofty pilgrim centre that was not easy to approach. Learning to appreciate Karnatik music has almost been translated to learning to be Hindu, if not brahmin. Generalizations are dangerous, and I must add the rider that there were and are exceptions. Nevertheless, a close observation of musicians' attitudes over the last century – and I have spoken to some of them – leads me to believe that Karnatik music's slow movement beyond its limited socio-geographical boundary and its slower permeation into the cultures of their domicile has been largely due to the musicians themselves. This is where musicians from the Hindustani world outpaced their Karnatik counterparts.

That aside, any discussion on the recognition Hindustani music has found in the West must acknowledge the contribution of one individual: Ravi Shankar (1920–2012). True, Karnatik musicians made sporadic appearances on international stages and conferences from the 1960s. But these neither amounted to, nor quite developed into, full-fledged international engagements. Those Karnatik musicians who did migrate to the West were either involved in academic work or moved into the genre of Western and fusion music. Karnatik musicians often complain about what they see as the Indian establishment's bias against the south when it comes to representing India at international art festivals, or even recognizing musicians at the national level. These accusations are not without truth, and have contributed to the lowered levels of international engagement with the music.

Curiously, however, while Hindustani music has for long been the voice of Indian 'classical' music abroad, Bharatanatyam – rather than Kathak, Manipuri or Odissi – has become the poster face of Indian 'classical' dance on the world stage. Practitioners of other dance forms in the country complain of discrimination, just as Karnatik musicians do. Like Ravi Shankar's presence-marking role, the tremendous contributions of Rukmini Devi Arundale (1904–86) and T. Balasaraswati (1918–84) gave Bharatanatyam an international image. Unfortunately, Karnatik music did not have such figures who contributed, not by design but by context, in creating beautiful performance art and institutional structures. All those who followed have reaped the benefits of the contribution of these two women. This is not to diminish the individual stature of the inheritors of their legacy.

Here I can almost hear the reader ask in astonishment and admonition: 'But what about M.S. Subbulakshmi? Did MS not provide this same impetus to Karnatik music?' I am afraid not. Performing at international non-diaspora platforms such as Carnegie Hall, the United Nations and the Edinburgh Festival gave M.S. Subbulakshmi an almost unprecedented international profile. But those remained her personal successes. Her stellar performances did not take that one further step towards creating an international environment for the music itself. Her bhakti-oriented approach, combined with the brahminical mindset of her inner circle, limited the ambit of this spectacular musician.

An early facilitator for the presentation of Karnatik music and Bharatanatyam in the West was the music scholar Dr V.K. Narayana Menon (b. 1911). As the head of All India Radio and, later, of the Sangeet Natak Akademi, he knew that south

Indian classical arts were under-shared with the wider world. By arranging for Balasaraswati and Subbulakshmi to render performances at the Edinburgh Festival, he broke altogether new ground, though in the case of Karnatik music it did not develop into larger serious engagements.

When I refer to the lack of a world stage for Karnatik music, I am only stating a fact. I am not in search of international recognition for Karnatik music, nor am I bemoaning the fact that the music has not received its due. Each music has its character, its body, which defines the extent of its reception by peoples of the world. What I am critical about is the territorial attitude of the Karnatik music community – musicians, listeners and impresarios – an attitude and a temperament that exists even now. I object to their creation of socio-religious requirements for the appreciation or learning of the music. The beauty of the music as an aesthetic form must be presented for all to receive. Who stays on is determined by individual choice.

The Changing Scene

Over the last few years, however, Karnatik music has slowly but surely begun to make its mark in the international music community as a serious art music form. It is increasingly featured in festivals around the world. Ease of travel, information and listenership has made many non-scholarly non-Indians aware of this music. Along with this, something quite beautiful has happened as well: a new generation of Karnatik musicians has risen that is open to conversations with the world. It does more; it strives for that engagement. This school does not shrink from – if anything it welcomes – challenges involved in sharing Karnatik music worldwide. Of course, such outgoing openness is a professional 'given' of our times. Karnatik musicians have seen the spread of Hindustani music around the globe, and are aware of the benefits and processes of interconnectedness with the larger world. Being practical, they also recognize the economic vista this opens up to them.

Yet, if one discusses Karnatik music with many of its practitioners, what one will still receive is an essentially brahminical perspective to the music, not an aesthetic understanding of it. And so, while the Karnatik musician today is becoming wonderfully open to the world, the music itself remains closely held, like a richly dealt deck of cards. Unless we re-evaluate our musical priorities, I believe that we will not be able to share the music effectively. If Karnatik music is to be a quasi-religious Hindu experience suitably customized for the non-Indian listener, we are further disfiguring its essence. Some people will listen to Indian music only for this reason and we cannot stop that, but we should be clear that we are not presenting religious music. This separation will allow others easier access to the music – through its intent. Karnatik music needs a re-evaluation from within. Not a disassociation from the past or its social context, but a rediscovery that can reveal the music to all, while removing the constrictions of the past.

In North America

I will now specifically discuss the reach of Karnatik music in North America over the last three decades – focusing on the south Indian brahmin community on that continent. This particularism is of great interest to me for two reasons. First, North America today has become the most important geographical location, beyond south India itself, where Karnatik music has a strong and thriving community. Second, over the last decade or two, the model developing in North America is being replicated in various other countries that have large south Indian brahmin communities. I am restricting the discussion to this specific world of Karnatik music adherents, as they are not just listening populations, but a world community of impresarios, teachers, connoisseurs and musicians. The Karnatik music world created in Madras in the early twentieth century now extends to a global community, where the pattern established by the expatriates of North America has special significance. In order to establish a contemporary context, let us briefly look at the history of Karnatik music in the region.

In the 1960s, south Indian brahmins moved in reasonable numbers to North America, specifically the United States, and many carried with them spool recordings of their favourite Karnatik musicians. These recordings were treasured as a cultural connect with their home. On every visit to India, which may have been only once in a few years, they collected many more such recordings. They attended kutcheris and returned, both rejuvenated as well as replenished, to the United States. The recordings they took back were then shared with others who were yearning for quality Karnatik music. Those were days, we should remember, when cultural information about India was negligible in the Western media, which meant that news on Karnatik music or musicians would have been practically non-existent. Most Karnatik aficionados received information on the happenings in that world only through letters.

From the 1960s, Karnatik musicians of the stature of M.S. Subbulakshmi, K.V. Narayanaswamy (1923–2002), S. Balachander (1927–90), Palghat Raghu, Vellore Ramabhadran (1929–2012), Umayalpuram K. Sivaraman (b. 1935) and V.V. Subrahmanyam (b. 1944) started visiting the US on concert tours. Their journeys made news in south India. These artists were primarily invited by a few American institutes and organizations or for teaching assignments in universities. Irrespective of the aegis for these visits and their sponsors, the presence of such musicians in a land devoid of Karnatik music was a godsend for the small community of expatriate rasikas. We can well imagine the excitement of these people on hearing their music, their musicians in the US. Young south Indians who loved the art helped in whatever way they could to support these concerts. Many of the immigrants then were students, and yet they helped organize concerts, advertise and bring people to the concerts.

Karnatik musicians began being invited to North America 'by their own people' only from the 1970s. Some of the key figures in organizing tours and concerts were V.K. Viswanathan, V.V. Sundaram, R. Balasubramaniam, P. Rajagopalan, K. Venkataraman and A. Nagarajan. Musicians such as D.K. Pattammal (1919–2009), Veena Doreswamy Iyengar (1920–97), Sheik Chinna Moulana (1924–99), T.K. Murthy (b. 1924), M.L. Vasanthakumari (1928–90), Lalgudi Jayaraman (1930–2013), N. Ramani (b. 1934) and T.V. Sankaranarayanan (b. 1945) were invited by newly formed 'south Indian' organizations in America. The 1970s were romantic times. Karnatik music organizers in the US of the time narrate stories of having to drive musicians across the country for concerts, as air travel was prohibitively expensive. Musicians stayed in the houses of some of these enthusiasts (a practice that still continues) and established lifelong friendships.

These were years of discovery as well for the visiting musicians, the hosting organizers and the listeners. The rasikas, organizers and musicians were trying to create Karnatik environments in various cities, but the going was not easy. In the 1960s and 1970s, there were not enough south Indian brahmins in North America. One must also keep in mind the fact that even among the south Indian brahmin population, the number of Karnatik music listeners was not very large. It took Lyndon Johnson's liberalization of the immigration policy (1965) some time to establish a sizeable Karnatik community in the US. Before then, these pioneers had to try and get as many Americans as possible in the audience. Most concerts were held in university halls that were available for free or at a very nominal cost. The organizers put up posters in as many places as possible, personally called their south Indian friends to come and support the concert and brought in as many Americans as possible.

In the 1960s, the audiences for Karnatik music in the US were mainly American with a few Indians. By the 1970s, though, the demographics seem to have become more or less equal. Musicians sometimes had to live in the houses of these friends for months while they waited for concerts to be organized. The wonderful thing though was that these hosts were doing what they did out of passion for the music, respect for the art. People from that time still treasure these memories. For the expatriates, this was a way of connecting with their culture, home and country.

By the end of the 1970s and early 1980s, south Indian organizers expanded their invitations to include Hindustani musicians like Bhimsen Joshi (1922–2011), Lakshmi Shankar (b. 1926), Pandit Jasraj (b. 1930), Prabha Atre (b. 1932), Hariprasad Chaurasia (b. 1938) and Parveen Sultana (b. 1950). These tours were organized in collaboration with aficionados of Hindustani music. Even until the late 1980s, the number of south Indian brahmins in the United States was not enough to sustain too many tours by Karnatik musicians. There were one or two tours in a year, or even less, and financial viability was a concern. Many concerts were held in houses and each individual in the audience made a contribution towards the artist's fees. The organizers had to make sure they broke even after meeting all the overheads and that the musicians made a little money. What kept Karnatik music alive in those early years was the sheer passion for music among the organizers.

The academic community in the US had begun to develop an interest in Karnatik music from about the 1950s. Ethno-musicologists Harold Powers (1928–2007) and Robert Brown (1927–2005) travelled to India and engaged with Karnatik music. Brown influenced T. Viswanathan (1927–2002), flautist and brother of T. Balasaraswati, to come to the US for ethno-musicological studies. 'Vishwa' went to UCLA in 1958 on a Fulbright scholarship. Brown, who was at Wesleyan University in the 1960s, was in fact influential in bringing many Karnatik musicians to teach and perform in the US. Mrdanga artist T. Ranganathan (1925–87), also a brother of T. Balasaraswati, had guided Brown in his doctoral work on the mrdanga in India and he came to the US to become the first Indian artist-in-residence in Wesleyan University. In the 1960s, Luise E. Scripps and Samuel H. Scripps (1927–2007) founded the American Society of Eastern Arts, which later became the Center for World Music. Luise Scripps was a lifelong friend and admirer of Balasaraswati and learnt from her in India. In fact, Balasaraswati is referred to as the patron saint of that Center. By the 1970s, musicians T. Viswanathan and violinist L. Shankar (b. 1950) completed their doctorates in Karnatik music at Wesleyan University, and violinist L. Subramaniam (b. 1947) his postgraduation in Western classical music at the California Institute of the Arts. L. Subramaniam and L. Shankar branched out into world music and fusion music, but T. Viswanathan became a prominent ethno-musicologist in North America and taught at Wesleyan University.

Around the same time, India was witness to the first Karnatik musician of American origin. Jon Higgins (1939–84) did his undergraduation and postgraduation at Wesleyan University. He developed a deep interest in Karnatik music and became a student of T. Viswanathan. He had the rare opportunity of performing at the Tyagaraja Aradhana in Tiruvaiyyaru among other venues in India and also released records. Among the Karnatik community in India, he was popularly known as Higgins Bhagavatar. Jon Higgins was a remarkable musician and was also a living example of his guru's teaching methods. Moving from Wesleyan, Jon Higgins, along with the mrdanga vidvan Trichy Sankaran, was instrumental in establishing a strong Karnatik music presence at York University, Toronto. In the 1960s and 1970s, the establishment of Karnatik music studies in the US created an opportunity for musicians such as T. Brinda (1912–96), Ramnad Krishnan (1918–73), K.V. Narayanaswamy (1923–2002), T.N. Krishnan (b. 1928), ghata vidvan Vikku

Vinayakaram (b. 1942), violinist V. Tyagarajan (1927–2005) and kanjira vidvan V. Nagarajan (1930–2002) to visit, teach and perform at universities and institutes such as Wesleyan University, San Diego State University, University of Washington, California Institute of the Arts (CalArts) and Center for World Music.

A few Karnatik music enthusiasts, like James A. Rubin (1927–91), came to Madras on as many as twenty visits and recorded concerts of Karnatik musicians from the 1960s to the 1980s. Many recordings of the past greats of Karnatik music are found in the libraries of Harvard University (to which the James A. Rubin collection was donated) and Wesleyan University which, as we have noted, hosted many Karnatik musicians as visiting faculty and performers. Even today, Wesleyan University has a vibrant Karnatik music department. Many ethno-musicologists of both North American and Indian origin have completed their postgraduate and doctorate degrees from Wesleyan University. Visiting musicians and scholars have participated in events at the university, but as far as appointments of professors and teaching assignments are concerned, there has been an inclination to appoint musicians from the Dhanammal school, or those associated with or influenced by the style, as a result of the family's associations with Wesleyan. This is not a criticism, merely an observation.

From the mid-1980s, the NRI's Karnatik world in the US changed rapidly. Two major organizations, Carnatic Music Association of North America (CMANA) and the Cleveland Thyagaraja Festival, were sponsoring tours. Karnatik musicians began travelling more regularly to the US, and the audience composition also began changing. By the 1980s, the audience was predominantly south Indian brahmin. Even though the 1980s saw more musicians tour North America, it was only in the mid-1990s that the terms of engagement we see being played out today were established. More Indians were moving to North America, creating the critical mass to sustain a 'sabha' in cities like New Jersey, Los Angeles and San Jose. One of the game changers was the financial strength of the professionally successful Indian expatriate. Financial and personal stability are major contributors to an increased interest in the arts, especially art music. Many of these people had been raised in homes where Karnatik music had a strong presence. They may have learnt music, their parents or grandparents may have been kutcheri-goers, listening to radio concerts may have been part of the atmosphere at home, and weddings in the extended family may have included a Karnatik kutcheri. Perhaps Karnatik music disappeared from their life while they tried to adjust to a new sociocultural environment and attain financial and emotional stability. Once they attained that security, their interest in music was rekindled. And they were, in their new situation, not just rasikas, but promoters of the art. It is significant that many of these individuals who were at the cusp of Karnatik music's transformation in the US were not from affluent families, but were middle-class brahmins from cities, towns and villages across south India. By the mid-1990s, the number of tours by Karnatik musicians gradually increased and senior, popular and upcoming musicians were touring the US.

The 1990s were an important phase in the development of the North American touring system. Many organizations and individuals began to sponsor and organize tours. The system was very simple. One organization contracted musicians for a concert tour of North America and sold the concerts to city-based sabhas across North America. The musicians were paid an agreed amount for every concert. Each city 'sabha' negotiated the price for the concert with the promoter and took care of the local logistics, including hospitality for the artists. In all tours organized by the south Indian community, the artists were and still are hosted by south Indian families. The tour promoter took care of all the expenses, including travel. This basic economic model is still followed by the promoters and musicians, but the financial advantages are far more for all concerned.

The 1990s were also significant for another reason. Among

the Indian migrants were many people who had learnt Karnatik music in India They now became music teachers. Their levels of expertise varied, but that did not stop them from turning their homes into little schools of music with young boys and girls, mostly brahmins, as students. By the late 1990s, suburbs in many cities had more than one teacher, sometimes teaching up to a hundred children. For the parents, this was a way of connecting their children to south Indian culture and, as many of them were brahmins, they saw Karnatik music as a very important part of their cultural identity. With the number of migrants increasing and tours becoming common, this period built up the momentum for Karnatik music.

Simultaneous with these developments, right from the 1960s, were the construction of temples and celebration of Hindu festivals in the US. While these activities seemed to cut across caste and language identities, Karnatik music still had a primarily brahminical association. This explains why it took so long to create a sustainable community for this form.

As more children learnt Karnatik music, parents wanted their children to be exposed to quality performances, thereby increasing the demand for concerts. A larger number of migrants, more tour organizers, many more cities that could host Karnatik music concerts, teachers in a large number of cities and young aspiring students led to the spread of Karnatik music across North America. By the end of the millennium, the audience composition in kutcheris became 100 per cent Indian. This was a dramatic transformation from the 1960s when there were hardly any Indians in the audience. The Karnatik community had become self-sufficient and did not need the support of Americans to invite musicians or fill halls.

The Cleveland Festival

In 1978 was born a festival that changed the dynamics of Karnatik music in North America. In Chennai the December music season became the central event around which other Karnatik music concerts happened through the year. By the mid-1990s, the Cleveland Thyagaraja Aradhana established itself as the central event for North America.

The Cleveland Thyagaraja Aradhana was the first Karnatik music festival in North America. Before this, Karnatik concerts had occurred as stand-alone weekend events in different cities. The festival organizers began sponsoring artists for both the festival and a tour. This helped cover the costs of the festival itself. Beginning as a single-day event, it expanded to a few days and began sponsoring many more musicians. It then became a week-long festival, where a number of great musicians from India performed and listened to other musicians. It was a unique environment, where Karnatik musicians stayed the whole week at Cleveland. Many also volunteered to help organize the festival. The Cleveland festival recreated the era of the 1940s, when musicians travelled for concerts and spent days together singing, discussing music and listening to each other. Karnatik musicians who had settled in North America also got an opportunity to perform. Soon, lectures by eminent musicians were included and then unique dance dramas, musical operas and rare combinations of artists all became part of the schedule. Cleveland by itself was not really a centre for Karnatik music, but the support that the organizers – some of the early pioneers in Karnatik music promotion such as V.V. Sundaram, K. Venkataraman and R. Balasubramaniam – got from the Cleveland State University made this possible. The whole festival was and is still run on volunteerism, something that is commendable and demonstrative of the interest in Karnatik music among its micro-community.

The highlight of the festival for many has been the first weekend when there was the rendition of Tyagaraja's pancharatna kirtanas – a very glamorous event, led by the leading lights of Karnatik music. The inclusion of music competitions in the schedule changed the intensity of interest. For both parents and teachers, this was an opportunity to present the talent of their children and students at a national-level event. The fact that visiting musicians from India were judging these events made them more prestigious. The children's music was being evaluated by 'experts'. The competitions increased the participation of the NRI population by leaps and bounds.

The festival itself became the most important event in the calendar year for a North American interested in Karnatik music. The visiting Karnatik musicians valued performing at this festival in front of such an audience and the opportunity to spend a week listening to their colleagues. The Cleveland Thyagaraja Aradhana committee also began to give awards to Karnatik musicians from India and to teachers and organizers of repute in North America. This covered the three main sets of people who contributed to the event's uniqueness. The Cleveland Thyagaraja Aradhana had gone beyond trying to replicate the December music season; in fact, it was trying to become the Music Academy of North America.

In all this, it is impossible to ignore the use of the Tyagaraja aradhana as the central event around which the festival was structured. Historically, the festival began as an expansion of the celebration of Tyagaraja by the local community, which included the rendition of pancharatna kirtanas and compositions. The Tyagaraja aradhana is traditionally a congregation of Karnatik musicians that takes place in Tiruvaiyyaru (the site of Tyagaraja's work and the place he died in) around the date of his death. The aradhana in Tiruvaiyyaru includes a congregational rendition of the pancharatna kirtanas, short concerts by musicians and the rituals involved in an aradhana, or prayerful remembrance, for a saint. The Cleveland festival is conducted around the Easter weekend holiday, rather than the dates of the actual aradhana. Other than the rendition of the pancharatna, and of late a large image of Tyagaraja in the background, the festival is not really centred on Tyagaraja. Concerts are not limited to his compositions either.

Initially, the pancharatna rendition was a local event and included only musicians and teachers living in and around Cleveland. Later, as invited musicians became part of the festival, it became a showcase event. However, the use of Tyagaraja and the rendition of the pancharatna are important because they give the event a sanctification that puts it on a parallel with the Tiruvaiyyaru aradhana. The Tyagaraja connection – even though the festival has grown beyond it – has given the festival a halo. With almost the whole community of musicians and listeners in the US, largely brahmins, being present, there is no shortage of religiosity surrounding the pancharatna rendition. This takes us back to the earlier discussion on the brahminization of Karnatik music in the early twentieth century. Then too, Tyagaraja was virtually the axle for the wheels of change.

The Cleveland festival was only continuing the established practices within Karnatik music, but this led to a transference of the same parameters to the American context. The festival is today a unique combination of the December season, the Music Academy and the Tyagaraja aradhana. It is also the most important Karnatik music festival outside India.

Technology to Bridge the Gap

By the twenty-first century, the number of young Indian Americans learning Karnatik music was large and many were serious about the music. Expatriate Indians felt that, during their yearly visits to India, their children could benefit from learning Karnatik music from senior musicians. Some were already doing so even in the 1990s, but the new century saw an explosion of NRI children spending summers in India to learn from the maestros. To the parents, this was the equivalent of sending their child for a postgraduate degree in an Ivy League university. It was both about the quality of training and a certain status they got from being 'India trained'. Around this time, young talented musicians from North America started performing regularly at sabhas in Chennai, even during the December music season.

Meanwhile, literal and metaphorical changes have occurred in the way concert tours are organized and travel arrangements are made. The way of teaching, listening and sharing music has also changed. Musicians, rasikas and organizers are in constant touch with the Karnatik music community in India. All these changes have been the result of technological advances related to the Internet, especially since 2000. Technologies such as e-ticketing, Skype, mp3 format, YouTube and Internet-enabled phones have changed the face of Karnatik music, not just in North America but around the world.

We have, in this essay, travelled with the North American south Indian brahmin from the mid-twentieth century until the twenty-first century. The last ten years have been quite dynamic and complex. I have mentioned the technological changes briefly, and that they have changed the way we converse with the music both directly and indirectly. This apart, other social changes and the demanding nature of modern life have also had an impact on Karnatik music and its overseas engagement. With the given historical context, let us now analyse the state of Karnatik music among the NRI community, and the role technology has played in it.

In the 1990s, some teachers came up with an interesting solution to enable long-distance teaching of Karnatik music. They would record a song and courier it to their student. The student in turn would learn from the cassette and record his learning and send it back. The teacher would listen to this and respond with her comments. It was a cumbersome process, but seemed like the only way to engage with a student who lived far away. These cassette classes were supplemented with personal lessons whenever the teacher – often a prominent musician – visited the student's city or the student travelled to India.

In the 2000s, when calls to India became inexpensive, this

complicated system was replaced by telephone classes. This made learning easier, and also expanded the pool of teachers. The possibility of telephone classes was a great way for many teachers and retired performers to supplement their income. These classes soon became one of the biggest sources of income for many. Today, we have teachers conducting half-hour or one-hour classes on the telephone with students all over the globe, with the payments being made through online transfers. Usually, a teacher would line up between two and four classes in two hours depending on the duration of each class. The timings were based on the student's time zones and the teacher's convenience. This system continues to date, but through far simpler and interactive technologies, like Skype.

On the face of it, this does seem like an elegant solution provided by technology. But behind this lie some serious problems of learning. Many teachers use Internet-based video and audio technologies to teach students, and even now, the majority of their students are from North America. The question that needs to be asked is: what is special about learning directly from the guru? What is learnt? These questions should provide us with clues to what is lacking in technology-based learning.

Sitting in the physical presence of the guru is not just about repeating what is taught. Technique is not always conveyed as instructions or verbal communication. It is imbibed through an intimate observation of the guru. The student wants to sing or play the phrase of music exactly as it sounded when heard from the guru. It is in this search that technique is acquired. What the guru transfers is sincere absorption of the music. The guru's personal presence is an important part of this transfer. Whether it is an instrument or vocal music, technique is not just about the position of the fingers, hands, neck or shoulder, but also the relationship between all these and the musical idea. The result of this combination is the music.

E-guru

When the guru is physically present, such intimate observation is possible. On the telephone it is lost. Through video-based learning technologies, the guru's physical absence makes the reception flawed. It is not a question of visual clarity, but rather the lack of physical reality. When the sound is heard directly from the guru, the student has a ringside view of the teacher's intimate conversation with the music itself; in this there is a truth to the music that cannot be replaced. This totality then is what is recieved in guru–shishya learning. It is crucial that every student learns this quality of sound, music and presence. Without it, their music will be unaesthetic. Any technology that processes this reception will filter out the human immediacy of the experience.

But music is also beyond technique. Music is ultimately about what it does to the person. Does one, can one, learn this impersonally? This is not learnt but is felt with the guru every time music is rendered in a class. Until they discover themselves as persons and musicians, students imbibe this quality of the guru. One might say this 'imbibing' is akin to imitating. I do not contest that, but such 'imitation' is not wrong as it is the door to discovering that musical person inside. That which moves us, stirs us, which we refer to as elevating or transcending reality exists only because this inner self exists in the music. If the teacher does not convey this to a student subconsciously during teaching, she is not a teacher. This cannot be experienced by the student through a long-distance classroom environment. We can watch the majesty of the tiger, hear the roar of the mountains, feel the silence of the river on television and they are stunning and impressive. But it is only when we are in the actual presence of tiger, river or mountain that we feel the inner soul of their existence. Learning music is no different.

For the teacher too, these limitations truncate their level of engagement with the student. Through the computer monitor or the telephone, the teacher does not really relate to the student's music. The class is about getting the line of music correct. Sometimes, even that is compromised because the class has a time limit. The teacher is not observing the student with sincerity, transferring every line as a physical creation of music. Only through such creation does the transfer of technique, mind and soul of music occur. In most Internet classrooms, each line is a fragment of music. For such a teacher, the class becomes just another log entry. It is also almost impossible for him to retain the level of concentration required for teaching through these technological devices. This means that the teacher is not completely involved in the process of teaching, and is only providing a service.

Music lessons from gurus were not time-bound. The class could go on for hours or end in less than an hour. It is not the amount of time spent with the guru that mattered, but the quality of the time. Often in Internet-based teaching, this space does not exist. I remember some classes in which my guru just sang and I listened. Did I learn anything? Much more than I am aware of. This was also teaching, as was the repetition of one line a hundred times until my guru was satisfied that I had learnt it the way it should be. Both these experiences are rare, even non-existent, when learning through technologies.

I must say here that the idea of value for money, which has been around for a long time, has also today engulfed Karnatik music learning. Whether it is learning Karnatik music through Skype, or learning from a teacher in the US, I have heard many parents discuss whether the class was actually for an hour, whether a kirtana was completed in two classes. The method of evaluating music learning has undergone a huge shift. This attitude is more rampant in Internet teaching when the parents want to make sure that the half-hour class is at least that much. To further complicate the issue, the music teachers are not wanting who would short-change their students of good learning in order to finish on time. Therefore, it is important for both parents and students to be vigilant.

While I have been highly critical of these technologies, I do recognize that they have provided a great opportunity for many to learn from a teacher in India, and also provided a source of income for many teachers who may not be financially stable, especially because teaching Karnatik music in India is not a financially lucrative profession. But I strongly feel that learning via the Internet or telephone cannot be the primary method of learning Karnatik music. These technologies provide an opportunity to many to learn Karnatik music and improve their skills. Besides, we cannot deprive those who are interested only because they are in a different geographical location. But for those who really want to learn Karnatik music, these methods can only be supplementary to direct lessons. These students must make the effort to come to India every year at least for a few months to learn directly from the guru. This will give them an opportunity to experience the magic of a real classroom, and give the teacher a way to touch the student with true musical transference. For those whose learning of Karnatik music is casual and for teachers who do not really care about quality in music, none of these criticisms apply, since to them Karnatik music is not what it should be.

Time to Bridge, Two-way

During the 1980s and especially the 1990s, the interest of youth in this art form was kept alive by teachers who began music schools in their homes. Many of these teachers had trained under musicians in India and gave youngsters living in a culturally alien environment the opportunity to learn in a traditional manner from a guru. They also sent students for advanced training from a guru in India. I am sure that, in some cases, a student's move to an India-based guru would have caused heartburn, yet many gurus in North America encouraged their students to seek training from senior maestros in India. Performers from India who today see so many young students attend concerts in various North American cities should thank these quality teachers who have given them a new generation of committed listeners.

Internet teaching has stabilized and disturbed, enriched and impoverished the Karnatik music education environment in North America. Migrant teachers still continue to teach a large number of students, but now they have to compete with teachers living in India. This trend cannot in itself be critiqued; it must be accepted as the result of a shrinking world. But it has led to two developments. Many musicians who teach via the Internet are not only India-based teachers, but also travelling performers. This means that they travel around North America as performers and meet many young students and their parents. It is normal for parents to ask their children to sing in the presence of visiting musicians. In fact, for years, visiting musicians taught many young students a few kirtanas when they visited a city. And teachers in North America were aware of this. But now North American teachers complain about 'student poaching'. After listening to young singers many teachers and performers who are on tour offer to teach these students, knowing fully well that they are being trained by a committed teacher. For the parent, the opportunity to have their child trained by an 'India guru' becomes important, forgetting that their child's musical quality has been nurtured by the local teacher. This affects both the spirit of the teachers and the relationship between touring musicians and music teachers in North America.

Most performing musicians who listen to young singers while visiting their homes are now looked upon with suspicion. Touring musicians who conduct workshops for students are seen as competitors. After all, at the end of a workshop, the musicians often do take over many students. Every individual has the right to choose her teacher, but if informal singing sessions or workshops are used as arenas to capture NRI students, it is a practice that deserves to be critiqued. We must remember that the quality of a teacher is not determined by whether they live in India or North America. There are good and bad teachers everywhere, and to make a choice based on geographical location is just wrong.

I understand that every musician needs to make a living and not all can be successful performers. In such a situation, Internet classes, travelling to the US for classes and workshops are important. As long as the intention remains true to the art, there is no problem, but when the idea is to 'make hay while the sun shines', it hurts both the art and its ecosystem. This is where we are today.

The strength of the dollar against the Indian rupee has come to define all these aspects of Karnatik music. Musicians try to teach as many students as possible through the Internet and during their travels to North America. They spend over a month making journeys to certain cities specially to teach. In addition to teaching, it is also beneficial for teachers to make these students present their first concert (arangetram, in Tamil), which is seen as a day of graduation. The costs of an arangetram are very high and include arranging for excellent accompanists if the student is a vocalist, or a good vocalist if the youngster is either a violinist or a mrdanga artist, and usually from India. The guru is treated with great respect and rewarded financially for bringing the student to this level of proficiency. All this is fine if the young student is actually ready, but unfortunately, the guru often rushes a student to this stage. Added to this is the competition between parents to push their child to perform first, putting pressure even on teachers who are sincere about their teaching.

There is no doubt that there is immense potential in many young musicians in North America, but the prevailing attitude of students, parents and teachers is ruining the possibilities for Karnatik music. All the stakeholders have to look at themselves and the music if we want to create a sustainable future. My criticism of musicians teaching students from North America is only directed at those whom I see as being opportunistic. Unfortunately, their number is quite large and hence generalizations are inevitable. The whole learning environment has become a complex cesspool where everyone wants to take full advantage of the situation. In spite of these developments there have been and still are teachers in both places who have stayed committed to the music.

Interestingly, the situation with accompanying artists settled in North America is almost exactly the opposite of what happened with NRI teachers. It is the accompanying artists who have really benefited from tours by musicians from India. Many vocalists and instrumental soloists tour North America without accompanists from India as this could reduce the overheads. Quality performers, like quality teachers, exist everywhere. But when the choice of accompanists is made on the basis of economics rather than musical quality, it becomes a sensitive issue. Many main performers travel to North America and perform with substandard accompanists only because they can make more money. For the American musician, it is a great opportunity to accompany a top-ranking Indian musician.

This has led to some ill feeling among accompanists in India, who feel that the musicians who call them for concerts in India ignore them for North American tours. The problem is also that some 'main artists' go to the US on teaching assignments, and then accept concerts in a few cities and perform with almost any musician, irrespective of quality. While the sense of musical quality is highly subjective, there are certain parameters that can be judged by most people. If the choice of accompanists does not meet even these criteria, there are serious problems. Irrespective of whether they are from India or North America, musicians must choose their accompanists on the basis of musicianship and not financial advantages and personal favours. Vocalists and solo instrumentalists present concerts with accompanists who are not ready to be on stage in the name of encouraging local talent. These trends bring down the quality of Karnatik music.

This shallowness has extended itself to concert opportunities for young students of music. In the name of providing opportunity for talent, even the Cleveland Thyagaraja Aradhana Festival has begun to feature group presentations and concerts by young students who are not ready for the stage. In one such recurring event, young students are selected from all over North America by a panel of musicians who listen to their recordings. The selected group learns compositions for the thematic presentation over the Internet from many great musicians in India. It saddens me greatly that some senior and respected musicians participate in this charade. After a few months of training, both on the Internet and from special guides who travel from India for this purpose, these students perform during the Cleveland festival. Every participant pays a fee for being part of such a 'privileged presentation'. The excitement of seeing their children on stage causes parents and teachers also to push them on stage.

Unfortunately, many of these children are not ready to perform. More importantly, such events delude the children and parents about their abilities. They do not remember that this does not represent their true musical quality. It even creates a competitive spirit among teachers who try to send more of their students to these presentations. Even here, students of the Internet teachers are an important part of the group. To me, these events are dangerous as they create a false idea of Karnatik music. Getting on stage – even at an important festival such as Cleveland – has become relatively easy, reducing the value of the music and its learning, and diluting its presentation. Today, we even have a televised contest, especially for musical talent from North America. As much in India as North America, this has made people believe that such shows spot rare talent and provide opportunities to young musicians who may have never seen the light of day. Talent usually finds its way, arduous though the path may be; this 'idol' believes he has found the way, only to see it vanish with the show lights.

I have named the Cleveland festival in this critique because it is the benchmark for Karnatik music festivals outside India and wields a great influence over teachers and students of Karnatik music in North America. I have the greatest respect for the festival and what it has achieved, but I am disappointed at the populist direction that it has taken. At such an important festival, a premium must be placed on the young students, whether they perform individually or collectively, and every music competition must set high standards of quality. In my mind, these are lacking today and the organizers have to re-look at ways to engage with talent in North America that will have a far-reaching and a long-standing positive impact on Karnatik music. Of course, the musicians who benefit from the festival and its significance are party to these developments. Their own tours are often clubbed along with the festival and the teaching opportunities that they have in the US. Understandably then, it serves their interests to please the Cleveland organizers, powerful impresarios from other cities and the parents of the strong Karnatik music student community.

Since we are discussing music concerts I also need to talk about the state of Karnatik music tours in North America. There was a time when only US-based outfits organized tours, but today the scene is very different. Since all the logistics of a tour and the confirming of concerts can be done over email, individual musicians in India organize their own tours. This has increased the number of tours in a year to close to thirty. This is wonderful, as more musicians are able to travel, teach and perform. Depending on the differing levels of popularity and seniority of the musicians, the manner of organizing the concerts too varies. While some still perform a number of chamber concerts, others have professionally organized tours. On the whole, some of the larger cities have concerts almost every weekend.

From a time when a US tour was a matter of prestige, today it has become a matter of routine. My only concern is whether we are reaching a tipping point. How much can the community sustain? Today, though there a number of musicians, students and rasikas in many cities, the audience numbers do not reflect this strength. The bigger cities, such as New Jersey and San Jose, have numerous organizations that can host concerts and also teachers of music. This has led to a highly competitive atmosphere between various groups. When one group organizes concerts, the other group will not attend. Communities seem more reluctant to come together at these events. In this conflicted environment, audiences are splintered, or more obsessed with their own little concerns. Along with this is the fact that most parents in the US seem more interested in their children performing rather than attending concerts. Singing in local groups, Tyagaraja aradhanas, attending the Cleveland competition are all directly linked to the growth of the young student, while attending concerts is only an addition. The focus has shifted from listening and learning from other concerts to getting the students on stage. It is also true that there are just too many concerts, and that leads to listener fatigue. The present situation is the result of a combination of changes in tours, teaching, learning and performance opportunities. Could it also be that, since many young students travel to India to learn and for the December music season in Chennai, they feel that they have received the required listening experience?

Right from the late 1990s, young musicians from North America have been trying to perform in Chennai, especially during the December music season. Having their names published along with the great names of Karnatik music, presenting a concert in Chennai during the much-talked-about season is considered a personal achievement. As a result, young NRI musicians apply to various sabhas in Chennai for an opportunity. This, once again, has resulted in organizers and parents of young aspiring musicians twisting the environment. The organizers realized that many parents can be exploited by charging a fee for the opportunity, and many parents were more than willing to part with their money to gain for their children an opportunity to perform in the season. This 'pay to perform' culture has now extended to even India-based musicians, though no one will officially admit it. Some organizations began NRI festivals, providing opportunities only to NRI performers who travelled specifically to perform during the music season. This monetization of concert opportunity, especially during the December music season, for which both the NRI and the Chennai sabhas are responsible, is deplorable.

Of course, the sincerity of young NRI performers too needs to be examined. A lot of them come to perform during the music season as it is considered the big stage, but do not have a long-term commitment to Karnatik music. Singing during the music season and having their reviews published in leading newspapers seem to be an end in itself. They come back every year for the same thing. But what this actually does is to deny concert opportunities to sincere and committed youngsters living in India who want to make Karnatik music their life. Besides, this also affects talented youngsters from North America who are not willing to pay for a concert. With only limited slots available in the sabhas and the willingness and capacity of NRIs to pay for opportunities, talent is ignored.

For many young NRI aspirants, Karnatik music is just another phase in their lives, and they will move on to other things. It is not a question of whether they take up Karnatik music as a profession, but rather their commitment to the art form and the space that it will occupy in their lives. It is also true that singing during the December season or in Chennai is also used as part of 'résumé-padding' for college admissions. Videos of concerts are used to present their talent to colleges.

There are students of music everywhere who do not approach Karnatik music with the seriousness it requires. This does not bother me as long as they are not eating into the opportunities of genuine artists. The December music season is an important time for young talent, a time when they can be heard by Karnatik music listeners from all over India and the world. If the financial strength of the NRI deprives the real talent of space during this time, we have a serious problem.

The Prospect Remains Bright

Despite these issues, there have been some talented musicians emerging from North America. These young musicians grew up in households where Karnatik music was integral to life. Some had mothers who taught music, others had parents who were active in organizing concerts or were ardent listeners and some had the opportunity to host great musicians in their homes. Invariably, all these were brahmin families. Many of these young musicians were trained by teachers from India who had migrated. After attaining a certain level of expertise, they learnt from musicians in India either by travelling to India every year or from musicians who went to North America to teach for a sustained period every year. More than how they learnt their music, it is their seriousness that needs to be commended. In spite of the fact that they had to travel every year to India only for their music and spend the rest of the year working hard on it, they never gave up. This is not just heartening, but very important for Karnatik music.

Living in a very different society, they have had to live with two different identities. Their Karnatik identity is inside the home and within the Karnatik music community; beyond those walls, they are regular North Americans. It is beautiful that they straddle both these worlds and see no contradiction there. A few of these American-born talents are making a mark for themselves as performers in India too. These are in a way the first wave of Indian American Karnatik musicians. It has not been easy for young NRI musicians who have had to fight the stigma of being 'foreigners'. Sabhas, especially in Chennai, view young musicians from North America as a lot that will appear for the music season and pressure them for concerts, with some being willing to pay for slots. Perhaps they will spend a few months here to learn, but eventually they will leave to return to their own world. Some even feel that since they are from North America, they cannot be as good as musicians from India. But what hurts many serious young musicians is the comment that 'local musicians have to be given preference' over them. The point they make is that it is quality that should determine opportunity, and not where they live.

While some still shuttle between the US and India, a few have even taken the big step of relocating to India, hoping to achieve recognition as quality performing musicians. In deciding to create a base for themselves in Chennai, 'the Mecca of Karnatik music', these young musicians show an intent towards their music that is refreshing. Chennai is the place to make a name for yourself if you want to be somebody in Karnatik music, and these young entrepreneurs have taken the risk of challenging the Karnatik citadel with just their talent. This is a wonderful development and I hope that they inspire more real young musicians to take their music seriously. It will not be easy, socially, culturally or financially, but the move can be eventually rewarding.

There are others who have learnt music with the same commitment, but chose to stay on in North America. They too are important for the health of the music in that continent. Commitment to music is not about being in India; it is about the music. They will inspire a new generation of performers, teachers and rasikas and will build Karnatik music. We must nurture such individuals. The real test for Karnatik music will be to see if musicians born and brought up in the US can live there and be professionals. This may be many years away, but is important to imagine. There could be domestic concert tours of North America, just as musicians in India tour the rest of the country. Respect for concert performers of quality living in North America must be at par with the respect shown to the ones in India. Performers and teachers of Karnatik music who live in the US are the ones who will change the dynamics of the art there.

The growth of Karnatik music in North America is an important case study in how the music has developed in a different sociocultural environment, and the role of the migrant community in its growth. It gives us an idea of the changes in patterns and attitudes that influence the direction that the music takes. It also gives us insight into the Karnatik community, no matter where the domicile may be. In the last half a decade or more, other countries have followed the patterns set by the North American NRI, whether it is learning, teaching, performing or the organizing of festivals.

Maybe opportunism cannot be condemned in the new world we live in, but we must protect the music from the consequences of it. Selflessness seems outdated, but musicians need to discover it to change. And those changes will not only influence Karnatik music in North America, but also everywhere else around the globe. This is a spectacular opportunity to create conscious aesthetic communities across the world that will preserve and enrich Karnatik music within different cultural contexts.

22

The Musician and the Machine

I often begin the examination of a subject by looking at the etymology and meaning of the word or words that define it. I find this process revealing, as the genesis of a word also gives us an insight into its journey. Of course no word is born of itself, neither does it journey alone. In exploring this traveller's tale of linguistic meaning, we can trace the flow of man's imagination. And by doing that we will find that the thought that created the word is far removed from its present expression. This constant transformation is part of both that word's existence and our own.

So let us look at the word 'technology'. It conjures up images of computers, airplanes, televisions, digital audio devices. The numerous inventions that have changed our lives rush into our mind's eye. In the modern world, technology almost always means devices that were created during and after the Industrial Revolution. More recently, it has come to be used almost synonymously with the computer and digital age. The impact of computerization and digitalization on recent history has come to determine our understanding of technology. Technology is not metaphysical in nature; its natural home is not the human mind as much as it is the human stage. It has a tangible and temporal existence. Technology necessarily indicates a device. It cannot be only an idea; it is an actual 'thing' that exists as matter, something we can use in the material transactions of our lives. But there is more to the word, as I shall try to explain.

The etymology of the word indicates both a connection to and a diversion from its original interpretation. 'Techno' is from the Latin 'technicus' and the Greek 'tekhnikos', the root for both (techne or tekhne) meaning art, craft. In other words, useful or applied techniques. 'Logy', of course, is from the lovely Greek word 'logos', meaning discourse. Technology, as a concept, is the area of knowledge that deals with the craft of techniques. At a conceptual level, the word 'technology' goes beyond the limiting reference of a device to the idea and intent that can be applied through technique. When this idea and intent embody themselves in a device, technology is created. In many ways, this can be related to the earlier discussion on imagination and creativity. Imagination here can be interpreted as the conceptual idea of technology and creativity as its manifestation in temporal form. Technology, therefore, is a far wider idea than the mechanical signature of the digital age. Any idea that leads to the invention or creation of an applied device is technology. This would include the daggers and spears used by early humans, cooking techniques, wheels and transportation inventions and everything else that has changed the way we live.

In music, the word has a limited play. It seems, in any case, to relate only to the era after the arrival of that attractive child of the Industrial Revolution, the microphone. Tying sound to electrically generated sound waves, the microphone changed the way sound travelled. Both by augmenting volume and making the recording and indirect dissemination of music possible, it actually began the processes that led to the creation of a 'music industry'. The microphone is seen as the most foundational and impactful event in the music industry. Recording and dissemination devices grew in sophistication and incredible variety over the twentieth and twenty-first centuries. In this essay, I would like to examine the quintessential idea that led to technology beyond the physicality of its mechanistic expansion.

Music is a human creation. We received from nature sound with which to create music. We drew, wove, turned, coloured, textured and shaped the sounds, making music that transcended the reality that inspired us. The most natural expression of music was the voice. This was not a created device; it lived inside the body and the mind and expressed itself in the most intimate manner. But we also experienced the beauty of sound generated from all that surrounded us. The wind ruffling the leaves, air travelling through bamboo, the calls of the birds and animals, the waves and thunder, all of these generated sounds. Human beings heard music in these sounds, or at least the possibility of it. This led us to behold and use objects, natural objects, and to join them in the making of our music – and then fashioning them into shapes beyond their original design, to enlarge and enrich our sense of the musical. The debate about which was the first ever instrument is not important here (many believe it was the flute). What is important is the fact that humanity's first techno-musical idea was the recognition that a sound beyond the voice could also be music.

Any instrument that has been created for music is, at a basic physical level, a technological device. It is an apparatus that has been developed from an idea into a mechanical construct with its own attributes and strengths to express music. To the extent that every such instrument is directed to a clear musical intent, it is a unique creation of technology. Whether they are chordophones, aerophones, membranophones or idiophones, all such instruments are designed to and are used to present music and the aesthetics that defines it. Instruments in each culture and musical genre are different. They have evolved according to the times, availability of material, changes in the music and the influence of various other cultures.

The Musical Illusion of Voice

Beyond this, there is in musical instruments something that transcends their mechanized instrumentation – and that is the living ideation that they represent. If something that is in itself inert and lifeless can have a nature, character and a temperament of its own, then a musical instrument certainly does. And that comes from its altogether distinctive ability to create the music that the musician seeks. The true musician is honest to the music. What is being 'honest to the music'? Nothing more than an understanding of its past, present and the reason for its existence, as well as an adherence to that understanding. This holistic musical understanding is the result of both musicianship and musicology. The idea of a certain musical form and the instruments used in it have almost always evolved together. This has resulted in changes in both the instruments and the playing techniques. Reciprocally, instrumentalists have also influenced the music. In that mutuality, the instrument and the musician together become part of the same musical ideation.

In the context of Karnatik music, what interests me is the relationship between the music and the instrument. Every instrument, melodic and rhythmic, has its own aesthetic qualities, which contribute to the music's aesthetic experience. In most cases, the instruments are used in a manner that is true to the music's aesthetic form. But while the musical form and instruments have an interrelated existence, there are times when there has been friction between the music and how the instrument works its way within it. This problem has a connection to both the musician and the instrument itself. Just as the whims and fancies of vocalists affected Karnatik music, the attitudes of instrumentalists have also impacted the musical form.

Melodic instruments like the vina or the flute have had a long history. Along the way, they have changed in physical form and musicians have improved on their techniques of playing. I use the word 'improved', as the changes in the playing technique were made with the sole purpose of being able to communicate the musicality to the best of their ability.

Once again, I would like to reiterate that Karnatik music is primarily a vocal form. I have said this a few times before, but have not fully explained my position. What do I mean by this statement? Does this also imply that vocal music is superior?

Karnatik music, over the last few hundred years, has shown an inclination towards interpreting its 'sound' from the point of view of what is produced in the voice. The music itself seems to be drawn towards the aesthetics created by the voice. This is what I mean when I say that Karnatik music is primarily a vocal form. Does this have anything to do with the fact that ours has been culturally an oral tradition? Have we used the voice over every other medium of expression to convey, share, recollect, remember and articulate all that was precious in our moments of thought and reflection? Frankly, I do not know. But I cannot think of another form of expression that has had the sway of the voice. I might add here that the transcribed word, or writing, is basically an extended form of the human voice expressing thought.

My assertion does not place the vocalist on a higher pedestal, but places the human voice as the source for musical expression. Instrumentalists in the Karnatik tradition have always tried to sound like the voice, not like the vocalist. This distinction is both subtle and significant. In fact, they cannot sound like the vocalist, as the aesthetics of the instrument and the derived techniques determine the instrument's identity. Instrumentalists have tried to create the musical illusion of the voice. Voice has the quality of being an internally created expression of the human being, our primary aural expression. In some way, this has been sought through the instruments. Therefore, the likeness to the voice is a search for closeness to ourselves.

In this identification, I see no hierarchy, only different ways of connecting to the voice as the primary source of human sound.

All through, vocalists too have adopted a great deal from the style and understanding of instrumentalists. This exchange between the vocalists and the instrumentalists has been constant, but the primacy of the voice has never disappeared. We must also remember, at the same time, that all vocalists have not necessarily been the voice of Karnatik music. Some vocalists have been as disconnected to the voice as some instrumentalists, unable to give life to the musical expression of the voice. Therefore, the lack of understanding of voice as the soul of Karnatik music is a problem that is of musicians in general, not just of one section.

Similarly, the closeness of instruments to the human voice has more to do with musical movements and expression of the voice, and less to do with the timbre. Vocalists have been able to use instruments to understand nuances of the music.

When a vocalist renders a certain line, its exact movement has no physical presence; it is a response to an internal intellectual and emotional trigger. The musical phrase has its existence only in the listening faculty of the musician and connoisseur. In the case of an instrumentalist, by moving his fingers across, say the vina, he can not only hear the music but also see it. In this visualizing, he can chart the exact course that brought the musical phrase into existence. This has contributed and continues to contribute immensely to a better understanding of Karnatik music.

We may wonder whether Karnatik music has a specific identity. Yes it does, one that I have often referred to as its 'sound' – the collective aural identity that encompasses various ragas, talas, compositions and improvisations and their aesthetic interpretations. The sound of Karnatik music is not static, but a constantly changing entity. With every such change, instrumentalists have responded with technological changes to the instruments and the technique of playing. This brings our discussion of technology in Karnatik music to the role of tradition, or of what in our cultural context, is best described as sampradaya.

But what about 'new' sounds? In the abstract world of sampradaya, newness is not a product of novelty. It comes from a real and living sense of the past. This past is not about nostalgia, but about an evolving journey to the present. It is this that creates and sustains sampradaya. New sounds that are generated by an individual's personal taste are bereft of this soul, even if they are enjoyable. As a musician, I consider a truly aesthetic individual interpretation as that which establishes an individual artist or school of thought, yet gives us the aesthetics of the music contained within its sampradaya. As we analyse the use of various musical instruments in Karnatik music, it is essential to reiterate this idea of sampradaya.

At this juncture, I feel the need to investigate the use of some melodic instruments within Karnatik music and within the context of its current aesthetic form. We need to be very careful in the use of the words 'traditional' and 'non-traditional'. Neither tradition nor sampradaya refer to 'that which has been in practice for a long time'. There are musical negotiations that occur in every time frame between musicians and the music, musicians and history, musical practices and society. Within this basket of interactions exists the idea of sampradaya. This is not as complicated a situation as might at first sight appear.

I would like to turn here to the wisdom of the contemporary Karnatik composer 'Spencer' Venugopal on the subject of classicism. He has said, 'Classicism is not too vague for words; it is indeed too precise.' All one needs to do is replace the word 'classicism' with 'sampradaya'. One may feel that these are 'just' expressions. But if we were to take any one aspect of music and study its present and past, a certain clarity would emerge. Does this mean that there are no grey areas? Of course there are, but we cannot negotiate them as long as we are unwilling to revisit our own position in terms of the present and past.

In the context of musical instruments too, we must be very cautious about referring to certain instruments as traditional and others as imports. Sometimes that which we thought of as indigenous exists in its present form only because of sociocultural interactions. What determines the use of any instrument in Karnatik music is its ability to present the music with a sense of sampradaya and express all the various aesthetic dimensions we know it for. This idea goes beyond the instrumentalist and must be the concern of every Karnatik musician. All this must provide us the fragrance of the music's sound. It is in this context that the use of some instruments in Karnatik music disturbs me.

The Vox and the Box

The harmonium is said to have been brought to India by the French and has been adapted into various musical genres. Many schools of Khyal use the harmonium, Ghazal musicians use it and so do the Namasankirtana musicians in the south. The use of the harmonium in Hindustani music makes no logical sense. Considering the nature of svara in Indian art music and the inability of the instrument to create its myriad forms, I wonder how it has been adapted into the music. When the harmonium accompanies a Khyal musician, an aesthetic disturbance is felt every time the harmonium player improvises on his own or fills the gaps for the vocalist. This is due to the sudden transformation of the raga's melodies from its continuous fluent movement in the voice to the transiting broken svara positions on the harmonium. The music's aesthetics demands that the instrument produce this continuous movement, but the harmonium just cannot. We may not recognize this disparity, because the human mind has an immense capacity to fill in the blanks. So when we hear the harmonium, we actually create the fluid connections within our mind, masking the aesthetic anomaly.

Was Hindustani music itself less fluid in the past? While I am not an expert on that musical system, it does seem rather unlikely that it ever completely lacked gamakas. The extent of the curves and svara expressions could have been less, but not altogether absent. Any study of ancient Indian music systems and Indian music over the last 500 years would reveal that the idea of a svara was almost always more than a frequency position, and therefore, its expressiveness is an essential quality of the various musical forms of India.

In the south, the harmonium was used in bhajana sampradaya and Harikatha congregations from at least the late nineteenth century, if not even earlier. At bhajana renderings, there is almost always a harmonium accompanist. Here too, since all the musical ingredients belong to Karnatik music, there is a certain disconnect between the sound of the singers and the harmonium accompanist. But since Namasankirtana is meant to evoke religious fervour and not to produce art music, the singers need not focus as much on the gamakas of the ragas. In this environment, the harmonium may not sound as inappropriate. To many, the sound of the harmonium is an important part of the bhajana and Namasankirtana experience. Some musicians, who are highly trained in the Karnatik form, start focusing on the musical aspects in Namasankirtana as well (which I believe they should not), resulting in the harmonium becoming out of place. These days, Namasankirtana presentations tend to use the violin accompaniment, rather than harmonium. This may be a result of the art music training of these singers.

Some musicians have tried presenting Karnatik music on the harmonium. This is not just unnecessary but inadvisable. We need to recognize that the instrument in its present form is incapable of rendering the gamakas that give Karnatik music its aural identity. Then why even attempt such an experiment? In such cases, musicians are primarily relying on the listeners' natural ability to imagine gamakas between the gamaka-less svaras being rendered on the instrument. Memory completes every musical experience. But this cannot – and should not – be a reason for musicians to render Karnatik music on instruments that are incapable of expressing that which defines the music. Instruments such as the jalataranga also fall into this category. A lack of continuity, which is the quality Karnatik music needs, haunts these instruments.

Bending Pitches Right

The modern keyboard was only a digital version of the piano. Today that has changed. With the use of pitch bender (a device on keyboards that allows for the rendition of the moving forms of svaras with continuity), musicians are able to render svaras in the Karnatik sense. Svaras can turn, swerve, bounce and glide; they are not rigid frequency positions. Yet there is a problem. While I recognize that this is a far better proposition than a keyboard without the pitch bender (the pitch bender itself comes with different settings and possibilities depending on the keyboard), my concern is subtle. I have spent a lot of time listening to ragas and compositions being played on this instrument. While the gamakas appear – and at times can even pass as – correct, they are actually distorted. The distortion is not a result of the keyboard's sound, but due to the sound of the gamaka.

On the keyboard, gamakas do not have the necessary 'feel' through their movements. It sounds like a contrived connection between two positions. There is also an obvious, and unnecessary, emphasis at the two end points of a gamaka movement, which sounds artificial. When sung or heard on the vina or violin, the gamaka is both smooth and rounded, without unnecessary pressure at any unsuitable point. The pitch benders, on the other hand, give the distinct impression of being limited in fully expressing the details of a gamaka movement, or the necessary feeling of a gamaka's completion, whether during the movement or in the eventual effect. More often than not, these artists are performing with a violin accompanying them and this creates an illusion of appropriate movement, where in fact it does not exist.

There is a difference between an approximate gamaka and a gamaka interpretation. The gamakas rendered by Ariyakudi Ramanuja Iyengar and T. Brinda were very different, but neither were compromises. They were both precise musical interpretations of sampradaya. With the musicians playing on the keyboard, gamakas are almost always musical adjustments that even the musicians do not recognize. The danger here is that if musicians and listeners get used to this approximation of svaras, the aesthetic quality of the music will be manipulated. This is not evolution, as it is not a result of musical continuity, but of an enforced aberration caused by the need of certain musicians to force a technology on the music. While I have explained my position with specifics on gamakas and svaras, ultimately, what the keyboard, with or without pitch benders, represents as Karnatik music hurts the art form.

But this I do recognize: the keyboard has evolved to incorporate within its range the possibility of gamakas, though only as approximations at present. It is entirely possible that in a few years from now, we may have a keyboard that can present Karnatik music as it ought to be presented. Even now there are technologically advanced keyboards that are getting very close to the requirements of Karnatik music, but are yet to be used by Karnatik keyboard players. In the interim, how much will the present keyboard affect musicality? It is a question we must bend our minds to.

The Saxophone on Loan

Another instrument that has become a presence in Karnatik music is the saxophone. Even with the conscious changes made to its construction, the saxophone is incapable of rendering the sound of Karnatik music. Here too, it is often the violinist who provides cover for the saxophone artist. Most ragas that have a lot of gamaka, especially kampita gamaka, cannot be rendered on this instrument in their true sense. This has led to saxophone-using musicians rendering only ragas with relatively less gamaka, thus limiting their own exploration of the music. Is this gamaka-low or gamaka-less form perhaps another interpretation of Karnatik music? The question can be posed thus: who says Karnatik music exists only in its gamakas?

Karnatik music has always had and will always have numerous interpretations. But these interpretations evolve from the spectrum that dwells within its sound. Inability to comprehend or present one aspect of the spectrum cannot be accepted as an interpretation. Interpretation must be born from an internalization of all that exists within the music. This has to be the endeavour of every musician, vocalist or instrumentalist. Therefore, while adapting an instrument to Karnatik music, the musician must take cognizance of the various melodic movements that exist within the music and what they provide to its aesthetics. That which embodies the sound of Karnatik music is not an arbitrary set of musical expressions. Each contributes to the other. Whether a svara has a lot of gamaka or is without it is not an individual idea limited to the svara. It is born out of the raga itself, which is one element of the music. In this connected existence, we cannot separate gamaka-laden svaras from gamaka-less svaras. Unless we grasp the music as a whole and experience the interconnectedness of all its elements, we have not understood the music itself.

One of the counter-arguments against the kind of observations I have made about the harmonium and saxophone has been that, for long, musicians playing the flute and violin were unable to create the Karnatik sound that I have described in its comprehensive totality. This meant that their interpretation was limited. This is not entirely untrue. However, these musicians' own understanding of music was complete, and not limited by the limitations, such as they are, of their instruments. Most crucially, they constantly sought the Karnatik sound. This is why, over the years, these musicians have improved and adapted techniques so that the flute and the violin can present the canvas of musicality that is essential to Karnatik music. It is also significant that the morphology of these two instruments lent itself to such adaptations.

The Clarinet Is Set

There have been instruments that have been successfully adapted into the Karnatik system. These include the violin, of course, and the clarinet. In the case of the violin, changes were made to the tuning system, strings, position of the violin and fingering technique – all made possible by the fact that the violin inherently provided this possibility. The story of the clarinet is more interesting. We know that the clarinet was used for Sadir, the earlier form of Bharatanatyam, in the late nineteenth and early twentieth century. I am not certain whether it was used in its original form with buttons to render the notes. If it was, I imagine the instrument would have been rather inappropriate. But later, the clarinet was modified into a nagasvara-like wind instrument, allowing for all the svara movements that today make it Karnatik. Most of the buttons were removed and tone holes – like in the nagasvara – were used to allow for slides in the fingering technique in order to render all the gamakas.

And the Mandolin Is In

In the 1980s, the mandolin was brought into the Karnatik fold. What we refer to as a mandolin is actually an electric mandolin closer to an electric guitar. There was no reason to make any changes to its physical structure. Easy movement across the frets, the feasibility of negotiating the strings for melodic movement and the instrument's inherent capacity for creating and sustaining continuity of sound has brought every Karnatik cadence into the mandolin's versatile scope. It has lent itself to adaptation and has rightfully become part of Karnatik music. There has been no compromise of musicality in order to accommodate the instrument.

But There Is Nothing Like the Mike!

From instruments, let us move to technologies that have enabled a larger audience to hear Karnatik music. The advent of the microphone in the early part of the twentieth century completely changed the nature of Karnatik music. It has influenced both the musicians' musicality and the listeners' experience of the music. Some people have asserted that the microphone contributed to ideas such as nuance, subtlety and elegance in the Karnatik voice. Before the microphone, male vocalists sang at higher shrutis (pitches) so their voices would carry to the audience. This meant the men, who spoke at a lower pitch post-puberty, had to artificially render music at a higher pitch, involving a rigorous training of the voice. Did this also mean that the music was more about reach and impact rather than subtlety? Once the microphone arrived, men, it is suggested, could sing at their natural pitches. And since technology attended to the reach of the voice, they could concentrate more on the nuances of the music. The voice now became an instrument of musicality, not volume. This implies that with the advent of the microphone, Karnatik music itself may have become more subtle. Did the gamakas become more minute, filigree-like, fine, complicated because musicians could concentrate more on the beauty of tone, changes in volume and complexity of melodic movements?

While this seems like a logical conclusion, for a number of reasons, I am unable to accept the proposition. We know that there was a time when Karnatik music was presented primarily in the courts and temples. The devadasis sang and danced every day for the lord, some of them also performed in the court. They were part of royal processions. The nagasvara vidvans had two main occasions to present music: the daily ritual and the temple festivals. The brahmin musicians composed, performed and competed with other musicians in courts, temples and private gatherings. Within these various spaces of performance, different contexts, varying types of people and differing numbers, musicians of the time would have had to have a flexible interpretation of the music. We must also keep in mind that we cannot be certain about what constituted a large audience back then. While recollections of musicians give us an impression of large crowds, we have to be careful with such anecdotes. In terms of population, we are far more numerous now.

The more important question, however, is: did musicians adjust their idea of tonality, volume and subtlety depending on the context of their presentation? This is definitely possible. Musicians do that today too. They will tell you that when performing in chamber music settings, their music is far more nuanced than while singing at a large temple gathering, where they resort to aggressive singing. When these adjustments occur even with the presence of the microphone, I am certain that musicians did the same at temples, courts, processions, festivals and the like. As much as musicians would have had different musical approaches, some soft and subdued, others forceful and energetic, they would have changed their musical approach based on the context of the performance. As early as the eighteenth century, King Shahaji (1684–1712) in his *Ragalakshanamu* classified ragas into the categories of ghana (rigid and dense), naya (fluid and soft) and deshiya (from other regions). Ghana and naya have been understood by cross-referring the terms and ragas categorized under each with later musical forms. It is a unique classification, because for the first time, ragas were categorized based on the nature of their melodic movement. I strongly feel that the classification suggests the possible emotional experience derived from these ragas, without passing any value judgements on them. That would imply various modes of vocalization, nuance and sensitivity. It would then be fallacious to assume that sweetness of voice or tonality is a modern idea.

The fact that the vina was an important instrument also means that loudness may not have always been the primary focus of the music. Treatises advert to the importance of the vina, and gamakas are described in terms of the vina. Surely then, nuanced music is not a post-microphone creation. The description of 'Vina' Dhanammal's music too is significant. All great musicians talk about her singing as being extremely soft and subtle while she accompanied herself on the vina. We are told that the whole street where she lived would maintain silence when she sang. This indicates something crucial: a sensitivity in both the artist and the people around her. It also gives us an impression that her music had an intimate quality, which may have been personal to her music but was also an indicator of the music she inherited. In some memoirs, we are also told about concerts at the homes of musicians, where they presented ragas with great finesse. The fact that male musicians sang at a higher pitch earlier should not be the basis for judging their sense of voice. I would definitely think that the voice as an instrument of subtle expression in Karnatik music existed much before the microphone. The experience of nuance and subtlety itself is restricted by time; hence, placing a modern interpretation into a historical context may be erroneous.

There does seem to have been a period (early twentieth century) before the advent of the microphone when loud, open, aggressive singing (as understood today) was in vogue. I say this from the recollections of past musicians, and even recordings of some of those musicians in the later part of their lives. This was when kutcheris were being fashioned and sabhas formed in Madras and elsewhere. It was also a time when Karnatik music was being reconfigured for the new world. The devadasis were losing their hold over music and dance, and the nagasvara vidvans were still confined to the temple world. During this period of transition and experimentation with public concert singing, musicians, primarily male, sang with great gusto and 'open' voices so that their music could reach even the last person in the newly configured audience. This was also the time when Harikatha and theatre were very popular. It is likely that the Harikatha vidvans sang with great power, given that the focus of their presentation was not musicality, but a musical–textual–mythological–religious impact. Given the influence of Harikatha on Karnatik music, one wonders whether it played a role even in the idea of vocalization. In this period we hear about actors – who also sang – rendering their songs with great energy and power so that no one in the crowd failed to hear it. How much did these drama musicians influence the idea of the 'singing voice' of Karnatik musicians? We need to ponder these aspects when we try to understand the vocalization of musicians in early twentieth century.

The nagasvara and tavil vidvans never had to battle this issue, as these instruments did not require the microphone for reach. But in the early twentieth century, the nagasvara changed from being a short high-pitched instrument (timiri nagasvara) to a longer and lower-pitched instrument (bari nagasvara). Many attribute this change to Vidvan T.N. Rajaratnam Pillai – and to his assertion that he would render kutcheris like vocalists, seated, using the longer length to rest the instrument on the floor. The lowering of the vocal pitch of male musicians influenced his musicality as well.

No doubt the advent of the microphone resulted in a lowering of the male singer's pitch, but the argument that this change brought increased musical sense or nuance is misleading. That sense existed within the varied contexts in which the music was presented in the pre-microphone era. As male musicians lowered their shrutis, in the male-dominated environment of the times, it became the standard. This came to be seen as the ideal, most comfortable, most pleasing, beautiful shruti for Karnatik music and for the instruments rendering the music. I believe these are forced notions brought about by the action of the dominant group: the male singers. Did Rajaratnam Pillai imitate that behaviour? Quite possibly. Even today, this notion of 'ideal shruti' dominates the narrative of pleasantness and beauty in the tone of voices and instruments.

Quite apart from the question of shruti, there is no doubt whatsoever that the microphone has changed the nature of the Karnatik voice and ear. Initially, there was one microphone at the kutcheri, which was multidirectional and hence could pick up sounds from all the musicians on the stage. Today, we have dedicated mikes for every part of every instrument and the singers. Of course, the technology involved in the making of mikes is far more sophisticated than it was even a decade ago. Technology changes every six months and we can certainly expect more advances, but the impact of this technology on the Karnatik voice needs study.

The major transformation has been in the way sound is produced by singers. Almost all vocalists belonging to the pre-mike era, or even a couple of generations after the emergence of the mike would let the sound flow out of their voice in an open-throated fashion. Open-throated singing does not imply shouting. It is about letting the sound emanate from the voice, allowing for free movement of the muscles involved in voice production. The shape of the mouth is also open, creating a warm, clear and full-bodied sound. Students were always told to follow this technique. It allowed the students to understand the texture, throw and strength of their voices. After a while, students naturally developed techniques to modulate their voice and use its various shades to suit melodic movements.

Even after the advent of the microphone, musicians first learnt to use their voices without it and later to use the mike intelligently to derive the desired result from their rendition. The truth is that many musicians may not yet have mastered the craft of using the microphone. Yes, craft – for I feel that learning the use of the voice is art, while learning the use of the microphone is craft. We cannot substitute the latter for the former.

Today, the microphone is used at all levels, from small informal gatherings, music competitions to kutcheris. It has come to be a prerequisite for music, in turn affecting the voices of Karnatik musicians. Students and young musicians are singing for the mike – conditioned by the tone of the voice heard through the microphone – rather than allowing their voice to naturally express the music and judging its usage and tone without the amplification. This has a serious impact on their voices. Young musicians do not develop an experience of their own voices. With this lack of understanding, they do not explore its potential. In fact, they do not know the sound of their own voice. The voice is adjusted right from the beginning to sound 'beautiful' via the mike. This means that a young musician is adjusting vocal production for the microphone, without dedicating time to first understand the tone, range and power of her own voice. All these are understood only as a reflection via the microphone.

They develop vocal practices that hurt the music – their music and their voice. This has seriously affected the quality of voices we have in Karnatik music. The microphone is necessary if we are to render a concert for an audience of a thousand or more, but can be done away with in smaller settings. Most singers today are unable to render a concert without a mike even in small gatherings. They do not know the technique of comfortable, relaxed singing without amplification. I am not blaming the microphone for this situation, but rather our own lack of understanding of its purpose.

The microphone is meant to help the vocalist communicate her music to a large audience. There are certain qualities that come with its creation. The microphone is not an independent single device; as an acoustic-to-electric transducer, it includes the amplifier, speakers and the various technologies that go into this whole audio system. Depending on the technology used, each amplification system has its own strengths and weaknesses. I will not enter into the analogue and digital debate, except to state that both are necessary tools. Yes, every singer must understand the microphone, how to use it and how it can enhance the musical experience. But unless she understands Karnatik music via her primary expressional tool – the voice – the microphone will be of no use. Vocalists must spend enough time in developing the voice, giving it strength, range, felicity, suppleness and the beauty to create the music. Beauty is not about being sweet, but about being able to express Karnatik music. When the vocalist understands the voice first sans the microphone, she can easily adapt it for use.

It could be argued that this mike-influenced trend is all right – after all, Karnatik music today is heard through audio systems. I beg to differ. The voice and the music must come first, and the use of the microphone must be recognized as a craft that is to be acquired later. The craft can be always acquired, but abuse of the voice due to the lack of self-awareness is very hard to correct.

The impact of the microphone on Karnatik instruments has depended on the instrument in question. I will take a few examples to explain my point. The violin is an instrument that has a limited audience reach, as its volume is determined purely by the pressure of the bow on the string. If more than a certain amount of pressure is applied on the strings, the sound becomes harsh and loses musicality. In Karnatik music, the accompanying violinists tune their violin according to the shruti of the vocalist. But the vocalists and mrdanga artists have a greater reach due to the natural volume that can be generated. In the pre-microphone days, violinists struggled with this problem. They came up with many a solution too. Some resorted to forceful bowing, which was applied not only upon the string they were playing on at that moment, but also on the other strings. This increased the overall volume generated, though it did affect the clarity of the phrase. Mysore Chowdiah (1894–1967) introduced the seven-stringed violin. Most musicians today find this idea and Chowdiah's technique unmusical. What we need to factor in is the fact that he was looking for ways to increase the reach of the violin among the audience. He did not want be drowned out by the other artists on stage. Marungapuri Gopalakrishna Ayyar (d. 1968) even used the phono-violin, which had an attached gramophone player-type speaker.

In any case, violinists were struggling to be heard. To them, the microphone has been a great help. It has lightened their minds by removing anxieties about volume and reach, especially in the modern era of kutcheri music. This has consequentially led to improved techniques, and today, the violin is one of the best representatives of Karnatik music. The violinists who struggled in the pre-microphone days and then moved into the microphone era with older instrumental techniques were brilliant musicians who understood Karnatik music as a fluid melodic identity. Later musicians learnt from the music of the past masters and used the advantages of the microphone, concentrating on improving the technique to change the violin forever.

The vina too benefited from the advent of the microphone, making it adaptable to large auditoriums. Vina maestro S. Balachander took this to another level when he started using the contact mike. This is a small microphone, which is pasted on to the face of the main resonating chamber or 'kudam' of the vina. I will not go into the details of the way it is used, but the intention of this aid was to try and pick up at its source every nuance in every gamaka in a manner in which a regular mike placed a foot away, it was believed, may not be able to do. This was even more important to him because of his technique: extended gamaka-laden phrases on a string that had been plucked only once. This meant that the sound levels towards the end of the phrases were very low. He wanted all this picked up and the contact microphone seemed to be a solution. It did that job, but like a drug that has a major adverse effect, it has led to a different problem.

There is no doubt that any microphone used for the voice or instrument affects the natural sound. But we need to check the extent to which we are willing to surrender natural sounds for amplified sounds. Contact mikes have made the vina sound like a guitar. While listening to a vina kutcheri, we are unable to experience the music of the natural timbre and tone of the vina. This has desensitized the listener to an important quality of the instrument's sound. All things considered, the external mike, in my view, is a better option because its amplification stays closer to the natural timbre of the vina. Like I said before, any microphone removes us one level from the natural tones of voices or instruments. It is up to us to decide to what extent we want the microphone to dictate the sound of the instruments. Violinists also use contact microphones. While the quality of the contact mikes are excellent today, sometimes they can make the violin sound like a wind instrument.

The use of microphones has also affected the mrdanga. Today we have two microphones on either side of the mrdanga, allowing for the sound to be picked up individually. But, oddly enough, in old recordings – where only one mike might have been used for the whole stage – both sides of the mrdanga sounded in great balance. One cannot but mention Palghat Mani Iyer in this context as the musician who refused to perform with the microphone. It is a stand that gives us an insight into the importance that he gave to the idea of natural tone in Karnatik music.

In the last decade, mikes and amplification have been taken to a completely new level with many solo violinists and flautists using computer sound-processing systems. They manipulate the tone of their instruments to suit what they feel is appealing and powerful on the sound processors and then provide a feed to the public audio system. This means that what we actually hear is not the violin or flute, but a computerized interpretation of those instruments. What does this do to the idea of the natural timbre of strings vibrating through the wooden chamber, or the sound of the flute produced by the blowing and fingering of the musician alone? The lack of this natural timbre clouds the music. In fact, the wood, strings, leather and every other part of an instrument contribute to the vividness of Karnatik music. This is missing today, making the experience synthetic.

Do we need this level of digitization, computerization in Karnatik music? What are we conveying in the music? What are we sharing? In continuation of my thoughts on the aesthetics of Karnatik music, I feel that the music does not need to depend on microphone and other audio technologies. These can be used to the extent needed to reach out to people, and not more. But with the ideas that the 'kutcheri' has brought into the music, the aesthetic basis has been blurred, leading to a dependence on technologies like the microphone.

The idea of the instrument's natural sound that I proposed has been sometimes countered by musicians who say that this idea itself is subjective. They point out that the violin itself has been modified to suit Karnatik music. The strings used, tuning system and playing technique are different from that used in Western music. But the naturalness I am referring to is about the sound that the actual instrument produces, rather than that which is modified by an external device or is being processed 'downstream' by other technology. There, in its original state, the violin still sounds like the violin – no matter what kind of music is played. This is natural. When this is morphed by technology, it is not.

Another question to ponder over is whether the use of mikes in Karnatik music has inclined the music to more bravado and, generally, to loudness. We find that most musicians at concerts want and expect the volumes to be increased incrementally. While mostly they only ask for the volume of the feedback speakers on stage to be increased, at times they want volumes to be increased even in the audience section. Each one is shouting over the other to be heard. Where is the music in this? Audibility is important, but if volume levels reach a point where music vanishes, we need to start thinking. It is also necessary to consider how much the idea of the kutcheri – the drama, artificial frenzy, devotional exaggerations and pulsating finishes – itself has actually been the basis for this over-dependence on the microphone. All these elements, or at least some of them, must have existed even before the advent of the microphone, but I have no doubt that it has been used by musicians to artificially heighten them. With the movement of a slider, the volume can be increased, and with contrived movements closer to and away from the mike, impact can be generated. With the combined effort of all the musicians, the microphone can create hysteria. But again, this is not the fault of the device but of its misuse by musicians. This has without any doubt been detrimental to Karnatik music.

Musicians and audiences alike have lost the ability to sense nuance and feeling in music – a fact that has been made obvious and exaggerated through the use of the mike. This results in the loss of silence in our minds as a musical society. The decibel levels are so high that both the musician and the audience today are unable to maintain the silence of the mind that is so essential for the artistic experience.

Mikes, spaces of performance, sound and silence are all about acoustics and what that word means in the context of Karnatik music. Acoustics is not only about sound clarity; more crucially, it is the sense of hearing itself. I mean this in a specific sense – of hearing being about what is to be sensed. This 'what' directs the mind to the 'how'. Karnatik music requires an environment in which the ear can hear what it should hear and the mind is able to receive these signals and give the human being an aural experience.

Once again, we are back at the idea of aesthetics, which is ultimately what must help us decide how the music is to be presented. Once we are clear about that, we can look at the external requirements needed to make sure that the experience is real. Why are we presenting Karnatik music? What does our music contain? How should it be experienced? If music seems to be nourishing technology, rather than technology being of aid to music, we may have got to a hi-tech summit but also reached an aesthetic precipice. Sadly, that is where we are poised today.

Rapture Capture

Beginning with 78 rpm, 33^1/$_3$ rpm and 48 rpm records, spool tapes, long-play records (LPs), cassettes, compact discs (CDs) and mp3s, the recording industry has been the other major influencer on music. Of these different recording systems, spool tapes were primarily used by private collectors and All India Radio to record concerts. Recording gave music the chance for it to be preserved and heard numerous times. While a live kutcheri was only a one-time experience that lived in memory, a recording provided an opportunity for the listener to return to the same kirtana, the same line numerous times at a time of the listener's choosing. It also meant that music could be preserved for posterity and we could analyse and understand the music of musicians from different eras. Radio and television are closely related to the technologies of recording and transmission. In every one of these recording and sharing systems, there are many important advances, but what interests me here is the influence that the idea of recording has had on Karnatik music.

Recording presents some interesting conceptual conflicts. It gives us an opportunity to record rare musicians, styles, compositions and even a certain era of music so that we may try and understand music better. The rare recordings of past masters are a treasure house of aesthetic knowledge, musical genealogy and of chronology even within the life trajectory of the same artist. They give us insights not only into the musicians themselves, but the music that they had in turn inherited and a chance to compare practice with theory. The advantages for study and understanding are innumerable.

At the same time, recording raises an important creative question. The aesthetic evolution of Karnatik music often took place as a subconscious process. When a musician is seriously engaged with the art, over a period of time, her musical ideas change and develop. The musician's own previous renditions and exposure to music marinate in the mind. Each time the musician renders the raga, it comes alive again. The raga is new – a newness that comes from the freshness of the mind and its capacity to reinterpret the raga each time, adding to it new dimensions. The interpretations and musical discoveries come from an internal referencing system that draws from all the experiential influences. These derive their form not just as permutations but as carriers of aesthetic emotion. Therefore, the mind is not creating a formula; it is delving into the music's aesthetics. Even the known phrase is new each time because there is a living experience of aesthetics.

Recording, I believe, can actually affect this process. Over the last six decades or so, with the use of recording systems, musicians are constantly reiterating the music of the past in their minds. This is a reiteration of the technicality and musicality, of course, but it also means that the derived experience is being reiterated. While the process could be viewed as educative, such constant reference can also limit the natural growth process of creativity. The musician must let the received experience lodge in the mind, not as a frozen fixity but an organic impulse. When this occurs, the phrase or ideas that come from the reception are no longer independent technical and aesthetics ideas. They are part of the aesthetic direction of that particular musician.

With the availability of recordings, there is a tendency to constantly listen to the music one is inspired by. Over a period of time, the excessive listening blunts the musician's mind from being creative, trapping it. The end result is that the music really does not grow. This evolution of musical thought and experience is a result of music being in the mind for a period of time without being conditioned by the influencing source. Until even the 1980s, musicians learnt from their gurus and from attending the concerts of other musicians. When they received music in this manner, they were far more attentive, because they knew that they could not press the rewind button. They also treasured what was being received. Over a period of time, these influences became part of their music. This is the process of receiving, living and giving.

Music classes have now become recording sessions rather than places for sharing. The teacher and the student know that every musical phrase is being recorded, and hence the intensity is that much less. We do not realize how much music is actually lost in the process. Learning music is not just about the kirtana, alapana, niraval or pallavi; it is more about what the phrase 'says'. This is the quality of music in the greats that makes them immortal. What it says is not in the recorder, it is in the music as expressed by the teacher. To receive this, we need to be within every moment of the learning. This has all but disappeared. My fear is that, in a few generations, music may be technically more accurate and correct, but less musical.

From the 1980s, recordings became very popular, and especially over the last decade or so, students have had access to great music. But while they are constantly listening to music, their own music is hardly developing. This is leading to a stagnation of creativity. They are only parroting what the recordings give them. If they have a doubt, instead of spending time with their guru, thinking and singing and rediscovering the music for themselves, they just search for a recording. All this has reduced the important process of creativity that is generated from internalization of the learnt and heard music. Recordings become databases instead of being inspirations. This may cause Karnatik music to stagnate over the next century.

Flawless, Soulless

Music is human, organic when it is not sanitized by the idea of flawlessness. The 'flaw' that I refer to is not born out of musical inadequacy or genuine error, but is part of the extrapolation of emotion from the music. This emotion could be derived from melodic or rhythmic improvisation or during the rendition of a composition. Either way, music reaches us only if it is alive. It is alive when it is human; and when it is human, it holds within it this 'flaw'. This is part of the creation of music, and is 'perfection'. Perfection occurs not when every musical movement is in the exact frequency of the sounds, the sahitya is pronounced impeccably, the tala and laya are exactly as measured on the metronome. Real musical perfection is achieved when all the elements of music fuse together. They exist as a single entity and the collective experience creates the world of emotions for all. Within this, there is that flaw, life, sensitivity, expression that makes it music.

As I have said, the nature of a recording is such that a person will return to the same line of music numerous times.

This has made musicians, studios and recording companies believe that everything has to be clean and free of glitches. These are measurements based on tunefulness, rhythmic accuracy and the like, but not on music. Therefore musicians edit and sing only those sections that have to be made glitch-free. Every small shift in laya, in shruti, in a sangati, in pronunciation is corrected in patches. The fact that many of these were part of the musical experience is not relevant. Ultimately, the recorded kirtana or alapana is a patchwork of numerous corrections rather than an animate body of music. The kirtana is perfect in the sense of accuracy, but imperfect as a musical creation. This is the fallout of the recording industry. It has also influenced listeners and what they seek in Karnatik music. Today, many seem to be satisfied with correct musical rendition rather than experiencing a creation of artistic beauty. We want music to be superficially beautiful, without any creases or spots, to sparkle on the surface. But what about what is within? Where music actually has its true being, the surface is not creaseless, spotless or necessarily 'pleasing'. In fact, it is when the surface is flawed, and yet the rendition has the power to move a singer or listener musically, that music comes into its own.

I must emphasize that this whole discussion is about music beyond its technicality; I am taking technical perfection as a given. When it transcends a certain level of skill and ability, all perceived errors cease to be flaws, becoming instead the lifeline of the music. Even an 'error' by a musician immersed in the music is part of a musical experience.

Putting a Price on It

The kutcheri shifted the idea of Karnatik music to the arena of saleability. While court musicians of old did try to please the raja or their patron, I believe that Karnatik music was not a profession in the modern sense. The musician was respected by the patron, not based on every performance, but on the artistic value and honour he brought to the court. This was a valuation of what art gave to the kingdom and the people residing within. The musician's ability was respected as whole, and he was a treasure for the king or the patron. Every time he sang or composed, he was hoping to please the king, but he was also secure in his position based on how he contributed artistically to the court throughout his life. This was his value – not the product of a performance, but a holistic perception of his musicianship. But what of the modern kutcheri? It is the success of every performance that determines the value of the musician. Since success itself is conditioned by applause, which invokes a sense of victory, the musician is blind to the music. The approval of the audience at every kutcheri determines its success, and the ticket-buying public has brought with it a change in the mindset. 'Is this musician worth the money I pay for his concert?' is the unasked but very real concern of the listener. Everyone seeks to be won over by the performance. If we can philosophically reconfigure the thought of success and aesthetically its experience, we just may have success of a different kind.

In a situation where the kutcheri had already reduced the duration of concerts to a few hours, the recording of Karnatik music further complicated the relationship between music and listening duration. For example, the 78 rpm records only had about six minutes of playing time. Musicians tried presenting ragam–tanam–pallavi, alapana and kirtana, niraval and kalpanasvaras within that time. This must have been a serious impediment to music. The condensing of music was done not out of artistic choice, but rather because of the technological limitation. The attempt was to try and present the best aspects of the music. Initially, the musicians decided what the best aspects of the music were, but once the recording market came to be strong, companies had their own opinions. They now had a market, understood their customers and had to provide music that would sell. This is similar to the ticket-buying public, but the recording industry took it to another level. Music was packaged for the record and being redesigned for the market. Soon, this limited time and what the market wanted to enjoy within that duration were dictating the content. Compositions were chosen based on their duration, and sometimes rendition speeds were actually faster in the records. The medium was dictating the content of Karnatik music. The records were very popular, with some renditions of kirtanas setting a benchmark that stands to this day. Thus was born a Karnatik music presentation that was specific to the recording industry.

Right from its birth, the All India Radio (AIR) was an active participant in the propagation of Karnatik music. AIR participated in the time reduction and packaging of Karnatik listening experience. There was a new set of planning and execution that led to the one-hour (or even shorter) kutcheris on the radio. The radio also created packaged programmes based on deities, composers and themes, producing music just like the recording label. The publishing of Karnatik music via the recording labels and its broadcast through All India Radio had the same sort of impact.

With improvements in technology, the duration of recordings increased and the recorded music market developed. This market too had its own perception of what would sell. While some musicians tried to break free of these limitations, by and large the burden stayed. By the 1980s and most of the 1990s, recording companies were discussing the content of a cassette on the basis of the number of kirtanas the musician could accommodate. This was the culmination of over fifty years of the development of a record-listening culture. The companies believed that the more the songs there are, the more value for the money it delivers. It is also possible that the listening public were looking at the number of kirtanas in a cassette. The understanding of Karnatik music began to tilt towards Namasankirtana music. It would be wrong to blame only the recording industry for this. There is no getting away from the fact that this packaging of music was the result of an increase in the number of kirtanas, the longer tukkada section and the content of compositions in the tukkada section of the kutcheri. People had become used to it and wanted more kirtanas in the concert, more devotional fervour, and the tukkadas were appealing. Recording labels merely took advantage of this. Live kutcheris were not often recorded and sold. Most recordings were made inside studios, creating the music specifically for the buyer.

The result is that compilations of kirtanas on specific deities, places of worship, language and many other such themes developed. The parallel existence of what may be called devotional music within the recording industry also influenced the Karnatik content. It reached a point where we did not know the difference between a devotional and a Karnatik album. After a while, even this became passé and recording labels started using background music for Karnatik albums. They were already using this idea in devotional and religious music, and now it came into the art music as well. At one point, the whole idea of Karnatik music was lost, with ghastly presentations that were titled Karnatik music. Musicians too did not know when they were Karnatik musicians, devotional or semi-classical musicians.

But over the last decade or so, there have been some positive developments in the recording industry. Recording companies have released more live concerts, and these have caught buyer interest too. The Internet is a big reason for this change. Over the years, a number of recordings of yesteryear musicians have been shared online by numerous collectors from all over the world. Dedicated groups have been formed to share the music. There are serious copyright issues here that need addressing, but I have to agree that access to these concert recordings has increased the interest in listening to kutcheris instead of studio recordings. The unlimited space available in the virtual world and compressed formats such as mp3 have removed the limitations of time and space. Access to live concerts has rejuvenated the idea of kutcheri in the recording platform. Not only are concert recordings of current musicians being produced, but even rare recordings from the past are being released.

This is a welcome trend and needs to be encouraged. I feel that listening to imperfect recordings (in terms of recording quality) and to unedited live concerts can only have a positive impact on the listening culture of the audience. I am certain that it will improve the sensitivity of listenership and help in making them look for natural music that goes beyond the veneer of surface-level correctness. The idea here is not to appreciate a bad recording, but to recognize the fact that it helps listeners focus on the music and not let packaging define their experience. It is not that thematic recordings have disappeared, they continue to exist. That format is also attempted in the live concert space, one feeding off the other.

Miniature recording devices and the free sharing of music over the Internet have created a completely new set of problems for artists and record labels. Whether music ought to be free or not is a serious debate and can be argued from both sides. While music labels and musicians say that it eats into their revenues, proponents of free music say that it in fact supports the industry and the artists. Newer artists get more exposure, as their music can be uploaded on various websites and streaming channels. Established artists get access to a larger market, even translating into increased audiences at live performances. Beyond these debates and the obvious financial and copyright issues, what really hurts a musician is the attitude of the audience member who records the performance. While recording for educational and research purposes is not a copyright violation, a recording must be made only with the consent of the artists. Today we have numerous listeners attending concerts with tiny recorders. They record the concert and then share it with their friends. At no point are the musicians asked if they are comfortable with that recording. It is a lack of basic courtesy. It feels like something is being stolen from you. When artists perform, they give all that they have to the music and they expect every individual in the audience to respect that, rather than think that the ticket entitles them to abuse their privilege.

Let me also emphatically say that the music being rendered at a concert is the music of the artists on the stage. Even when rendering the compositions of great composers, the very nature of our music makes every rendition a personal one. Therefore, the excuse that musicians are only reproducing the music of Tyagaraja or Muttusvami Dikshitar holds no water. It is no doubt their composition, but every time it is rendered, the rendering is the musician's personal creation. This is the beauty of the oral tradition – a shared ownership.

Each kutcheri is a unique musical experience put together on a particular day by the artists involved. The role of every musician on stage is unique each time and at every moment of a concert. When a Tyagaraja kirtana is rendered at five concerts, it results in five separate art objects. If we listen to each of the recordings, we will realize that the experience is different. This experience is not just about the rendition of the vocalist or main artist, but crucially the exact roles played by every musician in the musical unravelling of the kirtana and the resulting emotive quality. My point is not about just the differences in the rendition of a kirtana or the improvisation, but the collective experience of every part of the kutcheri. It is the moral responsibility of every listener to treasure each kutcheri experience of every musician.

Technology has always been a reality of life. It will and has changed the way we lead our lives, and largely for the better. At the same time, we must have the capacity to take a step back and wonder whether in our excitement to move with the times we have lost an important part of life experience to technology. It is not a question of one being replaced by the other, but one actually morphing into the other. These are the exact questions we need to ask ourselves about Karnatik music. Technology has helped musicians, organizers and connoisseurs, but it has also led to the music itself becoming lifeless. Life in music is not about soft or pretty music. It is the capacity of music to emotively abstract the essence of life for us. This is done by the content and the way it is conveyed. It is this conveying of music which has today almost become hostage to technology. If the vehicle of the music becomes its owner and master, the music will lose its aesthetics. I am afraid that we may be moving in that direction.

Book 3

The History

'The purpose of studying history is not to deride human action, nor to weep over it or to hate it, but to understand it – and then to learn from it as we contemplate our future.'
– Nelson Mandela

23

The Raga's Trail

The aesthetics of Karnatik music are recognized by two principal concepts: raga and tala. They give it aural shape. But raga and tala did not just come about all of a sudden; they have evolved over a long period of time to their present foundational status in art music. To understand how raga and tala became what they are – giving art music the distinctive quality of being an end in itself and absorbing Karnatik music within themselves – it is necessary to trace their journey a task best done through the musical interpretations of successive generations of scholars over time.

I have already dealt with raga aesthetics and identity. It is my view that the raga is an abstract melodic identity. I have tried to suggest a sense of the raga through its various interconnected facets: technical, musical, acoustic, emotional, psychological and, most significantly, through the experience of its abstract aesthetics. But, over the last 200 years, we have moved away from this composite aesthetic towards another idea, based largely on musical theory, and that too we call 'raga'.

Thus we have two raga conceptualizations, both of which are profoundly influential: one that contains natural melodic identities and another born from theoretical possibilities.

Should my interpretation acknowledge the latter as ragas and accommodate them? In order to answer that question, I must explain the difference between the two ideas of raga and what it means to Karnatik music. For this, we need to go back to the way musical concepts were treated in ancient music between the first and the thirteenth centuries, and their later adaptations and interpretations.

Let us first observe the role of certain technical concepts in Karnatik music: frequency, pitch and tone.

Frequency is a measure of sound, not a musical entity. It denotes the number of oscillating waves per second. The frequency is higher when the number of waves is greater and lower when it is smaller.

Pitch, on the other hand, is directly related to the process of hearing and auditory recognition. The individual hearing a pitch recognizes the position of the frequency in auditory terms and may even at this stage begin to perceive its musical relevance. Musical relevance indicates only cognition of a pitch position (svarasthana) through auditory recognition, but pitch is not yet music.

Tone is sometimes used synonymously with pitch and has multiple interpretations. When we refer to tone, we are qualifying the pitch position in terms of melodic emotion, attitude or intent. 'Timbre' is also used in place of tone. Technically, the quality of timbre is the result of the overtones and the resulting harmonics that occur when sound is produced. This varies from instrument to instrument, person to person and even when the same note is played on a single instrument using two distinct techniques. Timbre is an important determinant of the nature of the sound we hear. But in music it is not the fundamental frequency or partial frequencies that are felt, nor even what is broadly termed 'the harmonics'. It is the perceived emotional nature of the instrument or voice and the emotional investment of the musician that connects with us. In human experience, tone and timbre are interchangeable. Another word, texture, too is a very close cousin. Therefore tone, timbre and texture in music manifest feeling as much as they do in spoken or written language. Parallels have been drawn between language and music, with some even calling music 'the language of sound'. But there are serious philosophical problems with such comparisons, especially because of the way language and music are constructed. I make this point here to clarify that I am not drawing that parallel. Just as in speech, tone in music is connected to accent, intonation and vocal inflection, all integral to the svara. Interestingly, the word 'tone' is derived from the Greek 'tonos', which means tension, a stirred state of mind. Tone, in music, is about a stirring as well. It is something calibrated, defined and very specific, born out of the svara's complex identity, which within a raga acquires a context and a connotation. Musical tone is defined by the raga; so you could have a frequency that is neither a pitch nor tone, for example, the sound of a stone hitting the floor, or a frequency that is both a pitch and a tone, svara. Pitch is part of music but not music; tone is musical and this qualitative difference is essential to understand the nature of music.

Music for the Gods, Music for Pleasure

Bharata, the author of *Natya Shastra* (between the second centuries BC and AD), discusses two types of music: gandharva and gana. Gandharva is taken as music meant for the gods, and not to please an audience. This can be interpreted as art music. Gana is a part of his natya, a form of theatre presentation, which included dance, drama, singing and melodies played on chordophones and aerophones, with rhythmic support from membranophones and cymbals. Dattila's treatise *Dattilam* (which is very difficult to date, but is roughly placed a little before or after the *Natya Shastra*) deals only with gandharva music. The musical structures of both gandharva and gana were the same, but since the latter was meant to support and enhance natya, liberties were taken by its practitioners with grammatical rules. 'Gandharva' can also denote the musical fundamentals of both types. I will be using this word in both senses, as ancient art music and as the musical system that governed the music of Bharata, depending on the context. Natya, in later treatises, dating from around the ninth century, was referred to as marga sangita, because sangita had replaced natya as the dominant form of theatre.

Let us now turn to the evolution, adaptations and interpretations of the raga. Shruti was an important fundamental in the music of ancient India. I have earlier described the term 'shruti' as the pitch position that the Karnatik musician chooses as the tonic. This is accurate in terms of contemporary usage and practice, but we need to explore the idea to understand its relevance in ancient music. This will reveal its relevance, or indeed irrelevance, in Karnatik music.

Bharata conducted an interesting experiment using two vinas, later referred to as dhruva vina and chala vina, to establish that there are twenty-two shrutis within one octave. In other words, he could identify twenty-two separate sounds in one octave. In ancient times, 'vina' was a generic term used for stringed instruments, including harp-like ones. I am not going into the details of how this experiment was conducted (although I am fascinated by Bharata's methodology to establish this fundamental basis for their melodic structure). He defines shruti as the least audible difference in pitch between two sounds. Dattilla on his part interpreted shruti as the sounding pitches themselves. If we were to draw two lines as close to each other as possible, but in a way that they are still perceivable as two distinct lines, we could say that they are the closest perceivable lines or that the space between them is the least perceivable space.

Thus a distinct possibility of twenty-two shrutis came to be recognized. And yet the ancients did not consider all of them as individual melodic sounds. This is the difficult part. What the ancients meant was that the twenty-two shrutis are the most closely positioned sounds that could be heard – they are not musical pitch positions. They are only sound possibilities. These twenty-two shrutis were notional sounds contained within the seven svaras in an octave (shadja, rishabha, gandhara, madhyama, panchama, dhaivata and nishada). But how were these notional sounds to be placed within the seven svaras, which actually have musical value? The ancient scholars gave each svara a certain number of shrutis that it held within itself: shadja had four, rishabha three, gandhara two, madhyama four, panchama four, dhaivata three, nishada two. Add these values together and they total twenty-two. Every svara was considered established on its last shruti.

Chart 11: The shrutis in the svara

When each svara is given a certain number of shrutis, what is it exactly that happens? This can be understood in two ways. One, the shadja's musical sound encompasses the four shrutis, which are its value. Two, if we move beyond what is sounded as shadja, we will be rendering shrutis contained within either rishabha or nishada. The musical sound of each svara is said to conceptually occupy the auditory space of the shrutis it contains. This is a brilliant, conceptual idea that establishes many important concepts in music. It differentiates between sound and music and also establishes the role of our auditory system in the whole. Shruti was a beautiful concept that established a tonal theory for both gandharva (art music) and gana (music in natya) and remained in the background.

Shrutis were then the sounds hidden within the seven svaras. This also meant that each svara had only one musical sound. Today, we have a very different system, where ri, ga, ma, dha, ni have multiple svarasthanas, which are given musical identity as svaras. This did not exist in gandharva music, though the opening to such an idea is indicated. In the gandharva system, there were two main methods of arranging svaras according to their shruti values. While the shruti values that I have discussed here were associated with the shadja grama, the other popular arrangement was madhyama grama. The difference between the two lay in the shruti values attributed to some svaras, but the shrutis in both added up to twenty-two. The svaras with the shadja grama shruti values were referred to as shuddha svaras.

As the fixed tonic today, sa enjoys a prominent position in popular perception. Before proceeding any further, I need the reader to forget for a while the fact that art music in India is based on sa, and to imagine each svara as a musical sound that is not dependent on the sa alone for its musical identity. Imagine a musical system where the tonic could change based on the melodic source. In other words, any of the seven svaras could assume the role of the tonic. Let us see how this works in the two gramas.

For this, we must turn to the concept of murchhana, which in Sanskrit has two meanings: stupefying and increasing or augmenting. While a beautiful rendition of a murchhana can be stupefying, it is in the second sense of increasing, growing like the waxing moon, that we use murchhana in gandharva. The arrangement of the seven svaras in a natural ascending and descending order was referred to as a murchhana. Therefore, in shadja grama, you could have seven sequences, each beginning with the different svaras, namely sa, ni, dha, pa, ma, ga, ri. The murchhanas were arranged in descending order. Each sequence had a name. There was another difference between the two gramas. The first murchhana in shadja grama began with sa, while in madhyama grama it began with ma followed by murchhanas in ga, ri, sa, ni, dha, pa. Murchhanas may well have been early sources for melodies used in music. There were also svara sequences that did not have one or two of the seven svaras known as tanas.

Gramas were also the foundation for melodic sources called jatis (pronounced with an elongated 'aa'). One should not confuse the jatis with ragas. At the very basic level, a raga is a single melodic entity, while a jati is a collection of melodic sources. The term 'jati' is used to address a collection of melodic sources, and also refers to each individual source. Also, without one tonic as the basis for all melodies, each jati could provide melodic identities with different tonics. At the same time, the melodic position of every svara was limited by a single pitch position.

I know this is very difficult to grasp because we are habituated to today's music. But for the sake of understanding, we can think of it in terms of Western art music, where every symphony is based on a different pitch position as the tonic of the scale. This is only an example to illustrate the possibility of tonic variability, not to compare the two systems.

At this juncture, I want to introduce two of the many characteristics of svaras used to describe jatis – amsha svara and graha svara. The amsha svara was the tonic svara, and as I have already indicated, could be any of the seven. The graha svara was the one on which a melodic composition based on a jati began. These were among thirteen characteristics used to describe every jati. The most curious aspect of Indian musicology is that, even in the sixteenth century and later, these terms were being used to describe ragas, sometimes indicating an interpretative change of the meaning and in other cases being inappropriately used. All this only caused confusion for musicologists. Very rarely were new musicological terms actually created to describe the music of different periods.

The svaras of the two gramas were recognized as the natural svaras of the respective gramas. This meant that they had shruti values of sa (four), ri (three), ga (two), ma (four), pa (four), dha (three), ni (two) in shadja grama. However, even Bharata mentions the possibility of some svaras acquiring a deviant pitch position in certain jatis. He explains this idea as svara sadharana.

But he is very clear that these svaras are only incidental additional notes that can appear along with their originals, usually in jatis where the respective natural svaras are weak. Having no value of their own, they cannot replace them. The word 'sadharana' itself among its meanings refers to a joint existence of two or more elements. Bharata speaks clearly about two types of sadharana: antara, referring to an augmentation of gandhara by two shrutis, and kakali, referring to the augmentation of nishada by two shrutis. This would mean that gandhara's shruti value becomes four, madhyama's two, and the same with nishada and shadja, because the total number of shrutis must remain at twenty-two.

Chart 12: Shruti values change in these sadharanas, but the sum must stay constant at twenty-two

$$G \qquad M \qquad\qquad\qquad G \quad M$$
$$\bullet \; \bullet \;|\; \bullet \; \bullet \; \bullet \; \bullet\;| \qquad \rightarrow \qquad \bullet \; \bullet \; \bullet \; \bullet\;|\; \bullet \; \bullet\;| \quad \textit{Antara Sadharana}$$
$$2 \qquad\quad 4 \qquad\qquad\qquad\qquad 4 \qquad\quad 2$$

$$N \qquad S \qquad\qquad\qquad\quad N \quad S$$
$$\bullet \; \bullet \;|\; \bullet \; \bullet \; \bullet \; \bullet\;| \qquad \rightarrow \qquad \bullet \; \bullet \; \bullet \; \bullet\;|\; \bullet \; \bullet\;| \quad \textit{Kakali Sadharana}$$
$$2 \qquad\quad 4 \qquad\qquad\qquad\qquad 4 \qquad\quad 2$$

But the sadharana svara can only appear for a fleeting moment and does not disturb the shruti values of the natural svaras in the gramas. The sadharana svaras do not have the status of the natural svaras of the gramas. The gandharva system was a seven-svara system with fixed shruti values attributed to each svara.

Deshi Sangita

The other form of ancient theatre that we are aware of is deshi sangita, which comes to us through treatises like *Brhaddeshi* (ninth century) and *Manasollasa* (AD 1131), culminating with *Sangita Ratnakara* (thirteenth century). The deshi sangita consisted of gita, vadya and nrtta. I will not go into the significance of this at length, but I will stress the point that sangita seems to have been oriented towards music rather than theatre. While many musicologists look at deshi as having developed from marga sangita, which is Bharata's natya, I would prefer not to take that stance. It is quite possible that deshi existed alongside marga sangita, but was recorded later as a separate system. With deshi gaining popularity or social importance later, scholars may have put it down into the texts. While doing so, the scholars made sure that they created descriptions of Bharata's marga, thus giving deshi historical validity and relevance. More significant is the fact that they used Bharata's musicological tools to understand its music, even though their writing reveals that they were aware of the disconnect between deshi and marga. The reverence to Bharata is seen across all these treatises.

Abhinava Gupta's commentary on *Natya Shastra*, which can be dated to the eleventh century approximately, is also important as it gives an idea about later developments in marga sangita. It would not be incorrect to say that Abhinava Gupta himself must have been influenced by the dominant music of his period, which may have been the music in deshi.

Bharata's gandharva music can be understood as classical. Then what about the music in deshi? Many writers tend to categorize deshi as folk. I think this is a mistake. It could have been independent of the marga tradition, or may have evolved from it. Either way, it was not social or community music. This is clear from a study of the systematic organization within the music. Some scholars may argue that there are some songs of social nature in deshi music. But I make my point on the basis of its grammatical and aesthetic structure.

Sarngadeva's treatise *Sangita Ratnakara* is taken to be the seminal text on Indian music that bridges the gap between Bharata and later scholars. I tend to look at it as defining an era of transformation. I do not believe that Karnatik or Hindustani music directly evolved out of *Ratnakara*, but rather that it established some basic foundations of later Indian art music.

Coming back to shrutis and svaras, both Abhinava Gupta and Sarngadeva expanded sadharana to include shadja and madhyama sadharana. Here svara positions were both augmented and diminished. We then come across the terms 'shuddha svaras' and 'vikrta svaras'. Shuddha svaras were the positions of the svaras as seen in the shadja grama, and vikrta svaras were those that occupied other shruti positions or had their shruti value altered due to a shift in the position of an adjacent svara. So we had four possible sadharanas and more svaras taking positions other than the shuddha. Second, it becomes clear that the altered svara positions were accepted as svaras by themselves and could exist without iteration in their respective shuddha positions. Sarngadeva describes seven shuddha svaras and twelve vikrta svaras. The idea of shruti was losing its notionality and becoming an actual sounding-pitch position. This meant that more 'notional' shrutis were becoming operational svarasthanas, transforming into svaras in music.

The other significant development was the fixing of the tonic. Unlike the jati melodies of gandharva, where each jati could have a different tonic svara, rendered in its own pitch position, in deshi the tonic was moving towards being fixed at one pitch position. Every raga had its own tonic svara, but they were rendered on this fixed pitch. In a post-ratnakara development, the music as a whole and the ragas were determined by the shadja or sa as the fixed tonic. We are going to leave svaras and shrutis here, and come back to them when we discuss the development of ragas from the early sixteenth century.

The Gamakas

An important feature of Karnatik music are the gamakas, which are a part of the musical expression of svaras. Gamakas are not mentioned in *Natya Shastra*, either by way of a technical description or in terms of their aesthetic value to music. But Bharata does talk about different types of alankaras, and some of them seem to be similar to the concept of gamakas. Alankaras are used in varnas, which are melodic movements that may ascend, descend, remain in the same place or perform a mix of these actions. Alankaras and gamakas share some names in common – kampita, for instance. Therefore, we could say that Bharata's alankara includes gamaka.

The term 'gamaka' is found in *Sangita Ratnakara*, with a description that is close to the contemporary understanding of this essential Karnatik quality. Sarngadeva describes a gamaka as 'a shaking of tone that delights the listener'. We should understand shaking to be a wide term that includes various forms of movements to the svara's tone. Another scholar, Parshvadeva, in a visual description says that a gamaka is a tonal shade arising from a svara using the shrutis of another svara. This effectively means that, in a gamaka, the svara is moving beyond its own pitch position and touching upon other svaras. Sarngadeva mentions fifteen types of gamakas. We may relate to a few descriptions of gamakas, but many do not directly match our present understanding.

The Raga Idea

Were the seeds of the idea of the raga sown in *Natya Shastra*?

Neither in *Natya Shastra* nor in *Dattilam* do we find 'raga' used in the technical or aesthetic sense that we use it today. Bharata even uses raga while describing the tuning of instruments by musicians for the gandharva (art music) that preceded a natya presentation. But the use of raga as a melodic source is only found in treatises about deshi music. First, the raga is used in conjunction with grama, calling it grama raga. The grama ragas did not belong to deshi, but were considered part of marga sangita. It is, therefore, possible that these were jati-based melodic concepts, or they may have been independent melodic sources that replaced jatis during later developments in marga sangita. But even if the raga was part of marga sangita, it was not considered for use in gandharva, but rather as melodic sources for natya. Raga, therefore, was first used as part of gana and not gandharva. Second, grama ragas apart, Sarngadeva also mentions upa-ragas and ragas, and names many under each category. These three categories of ragas are quite well known by his time. He also describes various singing styles of grama ragas and classifies them accordingly. He mentions sub-varieties of grama ragas and upa-ragas called bhasha, vibhasha and antarabhasha. These may have been styles of singing grama ragas that later evolved into ragas in their own right.

While discussing deshi sangita, Sarngadeva introduces us to deshi ragas. I would say that this is when we come a little closer to what we today call raga. Yet, we cannot be sure about the direct melodic descent of any of the ragas that developed from the sixteenth century. The deshi ragas are said to have evolved from grama ragas and uparagas, and are classified as raganga, bhashanga, kriyanga and upanga. In *Sangita Ratnakara*, Sarngadeva describes only deshi ragas that were popular during his time. There are enough indications in the treatise for us to believe that deshi music was moving towards fixing sa as the tonic or had already done so.

We have briefly gone through the journey of svaras, gamakas and ragas until the twelfth century. I have tried to capture the most important elements of ancient music, which were reinterpreted during the development of Karnatik music. These musicological ideas on shruti, description of jatis, gamaka and raga play a very important role in the raga's later theoretical development.

If we were to compare *Natya Shastra* with *Sangita Ratnakara*, it is clear that in deshi sangita music had greater focus as compared to marga sangita. Today, we use the term 'sangita' to refer only to music, but in the context of ancient music, it referred to deshi theatre. But even during the twelfth century, beyond theatre, there were renditions and musical contests in courts of only deshi music. Music as an independent presentation was already developing.

Other treatises written between the twelfth and sixteenth centuries too discuss the developments in Indian music. These include *Sangitaraja* of Kumbha, Maharana of Mewar; *Kalanidhi*, a commentary on *Sangita Ratnakara* by Kallinatha and *Sangitopanishat-saroddhara* of Sudhakalasa. By the fourteenth century, deshi music had become an independent presentation and was not just part of a theatrical production, nor a preamble to theatre. This does not mean that art music was a post-ratnakara creation. The idea of art music had been there even in pre-*Natya Shastra* days.

One of the fascinating aspects of literature on Indian music until the thirteenth century is the cohesive nature of its discussions. It covered the whole range from art, aesthetics, beauty, dance, theatre and, of course, music. It even touched upon the philosophical underpinnings of these. Over time, texts became purely technical and analytical, and focused only on the musical aspects, unlike the wider scope and engagement of many of the earlier works. Gopalanayaka (fourteenth century) is said to be the architect of a complete musical system and a presentation that was independent of theatre. He may have influenced or inspired the birth of the chaturdandi system of art music, which later acquired a wider reference range on account of the *Chaturdandi Prakashika* (1620). I will come to this in detail in a later essay.

The Mela Period

The next phase of raga development can be referred to as the mela period (sixteenth to twentieth century) and is directly connected to the raga as it exists today. There are numerous treatises written all over the country from the sixteenth century, but my focus will be on the information that we can gather from texts that pertain to south Indian ragas. The term 'mela' refers to an assembly, union or grouping. Here it refers to a grouping of ragas. This term is said to have been first used by Vidyaranya in his *Sangitasara* in the fourteenth century. This information comes from Govinda Dikshita, who authored *Sangita Sudha* (1614). No copy of *Sangitasara* is extant, nor has the name been mentioned in any other texts.

By the time we come to the mela era, Indian music has become tonic-based, with sa as the tonic, its fifth pa also serving as a fixed svara. The variability of each of the other svaras in terms of its pitch position (svarasthana) is also established. The svaras – ri, ga, ma, dha,ni – had more than one pitch position each. The primacy of gamakas as being part of the raga concept had also become well established. It is the coming together of these various concepts that gave us the raga. Despite rapid changes in the music, the terminologies used continued to be drawn from older texts, and the theoretical understanding was based on the music of an earlier age, especially as reflected in *Sangita Ratnakara*. This caused, and continues to be a cause for, a great deal of confusion in musicology.

I will now try and go through the various phases of the mela period without getting caught up in the different treatises.

'Pitch' and Svara Relationship in the Mela

The shruti concept was integral to ancient music because each svara had only one referred pitch position and the tonic svara (amsha svara) varied, depending on the jati. In this system, shrutis gave stability to each svara. This was precisely why shrutis were notional ideas – about the relationship between each svara – not sound pitches. In the newer system, this relationship was provided by the fixed tonic, namely shadja. The moment the shadja was fixed, every svarasthana was positioned on the basis of the sa. The intra-relations between the other svarasthanas were also on the basis of the sa. This automatically provided the opportunity to explore other shrutis in an octave as possible svarasthanas. By now, shrutis had become irrelevant.

The purpose of the mela concept is to find a way to collate and categorize all the ragas that were in vogue. The easiest way to achieve this objective was to categorize them on the basis of the svarasthanas. Pitch positions were not musical devices; they were the technical basis for svaras. The early authors seem to have been very conscious of the fact that music was based on practice and that the role of the theoretician was to provide the theory for practice. The first task was to ascertain all the possible pitch positions in practice. By this time, shruti was no longer a notional idea; shrutis were actual pitch positions or svarasthanas that could be used in music. This meant that there could be twenty-two svarasthanas since there were twenty-two so-called shrutis. But the early mela theoreticians were careful to convert only those shrutis under each svara that were being used as svarasthanas in ragas. Consequently, melas were created only when there were existing ragas that could be classified under them. This was commendable, but retention of the term 'shruti' and the continued harping on the relevance of the twenty-two shrutis and the number of shrutis attributed to each svara within the music was flawed.

The early mela period theoreticians, musicologists and scholars created multiple sets of the seven svarasthanas, each containing one combination used in music. Each set was called a mela. Under each set, they placed the ragas that contained these svarasthanas. I am taking care to use the word 'svarasthanas' rather than 'svaras'. As I explained earlier, svaras have a far more complex aesthetic identity, while svarasthana is only a pitch position. The scholars were aware that many ragas did not have all seven svarasthanas, but that did not stop them from allocating a mela for those ragas. All ragas that had a set of svarasthanas assigned to one mela were called janyas, meaning they were born from the mela. But in fact, the meaning was that they were born from that set of seven svarasthanas. The minimum number of svaras in a raga was five.

But they were confronted with another problem. How were they to signify a mela? They needed a name. The solution was simple. Each mela was referred to by the name of the most popular janya raga categorized under it. The raga given the title name had no special significance. Ramamatya, one of the earliest authors in the mela period, mentions fifteen melas in *Svaramela Kalanidhi* (1550).

The ragas that were being classified were naturally evolved melodic identities. They were born out of musical practice. Some of the raga names can be traced back to *Sangita Ratnakara* and could have evolved from deshi ragas. Irrespective of whether the ragas of this era were born from deshi ragas or not, they were abstract aesthetic forms that were created by practice and not theory.

From this initial stage of classification, many things changed. The mela's objective was to create a classification system that could place all existent ragas. A mela was not considered a melodic form or even a melodic source. But soon theoreticians began to feel that if there were fifteen sets of seven svarasthanas (abstracted from the ragas in practice), we could mathematically compute many more melas based on the variable svarasthanas for every svara. This computation was not based on the svarasthanas in use – the combinations were a purely mathematical exercise. This meant that the combinations of seven svarasthanas were not always reflected in any existent raga, thereby rendering these melas redundant. The number of svarasthanas extracted from the twenty-two shrutis was variable, depending on the region the theoretician belonged to and his own approach to shrutis. Nevertheless, the whole idea of shuddha svaras and vikrta svaras was borrowed from *Ratnakara*. The shuddha svaras were still being related to the shruti values mentioned by Bharata. Each musicologist came up with different numbers and names for the vikrta svaras they had included. By now, vikrta svara meant a shuddha svara with an augmented or diminished svarasthana. As you can see, once many svarasthanas were functional, the idea of shruti was irrelevant.

Taking into account the total number of svarasthanas they had determined, each one worked out different combinations of melas and came up with different numbers. Pandarika Vitthala in *Sadragachandrodaya* (1583–89) came up with ninety possible melas, Somanatha in *Raga Vibodha* (1609) worked out the possibility of 960. Obviously, Somanatha had taken into account many more vikrta svaras and hence was able to compute many more melas. But both recognized that their number was only a mathematical computation, as only nineteen melas in *Sadragachandrodaya* and twenty-three melas in *Raga Vibodha* were functional, i.e., janya ragas existed only for these melas. The rest were only mathematical combinations of svarasthanas with no musical relevance. In spite of their theoretical prowess, these scholars did not seek to overwrite music practice. But the theoretical possibility they outlined opened a window to drastic changes in the way ragas were treated in later mela texts.

Early Commentators and Venkatamakhin

Govinda Dikshita, a musicologist, scholar and administrator in the court of Kings Achyutappa Nayak (1560–1614) and Raghunatha Nayak (1600–1634), did not fall into this trap of computation. He classified fifty janya ragas under fifteen melas. But he raised another issue that had not been considered till then. Scholars referred to ragas that had all the seven svaras as sampurna ragas. It did not matter in what order or phraseology these seven svaras appeared, as long as they were part of the raga. Govinda Dikshita raised the point that only a raga that had all seven svaras could be given the privilege of being the title-holder for a mela. But he did not follow his own diktat in the case of two melas. This issue that he raised later became a rule.

Govinda Dikshita's son Venkatamakhin was the most important musicologist in south India. Within six years of his father authoring the *Sangita Sudha*, Venkatamakhin wrote the *Chaturdandi Prakashika*. Before I go into the classification system he adopted, I would like to point to the startling fact that his views on the approach to ragas differed radically from his father's. We usually associate such forthright disagreements with modern thought, but it has always existed in scholastic discussions.

Venkatamakhin followed the lead of scholars like Somanatha in theoretically computing melas. He accepted the position that there were a total of twelve svarasthanas with sixteen names, as some pitch positions were shared by two svaras. Using these sixteen possibilities, he computed a total number of seventy-two melas. His approach to classification was elegant and easy to comprehend. He split the seventy-two into two parts. The first half had the lower variety of ma (shuddha madhyama), and the second the higher variety (prati madhyama). Each mela was created by altering the svarasthanas of ri, ga, dha and ni, keeping shuddha madhyama constant for the first thirty-six and creating another set by keeping the prati madhyama constant. Using ma as the separating factor was convenient, as it is the only svara that has two varieties in pitch position. With sa and pa being constant, all the other svaras have at least three different svarasthanas.

Chart 13: The different svarasthanas of ri, ga, ma, dha and ni
Rishabha – 3 Varieties

Position	Svara	Name
2	Ri	Shuddha Rishabha (R1)
3	Ri	Chatushruti Rishabha (R2)
4	Ri	Shatshruti Rishabha (R3)

Gandhara – 3 Varieties

Position	Svara	Name
3	Ga	Shuddha Gandhara (G1)
4	Ga	Sadharana Gandhara (G2)
5	Ga	Antara Gandhara (G3)

Madhyama – 2 Varieties

Position	Svara	Name
6	Ma	Shuddha Madhyama (M1)
7	Ma	Prati Madhyama (M2)

Dhaivata – 3 Varieties

Position	Svara	Name
9	Dha	Shuddha Dhaivata (D1)
10	Dha	Chatushruti Dhaivata (D2)
11	Dha	Shatshruti Dhaivata (D3)

Nishada – 3 Varieties

Position	Svara	Name
10	Ni	Shuddha Nishada (N1)
11	Ni	Kaishiki Nishada (N2)
12	Ni	Kakali Nishada (N3)

Venkatamakhin also realized that all these melas were, essentially, possibilities and there was no janya raga that could fit into them. But he was adventurous. He placed ragas in eighteen out of the seventy-two melas, making them functional, and experimented with one more. Using the svarasthanas computed for the mela that would occupy the position fifty-eight, he created a raga that was only a combination of seven svarasthanas and called it 'deshisimharavam'. This was an artificial exercise, as he did not have a melodically created raga entity that possessed these svarasthanas. Naturally evolved ragas were not created after determining the svarasthanas. Rather, they grew out of the melodic movements that they contained. As the melodic possibilities grew, the contours of a raga expanded; yet the raga itself remained cohesive, aesthetically and cognitively. It is from these existent ragas that the mela was created or determined. Venkatamakhin was reverse-engineering the process. This step changed the idea of raga and raised a crucial question: can a raga be artificially created by manipulating svarasthanas? Venkatamakhin referred to the raga that held the title for the mela as the raganga raga. Even here, the raganga raga was only a janya raga to the mela. Venkatamakhin left fifty-three melas untouched. He, therefore, had nineteen melas, eighteen of which contained organic, natural janya ragas and one an engineered raga, deshisimharavam.

I must now briefly dwell on how the ragas and their ingredients were described in these texts. Many treatises continued to use the ageless *Sangita Ratnakara* as the base for their descriptions of ragas. This process included categorizing svaras in each raga according to their role as graha (tonic svara), amsha (dominant svara), nyasa (svara on which melodic movements can end), alpatva (svara used rarely), bahutva (svara used in proliferation) and the like. There are two interesting aspects to this. In the ancient period, it was the amsha svara that referred to the tonic, but now the term 'graha' replaced amsha. But what is of interest here is that though the music system had changed and was completely based on a fixed tonic (shadja or sa), svaras other than sa continued to be called graha svara in many ragas. This was part of the *Sangita Ratnakara* vocabulary that almost all scholars carried unquestioningly – in spite of the fact that the practice of the time did not reflect this nature. Ragas were also described on the basis of other characteristics. These included the creative possibilities they provided, inferred in the uttama (superior), madhyama (moderate), adhama (inferior) descriptions, sonant (vadi), consonant (samvadi), dissonant (vivadi) and assonant (anuvadi) svaras in the ragas, the number of svaras in the raga sampurna (seven), shadava (six), audava (five) and the gamakas used in the ragas. Most scholars used 'arohana' and 'avarohana' only to indicate an ascending or descending melodic movement in the raga. Later this changed, causing a serious shift in raga perception. Arohana became a summary of the raga's melodic movement, commencing from the madhya sthayi shadja to the tara sthayi shadja. Avarohana indicated the reverse movement.

The second Maratha king, Shahaji of Tanjavur (1684–1712), wrote his musical treatise *Ragalakshanamu* around eighty years after Venkatamakhin's *Chaturdandi Prakashika*, but he seemed to be unaware of this landmark work. *Ragalakshanamu* does not theorize on the possible number of melas and mentions twenty melas with janya ragas. Shahaji made a few important contributions. In *Ragalakshanamu*, we notice that all the ragas that are the title-holders of the melas have seven svaras. This seems to have become a condition-precedent. It was also the first text to use the term 'melakarta' to address the raga that held the title name. As we know, the mela is only a collection of seven svarasthanas taken from the janya ragas contained in it. The raga that gave the mela its name was originally decided on the basis of its popularity. But post-*Ragalakshanamu*, it came to be based on the fact that it had seven svaras. Nonetheless, even this raga was still a janya of the mela. Therefore, the use of 'melakarta' for the raga that held the title can be quite misleading, even though in its original context it may have meant only 'name giver'. *Ragalakshanamu* also came up with the imaginative idea of classifying ragas on the basis of musical aesthetics, as ghana (rigid and dense), naya (soft and fluid) and deshiya (from other regions).

In the early eighteenth century, Venkatamakhin's descendent Muddu Venkatamakhin decided to artificially create ragas for the remaining fifty-three of the seventy-two possible melas computed by his ancestor Venkatamakhin. He used the same method that had been used to create the raga deshisimharavam. This meant that all seventy-two melas were functional. The raganga raga needed to have only the seven svaras. It was around this time that arohana and avarohana came to be used to define the melodic structure of a raga. This created artificial janya ragas that were formulated from the non-functional melas. As these ragas had no aesthetic component to their identity, the simplest way to describe them was to mention the svaras that appeared in their arohana and avarohana. These svaras were after all based on the computed svarasthanas. This was another important marker in raga history. Even under the constructed melas, Muddu Venkatamakhin placed older, naturally evolved ragas. He not only gave names to all the fifty-three raganga ragas that he constructed, but also altered the names of older raganga ragas. This was done to accommodate the ingenious syllabo-numeric memory system that was evolved to identify the number of the mela from the name of the raganga raga, a system called the katapayadi samkhya.

As I move to the next major development, I must point out that the exercise of computation resulted in ragas being reinterpreted in terms of only the svaras they contained, rather than the aesthetic form of their melodic movements. This is also revealed in the use of arohana and avarohana as the defining characteristic of ragas. We must realize that once these systems came into practice, they were also being placed upon ragas that had evolved organically and were not determined by the arohana or avarohana. All ragas were being looked at through the prism of the arohana and avarohana, thus deconstructing their natural melodic features. We will look into the repercussions of this a little later.

Mela, Melakarta and Meladhikara

In the eighteenth century, we come across another treatise called *Sangraha Chudamani* (1750–1800). We know very little about the treatise or its author Govinda (not to be confused with Govinda Dikshita). This treatise completely sterilized the concept of raga and mela. Govinda combined the ideas of sampurna along with arohana and avarohana. In doing so, he decided that the ragas that held the name of the mela must have all the seven svaras in sequential order both in the arohana and avarohana. He also created a new term for the melakarta: meladhikara (the raga that has authority over the mela). Most ragas that evolved naturally did not have svaras in linear sequence and could not be meladhikaras. Only six older ragas were given the meladhikara status. Older natural ragas were listed within artificial melas whose meladhikara was a synthetic raga. The status of the raga that held the title for the mela had thus changed from being the most popular raga to the one that had authority over the mela. Initially it was a janya raga, then melakarta and now meladhikara. These were literal and metaphorical changes. The change was also artificial, because the 'title-holding' raga was not meant to have any real authority over the mela and was only determining its name.

Returning to the Two Ideas of Raga

The final transformation was the use of the term 'janaka raga' for melakarta or meladhikara raga. This totally changed the role of the raga that took the name of the mela. It was now looked upon as the raga that gave birth to the derivatives – janya ragas. As we have seen, many of the so-called janaka ragas were only artificial combinations of the seven svarasthanas, yet they were considered to have given birth to ragas that had existed for over 300 years. Therefore, natural, older ragas were now considered to have been derived from a raga, which was a product of the manipulation of a set of seven svarasthanas. This was a complete inversion of raga evolution. Unfortunately, this thought did not remain confined to theory but also had a profound influence on musicians, thereby seriously disconnecting raga from music, choosing instead to stay wedded to theory.

Two musical schools evolved on the basis of Muddu Venkatamakhin and Govinda. The former was followed by

Muttusvami Dikshitar and the latter is said to have been followed by Tyagaraja. In the Muddu Venkatamakhin system, as we have already noted, the raganga raga needed to have only the seven svaras, but not necessarily in sequential order. Hence many of the fifty-three artificially created raganga ragas had svaras that were not linear in construction in arohana or avarohana. Grudging Muddu Venkatamakhin no respect, I must say that all these creations would have remained as text had Muttusvami Dikshitar not composed kirtanas in them. As we have discussed earlier, a raga does not come to life unless a vaggeyakara endows it with a composition. It is because of Muttusvami Dikshitar that all the artificial scales created by Muddu Venkatamakhin came to be established. But are they in fact ragas?

Tyagaraja is said to have used the system created by Govinda. Though Tyagaraja does not directly refer to either the treatise or the author, this deduction is made on the basis of the ragas used by him. Govinda had created a completely linear scale as the meladhikaras of the melas – and these were brought to life by Tyagaraja.

If we were to study the older natural ragas, we would find that their melodic form is not linear. This works in the raga's interest. It is the divagating, curved movement of melody that gives to raga its character and, in a sense, its colour. 'Raga' in Sanskrit, of course, carries the connotation of colour, as also of feeling and emotion. It is this quality of the raga to take a wander, so to say, and to digress that also provides the possibility for a further expansion in its melody. When a raga is straitjacketed with a linear sequence of svaras, it becomes almost impossible for it to develop the curvatures and meandering phraseology that define its character. Though I do not accept the efforts of Muddu Venkatamakhin and Govinda in principle, I feel that Muddu Venkatamakhin at least used his knowledge of raga aesthetics and recognized that his synthetic creations needed to be non-linear in form. Tyagaraja not only used Govinda's linear ragas, but himself went on to create many scales artificially, with less than seven svaras and svaras in non-linear form in the arohana, avarohana or both.

In the post-Tyagaraja era, many composers have constantly tried to devise new synthetic ragas by dropping some svaras or creating non-linear formulations from their janaka ragas.

The meladhikara system attributed to Govinda is now accepted as the standard in Karnatik music. This is unfortunate, as it has also led to the enforcement of raga characteristics from this system on to ragas in Muddu Venkatamakhin's system. To this end, the ragas used by Dikshitar were altered to fit into Govinda's classification. Sometimes Muddu Venkatamakhin's ragas have been completely ignored and Dikshitar's compositions have been retuned into ragas of the other system. Our understanding of Muddu Venkatamakhin's treatment of ragas comes from the magnificent treatise written by Subbarama Dikshitar, namely, *Sangita Sampradaya Pradarshini* (1904). It is also true that many ragas found in both classification systems are treated very differently, giving one raga two distinct melodic identities. Instead of celebrating multiple interpretations, we have ignored Muddu Venkatamakhin's system and considered only the ragas as described by Govinda and followed by Tyagaraja to be the standard. Though I have been critical about the mela developments, the fact is that we have accepted the mela system, and given that, we should at least have two mela systems of classifications. Instead, we have a unified one.

This journey of the raga and its classification presents some important challenges and contradictions. If we were to take into account all the types of melodic sources, we have today a collective body of melodic sources that we call raga.

Organic and Artificial

Ragas that evolved from melodic phraseology developed through time and remained cohesively held together by the aesthetic cognition of unity. These ragas may have seven svaras or even less. They cannot be purely defined by the sequence of the svaras in the arohana or avarohana. Examples of this are surati, ritigaula, anandabhairavi, gaula and saveri. There are ragas that were artificially created containing all seven svaras in sequential order in the arohana and avarohana, such as simhendramadhyamam, dharmavati, vachaspati and ramapriya. Then there are ragas that were artificially created containing all the seven svaras non-sequentially positioned and determined by the arohana or avarohana. For example, karnaranjani, nalinakanti, amrta behag, kokilavarali and malavi. There are also ragas that have less than seven svaras, which are in sequence in arohana and avarohana. Examples are jayantasena, mandari and jayamanohari. And now we even have synthetic ragas that have just three svaras. Lastly, there are the natural and organic ragas that have been incorporated from Hindustani music, like behag, hamir kalyani and sindhubhairavi.

With these conceptual changes to raga and the adaptation of many forms of contrived svara sequences as ragas, we are faced with an aesthetic challenge. Do all these different types of ragas have the abstract nature that is a creation of the raga's musical heritage, phraseology and its psychological recognition? An aware listener can sense this by listening to just one phrase. In an artificial raga, the musician and the listener have to constantly connect with all the svaras present and their sequence. They cannot transcend this level of engagement and move to the real level of aesthetics of phrase forms. Why is such transcendence important?

Let me suggest an answer to that question. A raga belongs not to the literal but to the inferred. The inferred comes alive when the perceiver can be invited into the sound of the raga, which is born from every svara, every phrase, every phrase connection and the raga as a whole. This experience is only possible when the listener does not need to be reminded of the technical nature of the svara or its sequence. Synthetic ragas lack the abstractive nature both in form and in the way they can be received. In order to try and conceptually elevate these ragas, musicians have sought to artificially impose phrase forms on them. But almost always, these imposed aesthetic markers do not succeed as the raga is, at its base, only a collection of svarasthanas. Whether the musician is rendering an alapana, kalpanasvaras or a composition, the melodic flow has to constantly traverse all the svaras present in the raga. It is only their reiteration that provides ragas with an aesthetic identity. Whether they are pleasant to the ear or not is not the question. Do they aesthetically form a raga? The naturally evolved ragas are not defined just by the svarasthanas and their order. They come to life as aesthetically connected phrases. Within this is the musical heritage and the psychological connection. Musical heritage does not refer to theoretical record, but the aesthetic continuum of the complex melodic identity that is a product of music.

Among the various types of artificially created ragas, I find that the ones with a non-linear sequence of svaras in the arohana, avarohana or both provide the most possibility of aesthetic abstraction. Perhaps this is the result of the non-sequential positioning of the svaras. Naturally formed phraseology is based on melodic flow and combined form. This leads to important phrases being such that the svaras are non-sequential, jumbled, skipped or repeated. In an artificially created raga with non-sequential svaras, the presence of a complex pattern in the arohana or avarohana immediately provides a phrase that can be used as a marker. I also find that the presence of meandering or non-sequential phrases in these ragas provides the possibility for a musician to use the available non-sequentiality to create more such phrases by exploring openings that exist at the point of melodic turn fixed by the non-sequentiality. That said, it is still limited by the raga being confined to the arohana and avarohana.

Ragas have regularly been adopted from other musical systems, such as Hindustani music. All these are complex raga forms and are defined by various phrases, not just by arohana and avarohana. Until the early part of the last century, when these ragas were adapted, musicians and composers gave them an abstract identity within Karnatik music. Unfortunately, most ragas that have been absorbed from Hindustani music over the past three or four decades have also been broken down to an arohana and avarohana format and rendered like synthetic ragas. This is a serious destruction of the raga from its Hindustani form and a lack of serious adaptation within Karnatik music.

The meladhikara system has had a serious effect on natural ragas, because they have been placed as janya ragas of artificially created ones. Every phrase found in the compositions in these ragas has a history. Their history exists in the induction of each phrase or movement and its integration into the raga's melodic whole. These are recorded in compositions and treatises from the mela period. With the word 'janya' indicating 'evolved from', musicians and musicologists forget the antiquity of the natural ragas. They have tried to cleanse these ragas of phrases and svaras that may be in divergence with their synthetic janaka raga. It is plain to see that this is an imposition, because the natural ragas are aesthetically independent, and have not evolved from the janaka ragas. The only reason they have been placed within the mela system is to bring them within the fold of a certain classification. The other problem is that the arohana and avarohana are determining raga features. This leads musicians and musicologists to create an arohana and avarohana to summarize ragas. With natural ragas, that is very difficult to do as multiple phrases and different approaches to the same svaras give these ragas their nature. It is unfortunate that, by pressing this rule on to older ragas, musicians and musicologists have boxed those ragas into an enforced arohana and avarohana, stripping them of history and aesthetics.

Gamakas are part of the life of every raga and these have also evolved through the mela period. They seem to have become more and more complex, giving Karnatik music an intricate melodic expression. In its present form, every svara is fluid and – depending on the raga and phrases – moves, merges and blends with every other. Many shrutis have become svarasthanas, and all the auditory space between these svarasthanas is used by the svaras as part of their gamaka forms.

What role does shruti play in aesthetics? Absolutely none. Yet, even now, musicologists and musicians try and determine the position of the twenty-two shrutis within this fluid identity. Within the melodic movements there are possibly more than twenty-two hidden shrutis, but it is of no consequence. The svarasthanas today provide clarity to the various manifestations of svaras and all the svaras are determined in relation to the tonic sa.

The Tamil Tradition

Some readers may feel that I have completely ignored the Tamil tradition in looking at the development of raga. But the fact is that today's Karnatik music is based on Sanskrit theorization. Ancient music in Tamil land is understood through *Silappadigaram*, which dates back to approximately the second century. That is essentially a love story, but built into it are descriptions of the various Tamil kingdoms, their cultures, art and music. The truth is that music-related information in this epic is scattered, brief and only indicative. It is from the commentaries, *Arumpada urai* and *Adiyarkunallar's urai* (between the ninth and eleventh centuries) that we learn about the music in *Silappadigaram*.

We do know that right from around the sixth century, deshi music had probably influenced and merged with the music in Tamil land. Therefore, expecting a clear separation between Tamil and Sanskrit music is not sensible. 'Pann', often considered to be the parallel to raga, has also had different meanings. The pann mentioned in connection with the music in *Silappadigaram* must have been very different from that said to be used to render the Tevarams around the eleventh century. Ancient music interpreted from *Silappadigaram* seems close to the music described in *Natya Shastra* and *Dattilam*. Karnatik music evolved during the Vijayanagara Empire and the Maratha kingdoms. This made the music Sanskrit- and Telugu-based, not to forget the influence of the Kannada bhakti saints. Tamil composers in the Karnatik tradition also followed the ragas and talas established through these various influences.

Raga Melody and Theory

The mela system is a mixed bag. While the initial theorists were brilliant in having created such a concept of classification, they were also acutely musical and did not ignore practice. But later theorists succumbed to the lure of mathematical computation. With this began the collapse of musicality in the mela system. Karnatik composers and musicians were so enamoured by these formulations that they too began using dry theoretical systems in the practice of music. They breathed life into the theorists' fancy ideas, and in doing so, surrendered the music to theory. In the history of musical systems, it is usually theory that follows practice, but here, probably for the first time, practice followed theory. This whole discussion is about aesthetics, not about whether the melodies in the synthetic ragas are beautiful or not. Maybe the solution is to create a new classification, a system that separates natural organic ragas from constructed ragas. But beyond all these arguments, the sanctity of the raga should remain. A raga is not a jugglery, manipulation, a clever arrangement or an egoistic display of prowess. Raga is a reflection of life's moments and emotions in melodic images. These moments have not been fashioned to make us feel sorry or happy about the many swings in our personal lives, but to touch us with the magic of a single encounter as when we stand with humility beholding a 500-year-old banyan tree. Can an artificial svara construction, which we have labelled as a raga, gift us this abstraction? This is the real question.

24

The Tala's Beat

Travelling with the raga has been challenging enough. But keeping step with the journey of the tala system has been a formidable task. Needless to say, for me, both ventures have been riveting.

Tala has evolved into the highly precise, definite system it is today. One might even say it has metamorphosed. As is true of many things, that story is part clear and part obscure. There are stages in its metamorphosis that cannot be completely understood.

This much is, of course, manifest: tala is not just about time measurements; it has played a far more complex role and exercised a deeper influence. Its role is best defined as a stabilizing force in the music, both in compositions and in the terrain of manodharma. While we can try and work out the measurements, master the timings, their intricacies, their creative variations that seem almost as infinite as fractions of time, we cannot be sure about how and why exactly some of these changes have occurred.

And so, as I begin our investigation into the tala system of the ancients, I am aware that this can be extremely confusing for the reader – the technicalities of time and measurement used in gandharva music can be mind-boggling. I will keep that fact in mind as I try and unravel it.

I commence the study by looking at those aspects of the ancient tala system that are relevant to our understanding today.

In Karnatik music, we have two types of tala. The first is the suladi sapta tala system and the other the chapu talas. I will, however, also discuss two others that are not in vogue but are intimately related to the way we render many kirtanas: the deshadi and madhyadi tala. Going beyond its structural form, tala also involves ideas of laya, divisions, placement of the songs and terms used for measurement.

Musicians often use the words 'akshara' and 'matra' in relation to talas. Lexically speaking, akshara means imperishable, indestructible, fixed or firm, apart from meaning 'a letter of the alphabet'. And matra refers to measure, a standard or correct unit. We can infer that both words indicate something that has been set out, prescribed, as a unit that holds or frames a moment in time. But there is no consensus on what these two words really denote in the context of Karnatik music. Scholars take two positions on this subject. The first maintains that akshara relates to the number of beats in a tala: for example adi tala has eight beats. This means that there are eight divisions or kriyas in the tala. Matra is the word used to denote the number of svaras or syllables that fill each pause between the beats. This would mean that if I rendered four svaras between every beat in adi tala, a total of thirty-two svaras would comprise one avartana. The matra would be four. The matra is variable, depending on the laya and the connected nadai being employed.

The second view is that 'akshara' means the number of svaras that fill the gap and matra denotes the divisions. Keeping these ideas of akshara and matra in mind, let us now visit the gandharva (art music) tala system described in *Natya Shastra*, *Dattilam* and in later treatises to discover the true import, meaning and, most importantly, the living action of tala from a somewhat different perspective.

Has Karnatik music fitted itself into the various tala moulds, or has tala grown into Karnatik music? How has tala's stabilizing role actually worked?

Tala organization in gandharva music was an intricate formulation. It was a precise system with great clarity on the nature and purpose of tala. It covered the entire gamut of principles that govern time, its manifestation in music, organization, function and execution. This whole set of ideas was driven by the fundamental thought that tala was created for music and had its being in what is being rendered. It is important to understand this basic position. Talas were not general structures into which music was composed, but rather created to accommodate the types of compositions that existed. Naturally, this meant that talas were reorganized, modified and changed, sometimes beyond recognition, in order to give melody a rhythmic structure. This, we must understand, is very different from how we view and treat tala in Karnatik music in the modern context. Talas have fixed structures today. Melody is created keeping these talas and their features in mind. There is an inversion of thought in this, because the tala is not designed for the composition based on its melodic form, rather compositional forms are designed to fit into existent tala structures.

Gandharva music had five basic talas: chachatputa, chaachaputa, satpitaputraka, udghatta and sampakveshtaka. Of these talas, the first three were the most important. I will not go into the exact structure of each. My intention in presenting the ancient tala system is for the reader to understand how many of the terms and principles that existed in ancient music are today used in a completely different context and also realize that we have adopted different ideas that were not part of gandharva.

All talas in the gandharva system were based on three units of time, known as tala angas. These were laghu, guru and pluta. At this point, I must request the reader to put aside the idea of laghu as used in contemporary Karnatik music. When I say time units, I mean that these three angas were defined by the span of time they covered. In order to bring the idea of this 'span' under one common denominator, they created the idea of matras. Using this basic measure of time, each of these angas was given a time value. Laghu was the smallest of one matra, guru was two matras and pluta was three matras.

But what was the value of the matra?

The matra did not have a definite empirical value. It was a base measure created by observation of life, rather than by mathematical computation. Matra had to be a very small quantity and was, therefore, described as 'the time taken to flutter the eyelids five times' (five nimeshas). This builds into the concept a sense of life and beauty, establishing the idea that music is art and not science. Laghu, therefore, is the time taken to flutter the eyelids five times, guru ten times and pluta fifteen times. Later, this matra was expressed as the time taken to utter five short syllables (laghu akshara).

Our natural reaction to such a concept would be that this is irrational. It could take one person less time and another more to utter short syllables or flutter her eyelids. The ancients must have been aware of this simple fact of life. Then why did they use the nimesha as a base measure? I propose two ideas. Firstly, five flutters of the eyelids was a notional measure, connected to life. Secondly, this minuscule variability between each individual also means that time in music is not a rigid stuffed box, but rather a sentient entity framed in the physicality of its form.

But laghu, guru and pluta that were measured by the number of matras could also expand to mean double or quadruple the number of matras. This was made functional, based on the concept of marga (literally, path). In gandharva, there were three functional margas: chitra, vartika and dakshina. The values one, two and three matras for laghu, guru and pluta that I spoke of earlier was in chitra marga. In vartika and dakshina marga, the matras would double accordingly. Laghu in vartika marga was two matras, in dakshina four matras. Guru and pluta would also change according to their respective values in chitra marga. Marga was, therefore, a path where the length of time that each matra took would expand. If, for example, guru in chitra marga took one second, in vartika marga it would take two seconds and in dakshina four. This was the basic principle. Therefore, in the tala chachatputa, which consisted of two gurus, one laghu and one pluta, the total number of matras in chitra marga is eight $(2+2+1+3)$ and sixteen $(4+4+2+6)$ in vartika marga. The time taken for the tala would be proportionately longer. This is basically a change in the laya of the tala and the connecting principle between every anga. The matra is the basic time measure, and all the other values are calculated accordingly. The interrelationship between the angas or that of the angas with the marga is based on the value of the matra.

In the contemporary practice of Karnatik music, we have three different senses of laya, which we refer to as chauka, madhyama and durita. These three states are not clearly interrelated in their experience. They change purely based on a feeling of laya. A kirtana may be rendered in chauka laya, but if it were to be rendered in a slightly faster speed, it may still be referred to as chauka. There is a certain arbitrariness in this. In the gandharva system, all the margas that determine a change in laya are connected with each other through the matra measure and give cohesiveness to laya variability – and therein lies an important difference between the gandharva and modern Karnatik systems.

Having noted that all talas in gandharva were combinations of laghu, guru and pluta angas, we can ask: but how were these talas expressed in action? There were nishabda kriyas and sashabda kriyas, just as there are today. But there is a subtle difference between how we view the kriya and how it was in the ancient system. Today, the kriya comprises not only the actions that divide the tala, but is also synonymous with the angas. For example, the anga druta also means the kriyas slap on the thigh and a flip of the hand; or a laghu, which is a variable time unit, is defined by a slap on the thigh and counting of the fingers. Therefore, when I use the term 'druta', the connoisseur actually visualizes the kriyas rather than understanding the measure. This almost interchangeable understanding did not exist in the gandharva talas. Kriyas were movements of the hands used to give the angas of the tala a visual representation. They represented the total time unit of each of the angas, but did not mean the time unit itself. Depending on the tala, the kriyas changed even if the same time unit was used in two different talas. By this I mean that there were no two actions that constantly only referred to a guru. The time unit guru – depending on the context in the tala – could be represented by other actions.

Another possibility in these talas was extending the total duration of the tala without changing the marga. That is, in chitra marga itself, you could make a tala take a longer time span to complete its form. This is very similar to what we use today, namely 'rendu kalai' and 'naalu kalai', achieving the extension by doubling each kriya in the tala. In gandharva, since the kriya was independent of the angas, a different system was employed. When they needed to double or quadruple the time span of a tala, all the angas were first reduced to the time value of the guru, becoming gurus. Since the values of the three angas were one, two and three, one could create a guru by combining two laghus or obtain three gurus by combining two plutas. Following this, the total number of gurus were split into pairs. I am not using the technical terms that were used to describe these different states, so that we can understand the concept without getting caught in jargon.

Chart 14: The gandharva technique of doubling or quadrupling the time span of a tala

Chachatputa					*Total*
Basic form	Guru	Guru	Laghu	Pluta	8
Matras	2	2	1	3	
Doubled	2 Guru	2 Guru	2 Laghu	2 Pluta	16
Matras	4	4	2	6	
Redistributed	2 Guru	2 Guru	2 Guru	2 Guru	16
Matras	4	4	4	4	

One may ask how the talas were differentiated if all the talas were equalized into pairs of gurus. This is where the separation between kriyas and angas help.

In their doubled or quadrupled state, the talas retain exactly the same number of sashabda kriyas as in their initial state. Also, the kinds of sashabda kriyas used in the primary state are not removed from the tala, but only altered in the order of their placement. From this, we can deduce that all the added kriyas were nishabda kriyas. These were not added arbitrarily either. By creating clear rules on how these extra nishabda kriyas need to be added and how the sashabda kriyas were to be placed when the tala was doubled or quadrupled, musicians could easily comprehend the tala in operation by observing the kriya. This method of extending the total duration of the tala is not found in deshi music.

Another important tool was used to enhance this comprehension. In Karnatik music today, the finger-count kriyas are associated with the laghu.

The use of finger counts in the gandharva system is fascinating. While the kriyas that were used to divide the tala consisted of various hand movements, such as clapping, waving, raising or bringing down the hand with an open palm, finger indications were not specifically used for these kriyas. Fingers were used to indicate the guru pair that the musician reached at that very moment when the tala was rendered in its double or quadruple state. This was necessary, since the whole tala was measured in these states as pairs of gurus presented as kriyas. All gurus were of the same time measure – two matras. It was then required that the musician also indicated which pair of gurus he was at. This is something like having a milestone on the road that indicates every kilometre travelled (kriya) and then another signpost, say after every two kilometres (finger indications) that tells you that you are entering the next section.

All talas were said to be of two kinds: chaturashra or tryashra (tisra). Today if I said this, we would understand it as meaning one of two things: either the nadai or the laghu jati. In the gandharva system, on the other hand, what that statement meant was that the total matras of the tala were either a multiple of four or three. For example, chachatputa tala was a total of eight matras and, therefore, chaturashra; whereas chaachaputa tala made up of one guru, two laghus and one guru (2+1+1+2), totalling six, was tryashra. Among the basic five talas, only chachatputa was a chaturashra form.

So far, the concept is utterly clear. But now we move on to a land of mystery as we look at the tala within gitakas, the compositions used in art music (gandharva). It would be very difficult for me to explain this in writing, but I shall try and convey one point significant to our discussion. All the gitakas were extremely rigid, tala-bound compositions. Fascinatingly, when we look at the tala structures in the gitakas, they seem completely independent of the primary talas we talked of earlier; so you do not have a complete gitaka in any of those talas. Depending on the structure of the gitakas and its sectional divisions, the tala angas are combined to structure the composition. The new anga combinations used in these compositions were chaturashra or tryashra structures, or a combination of both, and had new names given to them. Sometimes, the basic talas appear within the gitakas, but only in one part of the whole composition.

Here we learn one more thing that completely changes our idea of tala. We know the tala as a cyclical form. So if we render a kirtana, the same tala is presented multiple times throughout its rendition. In the ancient system, the structure of the song dictated the tala and this meant that every section or subsection required different types of tala anga combinations. Tala here moved in complete linearity according to the form of the song. This is not to say that there were no cyclical repetitions of any section of the gitaka. If this was done, that section of the tala too was repeated.

The most logical question here would be: how were the talas as used in the gitakas even remotely connected to the basic talas described? This is very difficult to say. We must keep in mind that we are trying to understand a musical system that is around 2,000 years old and any lacuna that we perceive may have actually been extremely clear to the ancients. That aside, the tala angas in the gitakas are structured on the basic concepts of gandharva music. Matra is the basis of these tala structures, the angas and the kriyas are the same as mentioned for the basic talas, the method of doubling or quadrupling the length of the angas are the same and the gitakas are rendered in different margas. The most important connection, though, seems to be that the total tala matra count in one whole gitaka or any of its sections was always a multiple of four or three, and thus a chaturashra or tryashra form, just as in the basic talas.

The ancients also deal with laya in relation to the text, as we do today. While one matra is equal to five nimeshas or five laghu aksharas, in the context of music, one matra was rendered as two syllables of text. So, in chitra marga, the musicians rendered two syllables for a laghu, four syllables for a guru and six syllables for a pluta. They also described the laya in compositions based on the way the laya in the text varied. We describe the same idea of laya change today, based on the density of emphasis or text within a division of the tala.

Finally, as we do today, the ancients also defined the point at which the musical composition began within the tala. If they began together, it was called sama-pani; if the melody began before the tala, it was called ava-pani; if it began after the tala commenced, it was known as upari-pani. These ideas are called sama, atita and anagata by deshi scholars. There have been some differences in the interpretation of these ideas and the same concepts have been used with regard to the coordination between melodic instruments and the singing. What is of interest to me is that although the same terms are used within the modern context, our tala is cyclical – therefore, beginning before the tala commences would mean beginning at the end of the last cycle of the tala. This is a significant difference.

All that I have described above is gandharva, or art, music. From commentators and authors after Bharata, we learn about the talas used in his natya (theatre). Even though some information is available about these talas, we don't have the understanding that we get with the talas of gandharva (art music). We need not go into the details of talas in natya, but need to understand that they are said to have evolved from the gandharva tala. They are all known as bhanga talas. These bhanga talas are varieties and derivatives of the talas and tala principles put forth in gandharva.

I have tried to summarize the tala system used by the ancients and, in doing so, also provided some ideas on how we have retained certain aspects and changed some ideas. To further understand our contemporary tala system we need to move to deshi and post-deshi developments before we directly deal with what we have inherited from the seventeenth century.

The talas used in deshi sangita were also connected to the gandharva talas, as they are supposed to have been deshi varieties of khanda talas. The khanda talas were formulated by breaking up the anga time units to smaller and even smaller units. This process automatically resulted in the creation of time units that were smaller than a laghu (one matra). For example, a pluta could be divided into three laghus and the laghu too could be further divided into newer, smaller angas. It is said that these talas were called khanda talas because of the dominance of the laghus. Khanda refers to a breaking or dividing, and the word 'laghu' means short, concise, small, diminutive or brief. This is an important period during which the talas were being dominated by laghus and determined by its value. The dominance of the laghu continues in our contemporary system. In the deshi tala, we come across two time units that are smaller than a laghu, namely the druta and virama. We are familiar with the term 'druta', but let us not assume that the druta of the ancients was the druta we know. Druta is an anga, calculated as half a laghu. Since a laghu is one matra, the druta is half a matra.

The case of the virama is more curious, because it is not treated as an independent anga. It is, in fact, an extension of any one of the angas – druta, laghu, guru or pluta. The value of a virama was initially proposed as being half the value of the anga to which it is attached. A laghu virama was one-and-a-half matras, a guru virama was three matras and a pluta virama was four-and-a-half matras. As you can clearly see, the creation of smaller units led to the tala angas becoming values in fractions, making talas very complex time measures. Another effect of the minuscule time-unit angas was that talas also became very large in the number of angas they had and, as a result, unwieldy. The breaking down of tala time units into smaller units resulted in the disappearance of guru and pluta from further developments in tala, the establishment of virama as an independent important measure and the centrality of the laghu in understanding tala. These three developments went on to shape the Karnatik tala. There was another, larger, time unit in the deshi system: the nishabda, which was four times the value of the laghu. This too disappeared.

In this already complicated environment, there seems to be another idea that gained currency, but curiously enough only with reference to the laghu. For long, angas were explained in terms of the number of matras. As I pointed out earlier, one matra was equal to five nimeshas or five laghu aksharas and the laghu was equal to one matra. But in a new development, variability was permitted in the time unit of laghu. Some scholars pointed out that a laghu could have four, five or six aksharas. This should automatically mean that the number of aksharas rendered in druta, guru and pluta would also change accordingly. This idea of laghu, with a variable number of aksharas, is a subtle but important development. In the story of shrutis, we noticed that the notional shrutis became actual svarasthanas and in a similar development, we will now see how the notional idea of 'laghu aksharas' change through a period of time to actually mean the number of aksharas rendered.

In works contemporary to and after *Sangita Ratnakara*, we find newer ideas to measure the duration of the angas. Here, the value of a kshana is the time taken to pierce a hundred lotus petals; time measures for the laghu, guru, pluta were determined based on this.

Some time later, the situation was further complicated when the measure of the virama was taken as being a quarter of the laghu's value. The musical difficulties here are plain to see. Tala angas – such as druta virama becoming three-fourths of a matra, druta being half a laghu and virama a quarter of a laghu – would have made keeping tala a nightmare. As we can see, from the deshi period, there seem to have been many rapid changes brought about by further dividing the basic angas, assigning them values and trying to understand them in terms of music. In *Sangita Ratnakara*, Sarngadeva mentions 120 talas. We cannot be sure how many of these were used in the compositions of deshi sangita, which were prabandhas. Interestingly, some of these talas have come down to us not in their original form, but reinterpreted according to the newer system devised in the seventeenth century.

There is almost no doubt that the reorganization and standardization of the numerous talas and their complex valuations was the contribution of the Haridasa saints. From about the fourteenth century, the Dasakuta and Vyasakuta (both Haridasa sects) were actively involved in bhakti music. They had inherited the deshi tradition of music and played a critical role in structuring our modern tala system. It is believed that they dispensed with so many talas which were made of numerous angas of even fractional values. They rationalized the system and formalized about nine talas. Of this, the Karnatik system retains seven talas, known as the suladi sapta talas.

I will use Venkatamakhin's *Chaturdandi Prakashika* to explain how we inherited suladi talas. *Chaturdandi Prakashika* gives us details of eight talas, which are presented in the form of svara patterns known as the alankaras. Even at this stage, the anga unit values were not completely finalized. Venkatamakhin indicates in the alankaras that the laghu can be four or five aksharas long. At six or seven, it is called a laghushekhara. The druta's time unit is fixed at two aksharas and the virama is used only as an extension of the druta and is equal to one akshara (half the value of the druta). While the virama is still in use, only in the case of jhampa tala, he brings in a new anga – anudruta – that is independent but has the same value as the virama. The transformation of the virama into an independent anga called the anudruta is a startling development. In an earlier period, the virama was an extension of any anga with half its value; later, it was considered a quarter of a laghu. Now the virama has come to be an independent anga of one akshara. At the same time, while enumerating these eight talas, in two cases, Venkatamakhin provided two methods of dividing the tala into angas. In these, he used the older anga guru, but with a value of ten aksharas, even if the laghu is four in the same tala. This appears to be a case of holding on to older tradition when the present practice may have moved ahead.

Chart 15: The eight talas

Jhompata

Structure	Druta		Druta		Laghu				Total
Aksharas	2		2		4				8
	S	R	G	M	P	D	N	S	
	S	N	D	P	M	G	R	S	

Dhruva

Old Structure	Laghu				Guru										Total
Aksharas	4				10										14
	S	R	G	M	G	R	S	R	G	R	S	R	G	M	
	R	G	M	P	M	G	R	G	M	G	R	G	M	P	

New Structure	Laghu				Laghu				Laghushekhara						Total
Aksharas	4				4				6						14
	S	R	G	M	G	R	S	R	G	R	S	R	G	M	
	R	G	M	P	M	G	R	G	M	G	R	G	M	P	

Matya

Structure	Druta		Laghu				Laghu				Total
Aksharas	2		4				4				10
	S	R	G	R	S	R	S	R	G	M	
	R	G	M	G	R	G	R	G	M	P	

Rupaka

Structure	Druta		Laghu				Total
Aksharas	2		4				6
	S	R	S	R	G	M	
	R	G	R	G	M	P	

Jhampa

Old Structure	Anudruta	Druta		Laghushekhara							Total
Aksharas	1	2		7							10
	S	R	G	S	R	S	R	G	M	-	
	R	G	M	R	G	R	G	M	P	-	

New Structure	Druta virama			Laghushekhara							Total
Aksharas	3			7							10
	S	R	G	S	R	S	R	G	M	-	
	R	G	M	R	G	R	G	M	P	-	

Triputa

		Druta		Druta		Druta-virama		Total
Structure		Druta		Druta		Druta-virama		
Aksharas		2		2		3		7
	S	R	G	S	R	G	M	
	R	G	M	R	G	M	P	

Ata

Structure	Druta	Druta	Laghu				Laghu				Total
Aksharas	2	2	5				5				14
	S R	- G	- S - R G				- M - M -				
	R G	- M	- R - G M				- P - P -				

Eka

Structure	Druta
Aksharas	2

Author Venkatamakhin mentions that since such a form does not offer any aesthetic pleasure, the tala is changed by substituting adi tala for eka tala. Adi tala's form is given as follows:

Structure	Laghu			
Aksharas	4			
	S	R	G	M
	R	G	M	P

Each alankara is rendered in ascending and descending order of the natural sequence of svaras, i.e. S, R, G, M, P, D, N and S, N, D, P, M, G, R.

One thing is very clear. By this time, akshara literally meant the number of syllables or svaras rendered within that anga. It was also this akshara that defined the time unit of the anga, and not a notional idea of matra. When we actually sing the alankaras mentioned for each tala, this fact becomes apparent. If a musician were to render the alankara for rupaka tala, she would sing sa ri within the time unit of the druta (druta: two aksharas), sa ri ga ma within the time unit of the laghu (laghu: four aksharas).

The aware reader may wonder why there are eight alankaras in Chart 15 (The eight talas), when students of music today learn only seven. You may also notice that the jhompata tala alankara does not exist today. In fact, the mentioned svara pattern for this tala is the first basic music lesson. It is taught in adi tala and not as part of the alankaras. I will explain these aspects a little later when I discuss the evolution of the foremost tala in Karnatik music, namely the adi tala.

Other than this, anyone familiar with the alankaras will notice that almost all these talas look very different in structure and in some cases the svara patterns are also different from contemporary practice (see Chart 16).

Before I proceed further, I must also state that Ahobala in *Sangita Parijata* (seventeenth century) has also published the seven suladi talas. There are differences in structure between these alankaras and the ones published in *Chaturdandi Prakashika*.

Chart 16: The alankaras as rendered today

Dhruva

Structure	Laghu				Druta		Laghu				Laghu				Total
Aksharas	4				2		4				4				14
	S	R	G	M	G	R	S	R	G	R	S	R	G	M	
	R	G	M	P	M	G	R	G	M	G	R	G	M	P	

Matya

Structure	Laghu				Druta		Laghu				Total
Aksharas	4				2		4				10
	S	R	G	R	S	R	S	R	G	M	
	R	G	M	G	R	G	R	G	M	P	

Rupaka

Structure	Druta		Laghu				Total
Aksharas	2		4				6
	S	R	S	R	G	M	
	R	G	R	G	M	P	

Jhampa

Structure	Laghu							Anudruta	Druta		Total
Aksharas	7							1	2		10
	S	R	G	S	R	S	R	G	M	-	
	R	G	M	R	G	R	G	M	P	-	

Triputa

Structure	Laghu			Druta		Druta		Total
Aksharas	3			2		2		7
	S	R	G	S	R	G	M	
	R	G	M	R	G	M	P	

Ata

Structure	Laghu					Laghu					Druta		Druta		Total
Aksharas	5					5					2		2		14
	S	R	-	G	-	S	-	R	G	-	M	-	M	-	
	R	G	-	M	-	R	-	G	M	-	P	-	P	-	

Eka

Structure	Laghu			
Aksharas	4			
	S	R	G	M
	R	G	M	P

The significant changes between the suladi talas as we know it and as depicted by Venkatamakhin are that, today:

- we have only three angas (laghu, druta and anudruta), while the talas in *Chaturdandi Prakashika* have other angas, such as guru, laghushekhara and druta virama;
- all talas, except rupaka tala, are devised to begin only with a laghu – a post-*Chaturdandi Prakashika* tala standardization;
- the length of the laghu can be anything from three to nine aksharas, depending on the tala, and so the laghushekhara has been done away with; and
- no tala begins with an anudruta.

The biggest change is the independence that druta and anudruta time units have in relation to the laghu. This was no surprise, considering that laghu had for long been a vacillating unit.

We should keep in mind that when the seven suladi talas were first formulated, the laghu value attributed to each tala was fixed for that particular tala. This meant that ata tala indicated only a laghu value of five, and rupaka tala a laghu value of four. But as early as the fifteenth century, it is likely that the idea of laghu jati may have been incorporated. The earliest treatise that mentions the jati concept seems to be *Sangita Suryodaya* (1509–29). From this we can be certain that, in practice, the idea of jati variability in the laghu may have been present from around the mid-fifteenth century. In *Sangita Parijata*, there is a description of a possibility of eight jatis of the laghu. However, other treatises refer to jatis only in terms of the five time unit values we give them today, i.e. four, three, seven, five and nine. This is seen in texts such as *Tala Chandrika*. Here, though there are many remnant aspects of the older tala system, including angas like the guru. The author refers to the five jatis being implemented in these talas. Since the tala chapter in *Chaturdandi Prakashika* manuscript is missing, we cannot be sure if Venkatamakhin had written about the laghu jati concept. It is from the implementation of this variability that we get the thirty-five talas in the suladi system now prevailing. Changes in the tala structure that brought it in line with the one we use today must have occurred by the end of the seventeenth century or the early eighteenth century.

It is in *Sangita Saramrta* authored by King Tulaja (1728– 36) that the seven alankaras as learnt by music students today is recorded. Though the tala break-up of the alankaras is not explicitly given, from the way the svaras are divided we can deduce the tala structure. Tulaja also speaks about Purandaradasa (1484–1564) with great reverence and proclaims him a 'master' of the compositional form suladi. Suladis were compositions of the Haridasas, which used at least five of the suladi talas. It is like a talamalika. In the suladis that we have in notated form, we find the use of all seven talas and the ragana mathya tala. One of the suladis has a section in the tala called tisra jati ragana mathya. If we accept that this suladi may have remained unchanged over 400 years, it reaffirms the point that the idea of laghu jati was in vogue for sometime before it was documented. Unfortunately, we do not have an oral singing tradition of suladis. Talas such as ragana mathya and dhruva rupaka were part of the deshi and chaturdandi tradition, but became obsolete due to the establishment of the suladi sapta talas as the basis for tala varieties.

The one thing we are unable to make out when we study the suladi talas is whether the laghu involved any finger counting as we do today. I sometimes wonder if four, five or seven aksharas could have been maintained just with a slap on the thigh or hand – one sashabda kriya. We may never know the answer to this question. But one possibility is that when the speed of music slowed down, the musicians may have needed more support to sustain the laya – finger counting helped. It seems that the idea of finger counting came back into our tala system with a completely different role than when it was used as part of gandharva.

There are two other talas that are prevalent today that do not fit the suladi tala scheme: mishra chapu and khanda chapu. Some scholars attribute these talas also to the Dasakutas and Vyasakutas (two groups of Haridasa saints). However, we cannot be sure about this claim. I have already described these two talas. They are unique because of the unequal distribution of kriyas in them. But we could look at the kriyas in a slightly different manner. Since these talas do not have any of the angas – laghu, druta and anudruta – we could treat each of the kriyas as anga separations. If we do that, we perceive the tala as made up of angas with the following akshara values: mishra chapu has $1+2+2+2$ and khanda chapu $2+1+2$.

Chart 17: Mishra chapu and khanda chapu

Mishra Chapu

1	2	2	2

Khanda Chapu

2	1	2

Chart 18: An example of how the mishra chapu and khanda chapu are similar to gandharva talas

Chachatputa

2	2	1	3

As is clear, if we treat each of the kriyas as angas, these chapu talas are similar in the unequal division of the tala to gandharva.

Another theory about their origin is that they may have come from the bhajana or Harikatha tradition, where musicians used castanets to maintain rhythm. Then, especially if the music was rendered at a faster pace, a tala of seven beats may have been maintained with just two clicks of the castanets, dividing it into 3+4 (mishra chapu) or five beats into 2+3 (khanda chapu). When the pace of these talas slowed down, the other divisions could have crept in.

Among all the talas used in Karnatik music, the most common is adi tala. Today, adi tala is considered the chaturashra variety of triputa tala.

Chart 19: The adi tala

Structure	Laghu				Druta		Druta		Total
Aksharas	4				2		2		8
	S	R	G	M	P	D	N	S	
	S	N	D	P	M	G	R	S	

This is because, with the possibility of laghu jati, the adi tala structure can be accommodated into the thirty-five talas. But adi tala itself has a very long history. Once again, the probable ways in which it may have evolved are many, but the question of its origin demands enquiry even if we cannot actually find a resolution.

Adi tala is connected to the deshi tradition and therefore first mentioned in *Brhaddeshi* (ninth century), authored by Matanga, though the form is not described. Adi is described as the source for all talas in *Manasollasa* (1131). It is given a form of one laghu. A laghu, as we know, even in the early deshi period was a time unit of one matra. There is another version of this tala that is very different, consisting of druta-virama, druta and druta, which would give us a total of one-and-three-quarters matras. *Manasollasa* also describes two other talas, which are of interest. Dvitiya, which consists of two drutas and a laghu in that order, and a tala tritiya that is one laghu and two drutas. The similarity between these talas and adi tala in their anga form is obvious. The Tamil treatise *Panchamarabu* also speaks about adi tala with the structure of one laghu. Most treatises describe the structure of adi tala as consisting of only a laghu.

Now we need to come to the first alankara presented in *Chaturdandi Prakashika*. Here jhompata tala has exactly the same structure as dvitiya tala – two drutas and a laghu. As I mentioned before, the idea of akshara had become literal by this time, which meant that, in the laghu, four aksharas were rendered, and two aksharas in each druta. Jhompata tala is the inverse form of adi tala, which is one laghu and two drutas, both adding up to eight aksharas. Did this inversion give us the adi tala? When did the name change occur?

It is interesting that in Kathakali, they use a tala called chempata tala, which has eight kriyas.

The last alankara in *Chaturdandi Prakashika* is the eka tala alankara. Venkatamakhin makes a very interesting observation here. He says that this tala is made up of only a druta, but since this has no beauty, eka tala is substituted by adi tala, which is made up of only a laghu. This adi tala mentioned by him is similar to the adi tala described in the deshi texts.

The description of jhompata tala and adi tala in *Chaturdandi* are important. The alankara mentioned for jhompata tala is the first lesson learnt by any student of music – sa ri ga ma pa dha ni sa / sa ni dha pa ma ga ri sa and is rendered in adi tala. The alankara given by Venkatamakhin in adi tala of one laghu is today rendered in eka tala of one laghu.

Muttusvami Dikshitar had composed seven kirtanas, one for each day of the week. These compositions are also supposed to be in each of the suladi sapta talas. The kirtana 'Divakaratanujam' in raga yadukulakambhoji is set to adi tala according to Subbarama Dikshitar. This kirtana is notated in his publication *Sangita Sampradaya Pradarshini*. It is possible that he was following the Venkatamakhin tradition and therefore sticking to the adi tala made up of one laghu. But the problem here is that the notation reveals that his adi tala is made up of a laghu and two drutas. Later scholars have published the same kirtana and referred to the tala as adi. This shows us that as much as jhompata and adi seem connected, so do adi and eka.

There is another possibility. Among the talas given for Tyagaraja kirtanas, we come across two distinct talas though they are not in vogue today. These do not seem connected directly to the suladi talas or the chapu talas. They are known as deshadi and madhyadi. Both talas are exactly the same in form. They consist of three slaps on the thigh, followed by the flip of the palm. The difference between them lies in the point in the tala where the composition begins.

Chart 20: The deshadi and madhyadi talas

Beats	1	2	3	4
Deshadi				x
Madhyadi		x		

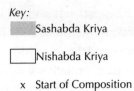

Key:

▓ Sashabda Kriya

☐ Nishabda Kriya

x   Start of Composition

The word 'deshadi' gives us a clue that this tala may have been incorporated into Karnatik music from some other region. Deshadi and Madhyadi talas have a connection with adi tala and eka tala because they are also made up of four kriyas, like eka tala, and have exactly the same number of sashabda kriyas as adi tala.

Chart 21: Deshadi and madhyadi talas have a connection with adi tala

Both Desadi/Madhyadi and Adi comprise 3 sashabda kriyas

Beats		1	2	3	4	5	6	7	8
Deshadi/Madhyadi									
Adi									

Both Desadi/Madhyadi and Eka have 4 kriyas

Beats		1	2	3	4
Desahdi/Madhyadi					
Eka					

The fact that we now render all Tyagaraja kirtanas in deshadi and madhyadi as adi tala of eight kriyas is significant.

The teen tal in the Hindustani system has a total number of sixteen beats, but the tala is split into four fours, with each four being rendered as two slaps, one flip of the palm and another slap on the palm. The emphasis is also only on the first, fifth, ninth and thirteenth beats, which splits the tala into 4+4+4+4. One cannot miss the relationship between the teen tal and deshadi/madhyadi tala. It is possible that this has something to do with deshadi's foreign origin.

Jhompata tala, adi tala, eka tala, deshadi and madhyadi tala and teen tal are all manifestations of four. Right from the beginning, it is only jhompata tala that consisted of eight aksharas. Jhompata tala may have inversed its form due to the unwritten rule that evolved after Venkatamakhin's period that talas must start with a laghu. But we cannot be sure when this tala began to be referred to as adi tala.

I had mentioned in this essay that, in the gandharva system, musicians could increase the total duration of the tala by adding nishabda kriyas. This idea is not expressed in deshi talas. The concept seems to have resurfaced suddenly in the eighteenth century. We achieve this today through the process of rendu kalai or naalu kalai – the doubling or quadrupling of each kriya. It is said that in the past, musicians used to render pallavis in even sixty-four kalais. Did this mean that sixty-four repetitions of each kriya were executed or were the musicians sustaining the time duration of sixty-four kriyas mentally after one single sashabda kriya – a slap on the thigh? If it was the latter, the concept changes and becomes closer to the gandharva system of marga. If every kriya was executed, it is more like the gandharva method of doubling or quadrupling the number of kriyas.

The two words 'nadai' and 'gati' have also been debated widely. I have used these synonymously to mean the number of svaras or syllables rendered between two beats of a tala, which can be in the jati values: chaturashra, tisra, mishra, khanda and sankirna. Many musicians and scholars have felt that these two terms mean different things, while others maintain that the difference is only linguistic. One interpretation is that gati refers to the number pattern derived from clubbing svaras together in a line of melody or rhythm, in any given nadai. This grouping also uses the basic jati values (4, 3, 7, 5, 9) (see Chart 22). Nadai, it is said, refers to the number of syllables being rendered between two beats (see Chart 23).

Example: Tisra Gati – 3 svara patterns with matras of 4 aksharas.

Chart 22: Tisra Gati – 4 aksharas in a matra with patterns of 3 svaras

S	R	G	R	G	M	G	M	P	M	P	D
P	D	N	D	N	S	S	N	D	N	D	P
D	P	M	P	M	G	M	G	R	G	R	S

Chart 23: Two kinds of nadai

Chaturashra Nadai – 4 aksharas in a matra

P M G M | P D N D | P M G R

Mishra Nadai – 7 aksharas in a matra

G M P M G M P | D N S N D P M | N D P M G R S

I believe that both words mean exactly the same thing, which is the number of svaras between every beat in a tala in the number values of the five jatis. Any line of melody will have groups of svaras based on the nature of the raga, composition type and syllabic structure. The five jati values will naturally exist within this. There is no need to superimpose the terminologies nadai or gati on to this concept. It will only lead to confusion. The reason we seek a term for the number of syllables is because, over the last 150 years, we have included within our music other complex mathematical structures that are based on such grouping of rhythmic syllables. Maybe a completely new word will solve this imbroglio.

Before I wind up this discussion, I would like to go back to how I began with the description of matra and akshara. This is one of the basic battles in tala. From this journey of discovery, it is clear that matra was initially used as a measure of time unit (anga), and the matra itself was equated to the time taken to flutter the eyelids (nimesha) five times or utter five laghu aksharas (short syllables). It was later that the notionality of laghu aksharas disappeared and with it the matra. The anga was then being understood in terms of the number of actual syllables (aksharas) that was being rendered within a given anga. Akshara has always referred to the actions within a time unit. When treated as a notional idea, as the laghu aksharas, it was the utterance of short syllables. When aksharas became the measure, it referred to the actual number of syllables rendered within a time unit. In contrast, matra was the whole time unit within which all these actions could be measured or sensed. Looking at the origins of matra and aksharas and their transformations, I feel that we should use the word 'akshara' to mean the number of syllables or stresses that are applied between every beat in a tala, while matra must denote the beat itself – the time unit. Therefore, adi tala is made up of eight matras and eight, sixteen or thirty-two aksharas, which reflects the rendition of one, two or four aksharas per matra, depending on laya being kizh-kala, sama-kala or mel-kala, all this in chaturashra nadai. If the nadai changes the number of aksharas will change accordingly.

Tala is a complex feature of Karnatik music, and one with a fascinating evolutionary history. I have separated the changes associated with raga and tala, but we need to look at them together to understand how they shaped the music. While writing treatises, authors have been able to give numerical and structural details about talas, and in the case of melody, information about the svaras, gamakas and ragas. But on the question of what the music actually sounded like, I have no answer. We are trying to reconstruct music from textual material and this is bound to have its limitations, but that does not make the process redundant. In trying to recreate what might have been, we also learn a lot about our own present practices. Recognizing the threads that may have led to where we are today, and also accepting the fact that some of our practices are relatively recent, will enable us to bridge what is invaluable in antiquity with what is desirable in contemporary practice. Unless every one of us continues this search and learns more, stands corrected and continues to question, the past will remain shrouded and the present and future will be in a state of some disarray.

These technical aspects of time and measure are of no consequence if they do not dissolve into the experience of music. The nuts and bolts of measuring time are the physical frame of laya and tala. But when the space created within is filled with raga, sahitya and svara, time manifests in its metaphysical form. This is beautiful. In order to lose oneself in this plume of experience, one must work on every method and technique, if only to transcend it. The reader would have noticed that I do not use quotations from others to embellish my argument or to supplement my thoughts. But I will depart from my practice to end this essay with a quote from Albert Einstein: 'Not everything that counts can be counted, and not everything that can be counted counts.'

25

A Thing Composed

The various compositional forms in Karnatik music have travelled and changed through the centuries to reach their present shape and form. When I say 'reached', I do not suggest that they have arrived at some destination. The journey continues. But these forms can be said to have now arrived at a certain fullness that makes it worthwhile for us to trace the trajectories they have taken.

Gita

Scholars of music instinctively use the word 'gita'. It has been used differently, its meaning varying according to the context. In a generic sense it means just 'music'. But it also refers very specifically to various constituents or types of music, such as an arrangement of svaras that are pleasing, as a blanket word that encompasses melody, a melodic structure, a melodic composition, melodic aspects of theatre and the music that specifically relates to the theatrical presentation within the deshi tradition. The last connection assumes relevance when we try to understand why gita is used as a technical term for certain compositions of Purandaradasa (1484–1564). These have traditionally been learnt and still are by all students of Karnatik music as the very first compositional form taught.

In the context of Karnatik music then, are gita and sangita the same? To answer this question, one must turn to their usage in tradition, specifically in the deshi tradition.

There, sangita subsumed gita. Let us see how. In the deshi tradition, the word 'sangita', which we use generically to denote music, was employed very pointedly to refer to the composite ingredients of theatre, similar to natya of the marga tradition (*Natya Shastra*). This sangita of the theatre had three elements: melodic component (gita), dance (nrtta) and rhythmic accompaniment (vadya). It does seem that in this tradition, music or gita was the most important of the three elements, just as natya was the dominant element in the marga tradition. There are differences between the natya and nrtta used to describe the dance element in marga and sangita respectively, but those need not detain us in this essay.

In the description of the music that is used in sangita, we come across three paddhatis or ways, paths, roads: shuddha, gaundali and perani. The shuddha paddhati was an older and therefore 'purer' (or shuddha) system, while the other two evolved out of it. The gaundali and perani paddhatis also came to be called deshi. The shuddha paddhati itself may have evolved at some point of time from an even older tradition, even possibly from the natya tradition, but we cannot be sure. Central to the music in sangita were the prabandhas, a compositional form no longer in vogue. The prabandha form contained texts either in Sanskrit or the regional languages, sung in one of these paddhatis. They are not to be conflated with the prabandhas of later periods or other literary traditions. Initially, 'gita' was used for prabandhas in general. The prefix 'shuddha' came to be used with prabandhas as well. Scholars maintain that only shuddha prabandhas were to be sung in the shuddha paddhati. Then 'gita' was used to refer only to prabandhas used in the shuddha paddhati. The prefix 'shuddha' came to be applied to prabandhas in order to differentiate these from prabandhas used in the gaundali and perani paddhatis. The gaundali tradition may have evolved in the Karnataka region. Influenced by the local language and dialects, the prabandhas used in it were called suda. This new cognomen, suda, slowly replaced gita. Soon prabandhas used in shuddha paddhati became shuddha suda and the prabandhas used in gaundali became salaga suda. Salaga was a corruption of 'chhayalaga', meaning 'shadows' of the shuddha sudas. With these transformations, gita came to include both shuddha and salaga sudas.

Soon, the salaga sudas became the prominent form of prabandhas, and the word 'gita' came to refer exclusively to them. It is from this deshi prabandha tradition that Gopalanayaka is said to have created the purely music-based presentation called chaturdandi. In a continuation of this tradition, we find Venkatamakhin's *Chaturdandi Prakashika* using the term 'gita' only in the context of the salaga sudas and prabandha only for shuddha sudas. Thereafter, prabandha becomes the purer term, connoting shuddha suda, while gita refers to salaga sudas.

From the gita's journeys so far, we infer that the application of the word that signified music in its broad sense was narrowing; it became pointed, like a tree branch, then a twig, then a pencil, eventually ending at a narrow lead point.

But the sharpening does not stop here. From around the regions of Karnataka, we get the Haridasa sect, which was part of the religious movement that propagated the philosophy of Madhvacharya. Its adherents were known as dasas (devoted followers). Their music was connected to the prabandha tradition. They also handled another compositional form, called suladi – complex compositions that used the seven talas (suladi sapta tala). From *Sangita Saramrta* (1729–35), we deduce that suladis evolved from salaga sudas. The suggested etymology for suladi makes for an interesting note here. Some Kannada scholars believe that the word comes from 'sulu' and 'hadi', or the easy way to attain bliss and salvation, a reference to the devotional focus of the music of the dasas. We have only three notated versions of suladis composed by Purandaradasa available for our reference in *Sangita Sampradaya Pradarshini*. As suladis became the popular compositional form, 'gita' was used to refer to them. Soon, other simple compositions, structurally very different from the suladi composed by Purandaradasa, were called gita. This new 'gita' had no direct connection to the prabandha tradition in form, only in reference. As a newer compositional form replaced the older one, 'gita' came to stand for the new entrant. And thus the transition moved from the shuddha prabandha to the salaga suda, then on to the suladi before finally settling down to refer to the gita of Purandaradasa.

The reader must make the acquaintance here of a form known as lakshya gita. These compositions also belong to the chaturdandi and prabandha traditions, and much like the gitas are not rendered as part of kutcheris. Lakshya gitas are composed in Sanskrit, Kannada, Telugu and Marathi, sometimes even a mixture of these languages, with colloquialisms and slang. They do not fit into our understanding of melodic expansion or progression in compositional forms. The overall experience is rather quaint. They are meant to summarize the melodic characteristics of a raga. In *Sangita Sampradaya Pradarshini*, most ragas described are followed by a lakshya gita. Only twenty-eight ragas do not have lakshya gitas out of the 191 ragas described in *Pradarshini*. While these also belong to the chaturdandi and prabandha traditions, their different sections and musical form are very different from the deshi music of the twelfth century. These lakshya gitas are related to the chaturdandi tradition established in Tanjavur by Govinda Dikshita (seventeenth century). In *Sangita Sampradaya Pradarshini*, lakshya gitas are attributed to Venkatamakhin (seventeenth century). But it is the opinion of most musicologists that while some of these are the creations of Venkatamakhin, most others must be compositions of his descendant Muddu Venkatamakhin (eighteenth century), as the ragas in which these lakshya gitas are composed include the fifty-three raganga ragas that are said to be his creations and did not exist in Venkatamakhin's days. There are even compositions called prabandhas notated in the *Sangita Sampradaya Pradarshini*, which are named after some of the varieties of prabandhas mentioned in *Sangita Ratnakara*, but they do not seem to be connected musically.

In the evolution of Karnatik music, the contribution and role of lakshya gitas was to essentially condense the melodic movements of a raga in a nutshell, thereby providing the musician an aesthetic construction of the raga in miniature.

Varna

Art music masterfully uses Sanskrit words and phrases for its own internal classifications. To be able to apply a generic word of broad application with logic and felicity to a specific entity is an accomplishment. Varna, which means, colour, hue, quality or class, has been utilized in Indian art music in many contexts with different meanings; in this instance, it defines a distinctive compositional form. Varnas give the listener the experience of raga melody through the syllabic form, vowel extensions or emphasis as well as in its svara state. All these sometimes in multiple layas.

As discussed in an earlier essay, there are two kinds of varnas: pada varna and tana varna, each with a distinct characteristic and intent.

The very first varnas can be traced to the late seventeenth century. In a little town called Karvetinagaram, in the present Chittoor district of Andhra Pradesh, the brothers Govindasamayya and Koonasamayya seem to have composed the very first var on record. They composed varnas in ragas such as me navaroj and kedaragaula, and were followed very closely by the multifaceted vaggeyakara, Melattur Virabhadrayya (early eighteenth century). Melattur, a small town in the Tanjavur delta, has been a centre of traditional dance and music of a devotional bent since the seventeenth century. Like almost all the scholars, musicians, composers and dancers living in Melattur, Virabhadrayya's ancestry can be traced to the Telugu-speaking regions. His varnas were in ragas such as huseni, anandabhairavi and punnagavarali.

Pada varnas, the first type composed, were characterized by their melodic flow, which was similar to the compositional form pada. How they actually came into being is very difficult to trace, but they do appear from the late seventeenth century. The significant point here is that the pada varna was probably composed for Sadir, which shows that the varna tradition is associated with the evolution of Bharatanatyam.

Soon, many composers appear, among whom Pacchimiriyam Adiyappaiyya (eighteenth century) occupies a very important place. What makes his position special in the annals of Karnatik music is the sheer grandeur of his only surviving varna, viriboni, in raga bhairavi and khanda jati ata tala. In a way, viriboni can be said to have standardized the structure for a tana varna that held its ground only for a short period of time.

It is in the varna of Adiyappaiyya that we see the emergence of the tana varna as a separate aesthetic variety. Scholars believe that the tana varnas are to be rendered only in ghana ragas, probably because of the aesthetic similarity between the tana and tana varna. 'Ghana' used in congruence with raga also indicates a dense and rigid melodic aesthetic. Bhairavi does not have such an aesthetic, which would lead us to wonder what possible connection there could be between ghana ragas, tana and tana varna. Maybe this was a logical framework that was not followed by all vaggeyakaras. But if the most revered tana varna in the history of varna is not in a ghana raga, it is difficult to reconcile with this analysis. We are also not sure about what performance contexts the tana varnas were rendered in.

Following Adiyappaiyya, there were numerous composers who composed varnas of both pada and tana varieties, including Ramasvami Dikshitar (1735–1817) and the prominent tana varna composer Pallavi Gopala Ayyar (mid- to late eighteenth century). Until Pallavi Gopala Ayyar, the varna seems to have retained its older format, where the charana is relinked with the anupallavi of the varna through multiple avartanas of charana, rendered after the ettugada svaras. Pallavi Gopala Ayyar may have been the first to edit this format into the modern structure now in vogue. Ramasvami Dikshitar was a prolific composer of varnas, and it seems unusual that his son Muttusvami Dikshitar (1775–1835) did not compose any. But in *Sangita Sampradaya Pradarshini*, Subbarama Dikshitar attributes two varnas to Muttusvami Dikshitar, though they do not contain his signet. One of the varnas is the popular pada varna 'Rupamujuchi', which has over the last century become iconic in Bharatanatyam. Other scholars attribute this varna to his father. Those who favour *Pradarshini*'s attribution believe that Muttusvami Dikshitar composed it for the arangetram (formal, first performance) of his student Kamalam, a devadasi. The other varna in raga sriranjani is a unique composition said to have been jointly composed by Ramasvami Dikshitar, Muttusvami Dikshitar, Chinnasvami Dikshitar (1778–1823), who was Muttusvami Dikshitar's brother and Shyama Shastri (1762–1827). Shyama Shastri has also composed tana varnas.

We also come across mention of varna as a compositional form within dance-based dramas called Nirupanas, which were composed during the rule of King Sarabhoji (1798–1832). But these varnas are structurally very different from the pada varna and tana varna. Were these some samples of an older varna format, or were they different compositions using the same nomenclature? It is very difficult to say.

The pada varna got its prominence from the compositions of the Tanjavur quartet (first half of the nineteenth century). The four brothers who made up that quartet – Chinnayya Pillai, Ponnayya Pillai, Sivanandam Pillai and Vadivelu Pillai – were all students of Muttusvami Dikshitar. They were prolific composers for Sadir, and established the pada varna as an important compositional form. Though Tyagaraja himself did not compose any varnas, almost all his students including Vina Kuppayyar (1798–1860) and later Kuppayyar's son Tiruvotriyur Tyagayyar (1845–1917) made significant contributions to varnas, especially tana varnas. We must keep in mind that many nattuvanars may well have been great varna composers, but due to the lack of information, we are unable to trace either their authorship or even sometimes the varnas themselves.

Among modern composers of pada varnas and tana varnas, Papanasam Sivan (1890–1973), Lalgudi Jayaraman (1930–2013) and Dr Balamuralikrishna (b. 1930) figure prominently. In many twentieth-century varna compositions, due to a lack of understanding regarding the aesthetic differences between pada varnas and tana varnas, it is almost impossible to differentiate between them, except by using the superficial aspect of the existence of lyrics or the lack of it in the svara sections of the varnas.

Varnas of the tana variety are the first complex compositions learnt by any student of music. Both tana and pada varnas with their distinct self-descriptive aesthetic nature give Karnatik music the thrust towards raga exploration.

Svarajati

We come now to a musical form that has two interpretations, one associated with Bharatanatyam and the other with Karnatik music.

Melattur Virabhadrayya appears as one of the earliest composers of the svarajati, which is used in Bharatanatyam. He composed a svarajati in huseni set to adi tala, 'Sami ne ne ralla'. This svarajati was obviously very popular, as many composers composed svarajatis in huseni with almost that exact melodic structure. Among them was 'Emandayanra' in raga huseni set to rupaka tala. According to Subbarama Dikshitar, this was a composition with the matu provided by Melattur Venkatarama Shastri (eighteenth century) and the dhatu by Pacchimiriyam Adiyappaiyya. Though it is traditionally believed that even the svarajati is structured such that the charana connects to the pallavi, this svarajati ends with the charana. The very same Adiyappaiyya in his 'Viriboni' used the older varna format connecting the charana with the pallavi. Is it then possible that the svarajati began this practice of ending a composition with the charana and that was later followed in varnas? Another svarajati in huseni, with the same melodic structure, is attributed to the Tanjavur quartet.

To Shyama Shastri must go the credit for having created the svarajati form now so well established in Karnatik art music, and his three svarajatis in ragas bhairavi, todi and yadukulakamboji stand out as examples of his great musicianship. But the Nirupanas of Tanjavur also contain a compositional form called svarajati. This is very similar to Shyama Shastri's svarajatis in the multiple svara–sahitya passages and in the correspondence between the length of the svara and sahitya. It is possible that Shyama Shastri adopted it from this dance-drama tradition.

Kirtana and Pada

Kirtanas are known to be wholly devotional and spiritual in intent and content, whereas padas contain erotic poetry as the lyrical theme, but in structure they seem the same. The question then: is the pada different from the kirtana? For any connoisseur of Karnatik music, this would appear to be a naïve query. Almost all rasikas will explain that what differentiates the pada from the kirtana is the slow pace of the pada and its fluid melodic structure.

The padas are invariably sung in chauka-kala, highlighting the raga's subtle expressions and bear the clear stamp of the Vina Dhanammal tradition. Padas in their essence are gentler than kirtanas and have the erotic content deftly woven into their aesthetics. But when the very same pada is rendered by some musicians from Andhra Pradesh, it can sound very similar to a kirtana, negating the point about their essential difference. The learning from this is that musical interpretation can influence presentation effects; they cannot alter aesthetic structures.

In the early stages of their evolution, the pada and kirtana were interchangeable terms. It did not matter whether the lyrical content was bhakti or shringara. Annamacharya (1424–1503), for instance, composed kirtanas that had both bhakti and shringara content. Annamacharya has been addressed as Padakavita-pitamaha and Purandaradasa's devotional kirtanas are called padas. Pada and kirtana were words that may have been used for many types of compositions or poetry, but during the fifteenth and sixteenth centuries became associated with this specific compositional form.

Annamacharya's compositions have a pallavi–charana structure and some have pallavi–anupallavi–charana. These four-line charana constructions are also called vrttas or vrttabandhas. Some scholars assert that it was Annamacharya who gave the pallavi pride of position – being the first section in a kirtana – and established the rule that the two pallavi lines must be of equal length. We have already discussed the difficulty in confirming the existence of anupallavi in a kirtana. It is from the observation of dvitiyakshara prasa in the first line and the third line that we can separate the composition into pallavi and anupallavi. Whether he used the anupallavi at all is a difficult question, but some of Annamacharya's compositions do have the dvitiyakshara prasa that helps us conclude that they might have been anupallavis. Most of his kirtanas have three charanas, but there are exceptions. We must accept, I think, that the kirtana tradition in the south was Annamacharya's contribution. Since there is no tradition of singing his compositions, and because the copper plates from the Tirupati temple on which his compositions are inscribed lack tala information, it is very difficult to determine the details of his kirtanas. Musicians who have tuned his sahitya have sometimes treated the second line of the kirtana as the anupallavi, creating a one-line pallavi and one-line anupallavi structure. At other times, they use it as a two-line pallavi structure.

We face similar problems with the compositions of Purandaradasa as we do not have an oral tradition of his compositions. In his padas, the dvitiyakshara prasa is very clear, and hence we believe that it must be an anupallavi. The next section is taken as the charana. Sometimes there is also a tendency to club two couplets together to bring about a four-avartana charana, establishing a concordance between the pallavi–anupallavi–charana, a pallavi of two avartanas, an anupallavi of two avartanas and a charana of four avartanas. But it is quite possible that all the sections were of equal length – that is, couplets of two avartanas each. We have kirtanas of this type even in Tyagaraja's creations. As in Annamacharya's kirtanas, sometimes the second poetic line is treated as a part of the pallavi, at other times as a single line anupallavi. The question is whether the first two lines could have been an integrated section with the prasa, without a separation of pallavi and anupallavi. The lack of an oral tradition or written music tradition makes it very difficult to visualize the musical form of the pada or kirtana as visualized by Annamacharya or Purandaradasa. We can only use the prasa yardstick to come to conclusions. It appears that both Annamacharya and Purandaradasa have compositions that seem to have an anupallavi and many that have only a pallavi–multiple charana structure.

We must also acknowledge the influence of Bhadrachala Ramadas in the seventeenth century, whose kirtanas also follow the dvitiyakshara prasa rule, leading us to believe that it is a separate anupallavi section.

We know that dvitiyakshara prasa tradition was born out of the Tamil poetry tradition. Among Tamil scholars, there is also a claim that the anupallavi was first found in the kirtanas of Muttutandavar. The problem with this assertion is that it is difficult to date Muttutandavar, though some attempts have been made to place him in the fifteenth century. But this cannot be clearly established. Narayana Tirtha (seventeenth century) is also given credit for developing the anupallavi section in a kirtana. But it gets complicated as some traditions of rendering the tarangams of Narayana Tirtha use the term 'udgraha' instead of pallavi. Maybe this was only to claim antiquity. What is clear is that, from the seventeenth century, the formats pallavi–charana and pallavi–anupallavi–charana became popular.

There is a temptation among scholars to try and link this compositional type to the prabandha tradition. Some believe that Narahari Tirtha (late fourteenth century) of the Haridasa tradition created the pallavi–charana structure, which was later established by Sripadaraya (1404–1502). They also strongly believe that pallavi–anupallavi–charana was created through the reorganization of the sections in the prabandhas: the udgraha, melapaka, dhruva and abhoga. Scholars with an 'Annamacharya orientation' have theorized that the Annamacharya kirtana evolved from the ela prabandha found in *Sangita Ratnakara*. But such conclusions are very difficult to validate.

I am sure there are many more theories. We cannot be certain about these conclusions, as it is possible that another tradition of kirtana existed locally in many of these areas. The human mind is capable of creating very logical correlations, which may not be the way in which transformations took place.

Let me propose another possibility. Originally, padas must have been multiple four-line poetic-musical forms, as the Tevarams are. In these poems, all the four lines adhered to dvitiyakshara prasa. The uniformity of the four-line structure may have also reflected in the melodic progression, which in turn would mean that the same melody was used for each set of four-line poetry. In the first transformation, the first four lines must have been divided into two sets of two. But why such a transformation? The most likely reason is the melodic imperative. Most vaggeyakaras and scholars state that compositions are musical creations. They give primacy to music and poetic alliteration that together give a composition its form. By splitting the first four lines in two sections and retaining a longer four-line charana, there were now three stages of raga development, yet the prasa of poetry was retained. As time went by, instead of all four lines of the pallavi and the anupallavi adhering to dvitiyakshara prasa, only the first lines of each needed to. Hence, the prasa in the charanas of all compositions remain independent of the pallavi and anupallavi. This development may have been completely independent of deshi tradition. Of course, all this is conjecture as much as the other theories are. The dvitiyakshara prasa is found in all kinds of compositions, including kirtanas, varnas, svarajatis and javalis.

The devotional kirtana tradition was absorbed into Karnatik music. Annamacharya and all the Haridasas were part of the bhakti movement in different regions. They were scholars and musicians, yet the objective of their compositions was religious.

Padas that became shringara padas owe their status to the seventeenth-century vaggeyakara Kshetrayya. He travelled through Madurai and Tanjavur, later moving to Golkonda. We know that Kshetrayya visited Tanjavur during the reign of Raghunatha Nayak (1600–33) and Vijayaraghava Nayak (1633–73). He was a prolific composer and is said to have composed around a thousand padas. His visit to Tanjavur had a deep impact on local musicians, so that from the seventeenth century onwards, we have many vaggeyakaras composing padas with both religious and erotic content. Padas of shringara seem to have been used primarily in Sadir and dance dramas. A contemporary of Kshetrayya, Karvetinagaram Sarangapani, composed shringara padas. Even during this period, there was no distinction drawn between the pada and the kirtana.

The question is whether Kshetrayya had a central role in the evolution of the kirtana as seen in the compositions of the trinity. Though kirtanas of the bhakti tradition played an important role in creating the modern kirtana, I am of the opinion that the padas of Kshetrayya seem to have developed a compositional unit that is very close to the ones used by later kirtana composers, such as the trinity. I believe that Kshetrayya's influence in the development of the modern kirtana in Tanjavur is far more than we give him credit for. If we were to look at the melodic form of a Kshetrayya pada and a Tyagaraja kirtana, there is a sense of similarity in the poetic and melodic interplay. All of Kshetrayya padas use the pallavi–anupallavi–charana structure and the melody flows similarly, though with some differences. This argument can be countered on the basis that my observations are based on contemporary practice. I concede that there is no definite way of confirming this; but I strongly feel that, beyond my musician's interpretations, the Kshetryya pada has the nature of a complex kirtana as associated with the trinity. Unlike the Kshetrayya padas, neither the poetry of Annamacharya or Purandaradasa seem to possess the form to be taken as complex compositions. When musicians try to create melody for them, even with the freedom to create a grand musical structure, the lyrics do not give the tunesmith the inspiration to create a kirtana à la Dikshitar or Tyagaraja. Musicians have attempted this, but the lyrics are unable to hold elongated musical curves, leaps, heavy stresses, miniature carvings and rapid sweeps, all associated with the dhatu in the monumental compositions of the trinity and of Kshetrayya. We should keep in mind that not all kirtanas of the trinity necessarily falls into the art music category.

In the seventeenth and eighteenth centuries, we come across

vaggeyakaras who composed in Tamil, including Papavinasa Mudaliyar, Arunachala Kavirayar and Marimutta Pillai. We could refer to their compositions as pada or kirtana. Other vaggeyakaras who composed padas/kirtanas in Telugu and Sanskrit around the same period included Giriraja Kavi, Melattur Virabhadrayya and Margadarshi Sesha Ayyangar.

The modern kirtanas – by which I mean the kirtanas that have prevailed through the nineteenth and twentieth centuries and are now standard – were the creations of the trinity: Tyagaraja, Muttusvami Dikshitar and Shyama Shastri. Each one of them contributed to the further exploration and consolidation of the kirtana form. It is around this time that the conceptual division between kirtana and pada may have begun to be felt and recognized. But one thing is clear: whether it was kirtana or pada, whether their lyrical content was bhakti or shringara, these two forms were reinvented from their own spheres of devotion or dance when they were absorbed into art music. This was a distinct gain to Karnatik compositions, as both kirtana and pada, in their own individualistic ways, became highly evolved musical entities, with a space for extended musical imaging and imagining within the Karnatik matrix.

Here we must turn our attention to the Karnatik krti. The word 'krti' today denotes the devotional kirtana. Some scholars assert that the word was derived from the Annamacharya tradition, where it was used to denote padas and kirtanas. Krti etymologically means 'that which carries skill'. In this sense, it could refer to any creation – music, sculpture or body of poetry. However, krti has now come to refer irreversibly to the compositional form of that name. 'Kirtana' or 'pada' are more appropriate terms, because they have been long associated with this compositional form, while krti is only a generic term that has been consciously adopted only over the last century or so to mean kirtanas. The use of the term 'krti' has also resulted in a futile and unnecessary differentiation between kirtanas and krtis. Some scholars state that kirtana is purely devotional in nature, while krti may also be philosophical in content and is art music. No such divisions actually exist.

Ghanam Krishna Ayyar (1790–1854), a contemporary of Tyagaraja, was a famous performing musician and vaggeyakara. He is well known for his padas. In the post-trinity period, we have had numerous vaggeyakaras, including many from the tradition of these composers, like Maha Vaidyanatha Ayyar (1844–93), Patnam Subrahmanya Ayyar (1845–1902), Subbaraya Shastri (1806–62) and Mysore Sadasiva Rao (nineteenth century), who were prolific composers of kirtanas. Other vaggeyakaras of importance in the nineteenth century included Gopalakrishna Bharati (1811–81) and Annai-Ayya (nineteenth century). To them, kirtana meant lyrics that were only devotional or religious.

Conversely, for Muvvanallur Sabhapati Ayyar (early nineteenth century) and Subbarama Ayyar (nineteenth century), who were vaggeyakaras of padas, padas were meant to be shringara padas. In the twentieth and twenty-first centuries, we have had many vaggeyakaras composing kirtanas, but very few composers of padas. It does seem that the devotional content has taken precedence over love and eroticism. Among the many vaggeyakaras of the twentieth century, Papanasam Sivan, Kotishvara Ayyar, M. Balamuralikrishna, Lalgudi Jayaraman, Tanjavur Sankara Iyer and 'Spencer' Venugopal stand out as those whose compositions have gained great respectability among musicians and listeners.

Some observations of U.V. Svaminatha Ayyar (1855–1942) are important at this juncture. A Tamil scholar who single-handedly brought to light Sangam literature, he wrote many books that help us understand the musical environment of the 1800s. His most important observation is regarding Tamil kirtanas. He says that until the early nineteenth century there were thousands of Tamil kirtanas that have now been lost as there was no one to sing or appreciate them. This seems like a castigation of what was perceived as excessive Sanskritization and Teluguization of Karnatik music. In an aside, he makes two very interesting observations. He mentions a woman Mayurattammal (seventeenth or eighteenth century) as a composer of kirtanas with the purity of Karnatik music and advaitic content. This is probably one of the first references to a Karnatik vaggeyakara who is a woman. These kirtanas were known to Gopalakrishna Bharati, the most prolific Tamil vaggeyakara of the nineteenth century. The second observation is about a Muslim, Mastan Sahib, whose compositions were rendered by a staunch Shaivite, Duraimangalam Shivaprakasha Svamigal. It would be logical to assume that these were Karnatik compositions, as U.V. Svaminatha Ayyar primarily discusses Karnatik music, Harikatha and Upanyasa.

Since so many kirtanas are attributed to several of these vaggeyakaras, there is bound to be controversy regarding the authorship. In the case of the trinity, there are claims and counter-claims. It becomes very difficult to resolve these conflicts because these vaggeyakaras had numerous disciples, and it is quite possible that only certain groups knew about some compositions. In spite of these possibilities, some scholars are definite about the spuriousness of certain compositions based on the lyrical and compositional structuring. For example, almost everybody accepts that 'Akhilandeshvari' in raga jujavanti set to adi tala has been wrongly attributed to Muttusvami Dikshitar. In the case of Dikshitar, there are many more kirtanas that might be of doubtful authorship. But how do we determine authorship?

It is my view that it is impossible to determine authorship based on the melody, as it has changed through generations of musicians handling these compositions. This can be determined only through a study of language and vocabulary. But as a musicologist pointed out, even that can be imitated. This leaves us without a solution. However, this is an issue that needs to be seriously studied without personal prejudice. But the spuriousness of authorship should not stop anyone from rendering them or appreciating the composition.

There are also cases of vaggeyakaras whose standing has been questioned. In the case of Svati Tirunal (1813–46), the matter even went to the courts. That particular controversy is a complex issue, with no clear resolution. People from both sides of the fence are constantly presenting 'new evidence' to establish their position. The complexity of the issue extends from the authenticity of the name 'Svati Tirunal' to the fact that other important vaggeyakaras, such as Vadivelu (of the Tanjavur quartet), have been court musicians and could well have been the 'true' makers of the court-originating compositions. From the different sources of information I have combed, I believe that Svati Tirunal was a vaggeyakara, but to what extent all the compositions that stand in his name in so many forms and styles can be attributed to him is highly debatable. This is a deeply polarizing issue and needs neutral scholarship.

Another vaggeyakara, Uttukadu Venkatakavi (from Uttukadu, Tanjavur district), is said to have lived before the trinity (probably early eighteenth century), but has been a cause of debate among musicologists and musicians, because there is no mention of him in any treatise, court document or publication. His style – which has been compared to that of poets like Arunagirinathar, the author of the tiruppugazh – is said to represent an older compositional method, but there is no externally verifiable evidence to support this. But it would be difficult to accept tiruppugazhs as musical compositions. No vaggeyakara of the period Venkatakavi is said to belong to reflects this older style. He may have been unique, but considering that so many vaggeyakaras, devadasis and performers have been mentioned and honoured by the culturally engaged rulers of Tanjavur, it seems unusual that a vaggeyakara with such a prolific record would not find even a little mention. The issue here is not about rendering compositions attributed to him. But if claims are made about the time and style of vaggeyakaras, there must be some external evidence to support such an assertion. Perhaps more research will reveal information that can substantiate those contentions.

Javali

The gait, melodic lilt and simple language of javalis combine to make them seem like a casual conversation in music. They are bound to leave any rasika with a feeling of joy. That the lyrics are sometimes seen as bordering on the prurient is of no consequence to a true rasika. The word 'javali' itself is a mystery. Some say that it refers to 'lewd poetry' in Kannada, while some have pointed to a Marathi etymology. This seems to be little more than a hypothesis, as Marathi scholars do not think it has a Marathi origin. The *Tamil Lexicon* mentions that javali is derived from the Urdu 'jhvali', but there is no corroboration of this possibility. What we can confidently say is that as a compositional form, it was established only in the mid-nineteenth century, when it became popular with the devadasi community who danced and sang javalis. There have been many javali composers in the nineteenth and early twentieth centuries, including Puchi Srinivasa Ayyangar (1860–1919), Vina Krishnamacharya (d. 1947), Karur Chinna Devudu (1861–1901), Dharmapuri Subbarayar (b. 1864) and Tatitopu Pattabhirama Rao (nineteenth century).

Ragamalikas and Talamalikas

Ragamalikas derive their distinct quality from the way the vaggeyakara visualizes the flow of one raga to another – a garland of ragas. The choice of each raga, their sequence, the changes in laya and the almost invisible exit and entry from one raga to another, gives the ragamalika its aesthetic beauty. Ragamalikas have been composed in many compositional formats, including kirtana, varna and tillana. Melattur Virabhadrayya seems to have been one of the first vaggeyakaras to use the ragamalika idea.

His ragamalikas were in the format of a kirtana. His disciple
Ramasvami Dikshitar followed his example, and went a step
further, composing a 108 raga–tala–malika. Muttusvami Dikshitar
was also a composer of brilliant ragamalikas. In the nineteenth
century, Maha Vaidyanatha Ayyar composed a ragamalika in all
the seventy-two melakarta ragas. There have also been tana varnas
in ragamalika, the most popular being the navaragamalika varna
in adi tala composed by Patnam Subrahmanya Ayyar. Among
contemporary composers, M. Balamuralikrishna has composed
two very popular tillanas that are ragamalikas.

Tillana

The very name, three-syllabled, with a double stress on the lingual
'l', conjures rhythm and a fast-moving sequence of non-lexical
syllables.

Once again, Melattur Virabhadrayya is the man of the
moment. His tillana in raga pantuvarali set to adi tala must have
been one of the earliest tillanas. The dominant view is that this
form came to Tanjavur from the north, especially considering its
closeness to the Hindustani tarana. But there are some scholars
who hold the view that the tillana can be traced to the older
compositional form, prabandha. Some prabandhas used rhythmic
syllables as part of their text. Scholars believe that it may have
been the forerunner to the tillana. Either way, there is no doubt
that even this compositional form gained great importance only
from the mid-nineteenth century, beginning with the Tanjavur
quartet. From then on, there have been vaggeyakaras who
have been significant contributors to the repertoire of tillanas,
including Patnam Subrahmanya Ayyar, Puchi Srinivasa Ayyangar,
M. Balamuralikrishna and Lalgudi G. Jayaraman among others.

The various compositional forms as we know them today
came into being in the last 300 years. By the end of the Nayak
period (1532–1673) and early Maratha rule in Tanjavur, it

seems that the prabandha, the primary compositional form in the chaturdandi tradition, had lost its importance. The pada and kirtana had come to stay. At the same time, older dance forms, such as jakkini, perani and dhrupada kelika, may have given way to the pada varna, svarajati and padas. But some seemingly older dance forms, such as jakkini, are found in the Nirupanas published in the period of King Sarabhoji and even said to have been performed in the Maratha courts. Even a Nirupana composition called prabandha, not related to the chaturdandi prabandha in any way, is found here. Older names are retained, even though the forms themselves have transformed. But there is no doubt that the eighteenth-century compositional forms had replaced older forms in their relevance. All these newer forms, which evolved from the early eighteenth century, crystallized from the mid-eighteenth century to the late nineteenth century to give Karnatik music its contemporary compositional foundation.

If we were to look at all these compositional forms and their history briefly described here, we find that most of them came into Karnatik art music from dance or religious music. This indicates to us the nature of 'art music' that may have been practised in the days before these compositions. The compositions have been absorbed in art music and not artificially planted into the tradition. Vaggeyakaras grasped the nuance of art music, introducing some of these forms into Karnatik music and stabilizing their aesthetic role within its intent. In some cases, performing musicians introduced certain compositional forms into Karnatik music and gave it an art music quality. But it is my view that musicians have also been at fault at times in not recognizing that absorbed compositions must be internalized within their new existence – art music. The fact that they have neglected to do so has increased the density of compositions in Karnatik music, making the form overly dependent on compositions. It is possible to have all these compositions within the spectrum of Karnatik identity, along with the various improvisational methods as long as we can treat them with the seriousness of art music and use them as the nucleus for creative departures.

Every composition holds within its heart two souls – the vaggeyakara and the musician. The composition belongs to both; neither can claim that the truth exists only with him. The composition can only blossom in this conjoint existence. But for this relationship to really create art music, the vaggeyakara must realize that his composition is a sea into which the musician must immerse in order to imbibe the music's essentials and expand its horizons. At the same time, every musician must realize that this delicate and fragile creation of the vaggeyakara is precious and must not be scarred by irreverence.

26

The Song Within

At the heart of the composition pulsates the idea of manodharma. To sense its vitality and, equally, its indispensability,
we have to examine the term and its actual aesthetic form.
Sometimes the recurrence of terminologies can be misleading.
We have to look at it critically to decide for ourselves whether our
manodharma systems have the antiquity that we constantly seek.

What does the word 'manodharma' mean? It is difficult to
find a one-word equivalent in English for this blend of two
highly evolved concepts. The word 'improvisation' is often used
to explain it in its actual working; I have used it too within these
pages. But manodharma is much more than just the ability to create
music on the spur of the moment. It is not about a technique.
Manodharma has a core to it, a still centre from which radiate
forms of creative musical expression. At that core of manodharma
is the intuiting, imagining, creating mind – 'manas', from which
comes 'mano'. But then manas contains a larger meaning than
'mind'. It encompasses all those faculties, impulses and gifts that
empower and propel the mind to creativity. Most importantly,
manodharma is also about the nature of the individual engaged
in such a creation. 'Dharma' here, is not just about righteousness,

virtue, impartiality or equity – the traditional connotations of that strong word – but about the integrity of action in the manner or mode of musical creativity. In 'manodharma', dharma is about a responsible free will, but also as much about what should be at the heart of that free will: respect for that which is being explored – Karnatik music.

Alapana

Any form of musical presentation that is not pre-composed is called anibaddha – untied or unbound. The pre-composed that is only rendered is considered nibaddha. Though contemporary scholars sometimes take nibaddha to mean compositions that are bound by tala, and anibaddha as those not bound by tala, the actual differentiation is more subtle. Anibaddha is music that does not have a fixed organization and that which the musician has not learnt before rendering it. Anibaddha is brought together by the musician at 'that moment' using the aesthetics of the music. This can be created with or without tala, within or outside a composition. Nibaddha refers to not only a composition with lyrics, but also to the rendition of a musical presentation of only svaras or melody, which has been structured in advance and memorized. This separation exists in deshi music.

We come across two words in deshi music that appear connected to our contemporary idea of alapana – alapa and alapti. Both refer to the delineation of a raga, but they are not synonyms. Alapa is explained as a rendition of the raga with the primary purpose of presenting its specific characteristics. This is almost like an academic exercise. Grama ragas are described according to various features, such as tonic svara, initial svara, the range of the raga, etc. In *Sangita Ratnakara*, after every grama raga, an alapa is notated. This is only a small set of svaras, which present the raga features in melodic form. Some scholars treat this alapa as nibaddha as it seems to have been a composed musical presentation. This alapa is not to be confused with alapana as we know it today.

The raga alapti is closer to our idea of an alapana. 'Raga alapti' is mentioned in connection with the rendition of deshi ragas. It is as an instantaneous organization and rendition of a raga. This would be a form of anibaddha music. During the alapti, a musician would explore the melodic movements in the raga using the paradigms that define its identity. Kallinatha (commentator of *Sangita Ratnakara*) makes an interesting comment when he says that the alapa and alapti can be brought together under the term alapanam. He says the role of alapti is not only to reveal the raga, but also conceal it. This may sound quite absurd, but I infer it to mean that the musician moves beyond the characteristic melodic features of a raga during alapti. She treads on the melodic movements clearly defining the raga and those that are commonly shared with other ragas – and in the course of the melodic development, brings clarity when the delineated raga once again emerges through a defining phrase. If the musician attempts to render an alapana today and confines herself to the textbook phrases associated with the raga, it is not an instantaneous creation, and in fact not an alapana. Only when the musician moves beyond them is she rendering an alapana. While this is done, the musician will constantly travel across phrases of melody that are textbook 'pat', those that stand on the borderline with other ragas and those that share common ground with other ragas. But she must with her own manodharma draw out from this flux the raga's cohesive identity. Kallinatha's analogy of a certain Devadatta entering and sitting in the royal court is very evocative. He says that until Devadatta is seated, he is clearly distinguished from all the other seated ministers. Once he is seated, he is one among them. Only when he rises once again to speak or present himself is he distinct. This gives us the idea that Kallinatha is looking at raga alapti as something that goes beyond rendering only the raga's defined characteristic phrases.

While raga alapti is very similar to the alapana as we understand it today, we must be careful not to conclude that they are the same in texture or presentation. They are only conceptually similar. The nature of today's ragas and the method of alapana are not similar to the alapti. There is also the word 'alatti' used in Tamil music literature that mirrors the idea of alapana.

In *Sangita Sudha* of Govinda Dikshita, we come across the term alapa once again. This treatise describes the chaturdandi tradition of music. Chaturdandi (literally, four pillars) has four modes of musical presentation: alapa, thaya, prabandha and gita, of which only the first is relevant in the context of this essay. While describing every raga, Govinda Dikshita provides a guide to an alapa in the raga that can give the reader a melodic concept of the raga. Obviously, for a musician who lived during his time, this would have made complete sense. The musician would have been intuitively aware of the melodic identity and texture of the ragas in practice, and interpreted the alapa accordingly. However, when we look back at this tool he provided, we find it difficult to aurally conceptualize the raga. The ragas Dikshita mentioned have changed over the years. Since music dwells not in a book but in the mind, this exercise, important as it is, is challenging. Yet it provides us an insight, however incomplete, into what the melodic movements may have been like and what the organization of an alapa meant. The alapa in *Sangita Sudha* is divided into six sections. The opening of the alapa is called the akshiptika, which introduces the raga. The next is the ragavardhani, where the raga is further elaborated. At the end of this elaboration, the alapa is brought to an intermediate rest: vidari. Then various kinds of elaborations that traverse different ranges of the raga are presented. These melodic movements can be ascending, descending or around a certain svara. This section is known as sthayi. This too is brought to a conclusion with a vartini. At the end of that is the nyasa, which establishes the svara on which the alapa ends. These divisions can be further subdivided if there are multiple ragavardhanis or sthayis in the alapa.

For every section, Dikshita has beautifully described the melodic direction that the phrases can take. For example, he wrote that, beginning from the rishabha in the tara sthayi, you need to descend to the madhya sthayi rishabha, and then ascend to the madhyama in the tara sthayi, then render a few tanas (melodic phrases) and rest at tara sthayi shadja. This was a sample of an akshiptika from raga gaula. He describes every section of the alapa in this manner.

I doubt that this meant the alapa was a fixed concept. It was probably an improvisation that was organized in a specific way. Within each section, the musician is given guidelines based on the melodic character of the raga. The musician must have used these as structural and melodic references within which he could expand the raga and present its emotional colour. Here we see that the alapa has a very different meaning in the chaturdandi tradition compared to the deshi. Now it is conceptually an alapti. *Chaturdandi Prakashika* also provides a description of the alapa technique, but does not use it to describe every raga.

However, as soon as we think that we have been able to decipher the alapa, we face another challenge. Manuscripts that contained notations – authorship unknown – of alapa and thaya collected by Raja Shahaji are preserved at the Sarasvati Mahal library, Tanjavur. The alapas are laid out in two main styles. One that is meant to be sung, as the notations provide the syllables 'ta nam' below the svaras. The use of these syllables raises some issues, as today, 'ta' and 'nam' are used for tana rendition and not alapana. The other style given for the alapa is to be played on the vina. There are also some changes in the nomenclature used for the various sections when compared to *Sangita Sudha*, but are quite similar to the names in *Chaturdandi Prakashika*.

These notations present us with two problems. If we compare the melodic movements in the notations for each raga with those in *Sangita Sudha*, we will find many differences. It is of course quite possible that the style of alapa renditions had changed by the time these notations were made. But the larger question is: why were they notated?

There is an important difference between the alapa being described at every stage of development and the whole alapa being notated. The latter indicates a certain rigidity in form. Was the alapa then a much more structured format than the free rendition that I had visualized in my reading of *Sangita Sudha*? Or were these notations only indicative of one possible way the alapa could be sung? I really do not have an answer. But the details of the notations incline me to the belief that the alapa was a fixed and rigid structure, and that my initial assumption regarding its open form needs reconsideration. While I come to this conclusion, I must remember that scholars have not described any musician as a composer of alapas, while composers of prabandhas have been acknowledged and even thayas are said to have been composed by Tannapacharya, the main guru for the chaturdandi school. Some twentieth-century musicians have tried to configure or even describe modern alapana methods using the chaturdandi alapa sections. This is only a way of giving structure to the modern alapana. It has no connection with the alapa of chaturdandi.

We first come across the nagasvara and tavil as distinct musical instruments of the temple during the fifteenth century. There is a lot of debate among scholars about how far these instruments date back. Some trace them to the Chola period (eleventh century) or even earlier, while others think they came from Telugu-speaking regions during the Vijayanagara Empire. We do not know what exactly these musicians played at the temples or royal processions until the eighteenth century, but we do know that, by the mid-eighteenth century, they must have been playing different ragas at different times of the day at the temple. We also know that Ramasvami Dikshitar formulated musical practice connected with the religious events at the Tiruvarur temple, both for everyday rituals and for special festivals. Ragas were chosen to depict the mood of the time in relation to the rituals in the temple. This is important as it indicates the anibaddha nature of the rendition in the temple. The rendition of alapana by nagasvara vidvans must have also influenced the emergence of the modern alapana and impacted the format of development. After all, they played for the ritual and for hours through the night during festivals, requiring them to improvise on a raga for an extended period of time.

In the nineteenth century, we come across clear examples of alapanas rendered by nagasvara vidvans and brahmin musicians. Sulamangalam Vaidyanatha Bhagavatar (1866–1943) in his description of musicians of the nineteenth century speaks about many musicians who excelled in alapana rendition, including vocalists Maha Vaidyanatha Ayyar (1844–93), Patnam Subrahmanya Ayyar (1845–1902), Kundrakkudi Krishna Ayyar (1816–89), nagasvara vidvan Shivakozhundu (1838–1911), violinist Tirukkodikaval Krishna Ayyar and even a sarangi vidvan Veerasami Naidu (nineteenth century). U.V. Svaminatha Ayyar writes that his father used to render alapana, but we do not get any further description of the method of rendition. He also speaks about Ghanam Krishna Ayyar rendering an alapana of athana raga at Tyagaraja's residence. He makes an interesting observation on Maha Vaidyanatha Ayyar, that he used the word 'shankara' instead of arbitrary syllables while rendering an alapana. I wonder what he would have said to the syllables used today in alapana.

Nevertheless, this is the journey of the alapana. Whether all these dots are directly connected or not is for each reader and researcher to decide. The formation of the alapana as we have come to understand it from the late 1800s is a culmination of many of these strains, along with the unseen and unheard travelling sounds of culture that moved between many different regions of the Indian subcontinent.

Tana

The history of the tana, or tanam, is one of the most difficult subjects to discuss in Karnatik music. The antiquity of the word makes the understanding of its contemporary usage extremely complex. In this section, I will first present the various meanings of the word tana in different musical systems, so we can explore whether these are relevant today and from where it may have come to the Karnatik idiom. But to an extent these are still conjectures.

It first appears in the context of murchhanas in gandharva music. Murchhana was the arrangement of the seven svaras in their natural sequence: sa, ri, ga, ma, pa, dha, ni. Each murchhana began on one of the seven svaras. When these sequences were made without one or two svaras, they were known as tanas. These are not arbitrary sequences. The gandharva system specified the svaras that could be removed to create shadava sequences (an ascending and descending sequence of six svaras) and audava sequences (an ascending and descending sequences of five svaras) in each grama. For example, in shadja grama, shadava tanas could be created only by removing sa, ri, pa or ni. For audava sequences, only the combinations of sa and pa, ga and ni or ri and pa could be removed. It is easy to compute the total number of shadava or audava tanas possible within these limitations. There are seven sequences, each beginning with one svara. Therefore, in shadja grama, a total of twenty-eight shadava tanas (7x4) and twenty-one (7x3) audava tanas were possible – a total of forty-nine. A similar calculation based on the rules for madhyama grama yielded thirty-five tanas, bringing the total to eighty-four.

These tanas, along with the murchhanas, seem to have been very early forms of melodic sources used for the Rig, Sama and Gatha – ancient musical compositions, usually containing non-vedic text of extended lengths, set to fixed lyrical metres, but not bound within a tala. But they may not have had any musical value even at the time of Bharata. Whether they were connected to the jati melodies or not is not clear, with each author giving us a different perspective.

By the time we come to *Sangita Ratnakara* (thirteenth century), the meaning of tana has changed. This change is closely linked to the change in perception of the murchhana itself. In the essay on raga history, we have already discussed kakali and antara sadharana in relation to the murchhana mentioned in gandharva music. These svaras could be included in a murchhana, but only rarely and along with the shuddha svaras, so that the shruti intervals were not upset. But we are not clear about how they were used. The same sadharanas are also mentioned in relation to murchhanas in *Sangita Ratnakara*. But by the time Sarngadeva wrote his treatise, both kakali nishada and antara gandhara had acquired independence and hence you could have murchhana sequences including both antara gandhara and kakali nishada as also with only antara gandhara or only kakali nishada. In all these cases, the respective shuddha svaras were omitted.

Soon murchhanas were being seen as svara sequences that were scales for melodic sources such as jatis and grama ragas. With this change in context, murchhana meant only a sequence of seven svaras, regardless of order and sequence. Now there were two types: sequences that were in the natural svara order and were known as krama murchhanas, and those that were deviant, known as kuta tana. Once again, 'tana' had changed complexion. Kuta tanas could omit one to six svaras. Which means that they could be sequences of only a couple of svaras, and became calculated combinations of svaras. Therefore, the total number of krama murchhanas and kuta tanas were computed using a unique calculating system.

The term kuta tana reappears in *Chaturdandi Prakashika*, but with a different meaning – a combination of svaras that reflects the characteristics of two ragas. I know this odyssey with the tana is like being trapped in a maze with no clear path. But we are still at the beginning of this mystery. It is only going to get more complex and I request the reader to bear with me.

Clearly, the word 'tana' has already travelled a lot. But to understand tana, we need to pick up another word – thaya – from the seventeenth-century treatise *Sangita Sudha*, which is sometimes linked with the modern tana by scholars. But it is not as simple as that. Thaya was the second 'dandi' of the chaturdandi system.

'Thaya' is a corruption of the term 'sthaya', which is an aesthetic concept that describes the phrases that make a deshi raga. The phrases of a deshi raga consist of gamakas, directional melodic movement and the melodic qualities related to the raga. Sthaya encapsulates the whole aesthetic idea of phrases. This being the case, sthayas are usually described in terms of the emotional effect they have on the listener, though some are explained in technical terms. Sarngadeva provides descriptions for ninety-six sthayas. Parshvadeva in his *Sangita Samayasara* uses the words sthaya and thaya to mean the same musical concept.

Thaya comes in a completely different avatar in *Sangita Sudha* and *Chaturdandi Prakashika*. What was this new thaya? *Chaturdandi Prakashika* does not give us much information. Venkatamakhin says, in accordance with the raga, resting on a svara, four tanas (melodic phrases) must be rendered on the higher four svaras in ascending order. Then four tanas must be sung in the four svaras in descending order. Here, tanas are musical phrases that are rendered with reference to each of these svaras. After this, a sthayi svara must be chosen and there must be a conclusion on the mandra sthayi shadja.

I know this description does not really tell us much about the structure of the thaya. We can try and compare this with the notated thaya that we have from the library of King Sarabhoji. But even that does not help us to really understand the aesthetic purpose of thaya as part of chaturdandi.

To add to this riddle is the presence of the syllables 'ta' and 'nam', marked in the notations, for the vocal rendition of alapa. Given that those are exactly the same syllables as used in modern tana, we could conclude that the alapa of chaturdandi is connected to the modern tana. The sounds tenna and tena, have all been used in both Sanskrit and Tamil literature as being part of musical presentations during different periods. These were considered auspicious syllables. Therefore, the use of such syllables does not establish any aesthetic connection.

I found that if we were to sing any of the alapas or thayas of the chaturdandi period, it could sound to some extent like tana. This is because of the nature of the melodic flow of the alapas and thayas, and our contemporary choice of speed in trying to render them. But we must be very careful to not presume that the modern tana evolved either from the chaturdandi alapa or thaya. The truth is that we have not been able to really make an aesthetic connection with the chaturdandi system in musical presentation. In raga and tala history, on the other hand, the evidence is far clearer.

Let us now move from thaya to another word that has been connected with tana – ghana. In *Ragalakshanamu*, King Shahaji has categorized ragas on the basis of aesthetic form. This is very unique in the history of raga. Ragas are usually slotted on the basis of their svaras or their melodic openness, which allows for improvisation and compositional rendition. Shahaji calls ragas ghana, naya and deshiya. The understanding of ghana as dense and rigid has had a huge impact on musicologists. In modern Karnatik music five of the ghana ragas – nata, gaula, arabhi, sri and varali – are considered ghana ragas apt for tana rendition.

Connected to the nature of ghana is the idea of the tana varna. These varnas are melodically dense – the rendition is rigid and every svara has an emphasis, making the aesthetic experience tight. There are many tana varnas in ghana ragas.

The result is that the use of tana in the context of tana varna composed in ghana ragas has led to some conclusions. Ghana ragas are the ragas in which tana is most apt. Tana varnas are so named because their aesthetic structure is dense and weighty (ghana), and hence sound like tana. This overlapping has led to tana and ghana ragas being irrevocably linked. The tana varna does resemble the modern idea of tana, and sounds beautiful in ghana ragas. However, consider this: there are many varnas from the eighteenth century that are not in ghana ragas. How then can we say that the tana was derived from a combination of the aesthetics of ghana ragas and the melodic form created by the tana varna?

Before we make the leap to the modern tana, we must once again look at ghana in the context of the music presented in the nineteenth century. Specifically, let's look at a musical and aesthetic style known as ghana marga. It seems to have been practised during the nineteenth century and is singularly connected with Ghanam Krishna Ayyar (1790–1854). Most musicians and scholars believe that the ghana marga is the source of today's tana. Information on ghana marga comes to us only because of Ghanam Krishna Ayyar's grand-nephew, the venerable U.V. Svaminatha Ayyar, whose books – among them, *En Charitram* and *Sangita Mummanigal* – provide a lot of information about Ghanam Krishna Ayyar, and specifically about ghana marga. Svaminatha Ayyar, in turn, was given all this information by his father, Venkatasubbayyar, a student of Ghanam Krishna Ayyar.

Svaminatha Ayyar says that ghana, naya and deshika are 'three types of music' and that Krishna Ayyar was a master of ghana. Deshika must be a corruption of the term deshiya. One needs to wonder whether Svaminatha Ayyar is talking about styles that are related to the melodic nature of the ghana, naya and deshiya raga? Or was he talking about three techniques that have different aesthetics, such as loud and weighty (ghana), soft and delicate (naya) and deshiya (using foreign techniques), which may not be related to the raga classification given by Shahaji or applicable to any raga?

Another famous musician we are aware of with the same prefix is Ghanam Sinayya, who seems to have been a contemporary of Kshetrayya, which places him in the seventeenth century. This would be about fifty years before Shahaji and over 150 years before Ghanam Krishna Ayyar. Were both the prefixes referring to the same musical feature or style? We will try and answer these questions.

But let us return to U.V. Svaminatha Ayyar's narratives in order to understand ghana marga.

During the reign of King Sarabhoji, Bobbili Keshavayya, a famous musician from Bobbili (Andhra Pradesh), performed in Tanjavur. He was a master of the ghana marga, and as he sang, it sounded like a lion's roar. The king asked if any of his court musicians could render this style, but there was no response. This style was not known to any musician in Tanjavur. Ghanam Krishna Ayyar, a court musician, stood up and said that he was willing to sing ghana marga if Bobbili Keshavayya would teach him. In a few days, he learnt from Keshavayya the techniques of singing 'tana' and 'chakratana', after which he requested that he be given a place away from Tanjavur, so that he can practise in solitude. It appears he also requested butter from cow milk, as the ghana marga would generate a lot of heat. All this was provided for. Svaminatha Ayyar mentions often that a person requires great deal of physical strength to render ghana marga. He says that ghana marga involves beginning the rendition with a humkara (roar) that arises from the navel. For the people around the place Krishna Ayyar was staying in during the days of practice, it seemed like the roar of a lion, we are told.

After some time, Ghanam Krishna Ayyar returned to the court and gave a performance.

He began with an alapana in the ghana raga punnagavarali, followed by tana in the same raga. He then rendered the first line from a small composition in punnagavarali composed by his father. He used this line as a pallavi, and to it added many sangatis and rendered hundreds of kalpanasvaras. Svaminatha Ayyar says that the specific nuances of ghana marga appeared here and there, like bright flashes of lightning.

Svaminatha Ayyar also mentions ghana marga in the context of the rendition of a kirtana. He says that in Ghanam Krishna Ayyar's compositions the murchhanas of ragas were clearly brought out. Then he says that when sung in ghana marga, the majesty of the marga and the lyrical structuring were beautiful.

Another mention of ghana marga occurs when he relates the method of learning that his father followed under Ghanam Krishna Ayyar. He says that his father learnt Krishna Ayyar's kirtanas, ghana marga, chakratana and many old kirtanas.

From the above information, we can make the following assumptions:

- ghana marga contains tana and chakratana;
- ghana marga is rendered in ghana ragas; and
- this does connect the raga classification of Shahaji with ghana, ghana marga and tana.

But there are also some problems:

- punnagavarali is not a ghana raga – even Shahaji has only called it a naya raga; and
- ghana marga requires a great deal of physical strength of a kind that is not related to tana singing as we understand it today.

The mention of ghana marga in relation to a kirtana is baffling.

I would like to bring in Dhrupad here, as I feel it has a bearing on ghana marga and even tana. The concept of bani in dhrupad is widely debated. There are four banis of Dhrupad referred to in the literature and in practice, each with a distinctive aesthetic, namely, Gaurhar, Dagur, Khandar and Nauhar. Of these, we are interested with Khandar Bani. The aesthetic effect of Khandar Bani is often described as vira rasa (triumphalism). The Khandar Bani uses a lot of gamak to achieve a certain aesthetic and is thus called 'gamak pradhan'. Gamak itself can be heavy, medium or of lighter kinds. The heavy kind of gamak is what we are concerned with. This kind of singing is said to be like kapalabhati yoga, as it comes from the navel. This gamak is a feature used widely in Dhrupad and can be even heard in the madhya laya alap sections, with increasing intensity in the faster sections of the alap. In Dhrupad, dhruvapadas (compositions) are also composed to create the aesthetics of Khandar Bani. A metaphor often used to describe the vocalization used in Khandar bani is 'voice like a lion'.

Could this be the ghana marga that Svaminatha Ayyar describes? We know that both Khyal and Dhrupad musicians visited Tanjavur, before and during the reign of Sarabhoji and some, like Ramadas, tutored Gopalakrishna Bharati in Hindustani music.

By the end of the nineteenth century, musicians also refer to a mode of raga rendition called madhyama-kala. This we are told was the older name for tana. If that is the case, what happened to the word ghana? A great musician of the nineteenth century, Sattanur Panchanada Ayyar was considered a master of madhyama-kala – even his name was prefixed with 'madhyama-kala'. Many senior vidvans say that madhyama-kala was very popular on the vina. Is this madhyama-kala the same as ghana, which later became tana?

Among vina artists in Karnataka and Kerala, there is a practice of rendering what is known as chitta tanas. These chitta tanas are composed pieces that are primarily used for practice. It is said that they help in mastering tana. Is there a connection here?

In *Sangita Sarvartha Sara Sangrahamu* (1859), the author Vina Ramanujayya has published notations under two headings: tanamulu and tannakaramu. The latter is supposed to be rendered vocally. The tana in raga nata that are notated in this category is actually an alapa, which is found in the old chaturdandi manuscripts. The author obviously believed that since the alapas used the syllables 'ta' and 'nam', they were tana.

The tanas in *Sangita Sampradaya Pradarshini* are published for forty-one raganga ragas (melakarta), which include traditionally accepted ghana ragas such as ritigoula and sri, many synthetic ragas like kanakambari and girvani. These tanas are attributed to Venkatamakhin, though they seem to be the creation of Muddu Venkatamakhin. One wonders how they got the name tana, as the word does not seem to have existed during Muddu Venkatamakhin's period. This title may have been given by Subbarama Dikshitar himself. A study of these notations show that these tanas are not much like today's tanas. They seem more like sets of short svara phrases in the ragas. Subbarama Dikshitar in another book, *Prathamabhyasa Pustakamu*, has also notated tanas only in six ghana ragas. Subbarama Dikshitar himself must have composed these.

Unconnected with these streams, we have musicians referring to a tradition where tanas are associated with the gait of different animals, for instance gajatana (tana rendered with an elephant-like gait) We really do not know the purpose of these techniques, as they do not seem to be used in the presentation of art music.

The reader must be wondering where all of this leads? There are these words we use and think are connected: tana, kuta tana, thaya, ghana raga, tana varna, ghana marga, madhyama-kala and, finally, tana as we know it. But one of the problems is that the same word may be used with different meanings in different contexts, making clarity very difficult. For example, tana in tana varna has a different meaning from that in kuta tana. In the latter, the sense is of a grouping of svaras. The tana and kuta tana in ancient music and kuta tana in chaturdandi have no relevance to the modern tana. Right now, I am unable to connect with certainty the alapa or thaya of the chaturdandi system with the modern tana. I think the aesthetic commonality that is perceived may be due to our own superimposition of contemporary aesthetic sense on the past.

The tana varna may have used rigid movements in the aesthetic structure, but composers right from the eighteenth century did not restrict themselves to ghana ragas. This would mean that the two were separated. One of the meanings of tana is 'a protracted tone'. Another is, quite simply, extension. So tana in tana varna may only refer to the fact that every syllable is extended using the ending vowel sound.

Where does ghana marga fit into all this? The usage of ghana in raga classification and in ghana marga may not be the same. The term ghana marga must have evolved from the observation of the ghana. Its heaviness, majesty, physicality are all condensed in the term ghana marga ('marga' meaning direction or way). Ghana marga must have been practised in the Tanjavur region in the seventeenth century, which is how Chinnayya acquired the prefix 'Ghanam'. The ghana marga may have been part of the chaturdandi tradition, but with this tradition becoming obsolete during the late seventeenth and early eighteenth century, ghana also may have been lost.

I think ghana marga is definitely connected to tana, but is much more than just tana. Ghana may have a connection with the heavy gamak used in Dhrupad. It is also interesting that this gamak is used during madhya laya alap section in Dhrupad (refer to tana being called madhyama-kala). Ghana marga uses tana and chakratana, but is also descriptive of a certain mode of rendering that has to do with a technique of physicality, heaviness and rigidity. Tana today does not involve ghana marga as a technique, but probably has within it elements derived from ghana renditions of tana and chakratana, especially in vocal rendition. Ghana marga was not restricted only to tana and chakratana and was used even while rendering kirtanas. We know that in Dhrupad, compositions were composed to create the aesthetics of Khandar Bani. It is also fascinating that the metaphor used to describe the 'voice' rendering of Khandar Bani is exactly the same as one used by U.V. Svaminatha Ayyar to describe ghana marga.

Consider this too: musicians who were experts of madhyama-kala were not mentioned as experts in ghana marga. It is, therefore, quite possible that madhyama-kala existed independent of ghana marga. We are also told that madhyama-kala was rendered by vina vidvans. Madhyama-kala is an important component of what is today tana. Here, maybe the vina style took precedence.

The connection between the ghana raga and tana is complex. The idea that certain ragas are ghana in nature has remained. But there is no consistency in the use of the word. Many times, ragas that are not considered ghana in the ghana–naya–deshiya classification are called ghana. The nature of the traditional ghana ragas and 'madhyama-kala' would have aesthetically matched, allowing for its natural integration. For long, this link seems to have been maintained, but by the twentieth century, the newly christened tana was extended to all ragas without the raga classification playing a role. This may have happened more in vocal rendition than the vina-playing of madhyama-kala. The vocal tana rendition is distinctly different from tana on the vina. It is much heavier, tougher. Vina tana is less aggressive, not because of the nature of the instrument, but because of a difference in technique and even the kind of tana phrases used.

The connection that we make between tana and tana varna is logical because of the melodic nature of both. But a similar connection can be made with mel-kala niraval or mel-kala kalpanasvara when sung in a certain way. It is important to remember that the modern tana is an organic creation with multiple aspects.

The human mind is never satisfied with knowledge of the bare facts. It wants to go behind them and ask how, why. So it is natural to wonder where the contemporary tana comes from. It is not from one source. The modern tana has within it madhyama-kala, ghana marga and the impact of the ghana–

naya–deshiya classification. It is not fixed by these factors, but built with aspects of their aesthetics. Madhyama-kala probably brought with it aspects to tana that evolved from the vina. The ghana–naya–deshiya classification may have initially influenced the melodic parameters of such an aesthetic. Ghana marga must have given the vocal rendition of tana a certain tough texture. From this synergy of musical aesthetics, we have today's tana.

Interestingly, in the presentation of music in the mid- and late nineteenth century, there are not too many mentions of tana or madhyama-kala. Even the references that do exist tell us nothing of where in the presentation it was rendered. Pallavis were rendered after a raga alapana without a tana in between. Tana may have really acquired its position of importance only in the late nineteenth and early twentieth century.

Niraval

Among the pivotal forms of manodharma, niraval holds a special position in exploring the relationship between sahitya, raga and tala, all inspired by the creation of the vaggeyakaras. In Karnatik music today, niraval is the most ignored. Most of the time, it is only used as a passing phase before rendering kalpanasvaras. With the possibility of so many ways of approaching niraval, the Karnatik experience is incomplete without musicians dedicating time to explore its many shades. But when did this form of manodharma enter art music consciousness? Did it always exist? The first indication of a manodharma technique that can involve a line in a composition is seen in deshi music. In *Sangita Ratnakara*, Sarngadeva speaks about rupaka alapti in the context of the rendition of prabandhas. Rupaka alapti has two varieties, pratigrahanika and bhanjani, of which the latter is of interest here. Bhanjani means breaking or splitting. There are two types of bhanjani. Sthaya bhanjani is the rendition of a portion of a prabandha with melodic variations. An important condition in this rendition is that the syllabic placement in the portion chosen must be kept intact as composed in the prabandha. This is very similar to niraval in Karnatik music. Once again this is a conceptual similarity and does not reflect melodic or stylistic similarity.

After *Sangita Ratnakara*, we do not come across any mention of a niraval-like presentation. We must remember that we do not know where, geographically, the music mentioned in *Ratnakara* was practised. Where did it travel to? Did it really disappear or was it not part of the tradition in the southern region? These are all questions to which there are no answers.

Chaturdandi presentations do not mention any niraval-like improvisation. Right through the eighteenth century, we are unsure whether niraval was rendered or not. But in the nineteenth century, we come across references that are very important. In his description of a few musical encounters, U.V. Svaminatha Ayyar gives us some important clues. First, when he is describing Ghanam Krishna Ayyar's performance of ghana marga at the Tanjavur court, he says that after choosing the line from his father's composition 'Yetrakaikellaam Kodukkum' and treating it as a pallavi, he rendered many sangatis for the pallavi and hundreds of kalpanasvaras.

Svaminatha Ayyar also describes Ghanam Krishna Ayyar's visit to Tyagaraja's house. There, two disciples of Tyagaraja, Kamarasavalli Nanu Ayyar and Tillaisthanam Rama Ayyangar, were rendering a kirtana of Tyagaraja, 'E Papamu', in raga athana set to mishra chapu tala. Tyagaraja then requested Krishna Ayyar to sing. Krishna Ayyar rendered an alapana of athana and took the pallavi line of the kirtana and rendered a lot of sangatis and kalpanasvaras. Later, at Tyagaraja's request that he sing something of his own, Ayyar composed an impromptu pallavi in athana – 'Summa Summa Varugumaa Sukham' – and rendered hundreds of sangatis and kalpanasvaras.

When Svaminatha Ayyar speaks about many or hundreds of sangatis, I do not think he is referring to the pre-composed or set sangatis that are today the rendered lines in kirtanas. This was on-the-spot improvisation; it has to be niraval. But he does not use that word. Was he not aware of it? Unlikely. A person who could use terms such as pallavi, kalpanasvara, anupallavi, charana, names of ragas and in his book provide lyrics for kirtanas would have definitely known the word niraval. It is quite possible the term sangati was used to also denote niraval. Niraval was not rendered to any other part of the kirtana than the pallavi 'E Papamu'. The twentieth-century practice is to render niraval primarily to lines from the anupallavi or charana. Very rarely is the pallavi of a kirtana used.

This leads me to believe that niraval was originally only sung to pallavis, as in ragam–tanam–pallavi. Another writer, Sulamangalam Vaidyanatha Bhagavatar, states that musicians rendered pallavis and kalpanasvaras. What I think is implied is that niraval was sung in the pallavi. This need not have been specifically mentioned, as it was understood. Also, the word 'niraval' may not have been in use. Even when discussing the music of Konerirajapuram Vaidyanatha Ayyar (1878–1921), who was a turn-of-the-century musician, Bhagavatar says that Ayyar improvised beautifully for the anupallavi 'Nigama' of the kirtana 'Sogasuga Mrdanga Talamu' in raga sriranjani. He does not use the word niraval here either. I believe that niraval must originally have been rendered only in ragam–tanam–pallavis, but towards the end of the nineteenth century began to be also used in kirtanas, when they became important presentations in art music. The line chosen for niraval too moved from the pallavi to other lines. But the word niraval seems like a twentieth-century addition to Karnatik terminology.

Kalpanasvara

Much like niraval, we have little information on kalpanasvaras. In the *Sangita Ratnakara*, there is the pratigrahanika form of rupaka alapti. Sarngadeva speaks about a form of alapti where the musician while rendering a prabandha renders raga alapti and returns to a line in a prabandha. This is repeated many times. Unlike kalpanasvaras, svaras here are not rendered as sol-fa syllables. In *Sangita Raja*, a text written after *Ratnakara*, there is a mention of pratigrahanika, which is rendered using the svaras themselves. This is similar to our understanding of kalpanasvara.

This is the last we hear of the idea until the nineteenth century, from which period we have enough information to try and reconstruct the practice and connect it with the twentieth century. There is absolutely no doubt that kalpanasvara was a very important part of Karnatik music presentation. The word kalpanasvara appears numerous times in the narratives about musicians right through the nineteenth century. It is looked upon as an exciting and captivating part of the musical presentation. Nagasvara vidvans are also mentioned as being proficient in kalpanasvaras as much as they were coveted for their alapana and pallavi presentation. Kalpanasvara too may have initially been used for pallavis. In many descriptions, authors say that musicians sang a pallavi and kalpanasvaras. Then this practice spread to kirtanas. In one instance that Sulamangalam Vaidyanatha Bhagavatar mentions, Maha Vaidyanatha Ayyar sang kalpanasvaras to 'Na Jivadhara', a kirtana in bilahari. Another information that is in contrast to this is that Umayalpuram Krishna Bhagavatar and Sundara Bhagavatar (nineteenth century), who were direct disciples of Tyagaraja, never sang kalpanasvaras out of respect for him. These two brothers presented what may be termed lecture concerts where they spoke about the meaning of the kirtanas and then sang them, evoking great emotion from the lyrical and musical output. They also may have not sung pallavis. The oft-repeated comment that Tyagaraja did not recommend the singing of kalpanasvaras may be misguided. The issue might have been that kaplanasvaras were originally meant to be sung only in pallavis.

As with tana, here too one must ask: where did niraval and kalpanasvara come from? They do not seem to have been present in Tanjavur or any other Tamil-speaking area. This is very difficult to answer, but one theory is that they may have come from the Telugu-speaking regions. One should remember that we cannot compartmentalize the flow of culture between regions based on linguistic or political geography. The appearance of the pallavi (which we shall discuss in another essay) and what we know of Bobbili Keshavayya lead us to believe that the pallavi may have been practised more in Telugu regions. Bobbili is situated near Vizianagaram in Andhra Pradesh. These places were rich in music and dance. He must have kindled interest in the pallavi, and with it niraval and kalpanasvaras, in the Tanjavur region and in the rest of the Tamil-speaking belt.

I must add that the practice of rendering shlokas, viruttams and ugabhogas in kutcheris may have been influenced by the overlapping nature of Karnatik musicians being Harikatha practitioners and rendering Namasankirtana, where verses from various texts are explained and then rendered in music to great emotional impact.

In this essay, I have tried to trace the history of manodharma in Karnatik music. This is only an overview and readers are requested to read specific works on each one of these aspects and spend time with the original treatises to further understand these developments. No historical narrative will provide us with all the answers. There will remain some empty spaces and shadows that we are unable to negotiate or wave away. Some of this may be reconciled by studying the music directly, yet the mystery will remain. This does not in any way weaken tradition or make it untenable. In fact, it is this enquiry that keeps tradition alive, vital.

That which lies within us, the song within, is more than a rendering technique. It is more than a concert method or a phraseological manoeuvre. It certainly has nothing to do with a singer's passing whimsy or fancy. It is not about deftness or cleverness either. This inner song comes, almost paradoxically, from the silence within, which one may even see as a solitude. But the song within does not live in solitary confinement. On the contrary, it is hugely active, reaching out and touching and engaging the song beyond – the composed song. It draws its own purpose and direction from the song beyond. And when that happens, the composition itself becomes manodharma's companion. They do not come one after the other, but depend on each other for their existence. Manodharma and compositions live in the music together, not separately, and shape the music's forward flow. How exactly they draw from each other or who draws what from the other we do not know, nor need to know. But we do feel their connectedness, in fact, their unity. Being in love, passionately, is about forgetting how you love; it is about feeling the love.

27

The Song on Stage

History is a complex labyrinth in which it is pointless to seek unequivocal answers. What we need to seek is clarity in the way we ask questions about the past. It is from this clarity that we can ask the questions that concern us today. In the context of Karnatik music, these would be: how was music actually presented? By whom? And where?

The Nayak period (1532–1673) would dominate any attempt at answering these questions. But before we get down to examining the evidence, I would like to say something about the deep gulf between Tamil scholarship and Sanskrit and Telugu scholarship. From the sixth century, deshi music and regional Tamil, Telugu or Kannada musical ideas had connected, which means that it would not be correct to define music on the basis of linguistic regions. To my eyes, the divisions that some scholars point to, betray linguistic chauvinism. I am not interested in the question of which of the scholastic traditions came first.

Most of my essays on the history of Karnatik music tend to centre on the Tanjavur belt. This could lead to the criticism that I have ignored other regions, particularly linguistic regions.

The Tanjavur region does not signify a language group. It was a fertile area for the arts, where Telugus, Kannadigas, Tamils and those whose mother-tongue was Marathi contributed to the development of the music that eventually came to be Karnatik music. While the focus is on the region in and around Tanjavur, the role of the vaggeyakaras and developments in other regions have also been included in the narrative. I have used Sanskrit treatises as the basis for theoretical understanding, simply because Karnatik music developed from the Nayak period when Sanskrit and Telugu were the official languages. The terms and system used today are related to these theoretical texts, and therefore this approach is logical.

Musical ideas in Tamil texts in the post-fifteenth-century period do not deviate much from the Sanskrit treatises. The differences are chiefly in the technical nuances that are not part of the story I am trying to tell. Other than Tanjavur, other large princely states, like Travancore and Mysore, and smaller ones – Ramnad, Pudukkottai, Ettayapuram, Bobbili, Karvetinagaram, Vijayanagaram and Pithapuram – supported dance and music. There have been great musicians from all these areas, many of whom travelled widely. There are also differences in certain practices in many of these areas, but the overall development of Karnatik music has been shaped by the Tanjavur belt.

Let us return to the Nayak kings – an apt starting point for this journey of discovery. The reign of Sevappa Nayak (1532–1580), the first Tanjavur Nayak, was a period of peace. He was known for his charity and numerous renovations of temples and tanks. Achyutappa Nayak (1560–1614), his son and successor, provided great support to artists. The Bhagavata Mela musicians who migrated from Telugu regions were gifted villages such as Melattur where they could live in and practise their art. But it is from the reign of Raghunatha Nayak (1600–1634) that music really became an important and independent presentation. The Kannada-speaking scholar Govinda Dikshita had brought the chaturdandi musical system to this region. As we have already seen, chaturdandi has a historical connection with deshi music. It was presented in four parts: alapa, thaya, prabandha and gita, in that order. Alapa and thaya, which we would like to believe were spontaneous improvisations, might have actually been composed presentations, unless the notations we have for reference were only samples. Even if that is the case, the texture of the presentation seems rigid. Curiously, we do not know anything about the use of percussion instruments in the presentation of chaturdandi. Were they used at all?

It is also clear from the descriptions available in literary pieces written by court poets that chaturdandi was presented on the vina. The vina itself was a very important part of this tradition. The vina's importance, especially in this school of music, continued through Muttusvami Dikshitar and was carried on through his shishya parampara. The kirtanas of Dikshitar are said to display the influence of the vina style in their aesthetic form. The vina is an ancient instrument and has been referred to in Puranas (narratives in Sanskrit eulogizing specific deities), Itihasas (traditional epic narratives in Sanskrit) and treatises for over 2,000 years. The term vina today conjures up Ravi Varma's painting of Goddess Sarasvati holding the vina. But in ancient times, the vina was a generic term for stringed instruments. Many vinas were like harps; even the yazh may have been a kind of vina. The transformation of the open-string vina to the one with the fingerboard was a significant metamorphosis in the aesthetic evolution of Indian art music. The Sarasvati vina was the result of the years of change that the instrument had undergone. Raghunatha Nayak is said to have designed the modern Sarasvati vina.

From the literary works of the period in the Nayak courts, we get details on the presentation of chaturdandi. There are descriptions of chaturdandi being played on the vina by women musicians or devadasis. Scholars refer to dasis who were part of the court as rajadasis, but they all belonged to the very same artistic community. I use the term devadasi generically for women musicians and dancers from this artistic community, as their roles in the court and temple were interchangeable. The separation between musicians and dancers did not exist among them.

There are detailed descriptions of how the vina artists prepared for a concert, tuned the instruments and performed chaturdandi. Fascinatingly, this description is similar to the way vina artists prepare the instrument before a concert even today. The terms used for some of the parts of the vina are exactly the same as today. The quality of the music is described, as is the manner in which the audience showered appreciation on the artistes. Members of the audience are said to have used phrases like 'oura raga', 'bale tayam', 'aha rakti pada' to appreciate the music. 'Bale' and 'aha' are used even today in appreciation. There is also a description of chaturdandi being played on another instrument, gotivadya.

The Nayak kings honoured their musicians handsomely. In fact, Raghunatha Nayak himself was a vainika of great repute. Interestingly, there are hardly any descriptions of chaturdandi being sung as such, but the existence of prabandha and gita that had sahitya and the mention of 'ta' and 'nam' as syllables to be used in the rendition of alapa go to show that singing did take place. Regrettably, we do not know much about the musicians or composers who were in the courts of the Nayaks. In fact, the most prominent composer mentioned is Kshetrayya who visited Tanjavur twice, once during the reign of Raghunatha Nayak and then in Vijayaraghava Nayak's time (1633–1673).

What else do we know about chaturdandi? Not much, but some scholars are of the opinion that it may have been aesthetically closer to Dhrupad rather than to what later emerged as Karnatik music. There are some bases for this view. Like Dhrupad, chaturdandi did not have niraval or kalpanasvara renditions. The dhruvapada rendered in Dhrupad seems to have been structured on the basis of the prabandhas. The reference to Ghanam Sinayya as a musician of great repute also indicates the prevalence of the 'ghanam' style in Tanjavur, which may have been closer to Dhrupad. Other than prabandha and gita, no other compositional form was used in chaturdandi even though the dance in the same period used many other compositions. To clinch all this is the fact that Venkatamakhin's father Govinda Dikshita was a Kannada brahmin from northern Karnataka or lower Maharashtra. Dhrupad may have originated from around the same region and dhrupad musicians also refer to the Kannada musician Gopala Nayak as a founding father.

This gives rise to the question: what was the music that existed before the chaturdandi? Iconography from the Chola temples (ninth to twelfth centuries) gives us a lot of information on the various instruments, and we can use these to trace their genealogy. Tamil or Sanskrit treatises do not give us enough information on performance and practice before the Nayak period. Incredibly, the commentaries on the *Silappadikaram*, *Sangita Ratnakara* and other treatises, which were from different parts of India, describe very similar theoretical foundations for music. We know that scholars travelled and carried with them the music of their region, and concepts and terms were reinterpreted within different cultures.

We cannot tell from Chola temple iconography and religious texts just how these musical instruments and presentations were divided on the basis of music type and musical hierarchy. But we have enough evidence to conclude that the devadasi and her chinna melam were highly respected artistes. We also know that the oduvars were devotional singers attached to Shaivite temples.

Valuable information on the music and dance in the courts of Raghunatha Nayak and Vijayaraghava Nayak has been obtained from various poems and stories written by court poets, courtesans and sometimes the kings. In Tanjavur, there was an auditorium where great concerts, dance performances and even discussions took place. It is clear that dancers were well supported during the Nayak period, for we gather the names of many dancers in the courts. The dance presentations used older compositional forms like perani and jakkini, and dance-music theatrical presentations such as Yakshaganas and Kuravanjis were very popular. We have details of ragas, talas, dance postures and movements from this period.

The frescoes in the Pattishvaram temple (1550–1600) also give us a picture of the way devadasis presented their art. One of them depicts a dancer in movement, with a nattuvanar in action and playing the cymbals. Closely following him is a mrdanga vidvan, another musician playing idakka, a third who seems to be blowing into the tutti, and a few women who are watching. From this, we learn about the importance given to the devadasi and her troupe as part of the religious and cultural activities of the court and temple. Significantly, almost all the musicians and dancers described in the courts are women. Women have played almost every type of instrument, including percussion, a fact borne out by the beautiful bas-reliefs in Darasuram's Airavatesvara temple (1150).

We first hear about the nagasvara in the fifteenth century. Iconography belonging to the Chola period displays many types of piped instruments, but there is no mention of the nagasvara. Scholars point to the vangiyam and say this became the nagasvara. Regarding the antiquity of the instrument, there has been some debate among scholars based on iconography found in the Chidambaram temple. Some say that they date back to the eleventh century, while others place these in the Nayak period. The first inscription referring to nagasvara appears in 1496 in Tirumala and, later, Nitturu and Devalapura (mid-sixteenth century). These are not Tamil regions, but today the nagasvara has become a prominent symbol of Tamil music. It probably established itself in the Tamil areas around the sixteenth and seventeenth centuries. I see the arrival of the nagasvara as a very important part of the musical development that led to what we call Karnatik music.

The frescoes in the Tiruvarur temple also give us some interesting clues. They are late Nayak and early Maratha paintings (1660–1700). I found on a recent visit to the temple that the chinna melam appears often, and so does a huge orchestra of musical instruments. The paintings of the chinna melam depict the devadasis dressed in pleated skirts and blouses of different colours and designs. The nattuvanars are of different ages – some old and white-haired, others young and handsome. The dancers hold many poses and the nattuvanar is almost always leaning towards the dancer with the cymbals in his hands. Behind him is the mrdanga player. His instrument is beautifully decorated with cloth in different colours and designs, very much like mrdanga artists do now. The dancer is accompanied by a flautist, a tutti and a shankha. Most depictions of the devadasi's troupe have a few women watching their performance from behind the nattuvanar or mrdanga player. In these frescoes, the performances are almost always part of a procession or a specific event.

The frescoes also depict musical orchestras – periya melam. What struck me as being of even more significance was the size of the musical orchestra. It was huge, and usually included many instruments, including different kinds of pipes such as yekkalam, karna and the nagasvara. Apart from these, there are multiple rhythmic instruments, like the kodikatti, maddalam and the almost extinct panchamukhavadya. There are also flautists and people blowing the shankha. Often, there is more than one musician playing these instruments. The nagasvara seems to be just a member of this large orchestra, and may not have had a special independent status. In smaller temples, there may not have been such a large orchestra, but was the music of the nagasvara part of serious music? We do not know.

At the same time, Portuguese travellers in the sixteenth century have provided descriptions of aerophones being played during temple rituals and processions in the Vijayanagara Empire. But we do not know what music they played. It is also clear that the chinna melam was treated as a separate artistic community. In the Tiruvarur frescoes too, we can make out that the artist has created an unwritten demarcation between the two melams. The way in which these artists are placed and the size of their figures are all telling. The terms periya melam and chinna melam may have come later, but their reference may be to the earlier size of the respective orchestras. Scholars still debate the reasons for these terms; I am only adding another possibility.

Post-Nayak Trends

The change of dynasty left an indelible impact on what was to become modern Karnatik music. I strongly believe that between the post-Nayak period and the late eighteenth century, Karnatik music may not have had an art music presence in Tanjavur and the surrounding areas. Govinda Dikshita and his son Venkatamakhin both played a large role in keeping chaturdandi central to the practice of art music during the Nayak period. But after the Maratha rule began in the late seventeenth century, the chaturdandi tradition slowly went out of vogue. The theory of ragas, talas and newer compositional forms were developing rapidly, but Karnatik music as we understand it may not have been presented as a separate form in the first half of the eighteenth century. Ideas of chaturdandi are found only while describing ragas in the theoretical texts of Shahaji (1684–1712) and Tulaja I (1728–36), but nowhere else of any significance. The Maratha period was very important to the developments in music. Ragas that belonged to other regions, which we may today call Hindustani ragas, were evident from the period of Shahaji. His raga classification is also evidence of this influence.

The visits of Kshetrayya to this region in the late seventeenth century might have been a catalyst for changes in both dance and music. After Kshetrayya's second visit, we have many composers of padas in the Tanjavur courts. Many of them were musicians during the reign of Shahaji. Using the then established pallavi–anupallavi–charana structure, many new types of compositional forms started emerging. With the emergence of these compositions, the content of Sadir must have changed. The older dance compositional forms took a back seat and these forms became dominant. It is important to note that all these compositional forms – pada, varna, svarajati, tillana – were connected to Sadir and not pure art music. We cannot forget Shahaji's own contribution as a composer, including padas and operas such as the 'Pallaki Seva Prabandham'. The music of the eighteenth century seems to have completely focused on compositional music and mainly Sadir-related music. This is the picture we get at least until the late 1800s. In the development of these compositional forms, we have to remember the active role of devadasis. They were all musicians and dancers, and their aesthetic sense must have influenced the way these compositions evolved, even though the composers were mainly brahmins.

This was also a period when padas with bhakti content were being composed, but I am not sure where they were being presented – maybe only at the courts and for congregational singing. The emergence of the tana varna in the mid- to late eighteenth century could be an indicator of a purely musical tradition emerging from Sadir. This type of composition tells us that, by the late eighteenth century, a focus on purely musical presentations beyond dance solos, bhakti kirtanas and dance productions was emerging. One may argue that these were only composed for learning and practice, but I sense that with such a development, the focus began to shift from dance or bhajana to art music once again.

Bhakti

The bhakti saints were using the same music as that of the Karnatik vaggeyakaras, and this must have led to a natural crossover of ideas. The passionate devotion in Narayana Tirtha's 'Krishna Lila Tarangini', the advaitic realization of Sadashiva Brahmendra and the bhakti movement – moulded by the saint Bodhendra, spearheaded by Shridhara Ayyaval and finally structured by Sadguru Svami – must have had an impact. This is reflected in some Tyagaraja compositions, such as 'Divyanamakirtana', that may be categorized as bhakti music rather than art music. If the belief that Tyagaraja was exposed to Bhadrachala Ramadas's kirtanas is true, it only reinforces my thoughts on this matter. Scholars also say that Tyagaraja was influenced by the Tevaram renditions in the temples. There is no doubt that he would have been exposed to the Tevarams emotively sung by the oduvars, but how exactly it influenced him we do not know. There is, however, no doubt that the intense bhakti of the saints and the brahmin environment in which Tyagaraja grew up contributed to the textual content of his kirtanas. This does not take anything away from his enormous contribution in creating, collectively with Dikshitar and Shyama Shastri, the kirtana as an art music composition. Tyagaraja was also influenced by theatre forms, particularly the Bhagavata Mela tradition and the musical operas of Shahaji. This is seen in his bhakti-laden musical operas 'Nauka Charitramu' and 'Prahlada Bhakti Vijayamu'. We must keep in mind that religion and bhakti were part of their lives, anchoring them. Any individual or movement that contributed to this core was contributing to the thoughts of the vaggeyakaras. In the nineteenth century, under the influence of the Marathas who migrated south, the bhakti movement was once again charged, deeply impacting Karnatik music.

It is also around the mid-eighteenth century that the nagasvara and the tavil may have acquired a separate identity as instruments of serious art music. It is in the eighteenth century that Ramasvami Dikshitar is said to have formalized the method of playing the nagasvara for all the Tiruvarur temple rituals. He also designated the ragas that were to be played at different times of the day in the temple. This is a valuable piece of information received through the oral tradition, which confirms that the nagasvara was, in his time, considered an instrument that could play all the Karnatik ragas and that the musicians themselves were respected. The emergence of the nagasvara and the tavil as the pivotal melodic and rhythmic instruments, respectively, in temples is a marker to remember. The Tiruvarur temple was a very important one that Shahaji Maharaja was attached to.

I have tried to draw some distinctions between various forms of art based on musical content in their presentation. Whether it was the dance-related rituals in the temples, other dance compositions, the nagasvara's role in the temple and society, or court music, the collective community was participating in creating and sustaining all these arts. This was not a new phenomenon, because for long, art was the product of a community of artists who worked beyond caste confines to provide culturally unifying artistic expressions. But I also feel that artists were aware of the distinctiveness of music in these various forms, yet allowed for the free flow of aesthetic concepts from one to the other. I make the last two observations based on the music that constituted these various spheres of social life, in which the court and the temple were inseparable.

Alapana

I am of the opinion that the modern alapana, which evolved through the renditions of many great musicians over the nineteenth century, may have been drawn from the nagasvara vidvans. It is well known that nagasvara vidvans played different ragas at different times of the day, and on most occasions, in the form of an alapana. During the festivals, alapana was a key portion of their musical presentation. It cannot be an accident that the main form of Karnatik music presentation in the nineteenth century was the alapana. It is said that musicians actually sang alapanas for over an hour or more. We have an idea of the duration of nagasvara presentations in the nineteenth century, so it is logical to presume that it would have been at least of the same duration in an earlier era.

By the end of the eighteenth century, we know of many composers. While many worked with diverse compositional forms, a few focused primarily on kirtanas. The trinity transformed the idea of the kirtana. But if someone were to ask what the trinity learnt as students of music, we would not really have an answer. Did they learn the alankaras? We know that the alankaras were published in *Chaturdandi Prakashika* as early as 1620, but do not know if they were part of the learning system. Did they learn varnas, padas and svarajatis? What we have is the folklore built by the Harikatha vidvans of the late nineteenth century, where they speak of Tyagaraja having heard the compositions of Bhadrachala Ramadas rendered by his mother. For the post Nayak period, we are unable to picture the way Karnatik music may have been presented sans dance. It may well be that when chaturdandi was in a low tide, a newer form of art music did not emerge immediately to take its place. This is the sense one gets from the fact that most eighteenth-century courts do not seem to have had art music presentations.

It is from the mid- to late eighteenth century that we see Karnatik music emerging to become what we recognize today. But this happened only because the brahmin musicians and vaggeyakaras, the periya melam musicians and the chinna melam artists were sharing an artistic space. The reader must discard the idea that the chinna melam was only about dance and rituals, or that the periya melam was only about temple music. It is clear from the information we have that the musical base was the same for all these groups. The creation of dance compositional forms, which started from about Kshetrayya's times, definitely influenced the texture of Karnatik music. The nattuvanars and devadasis were learning art music too, and were adding to its beauty. Besides, the nattuvanars too were composing. The brahmin musicians and the devadasis were rendering music in the royal court. Were their alapanas influenced by compositional forms such as padas, varnas and svarajatis? Quite possibly. The devadasi's art had many artistic dimensions, some of which found their way to the court. In this electric atmosphere, no movement in music could have been an isolated phenomenon. In the trinity, Muttusvami Dikshitar was probably most closely associated with the chinna melam and periya melam artistes. These musicians and dancers were closely associated with Ramasvami Dikshitar (Muttusvami Dikshitar's father) and his descendants, with many being their disciples. This must have led to a transfer of musical ideas between them. The nagasvara repertoire also included a large number of padas, chauka varnas and kirtanas, many being the compositions of Ramasvami Dikshitar and his son.

The Pallavi

The pallavi as a pivotal part of music presentation comes to us from the late eighteenth century. Vaggeyakaras such as Pallavi Gopala Ayyar (eighteenth and nineteenth centuries) and Pallavi Duraisvami Ayyar (1782–1816) had their names prefixed with 'pallavi' in recognition of their prowess in its rendition. But where did the pallavi come from? Again, a difficult question, but there are two possibilities. The idea of rendering a one-line composition after an extensive alapana and using that to improvise may also have come from the nagasvara tradition. This assumption is based on the fact that we know that most nagasvara vidvans until even the early part of the twentieth century did not play kirtanas. They also presented another piece, called raktimela, which is something like a pallavi and usually set to mishra chapu tala. It is composed in rhythmic syllabic form first and then converted to raga and used to create multiple complicated rhythmic presentations in melody. Considering that this is a form of composed music derived from rhythmic structures that have no lyrics suggests that the pallavi may have been a melodic line for improvisation used by the nagasvara community. Based on numerous anecdotes about Andhra musical stalwart Bobbili Keshavayya, we can deduce the possibility that it may have come from those regions.

Competitions

In my readings, I have found three different musical events where Bobbili Keshavayya was an important participant. I have already mentioned his presentation of ghana marga and the consequent learning of this marga by Ghanam Krishna Ayyar. Other than that, there are two more events, the first of which involves Shyama Shastri. A competition is said to have taken place between Keshavayya and Shyama Shastri, where the former rendered a pallavi in simhanandana tala to which Shyama Shastri responded with a pallavi in sharabanandana tala. The night before this contest, Shyama Shastri is said to have been worried about his performance and prayed to his ishta devata, Kamakshi. It is said that he then created the raga chintamani and the kirtana 'Devi Brovasamayamide'. The other story is also about a pallavi competition between Keshavayya and Pallavi Duraisvami Ayyar. It is said that Ayyar presented a pallavi in pantuvarali raga and mishra chapu tala and won the contest. These stories also seem to have a political undertone. In all three, the Tanjavur musician was victorious. Except for the incident mentioned by U.V. Svaminatha Ayyar in his memoir, the others are retold orally. Whether they actually happened or not is not important; they carry a musical insight. It is clear that pallavi singing was of great importance for musicians, and that competitions were quite common in the courts. It is also obvious that Bobbili Keshavayya was a musician of great repute and a master of pallavi-singing and ghana marga. This is why some scholars like to connect the pallavi tradition to Telugu regions.

Music contests continue to be common right through the nineteenth century. We know of two other competitions involving Maha Vaidyanatha Ayyar. One took place in Kallidaikurichi in 1856 involving two other musicians, Periya Vaidyanatha Ayyar and Chinna Vaidyanatha Ayyar. This was under the auspices of the Tiruvadudurai mutt and specifically Subrahmanya Desikar, who later became the head of the mutt. Another legendary contest is between Maha Vaidyanatha Ayyar again and Coimbatore Raghava Ayyar. This took place during the reign of Ayilyam Tirunal in Tranvancore. Most of these contests involved only the singing of alapanas and pallavis that went on for hours and renditions of various kinds of pallavis. It is safe to conclude then that alapanas and pallavis were the order of the day in the early and mid-nineteenth century. I have already indicated that the rendition of pallavis would have included some kind of niraval and kalpanasvara.

The British

In the nineteenth century, performances took place in the palaces of kings, residences of zamindars, in religious centres and temples. The nagasvara vidvans were performing in temples and the devadasis and the chinna melam were active both in temples and courts. By this time, the British were well entrenched in India and many performances of Sadir and Karnatik concerts took place in honour of the 'Raj's representatives'. According to U.V. Svaminatha Ayyar, Ghanam Krishna Ayyar performed in Madras in honour of Governor Thomas Munro. He is even said to have presented one song, which included in the lyrics a mention of 'Munro Sahib'. Not unlike vaggeyakaras of every era, Ghanam

Krishna Ayyar was trying to please the ruler. This concert must have taken place between 1820 and 1827 when Munro was the governor of Madras. Performances also took place in the presence of many well-read scholars and musicians in towns and villages. Those would have been the real tests for musicians, where they had to excel in front of their peers.

In all this, we should not forget the impact of the British. The most obvious example would be the violin. Balusvami Dikshitar (1786–1858) is said to have been the first musician to use the violin in Karnatik music. But in reality, the violin had already been used in Sadir, as part of the chinna melam. Paintings from Tanjavur with the date '1800' show the chinna melam including a violin artist. At this time, Balusvami Dikshitar would have been only about fourteen years old. He learnt the violin when he was in Manali (Madras). Therefore, the use of the violin in Sadir was older, and may have been in practice from the late eighteenth century. It is unfortunate that the Sadir presentation is not considered part of the Karnatik story. Art music presentations were taking shape during this period, with aesthetic influences from various impulses feeding into it. To me, the adaptation of the violin in Sadir is an important landmark. It is emblematic of the inclusive nature of art, the adapting of technologies and the integrating of them within the local artistic culture. The music in Sadir was the same as the music that was being shaped into Karnatik art music. The other instrument that found its way into Sadir was the clarinet, not to forget the harmonium, which entered Harikatha and Namasankirtana a little later. In the twentieth century, the clarinet became a kutcheri instrument. The Mysore court was also influenced by Western classical traditions. Muttusvami Dikshitar himself created sahitya to many English folk and light tunes that he heard the British bands play. Tyagaraja also shows some traces of this impact in a few compositions.

The Kirtankar and Harikathakar

In the nineteenth century, we need to look at the role of prasangas and Harikatha performances in the formation of Karnatik concert practices. It is evident that musical–religious discourse must have been a practice in the regions in and around Tanjavur for some time. According to U.V. Svaminatha Ayyar, the compositions rendered in the prasangas used Sanskrit or Telugu texts; so I presume it had limited reach. Svaminatha Ayyar goes on to say that there were not enough Tamil kirtanas to be used in Harikathas and Shivakathas. No composer had yet created a repertoire of Tamil kirtanas that told a complete story. The person who changed this was Gopalakrishna Bharati when he created his 'Nandanar Charitram'. He established a tradition for prasangas that was so popular that it could be compared to the cinema of today.

Gopalakrishna Bharati belonged to Nagapattinam, but later moved to a little brahmin village called Anandatandavapuram (very close to Mayiladudurai), and learnt both Hindustani and Karnatik music. He was a student of Ramadas, who taught him Hindustani music, and a student of Ghanam Krishna Ayyar. Gopalakrishna Bharati's 'Nandanar Charitram' changed the complexion of prasangas in the first half of the nineteenth century. Though Ghanam Krishna Ayyar was a great vaggeyakara in Tamil, it was Gopalakrishna Bharati who revived the tradition of Tamil compositions in Karnatik music. A Frenchman, Cice 'Durai', who was the collector in Karaikal, was so impressed with the 'Nandanar Charitram' presentation that he published it as a book in 1861–62.

Svaminatha Ayyar recounts the events that led to its publication. When Gopalakrishna Bharati presented the 'Nandanar Charitram' over three days in Nagapattinam, its first ever performance, the French collector found that his staff was coming to work tired and sleepy. He instituted enquiries which revealed that they were all at that performance. Cice 'Durai', who knew some Tamil and music, then decided to watch the presentation. So impressed was he that he felt it should be published. According to Svaminatha Ayyar, the music-cum-storytelling Bharati presented was so popular that everyone knew his kirtanas. It did not matter whether they knew music or not; they were humming the compositions as they walked in the streets.

Around the mid-nineteenth century, kirtankars from the west of India came to Tanjavur. In the Maratha kirtan tradition, there existed two streams: Varkari and Naradiya. The practioners of the former were saint-singers who sang the praise of the lord with stories thrown in. There was no caste distinction in this presentation. This tradition focused on bringing everyone together in the devotion to god. The Naradiya tradition was a scholastic exposition of katha, using a miniature tambura and accompanists. The Naradiya practitioners were brahmins and the format was very different from the Varkari. The audience needed to be well versed in philosophy and the scriptures. It is this Naradiya tradition that came down to Tanjavur. Some scholars believe that the kirtan tradition might have reached Tanjavur much earlier – as early as the early eighteenth century – but there is not enough evidence to confirm its prevalence in this region before the arrival of kirtankars such as Ramachandra Bava in the mid-nineteenth century.

This also gives us another piece in the caste puzzle that played out in Karnatik music from the mid-nineteenth century. The advent of the kirtan tradition is an inflection point in Karnatik music. Kirtankars brought with them their tradition of music and narration. It is very clear that this form was fashioned into Harikatha or Kathakalakshepam and became very popular in the Tamil region. Many artists adopted the methods used by the kirtankars to create a southern Harikatha tradition. They had numerous themes for their kathas that were known as Nirupanas, story summaries that were used for Harikatha. Based on these, they developed their stories and wove into them kirtanas and shlokas. Most of the Harikathas were based on Itihasas and Puranas, and were presented using many languages, including Sanskrit, Telugu, Kannada, Marathi and Tamil. Among the artists who presented Harikathas were also some who were well versed in abhinaya and used that to depict the story.

Most interesting for us in the Harikatha tradition are the artists. Many Harikatha giants of the mid- and late nineteenth century were very competent, and sometimes brilliant, Karnatik musicians. Many were also well versed in Tyagaraja kirtanas, which they used in the Harikatha presentations. Harikatha was extremely popular and hence financially lucrative; so many Karnatik musicians would perform a concert one day and a Harikatha the next, including the legendary Maha Vaidyanatha Ayyar. Some moved to Harikatha from concert music, such as Palghat Anantarama Bhagavatar (late nineteenth century). This overlapping is another important stage in the development of the modern kutcheri. In the shishya parampara of Tyagaraja, we find many Harikatha exponents. It is not in any small measure due to these artists that Tyagaraja kirtanas became a household name. The compositions of Muttusvami Dikshitar, on the other hand, were held very closely by his shishyas among the chinna and periya melams and further south among the brahmins in Ettayapuram and Tirunelveli. Tyagaraja kirtanas are said to be very accessible to the layperson, while Dikshitar's compositions are described as being like a coconut – tough outside but sweet inside. All these ideas may have been born from the fact that Tyagaraja kirtanas were not only presented in Harikathas, but also adapted for that form. Hence the rendition was probably straightforward. Tyagaraja kirtanas were also used in the bhajana sampradaya, leading to greater access in a simpler format. The nuance here is that these renditions also had an impact in the way Tyagaraja kirtanas were later presented in Karnatik kutcheris.

I must stress that the influence of the kirtankars was not only in the field of Harikatha, but also in the bhajana tradition in Tanjavur.

The modern bhajana sampradaya has also been shaped by the influence of the Marathi kirtankars. Among other things, it is also from this merging of ideas that all Tyagaraja compositions were treated with the same reverence after they were included within the art music umbrella. All these are significant developments and had a far-reaching impact on the twentieth-century kutcheri.

Mrdanga

The mrdanga, or different varieties of it, have been found in temple iconography and painting for over a thousand years and mentioned in even the *Patthuppattu* and *Ettuthogai* (first to third centuries), and later Tamil and Sanskrit treatises. Scholars say that the mrdanga was earlier called the tannumai. We do not know anything about the use of the mrdanga in the chaturdandi presentation. But right from the Nayak period, it features in Sadir presentation. The development of mrdanga techniques and mathematical systems must have evolved from the practice of dance and from the nagasvara and tavil vidvans, since they were one artistic group. This was the community that initially built a repertoire around the mrdanga. But in the mid- and late nineteenth century, other styles began changing the nature of its accompaniment.

The kirtan style of accompaniment came into the southern regions through mrdanga vidvans such as Tanjavur Tukaram Appa (1860–1900), Tanjavur Narayanasvami Appa (late nineteenth century), Tanjavur Sethuram Rao (1850–1920) and Professor Ramdas Svami (1845–1925). These musicians were very popular in accompanying Harikathas and bhajan presentations. With many musicians being both Harikatha exponents and concert musicians, mrdanga artists also inhabited two worlds, which made stylistic overlaps inevitable. Therefore, by the early twentieth century, two distinct schools of mrdanga had been established. Among the mrdanga vidvans of the late nineteenth century, Azhaganambiya Pillai of the Tanjavur school was a towering personality. The Tanjavur school evolved from the kirtan tradition, and the Pudukkottai school traces its roots to the nagasvara tradition. I would also add that the Sadir tradition must have influenced the Pudukkottai school, since artists from the same community were engaged in both. The fact that these two schools later became separated on caste lines has already been mentioned.

Nagasvara

The nagasvara tradition grew from strength to strength for most part of the nineteenth century. Nagasvara vidvans were celebrated as masters of alapana and pallavi. The temple festival concerts in which they performed may have lasted for hours, sometimes the whole night. Their concerts included pieces that were exclusive to the nagasvara/tavil repertoire, such as alarippu, mallari and rakti melam. Another interesting tradition – of the tavil vidvan playing a few strokes during the pause between phrases in an alapana – also evolved. We are still not sure about the real purpose of these pauses, though there are many theories. The tradition did not seep into vocal or other instrumental kutcheris. Some nagasvara vidvans included kirtanas as part of their presentation, but it was still minimal. The role of tavil vidvans too saw an upswing. By the early twentieth century, tavil tani avartanas were also important to the presentation. The bulk of the nagasvara concert was non-compositional, with pre-composed forms only being used as improvisational platforms. The manodharma was not only melodic, but also rhythmic. All this provided a large platform for the artists.

The Tanjavur Quartet

It is in the nineteenth century that the modern repertoire of Bharatanatyam took shape due to the contributions of the Tanjavur quartet: Chinnayya, Ponnayya, Sivanandam and Vadivelu (early nineteenth century) – all disciples of Muttusvami Dikshitar. They gave pada varna, shabda, svarajati and jatisvara the shape that has come to be the basis for Bharatanatyam. They were also composers of kirtanas in the tradition of Dikshitar. It is important that, among Muttusvami Dikshitar's students, many were from the devadasi and nattuvanar tradition. Therefore, the aesthetic impact of Dikshitar on them and, conversely, of their music on Dikshitar would have been powerful. The devadasis gave life to the compositions of the quartet. The repertoire of the devadasis as musicians and dancers was wide. It included pushpanjalis, kautuvam, kirtanas and social songs such as lalis (lullaby), talattu (cradle songs), unjal songs (sung to the swaying of the swing), pure nrtta pieces, varnas, padas, javalis, tillanas, ashtapadis and, in some temples like the Tiruvarur temple, dance operas such as the 'Pallaki Seva Prabandham'. Devadasis and the nattuvanars were hereditary artists. Whether it was at the temple or the court, it was art. The devadasi herself was part of the ritual, religious and social life of society, binding them together through her art. She was not alone; nourishing music and dance alongside her were the nattuvanars, the gurus. The role they played together in the creation of modern Karnatik music and Bharatanatyam was cardinal.

Dasis Take the Concert Stage

As the new century was welcomed, the situation of the devadasis began to decline. The anti-nautch movement was gaining steam, and they had begun to lose the patronage of the royals and zamindars. With stigma hovering over Sadir, many turned into 'concert performers'. For about a decade, they were very successful. Some of the popular devadasi singers included Bangalore Nagaratnammal, Coimbatore Thayi, the Kanchi Dhanakoti sisters, Tiruvidaimarudur Bhavani and the Enadi sisters. All these musicians performed by playing the tambura themselves, something that we do not hear of from the 1930s and 1940s. An interesting aspect of their music is that they did not all follow the same presentation style for concerts. Nagaratnammal, Coimbatore Thayi and the Dhanakoti sisters were masters of the ragam–tanam–pallavi. The Enadi sisters were known for javali renditions and never sang kalpanasvaras. They rendered many kirtanas, including some large compositions of Tyagaraja. We have already discussed the music of Vina Dhannamal. Maharashtrian scholar V.N. Bhatkhande (1860–1936), during his stay in Madras, observes an unusual detail while attending a concert by Bangalore Nagaratnammal. He says that, after the rendition of a song, the audience requested her to render only alap ('keval alap'). She is said to have sung three raga alapanas in what he felt sounded like the Hindustani ragas kanada, bhairavi and pilu.

Northern Visitors

An important feature in the development of music in the south has been the natural osmosis of influences from different parts of the country. In absorbing theoretical ideas, ragas, talas, composition types and presentation styles, the south has been welcoming. Many instruments from other regions were also used in Karnatik music. Around the eighteenth or early nineteenth century, the svarabat was used for Karnatik music. The sarangi was used for Sadir and Karnatik performances, and the dholak was used for Karnatik concerts. I am told the sarangi was also used for devotional Tevaram rendition. The Tanjavur court, as much the Mysore and the Travancore courts, had Hindustani musicians. Paintings in the Sarasvati Mahal library depict both Dhrupad and Khyal singers and musicians of many folk and bhakti traditions who visited Tanjavur. According to some scholars, Hindustani musician Maula Baksh (1833–96) visited Tanjavur around the 1860s and learnt Karnatik music from Subrahmanya Ayyar. Was this Patnam Subrahmanya Ayyar? Bhatkhande came on a musical pilgrimage to south India. He came in search of a theoretical authenticity for an all-India classical music tradition. His plan was to unite Indian classical music through scientific and logical study. During his visit to Tanjavur in 1904, he heard concerts by a taus player accompanied on the pakhavaj and a vocal recital of Khyal. These are indicators of the kinds of music practised in the south. A similar environment also existed in Mysore and Travancore. Maula Baksh and many other Hindustani musicians were both court musicians and regular performers at the Mysore palace.

Concert Performers

What about the music of the 'concert performers' of the later nineteenth century? I use this term with some hesitation. It has, I should say, been bandied about rather thoughtlessly for many years. We have already seen the concert content in courts and the parallel lives that many musicians led, as both Harikatha vidvans and concert artists. We know that the primary content of their performances were alapanas and pallavis. There is a description of the concert format followed by three great musicians of the nineteenth century – Maha Vaidyanatha Ayyar, Patnam Subrahmanya Ayyar and Kundrakkudi Krishna Ayyar – that is important at this juncture. This format must have been in vogue in the 1860s and '70s. Their concerts are said to have begun with a few kirtanas, but the major portion involved an alapana that lasted for hours followed by a pallavi.

Today we are used to a vocal kutcheri consisting of a violin and mrdanga accompaniment, sometimes joined by a khanjira and ghata. In the nineteenth century, all this was just evolving. There have been artists like Nannu Mian who accompanied Patnam Subrahmanya Ayyar on the dholak. It is said that vina artists also accompanied the vocalist.

The khanjira became a Karnatik instrument only in the mid- or late nineteenth century. The instrument itself was already being used in other regions, including Bengal. A sketch by the Flemish artist Francois Baltazard Solvyns (1760–1824), published as part of his collection of musical instruments in Calcutta, shows a person, whom he calls a fakir, playing a K'hunjery (the khanjira is even today called a khanjari in Karnataka). He describes the fakir as a travelling musician who goes from house to house receiving alms singing the praises of the divine. C.R Day, the British scholar, in his celebrated work *The Music and Musical Instruments of Southern India* (1891) says that the khanjira was also used in nautch (Sadir). U.V. Svaminatha Ayyar speaks about Tiruvidaimarudur Radhakrishnan as a great khanjira vidvan of the nineteenth century. But it was Manpundiya Pillai (1857–1921) who brought it to the forefront of Karnatik music. Manpundiya, the father of the Pudukkottai school of mrdanga, was a disciple of the tavil vidvan Mariappa Pillai. Manpundiya's disciple, Dakshinamurti Pillai (1876–1937), carried on the tradition of his guru and was one of the most revered percussion artists in the Karnatik tradition. Unlike the twentieth-century tradition of the khanjira vidvans sitting behind the mrdanga artists, Dakshinamurti Pillai used to be seated in front of the mrdanga vidvan because of his stature. It might also be that in the days before the roles of every instrument were fixed in a kutcheri, the khanjira vidvans had accompanied vocalists without a mrdanga vidvan present. Hence, Dakshinamurti Pillai was not just confirming his status, but also following a precedent. Hierarchies probably were in the process of being established.

The flute, before entering the formal concert stage in the late nineteenth century, was being used for over 150 years as part of the chinna melam. Sharabha Shastri (1872–1904) established the flute as a solo concert instrument. The other instrument that gained prominence was the ghata. The vidvans

Umayalpuram Narayana Ayyar (late nineteenth century) and
Pazhani Krishna Ayyar (1876–1908) are pioneers of the ghata.
The ghata was not a new instrument. It is said to have evolved
from the ancient kudamuzha, and must have been used in local
music traditions, including temple music. Sharabha Shastri is
said to have performed with only the accompaniment of Pazhani
Krishna Ayyar on the ghata. C.R. Day also speaks about the
ghata accompanying the vocalist. The scholar Bhatkhande makes
an interesting observation about a ghata performance that he
was present at in Tanjavur (1904). He does not name the vidvan
but says that while playing his solo, the vidvan tossed the ghata
into the air and caught it on its downward path within the tala.
This almost gymnastic technique is still popular among ghata
vidvans. The morsing also became part of the kutcheri ensemble.
Some of the earliest exponents included Mannargudi Natesha
Pillai and Adichapuram Sitarama Ayyar.

In the field of violin, Tirukkodikaval Krishna Ayyar was the
maestro who inspired a whole generation of musicians, including
vocalists and instrumentalists. He not only accompanied a
couple or more generations of musicians, but also presented
solo concerts.

The vina tradition was quite intact in the nineteenth century.
There were musicians of great repute from different regions in
south India. In Tamil areas, the tradition of the Karaikudi family
was intact. They had been vina artists for over seven generations.
The eighth generation produced the great Karaikudi brothers:
Subbarama Ayyar (1883–1936) and Sambashiva Ayyar (1888–
1958). Other great vainikas of the nineteenth century included
Vina Venkataramana Das (1866–1948) from Vijayanagaram and
Vina Sangameshwara Sastri from Pithapuram. These musicians
belonged to the latter part of the nineteenth century. The vina
tradition was also very vibrant in Travancore. In the tradition
of Muttusvami Dikshitar, his brother's adopted son Subbarama
Dikshitar (1839–1906) was a reputed vainika and scholar.

Towards the end of the nineteenth century, the nagasvara vidvans, tavil vidvans and artists such Manpundiya Pillai also had an impact on some leading vocalists. Their great interest in the rhythmic complexities and rendering of pallavis with complicated mathematical improvisations influenced many vocalists, such as Konerirajapuram Vaidyanatha Ayyar (1878–1921) and Kanchipuram Naina Pillai (1889–1934). This led to pallavis becoming more than only a line of melody with sahitya to a way of developing the raga using niraval and kalpanasvaras. The pallavis were structured in complex and difficult talas and nadais, making it challenging for all accompanying artists. Some musicians who were more interested in raga bhava, such as Tirukkodikaval Krishna Ayyar, believed that such exercises were detrimental to Karnatik music. In spite of differences in approach and preferences, by the 1940s, Karnatik music had given itself an identity, with the kutcheri as its end goal.

I have now placed the various players on the musical stage as Karnatik music became kutcheri music. Some actors remained, others changed so as to reach the kutcheri platform and yet others were unable to even approach its vicinity. The stage itself changed in character. It now referred to an actual location, no longer a metaphorical presence within society where music was created. Karnatik music entered the new world, the urban world. In making this transition, the music changed. It may even be said to have twisted itself into improbable positions to accommodate the notions of a new era. In so doing, the music lost more than it gained. The last hundred years have seen many geniuses, inspired artistes whose music is quite unparalleled, but in spite of their immense personal presence, the repercussions of the social, political, religious and intellectual adjustments of the late nineteenth and early twentieth century on them have been so great as to be impossible to erase. The focus has moved from 'art' to so-called and so-labelled 'classicism' and this changed the music and the musician. We have discussed many things, each distinct and important in itself, that are lost to us today within the single construct of classicism. In fact, our world has demolished a living reality with myriad dimensions at the altar of one grand hypothesis – classicism.

Not the Last Word

Through these twenty-seven essays I have tried to understand the journey of Karnatik music. My intention was not to find its destinations. It was rather to see and, withal, to touch the various currents on which that great music surges ahead. Finding myself in those currents, I have discovered more depths to them than I thought existed. I believe the readers of these essays will also find those depths and ones that I may have missed.

These depths have opened up layers of understanding within myself, which I never thought existed. I have come to see and know art, beauty, philosophy, aesthetics, society and the people – the devadasis, scholars, aesthetes, vaggeyakaras, sangita vidvans, nattuvanars, nagasvara and tavil vidvans, kings, zamindars, religious heads, Harikatha vidvans, aficionados, impresarios and rasikas – and have placed myself within their world as I had never done before. I began this search many years ago, if only to see why I am standing where I am. But in writing these essays, I have taken the search forward and tried removing myself from this personal space. In that very process, ironically, I revisited myself. In so doing I have seen another person, one that I had not seen while being who I was.

Now, seeing the art through the eyes of that very different 'I', have I got all my answers? No, because I never sought any. Are all the thoughts I have expressed accurate, perfect? They are not, and I am glad they are not. Any endeavour must have the philosophical nerve for correction; mine is no different. But this I know: the thoughts in it come from a quest, not an arrival. To the reader who has reached this page, all I ask is this: agree, disagree, argue, fight, battle with the ideas here, but as a fellow seeker. As for me, as I write the last words of this book I know of only one thing: my next question.

Select Bibliography

Books

Aiyer, P.S. Sundaram and Sastri, S. Subrahmanya. *The Sangita Sudha of King Raghunatha of Tanjore*. Madras: The Music Academy, 1940.

Allen, Matthew Harp. 'The Tamil Padam: A Dance Music Genre of South India.' Vol. 1.: Text. PhD diss., Wesleyan University, 1992.

Bakhle, Janaki. *Two Men and Music*. Ranikhet: Permanent Black, 2008.

Bhagavatar, Soolamangalam Vaidyanatha. *Cameos*. Chennai: Sunadham, 2005.

Bhagavatar, Soolamangalam Vaidyanatha. *Karnataka Sangita Vidvangal*. Sunaadham, 1994.

Bharathiar, C. Subramania. 'Sangita Vishayam.' *Mahakavi Bharathiyar Katturaigal* (7th edn.). Chennai: Vanathi Pathippakam, 2011.

Bhatkhande, Vishnu Narayan. *Majha Dakshinecha Pravas – 1904*. Indira Kala Sangita Vishwavidyalaya (trans.). Khairagarh: Indira Kala Sangita Vishwavidyalaya, 1986.

Chaudhary, Subhadra. *Time Measure and Compositional Types in Indian Music*. Ramanathan, Hema (trans.). New Delhi: Aditya Prakashan, 1997.

Clements, E. *The Ragas of Tanjore: Songs and Hymns from the Repertoire of the Karnatik Singer Natrajan*. London: Dharwar Gayan Samaj, 1920.

Day, C.R. *The Music and Musical Instruments of Southern India and The Deccan.* New York: Novello Ewer & Co.; London: Adam & Charles Black, 1891.

Deva, B.C. *Musical Instruments of India: Their History and Development.* Calcutta: Firma KLM Pvt. Ltd., 1978.

Deva, B.C. *Musical Instruments.* New Delhi: National Book, Trust India, 1977.

Dikshitar, Brahmasri Subbarama. *Sangita Sampradaya Pradarsini.* Ettayapuram: Vidia Vilasini Press, 1904.

Durant, Will. *The Story of Philosophy.* New York: Simon & Schuster, 1991.

Ellmann, Richard and Feidelson, Charles (eds.). *The Modern Tradition: Backgrounds of Modern Literature.* New York: Oxford University Press, 1965.

Gangoli, O.C. *Ragas and Raginis.* New Delhi: Munshiram Manoharlal Publishers Pvt. Ltd., 1935, Reprint 2004.

George, T.J.S. *MS: A Life in Music.* New Delhi: HarperCollins Publishers, 2004.

Guru, Kumara. *An Artist's Miscellany.* Madras: R. Venkateshwar & Co., 1946.

Hardgrave Jr., Robert L. & Slawek, Stephen M. *Musical Instruments of North India: 18th Century Portraits by Baltazard Solvyns.* New Delhi: Manohar, 1997.

Hindu Music from Various Authors (2nd edn.). Compiled by Raja Comm. Sourindro Mohun Tagore. Calcutta: I.C. Bose & Co., 1882.

Jackson, William J. *Tyagaraja: Life and Lyrics.* Madras: Oxford University Press, 1993.

Kersenboom, Saskia C. *Nityasumangali Devadasi Traditions in South India.* Delhi: Motilal Banarsidas Publishers Pvt. Ltd., 1989, Reprint 2011.

King Tulaja of Tanjavur. *Ragas of the Sangita Saramrta.* Rao, T.V. Subba and Janakiraman, S.R. (eds.). Madras: The Music Academy, 1993.

Knight Jr., Douglas M. *Balasaraswati: Her Art & Life.* Chennai: Tranquebar Press, 2011.

Krishnaswamy, S.Y. *Memoirs of a Mediocre Man.* Bangalore: Bhamati Books, 1983.

Kumar, Pushpendra (ed.). *Natyasastra of Bharatamuni*. Vol. 1. Delhi: New Bharatiya Book Corporation, 2010.

Kumar, Pushpendra (ed.). *Natyasastra of Bharatamuni*. Vol. 3. Delhi: New Bharatiya Book Corporation, 2010.

Kumar, Pushpendra (ed.). *Natyasastra of Bharatamuni*. Vol. 4. Delhi: New Bharatiya Book Corporation, 2010.

Langer, Susanne K. *Feeling and Form*. New York: Charles Scribner's Sons, 1953.

Lath, Mukund. *Dattilam*. Delhi: Motilal Banarsidass Publishers Pvt. Ltd., 1989.

Ludden, David E. *Peasant History in South India*. New Jersey: Princeton University Press, 1985.

Nevile, Pran. *Nautch Girls of India*. New Delhi: Ravi Kumar Pablisher and Prakriti India, 1996.

Pearson, Hugh. *Memoirs of the life and Correspondance of the Reverend Christian Fredrich Shwartz*. 3rd edn. Vol. 1. J. Hatchard & Sons, 1939.

Pearson, Hugh. *Memoirs of the life and Correspondance of the Reverend Christian Fredrich Shwartz*. 3rd edn. Vol. 2. J. Hatchard & Sons, 1939.

Pictures of Famous Composers, Musicians and Patrons. 2nd edn. Short Notes by P. Sambamoorthy. Madras: The Indian Music Publishing House, 1961.

Popley, Herbert A. *The Music of India*. Oxford: Oxford University Press, 1921.

Raghavan, V. (ed.). *Muttuswami Dikshitar*. Bombay: National Centre for the Performing Arts, 1975.

Ramanathan, Hema. *Ragalaksanasangraha*. Chennai: N. Ramanathan, 2004.

Ramanathan, N. *Musical Forms in Sangitaratnakara*. Chennai: Sampradaya, 1999.

Ramanathan, S. *Music in Cilappatikaaram*. Madurai: Sri Sathguru Sangeetha Vidyalayam, 1979.

Ramanujam, A.K. (trans.). *Nammalvar: Hymns for the Drowning*. New Delhi: Penguin Books, 1993.

Rao, Pappu Venugopala (ed.). *Sangita Sampradaya Pradarsini of Brahmasri Subbarama Diksitulu*. Vol. 1. Madras: The Music Academy, 2011.

Rao, Pappu Venugopala (ed.). *Sangita Sampradaya Pradarsini of Brahmasri Subbarama Diksitulu*. Vol. 2. Madras: The Music Academy, 2011.

Rao, Pappu Venugopala (ed.). *Sangita Sampradaya Pradarsini of Brahmasri Subbarama Diksitulu*. Vol. 3. Madras: The Music Academy, 2012.

Sambamoorthy, P. *Great Composers: Book 1*. 7th edn. Chennai: The Indian Music Publishing House, 2004.

Sambamoorthy, P. *South Indian Music. 6 Volumes*. Madras: The Indian Music Publishing House, 1969-77.

Sanyal, Ritwik and Widdess, Richard. *Dhrupad: Tradition and Performance in Indian Music*. Hampshire: Ashgate Publishing Ltd., 2004.

Sastri, K.A Nilakanta. *The Culture and History of the Tamils*. Calcutta: Firma K.L. Mukhopadhyay, 1964.

Sastri, S. Subrahmanya (ed.) *Samgitaratnakara of Sarngadeva*. 2nd edn. Vol. 1. Revised by S. Sarada. Madras: The Adyar Library & Research Centre, 1992.

Sastri, S. Subrahmanya (ed.) *Samgitaratnakara of Sarngadeva*. 2nd edn. Vol. 2. Revised by V.Krishnamacharya. Madras: The Adyar Library & Research Centre, 1944, Reprint 1976.

Sastri, S. Subrahmanya (ed.) *Samgitaratnakara of Sarngadeva*. 2nd edn. Vol. 3. Revised by S. Sarada. Madras: The Adyar Library & Research Centre, 1986.

Sastri, S. Subrahmanya (ed.) *The Samgraha-Cuda-Mani of Govinda & The Bahattara-Mela-Karta of Venkata-Kavi*. Chennai: The Adyar Library, 1938.

Sastri, S. Subrahmanya (ed.). *Sangita Saramrta of King Tulaja of Tanjore*. Madras: The Music Academy, 1942.

Sathyanarayana, R. (ed.). *The Kudimiyamalai Inscription on Music*. Mysore: Sri Varalakshmi Academies of Fine Arts, 1957.

Sathyanarayana, R. (trans. & ed.). *Caturdandiprakasika of Venkatamakhin*. Vol. 1. Delhi: Indira Gandhi National Centre for the Arts and Motilal Banarsidas Publishers Pvt. Ltd., 2002.

Sathyanarayana, R. *Music of Madhva Monks of Karnataka*. Bangalore: Gnana Jyothi Kala Mandir, 1988.

Sathyanarayana,R. (trans. & ed.). *Caturdandiprakasika of Venkatamakhin*. Vol. 2. Delhi: Indira Gandhi National Centre for the Arts and Motilal Banarsidas Publishers Pvt. Ltd., 2006.

Seetha, S. (ed.). *Raga Lakshanamu of Saha Maharaja.* Madras: Brhaddhvani, 1990.

Seetha, S. *Thanjavur as a Seat of Music.* Madras: University of Madras, 2001.

Seth, Vikram. *An Equal Music.* New Delhi: Penguin Books, 1999.

Shastri, K. Vasudeva. *Raga Alapanas & Thayams.* Tanjavur: Sri S. Gopalan, Saraswathi Maha Library, 1958.

Shringy, R.K. and Sharma, Prem Lata. *Sangitaratnakara of Sarngadeva.* Vol. 1. New Delhi: Munshiram Manoharlal Publishers Pvt. Ltd., 2007.

Shringy, R.K. and Sharma, Prem Lata. *Sangitaratnakara of Sarngadeva.* Vol. 2. New Delhi: Munshiram Manoharlal Publishers Pvt. Ltd., 2007.

Shringy, R.K. and Sharma, Prem Lata. *Sangitaratnakara of Sarngadeva.* Vol. 3. New Delhi: Munshiram Manoharlal Publishers Pvt. Ltd., 2007.

Shulman, David and Rajamani, V.K. *The Mucukunda Murals in the Tyagarajasvami Temple, Tiruvarur.* Chennai: Prakriti Foundation, 2011.

Sriram, V. and Rangaswami, Malathi. *Four Score and More: The History of The Music Academy, Madras.* Madras: Westland Limited for The Music Academy, Madras, 2009.

Sriram, V. *The Devadasi and the Saint: The life and times of Bangalore Nagarathnamma.* Madras: EastWest Books Pvt. Ltd., 2007.

Strangways, A.H. Fox. *The Music of Hindostan.* Oxford: Oxford at the Clarendon Press, 1914.

Subramanian, K.R. 'The Maratha Rajas of Tanjore.' K.R. Subramanian, 1928.

Svaminatha Ayyar, U. Ve. *En Charittiram.* Chennai: Mahamahopadyaya Dr. U. Ve. Svaminatha Ayyar Nul Nilayam, 1982.

Svaminatha Ayyar, U. Ve. *Ilango Adigalal Arulchaida Silapadigaram Mulamum Arumpada Uraiyum, Adiyarkunallar Uraiyum.* (10th edn.). Chennai: Mahamahopadyaya Dr. U. Ve. Svaminatha Ayyar Nul Nilayam, 2001.

Svaminatha Ayyar, U. Ve. *Sangitha Mummanigal* (2nd edn.). Chennai: Mahamahopadyaya Dr. U. Ve. Svaminatha Ayyar Nul Nilayam, 1987.

Tagore, Rabindranath. *Songs of Kabir.* New York: The Macmillan Company, 1915.

The Complete Kritis of Sri Tyagaraja. Compiled by Maddali Venkatasubbayya. Hyderabad: The Icfai University Press, 2008, Reprinted 2009.

Tirumalacarya, Tallapaka Cina. *The Tunes of Divinity (Sankirtanalaksanamu).* Vol. 1. Hikosaka, Shu and Samuel, John G. (eds.). Commentary by Krishnamurthy, Salva (trans.). Madras: Institute of Asian Studies, 1990.

Tirumalacarya, Tallapaka Cina. *The Tunes of Divinity (Sankirtanalaksanamu).* Vol. 2. Hikosaka, Shu and Samuel, John G. (eds.). Commentary by Krishnamurthy, Salva (trans.). Madras: Institute of Asian Studies, 1990.

Veeraraghavan, D. *The Making of the Madras Working Class.* New Delhi: LeftWord Books, 2013.

Venkatamakhin. *The Chaturdandi Prakasika of Venkatamakhin: Sanskrit Text with Supplement.* Madras: The Music Academy, 1984, Reprinted in 1986.

Viswanathan, Tanjavur. 'Raga Alapana in South Indian Music.' *Asian Music.* Vol.9, No. 1, Second India Issue (1977). PhD diss., Wesleyan University, 1975.

Vriddhagirisan, V. *The Nayaks of Tanjore.* New Delhi: Asian Educational Services, 1942, AES Reprint 2011.

Wade, Bonnie C. *Music in India The Classical Traditions.* New Delhi: Manohar Publishers & Distributers, 1979.

Watson, Peter. *Ideas: A History from Fire to Freud.* London: Weidenfeld & Nicolson, 2005.

Weidman, Amanda J. *Singing the Classical, Voicing the Modern: The Postcolonial Politics of Music in South India.* Durham: Duke University Press, 2006.

Widdess, Richard. *The Ragas of Early Indian Music.* New York: Oxford University Press, 1995.

Articles

Allen, Matthew Harp. 'Tales, Tunes, Tell - Deepening the Dialogue between "Classical" and "Non-Classical" in the Music of India.'

Year Book for Traditional Music. 1998. International Council for Traditional Music, 1998.

Auxier, Randall. 'Susanne Langer on Symbols and Analogy: A Case of Misplaced Concreteness?' *Process Studies*, 26 (January 1998), pp 86-106.

Coomaraswamy, Ananda K. 'Indian Art.' *Studies in Comparative Religion*. Vol. 15, No. 3 & 4 (Summer-Autumn 1983).

L'Armande, Kathleen and Adrien. 'One Hundred Years of Music in Madras: A Case Study in Secondary Urbanization.' *Ethnomusicology*. 1983. Society for Ethnomusicology, 1983.

Meduri, Avanthi. 'Bharatha Natyam - What are You?' *Asian Theatre Journal*. 1988. University of Hawai'i Press, 1988.

Peterson, Indira V. 'The Kriti as an Integrative Cultural Form: Esthetic Experience in the Religious Songs of Two South Indian Classical Composers.' Michigan: Asian Study Centre, Michigan State University, 1984.

Ramanathan, N. 'Adi-Tala: A Historical Study of its Structure.' *Sangeetham*. No. 3. pp.128-137. Kozhikode: October 2007.

Ramanathan, N. 'Concept of Art Music.' This article has been published in the Oct 2013 issue of the *Sangeetham* (Journal), Kozhikode. Since it is a long article, this issue contains only Part 1.

Ramanathan, N. 'Interpreting the "Graham" Part of the Cittasvara Passages in the Krti-s of Muttusvami Dikshitar.' 71st Annual Conference of the Music Academy, Chennai. The Music Academy, Chennai. 15 Dec 1997 - 01 Jan 1998.

Ramanathan, N. 'The Influence of Theory on the Practice of Music.' *Sruti Ranjani: Essays on Indian Classical Music and Dance*. Swaminathan, Viji (ed.). pp. 132-142. USA: SRUTI, The India Music and Dance Society, 2003.

Sankaran and Allen, Matthew. 'Social Organization of Music: Southern Area.'

Shortt, John. ' The Bayaderes or Dancing Girls of Southern India.' *Memoirs Read Before the Anthropological Society of London: 1867-8-9*. Vol. 3. London: Longmans, Green, & Co., 1870.

Srinivasan, Amrit. 'The Devadasi and her Dance.' *Economic and Political Weekly*. 1985.

Subramanian, Lakshmi. 'A Language for Music; Revisiting the Tamil

Isai Iyakkam.' Indian Economic & Social History Review, 2005.

Terada, Yoshitaka. 'Effects of Nostalgia: The Discourse of Decline in Periya Melam Music in South India.' National Museum of Ethnology.

Terada, Yoshitaka. 'T.R. Rajarattinam Pillai and Caste Rivalry in South Indian Classical Music.' *Ethnomusicology*. 2000. Society for Ethnomusicology.

Terada, Yoshitaka. 'Tamil Isai as a Challenge to Brahmanical Music Culture in South India.' *Music and Society in South Asia: Perspectives from Japan*. 2008.

Terada, Yoshitaka. 'Temple Music Traditions in Hindu South India: Periya Melam and its Performance Practice.' *Asian Music*. 2008. Texas: University of Texas, 2008.

Weidman, Amanda. 'Can the Subaltern Sing? Music, Language, and the Politics of Voice in Early Twentieth Century South India.' Indian Economic & Social History Review, 2005.

Newspapers & Journals

Music Academy Journals: The Music Academy. Madras.
Music Academy Souvenir: The Music Academy. Madras.
Sangeet Natak; Journal of the Sangeet Natak Akademi. New Delhi.
Sruti/Sruti Magazine for the Performing Arts: The Sruti Foundation. Chennai.
The Hindu (archives). Kasturi & Sons Ltd.

Lectures

Balasubramanian, Kudavayil. 'Musical Instruments in Ancient Times as seen from Literature and Archeological Source.' 85th Annual Conference and Concerts. The Music Academy, Madras. 2011.

Mitra, Falguni and Ranganathan, Sumitra. 'Between Structure and Form: The Four Banis as Aesthetic Typologies in Dhruvapada.' 86th Annual Conference and Concerts. The Music Academy, Madras. 2012.

Dictionaries

Apte, Vaman Shivram. *The Student's Sanskrit-English Dictionary*. 2nd edn. New Delhi: Motilal Banarsidass Publishers Pvt. Ltd., 1970.

Chambers, W. and R. *English Dictionary*. 1872.

McGregor R.S. *Hindi-English Dictionary*. USA: 1994.

Monier-Williams, Monier. *A Sanskrit-English Dictionary*. Oxford: Oxford at the Clarendon Press, 1899.

Onions, C.T. *The Oxford Dictionary of English Etymology*. 1966.

Roget, P.M. *Thesaurus*. 1805.

Acknowledgements

In the course of writing this book I have been helped by individuals who have been generous with their time and knowledge, enriching my understanding of art, philosophy, science and aesthetics. I must first thank Dr N. Ramanathan with whom I have spent hours clarifying doubts. Over the last five or six years, I have gained from his analytical approach to understanding matters pertaining to music. He is a most open-minded and catholic scholar. His attitude towards knowledge and respect for any individual from whom he can learn are rare qualities. I would like to acknowledge the guidance I have received from Dr R.S. Jayalakshmi, who has always encouraged my investigations into various aspects of Karnatik music and has asked most difficult questions. She has kept me alert. Her detailed sessions on ancient Tamil music, spread over the years, have been truly fascinating. I have engaged my good friends Dr Haribabu Arthanari and Kendra Leigh in many conversations through emails regarding science, life and genetics, all of which helped me grasp life's riddles better. I must also thank Kendra for sourcing several publications which became essential reading. There are some silent, wise philosophers who are always available whenever we need them, even if we do not pose any questions to them. Dr Shyam Krishnamurthy has been that person for me over the last so many years and he continued to silently help me in this journey. I thank Prema Rangachary and Krithika Rajagopalan for being my in-house critics and editors, pointing out all the errors that I would have missed. There have been so many other people who have answered my queries and helped in clarifying my doubts, including Hema Ramanathan, Dr Ritha Rajan, Sumitra Ranganathan, M. Subramaniam, K.S. Kalidas, Rajesh Garga, Keshav Desiraju and Siddharth Sriram. They have all helped in clarifying my thoughts. In the course of my writing, Sangeetha Sivakumar researched many Tamil books and articles, which are important inclusions in 'The History'. R.K. Shriramkumar helped greatly in standardizing the spellings for all the Sanskrit, Tamil, Kannada and Telugu words, and clarified all my doubts in the reading of Sanskrit treatises. K. Jagannatha Rao and K. Arun Prakash provided invaluable insights into the world of cinema and cine-music. R. Latha, a Karnatik music scholar, has been most helpful with sourcing material for my research. My students, G. Ravikiran, Vidhya Raghavan and Rithvik Raja have helped me gather all the data I required. I thank Vidhya Raghavan for having prepared the bibliography and my student, Vikram Raghavan, who put together the charts required for the book.

I am deeply grateful to the scholar-professor Dr David Shulman for having written a warm foreword that captures the spirit of the book.

Ajitha Gangadharan Sushama, who came up with the idea of this book and was my brilliant editor, is integral to how the book has come out. Her insightful, blunt edits and questions made me revisit many ideas and explain positions I had taken with greater clarity. This process was most rewarding and was a result of her personal investment in this book.

Be a writer's subject ever so wide, his writing needs a little corner for it to take shape. I was looking for a little corner-table in Chennai, where I could be whenever I wanted, to think, write or read. The elegant Chamiers Café became my hermit cave. I must thank Mathangi and her staff for tolerating my presence on many afternoons. I cannot forget the weeks I spent in the hillslopes at Anaikatti among the trees and the elephants (none of whom I ever saw!). It was in these sylvan gradients that I wrote most of the book.

I thank the following individuals whom I interviewed, for being part of the process by sharing their views on many subjects.

Dr Kudavayil Balasubramanian
Dr Chitra Madhavan
Dr R.S. Jayalakshmi
A.K.C. Natarajan
B.S. Purushotham
Ramakrishnan Murthy
Dr N. Ramanathan
Ramanujam (Arayar at Ranganatha Temple – Srirangam)
G. Rangarajan (hereditary vina vidvan at Ranganatha temple, Srirangam)
V.V. Sundaram
Sandeep Narayan
Siddharth Sriram

This book took me to many places in and around Tanjavur. In this connection I would like to thank all the priests, temple staff and devotees who contributed to my experience. I must thank Sathyabhama Bhadreenath of the Archaeological Survey of India for providing access to view the Chola and Nayak frescoes at the Brhadisvara temple and the people at the Sarasvati Mahal Library, Tanjavur for being most accommodative when I visited them for some information. This is a list of some of the places I visited:

Airavateshvara temple, Darasuram
Brahmapurishvara temple, Pullamangai
Brhadamba temple, Tirugokarnam
Brhadishvara temple, Tanjavur
Dhenupurishvara temple, Pattishvaram
Kampahareshvara temple, Tirubhuvanam
Nageshvara temple, Kumbakonam
Ramasvami temple, Kumbakonam
Ranganatha temple, Srirangam
Sarasvati Mahal Library, Tanjavur
Tanjavur Art Gallery
Tyagaraja temple, Tiruvarur

Index